An Introduction to

LAW IN GEORGIA

FOURTH EDITION

By Members of the Young Lawyers Division
of the State Bar of Georgia
Edited by Ann Blum and Anna D. Boling

**CARL VINSON INSTITUTE OF GOVERNMENT
THE UNIVERSITY OF GEORGIA**

The Carl Vinson Institute of Government
University of Georgia
© 1985, 1991, 1998, 2004 by the Carl Vinson Institute of Government
All rights reserved. First edition 1985
Fourth edition 2004
Printed in the United States of America
10 09 08 07 06 05 04   1 2 3 4 5

Library of Congress Cataloging-in-Publication Data

An introduction to law in Georgia / by members of the Young Lawyers Division of the State
    Bar of Georgia ; edited by Ann Blum and Anna D. Boling. — 4th ed.
        p.   cm.
    Includes index.
    ISBN 0-89854-211-1
        1. Law—Georgia—Popular works.   I. Blum, Ann, 1933–   II. Boling, Anna D.,
    1959–   III. State Bar of Georgia. Young Lawyers Division.

KFG81.I58   2004
349.750′8—dc22

                                                                                2004050207

Foreword

This fourth edition of *An Introduction to Law in Georgia* represents a continuing cooperative effort between practicing attorneys and education specialists. Its objectives are threefold and remain the same as they have in previous editions: to give young people an understanding of the laws that govern them, both nationally and in Georgia; to involve students in realistic situations and cases that demonstrate legal principles and actions; and to illustrate how the law affects their daily lives.

Designed for Georgia students, the textbook covers many of the civic and government standards set by the state for the ninth- through twelfth-grade social studies curriculum. It also addresses some of the Georgia Studies standards for the eighth-grade social studies curriculum. As a law-related education text, the book provides practice in analytical, evaluative, problem-solving, and participatory interdisciplinary skills.

Many people contributed time and energy to the development of this edition. We especially acknowledge the members of the Young Lawyers Division of the State Bar of Georgia, who contributed to development of the text for this edition. We are grateful to all who worked on this project for their efforts toward broadening the general knowledge and life skills of today's student, who is also tomorrow's citizen.

James G. Ledbetter
Director
Carl Vinson Institute of Government

Contents

PART 2 CIVIL LAW

PART 3 CONSTITUTIONAL PROTECTIONS

PART 4 CRIMINAL LAW

PART 5 IMMIGRATION

FOUNDATIONS

i1 Legal Rights and Duties

What is "the law"? Where does it come from? How is it enforced? Why do we need the law? How does the law affect members of society? How does it affect you? This book is intended to help you understand the answers to these questions. Before finding out how the law works in specific situations, however, it is important to have a general understanding of the law.

WHAT ARE LEGAL RIGHTS AND DUTIES?

We live in a world with many sets of rules. Families, social clubs, schools, stores, Sunday school classes, labor unions, governments, football teams, libraries—even school bands—all create rules. These rules establish duties and rights that affect your everyday life. But when is a right or duty a legal one?

What Are Legal Duties?

Think about the following situations:

SITUATION 1 At home, you are supposed to take out the kitchen garbage every day. For two days you forget. Your parents are angry.

Have you failed to meet a legal duty?

SITUATION 2 You belong to a music club and have been late showing up to meetings. The rule is that you must pay a fine if you are late to meetings.

Do you have a legal duty to pay the fine?

LAW TALK

constitutional right

contract

crime

due process

equal protection

law

legal duty

legal right

property ownership

tort

SITUATION 3 You are driving down a busy road. The driver behind you honks loudly and continuously as soon as the light turns green. You get mad. You think his conduct is dangerous and rude.

Is he violating his legal duties as a driver?

Duties may be established by social groups. A family is one type of social group. Situation 1 is an obligation to the family. It is not a legal duty; however, because you failed in your obligation, your parents—not the government—may enforce the rule.

Situation 2 is also a social duty. In this case, the social group is a club rather than a family. Although you have no legal duty to pay the fine, the club may kick you out if you do not.

Social groups can be very large. They may consist of the people in your circle of friends or in your community. A social group may be a nation or even the entire human race. Treating people politely is a social duty. However, as long as no injury results from rudeness (situation 3), it generally does not violate any legal duty.

SITUATION 4 Your religion requires you to go to church on Sunday. You want to go to a picnic at the lake instead.

Do you have a legal obligation to go to church?

Situation 4 involves another kind of obligation: religious duties. One of the most basic freedoms our society protects is the freedom of religion. Our government cannot prohibit people from following their religious beliefs. However, the practices of religious beliefs can be prohibited if they are harmful. In countries with state religions, religious and legal duties may be the same. In the United States, religion and government are separated; the government cannot enforce religious duties, which are solely between individuals and the institutions of their personal religions. In situation 4, you do not have a legal obligation to attend church.

SITUATION 5 You see an accident in which someone has been hurt. A crowd has gathered.

Are you legally obligated to stop and offer assistance?

Situation 5 involves the moral obligation of individuals to assist others. A moral obligation is what a person thinks is the right thing to do or not do. Under our laws, moral obligations to do something—that is, to carry out some action—are generally not enforceable. In this particular situation, you would not be arrested if you did not try to help the accident victim. However, your conscience might bother you, or you might feel that you failed to carry out a religious duty.

SITUATION 6 You hate your school. One night you throw rocks at the school windows, and you break several of them.

SITUATION 7 You find a wallet in a movie theater seat. It contains the name of the owner. It also contains $50. You are really broke, so you decide to keep the money.

Are you violating anyone's legal rights in situations 6 and 7?

The law does enforce a number of duties not to do something. In Georgia and elsewhere, the law imposes duties not to take or damage the property of others. You could be punished under the law for damaging public property (situation 6) and taking someone else's property (situation 7).

What is the difference, then, between a legal obligation and a social, religious, or moral obligation? Have you noticed the use of the word "enforce" or "enforceable" in the discussions of the situations?

An obligation is legal if it can be enforced by the government through the police, the courts, or some other governmental agency. For example, if you do not meet a legal obligation, like attending school, then the government can take action against you. If another person does not meet a legal duty to you, then you can take legal action against him or her. That is, you may use the power of government against the person.

What Are Legal Rights?

We have legal obligations, and we also have legal rights. For example, you have a legal duty not to harm others. Similarly, you have a legal right to compensation if you are wrongfully harmed by others. Like a duty, a right is considered to be legal only if it can be enforced by some part of government. Consider situation 8:

> **SITUATION 8** The rule at Everblue High School is "no talking in the school library." This rule gives students the right to have a quiet place to study and research term papers.
>
> The XYZ club decides on the spur of the moment to hold a meeting in the library. Its meeting is noisy. When told to be quiet or leave, the club members claim they have the right to talk during a club meeting.

Q Are the rights of either the students or the members of the XYZ club legal rights?

The "right" of the XYZ club would not be enforced by a court of law. Therefore, it is not a legal right. However, a school does have the legal authority to enforce its rule to maintain quiet in the library, and students have a right to expect that the school will provide a quiet place for them to work and study.

What Is the Law?

The law is more than legal rights and duties. It also includes the procedures or means of enforc-

A library has the right to enforce silence. Are there limits on how such rules can be enforced? Why or why not?

ing these rights and duties. The law consists of all legal rights, duties, and obligations that can be enforced by the government (or one of its agencies) and the means and procedures for enforcing them.

Some legal rights and responsibilities apply generally to all situations. Other rights and duties are more specific. For example, some legal rights and duties affect only buyers or sellers. Others apply only to tenants or landlords, parents or children, or employees or employers.

One other point should be made about laws. Laws only apply within the geographic boundaries of the governments that enforce them. This concept is referred to as a type of jurisdiction. A government has jurisdiction over people within its geographic boundaries. There are other types of jurisdiction. Jurisdiction, in its broadest sense, refers to the authority of a government or government entity. Government entities, such as courts, typically have authority over certain types of issues or cases. This concept is referred to as subject matter jurisdiction. A particular court can only enforce laws within its geographical jurisdiction and hear cases within its subject matter jurisdiction.

Governments have jurisdiction over certain areas and can enforce laws only in their jurisdiction. While you are living in Georgia, for example, you must perform the legal duties and may enjoy the legal rights of a state resident. If you move to Alabama, you move into the jurisdiction of Alabama law. That is, you will have to obey Alabama laws. Some Alabama laws are similar to those of Georgia; some are not. Furthermore, if you disobey laws in Georgia or Alabama, a case may be brought against you in court. However, the particular court must have the subject matter jurisdiction to hear the kind of case that has been brought against you.

O n l y   t h e   F a c t s

1. How does a legal duty differ from a social, religious, or moral duty?
2. What is a jurisdiction?
3. What does the law consist of?

T h i n k   A b o u t

1. Legal duties only apply in jurisdictions that have the power to enforce them. What about social duties? religious duties? moral duties? Do these change if you go to another state? another country? Explain.

TYPES OF LEGAL RIGHTS AND DUTIES

There are many federal, state, and even local government laws. How do these laws apply to individuals like you? The remainder of this chapter discusses some basic kinds of legal rights and duties.

The Duty Not to Harm Others: Torts and Crimes

SITUATION 9 Hank is deer hunting. He hears a noise, glimpses an animal, aims, and fires. It's a perfect shot—except that it hits and kills one of Mrs. Higgins's prize bulls. The bull had jumped the fence and wandered into the woods.

SITUATION 10 Cindy is a drug dealer. She makes her living selling drugs such as cocaine and heroin to people in her neighborhood.

Have Hank or Cindy broken any legal duties?

In Georgia and the United States as well as other countries, each person has a legal duty not to harm others. This duty extends to negligent (or accidental) as well as intended acts of harm. This duty also includes not harming people's property.

The law concerning these duties is called the law of torts, and breaching (or breaking) the legal duty not to harm others is considered to be a tort. If a person commits a tort, he or she has a legal duty to compensate (or pay) anyone who has been injured as a result of his or her actions. Situation 9 illustrates a tort. Hank has a legal duty to pay Mrs. Higgins for the loss of her bull. Mrs. Higgins could bring a lawsuit against Hank. In it, she could ask the court to require that Hank compensate her. (Chapter 10 provides more information on the law of torts.)

The basic need to protect people from the harm that others might do underlies much of the law. Because this protection is essential to a safe and orderly society, governments pass laws making certain harmful acts crimes. (Chapter 15 discusses crimes more fully.) Situation 10 illustrates a crime. In Georgia and elsewhere, selling dangerous drugs is a crime. Because Cindy has committed a crime, the state of Georgia could take legal action against her. If she is found guilty, the state could punish her with a fine and/or jail sentence.

What are the differences between crimes and torts? Generally, an act is a crime if it violates a criminal statute (or law). A tort is any civil wrong resulting from an act or failure to act for which the law allows a remedy (also called damages). Damages are determined on a case-by-case basis, according to the facts. If a tort is committed, the legal duty is to the person who was injured. For example, in situation 9, Hank would have to compensate Mrs. Higgins. However, the duty to obey criminal laws is a duty to the government or to society, not to an individual. In situation 10, then, Cindy would pay the fine to the state if she were found guilty.

Some acts, such as stealing a car, can be both a tort and a crime. That is, the thief has broken a legal duty to the car owner as well as the government. Each could take court action against the thief.

When a crime is committed, the case is tried under the criminal law. All other legal actions come under the general heading of civil law. The law of torts is part of the civil law.

Contracts

Like the law of torts, the law relating to contracts is part of civil law. Consider the following examples:

> Loretta buys a stereo for $300. She makes a $50 down payment and signs an agreement with the store to pay the rest of the money over the next six months.

> Barry's neighbor offers to pay him $5 an hour for raking leaves in his yard. Barry agrees.

These two agreements are contracts. A contract is an agreement that creates legal rights and duties among the persons who make it. These persons are called the parties to the contract. Each party takes on some duty to the other. These duties (and rights) exist only because of the contract. In the future, you may enter into a contract by borrowing or loaning money, renting or buying a home, or getting a job. Legal contracts—like other laws—are enforceable by the government. (Chapter 4 explains more about contracts.)

How do the duties and rights under contracts differ from the duty not to cause harm to others and the right to be free from such harm? The rights and duties under a contract are completely voluntary in the sense that nobody can force a party to enter into a contract. For example, you cannot be forced to enter into a contract to buy CDs from a certain music club. However, if you enter into the contract, you are required to meet the terms of that contract. In contrast, U.S. citizens (and citizens of other nations) are automatically subject to the duty not to cause harm to others.

Owning Property

It is after Christmas. Jack now owns a motorcycle. Karen owns her first computer. What, legally speaking, does it mean to own something? Suppose both Karen and her sister want to use the computer at the same time? Does one of them have more of a right than the other? What if Harold borrows Jack's motorcycle, crashes into a wall, and damages it? Does he have a duty to repair it for Jack?

An important type of legal right is the right to own property. Property can be stationary, like land. It may be something tangible that can be touched, such as a car or a jacket, or something that is intangible that cannot be touched physically, such the contractual right of a movie company to make a film of a book.

When a person "owns" a particular piece of property, his or her rights to that property are superior to (or greater than) the rights of anyone else to that same property. If you own a bicycle, for example, your right to use it is superior to anyone else's. In fact, someone else can only legally use it with your permission.

Generally, the government may not take away property without compensating the owner for its value. Property may be taken by other persons to satisfy claims against the owner (such as debts). But such claims must have been upheld in a court of law under the required legal procedures before the taking occurs.

THANK YOU FOR NOT WEARING FUR
Campaign for a Fur-Free America

LOVE ANIMALS DON'T EAT THEM
PEOPLE FOR THE ETHICAL TREATMENT OF ANIMALS

GET LIVESTOCK OFF OUR PUBLIC LANDS!

SAVE THE REEF
PROTECT LIVING CORAL

WARNING! I DON'T BRAKE FOR VIVISECTORS
Trans-Species Unlimited, P.O.B. 1553, Williamsport, PA 17703

HUNTING SPORT OF COWARDS

FIGHT FACTORY FARMING

BOYCOTT VEAL!

Are bumper stickers a form of freedom of speech?

Can owners use their property however they wish? The rights that arise from the ownership of property are not unlimited. The law can limit the ability of individuals to use property that they own. For example, an owner of a car cannot disobey the rules of the road.

The rights of individuals to use their property are also limited by the law of torts. Property owners have a right to compensation if their property is harmed. They also have a duty not to use their property in any way that will harm others accidentally or intentionally.

The rights to use or dispose of property may be limited by obligations in a contract. However, contractual obligations apply only if the owner of the property has agreed to them.

The legal duty not to harm others and the legal right to contract are basic to the laws of most, if not all, governments. The right to individual ownership of property is basic to American society but is absent in other legal systems. In some tribes, for example, property belongs not to the individual but to the tribe. In a pure communist system, property is owned by the state, and citizens are allowed to use the property.

Constitutional Rights and Limits

Would the following incidents violate your rights and freedoms?

SITUATION 11 You plan a trip to Nashville, Tennessee. At the state border, a Tennessee state patrol officer asks to see your permit to travel in Tennessee. You do not have one, and he will not let you enter the state.

SITUATION 12 You are strongly opposed to the government's foreign policy. You explain your views to a friend while taking a bus to a nearby town. When you get off the bus, you are arrested by a police officer who says that speaking against the government in a public place is illegal.

SITUATION 13 You are arrested. You are not allowed to talk to anyone. You are called before the judge and sentenced to prison for six years.

In each of these situations, your constitutional rights have been violated. As a member of a free democratic society, you have the right to travel wherever you wish in the United States (situation 11). You have other freedoms, such as freedom of speech (situation 12) and religion. You have a number of rights, including the right to a hearing before being deprived of life, liberty, or property (situation 13). These rights are based on the U.S. Constitution and its amendments, and they can be enforced and protected by the government. (Freedoms and rights are discussed in more detail in chapters 13 and 14.)

Georgia law requires a person to be 18 years old to apply for an unrestricted driver's license.

SITUATION 14 The last football rally was very rowdy. Several students were bumped and bruised. The principal has therefore banned all pregame rallies.

Is the ban a limit on your right to free speech and association?

Like the rights to own property and to enter into contracts, individual rights and freedoms are not unlimited. U.S. citizens have given the government the power to put reasonable limitations on the use of rights and liberties because these limitations are in the best interest of society. For example, although criminal laws limit peoples' actions, such laws are clearly desirable because criminal acts are harmful to everyone.

Similarly, we allow the government to license auto drivers to protect others from unsafe, unskilled drivers. We also allow limits on our cherished rights to freedom of speech and association, such as when there is a danger of people being injured (situation 14).

In other words, restrictions on individual rights have been allowed when exercising these rights would harm another person or society. The balance between preserving rights and protecting individuals and society often can be very delicate.

However, the government is restricted in its power to limit these rights and freedoms. Two main restrictions are stated in the constitutions of the United States and Georgia.

First, the government may take away the "life, liberty, or property" of individuals only with "due process of law." In simple terms, due process means fair treatment. The due process requirement is the foundation of individuals' relationship with the government. Due process means that the government itself is bound by law. For example, the president may claim that someone has committed treason and should be punished immediately, but that person cannot be deprived of his or her life, liberty, or property without a proper trial. This requirement restricts governmental activity that might endanger individual freedoms. It limits governmental actions to take away other legal rights.

Second, the government must provide "equal protection of the laws" to all individuals. Equal protection means that the government may not unfairly discriminate against individuals or classes of individuals. Each person—whether rich or poor, light- or dark-skinned, Muslim or Christian—is to be treated by the government in the same way.

However, there are some limits on the right to equal protection. For example, Georgia law requires a person to be 18 years old to apply for an unrestricted driver's license. Although it could be argued that this law discriminates against young people, such discrimination is allowed because it is made in the interest of public safety.

Only the Facts

1. How does a crime differ from a tort?
2. Who creates the rights and duties under a contract?
3. What does it mean to "own" a piece of property?
4. Name two constitutional freedoms.
5. What are the two restrictions on the power of the government to limit individual rights?

Think About

1. Why is the duty not to harm others —their persons or property—so important to an orderly society?
2. The desks in the classroom are owned by the school. List the rules that govern the use of this property.
   Now think about how these rules might change if each person in the class had to buy (and own) his or her own desk. What if the entire class had to buy all the desks and work out rules governing their use? Create rules to govern these new situations.
3. Think of situations in which you would allow the government to limit the right to freedom of speech. If you think there should be no limits, explain your reasons.

LOOKING AHEAD

At this point, you have learned something about legal rights and duties and how the law is defined. You have also been introduced to some terms and concepts that will be used throughout the book. As you encounter situations about specific areas of law in this book, ask yourself,

- What would be my legal rights in this situation?
- What would be my legal duties?
- How are these legal rights and duties enforced?

The duty not to harm the person or property of others and the right to protection from harm are basic concepts that underlie many laws and government actions. As you read, ask,

- Have the legal rights and duties in this situation been established to protect individuals or society from harm?

Often legal rights and duties come into conflict with each other. One person's right to breathe safe air may conflict with another person's right to run a business for profit, for example. In such situations, you might ask,

- Are there conflicts between certain duties and/or rights in this situation?
- Can the duties and rights be balanced?

The restrictions of "due process of law" and "equal protection under the law" are very important. Both concern the underlying concept of fairness. As you read, consider,

- Is the enforcement of these specific laws fair to both parties?
- Is this law unfair to some individuals? Is there any reason for such discrimination?

2 Sources of Law

LAW TALK

administrative law

code

elastic clause

ordinance

police powers

statutory law

In chapter 1, you learned that laws consist of legal responsibilities and rights. Where do laws come from? Who makes these laws? Can they ever be changed?

There are duties and rights associated with being part of a family, a social club, a football team, and similarly, a government. In some types of government, only one or a few persons may make the laws. In a representative democracy such as the United States, the citizens decide what the rules or laws will be. "We the people" elect representatives with the power to make and enforce laws at local, state, and national levels.

In the United States, the power to make and enforce laws is shared by the three branches of government. Elected representatives with the power to make laws form the legislative branch of government. The executive branch is responsible for seeing that laws are carried out. The judicial branch has the power to interpret laws (that is, to say what they mean and how they should be enforced).

In the state and federal government, these three branches are very distinct and separate. A system of checks and balances prevents any branch from having too much power. But, as you can see in figure 2-1, the separation of powers is not always as distinct at the local level. Notice that county commissioners have the responsibilities of both the executive and legislative branches.

The U.S. and state constitutions provide the framework for laws in Georgia. There are other sources of law, however. Statutes are made by legislatures, which are composed of elected lawmakers. Administrative law is determined by agencies. Finally, the courts determine case law.

FIGURE 2-1

Branches and Levels of Government

Levels of Government	Branches of Government		
	Legislative	Executive	Judicial
Federal	U.S. Congress: Senate and House of Representatives	President	Federal Court System (diagram, p. 27)
State (Georgia)	Georgia General Assembly: Senate and House of Representatives	Governor	Georgia Court System (diagram, p. 24)
Local (County/City)	County Commissioner(s)/ City Council	Board of County Commissioners/Mayor	City Courts

SOURCES OF LAW

Source 1—Constitutional Laws

The primary law of American society is found in its basic documents—the Constitution of the United States (or federal Constitution) and the various state constitutions. These constitutions form the legal framework of our society. In these documents, we, the people, have set forth our agreements as to how we should be governed (see figure 2-2). Each constitution clearly states that its authority comes from the people.

The U.S. Constitution is more than 200 years old. By comparison, the constitution that is used in Georgia is relatively new and has seen many changes. There have been eight revisions to Georgia's first constitution, which was written in 1777. The various Georgia constitutions were found to be either too vague or too detailed, or they had too many amendments. In 1976, the General Assembly established a committee to revise the Georgia Constitution. On November 2, 1982, 72.9 percent of Georgia citizens voting on the issue approved the state's 10th constitution. It went into effect in July 1983.

The Georgia Constitution is modeled after the federal Constitution. The federal Constitution is regarded as "the highest law in the land." Therefore, the rights of citizens cannot be mini-mized under the state constitution. Under the state constitution, however, those rights may be expanded.

Both the Georgia and U.S. constitutions determine the structure of their respective governments. Each establishes a legislative, executive, and judicial branch. Each constitution sets forth a process for enacting laws. Each also gives the

FIGURE 2-2

Preambles to Constitutions

WE THE PEOPLE of the United States, in Order to form a more perfect Union, establish Justice, insure domestic Tranquility, provide for the common defense, promote the general Welfare, and secure the Blessings of Liberty to ourselves and our Posterity, do ordain and establish this Constitution for the United States of America.

Preamble, Constitution of the United States

To perpetuate the principles of free government, insure justice to all, preserve peace, promote the interest and happiness of the citizen and of the family, and transmit to posterity the enjoyment of liberty, we the people of Georgia, relying upon the protection and guidance of Almighty God, do ordain and establish this Constitution.

Preamble, Constitution of the State of Georgia

government certain powers to act. Each sets limits on what the government may do and sets forth minimum basic rights of the people.

Both the federal and Georgia constitutions contain Bills of Rights. The first 10 amendments to the U.S. Constitution make up the Bill of Rights; the Georgia Constitution has 28 amendments in its Bill of Rights. The amendments deal with the right to bear arms, the right to engage in free speech, freedom of religion, freedom from unlawful search and seizure, the right to jury trials, and other rights.

Source 2—Statutory Laws

Laws enacted by state and federal legislatures are called statutes. Collectively, they are referred to as statutory law.

To be a valid law, a statute must meet three conditions:

1. Procedures set forth in the U.S. Constitution (for federal laws) or the Georgia Constitution (for state laws) must be followed in order for a statute to be adopted.

2. The constitution gives the government authority to enact law on a particular subject. Such authority must be stated in the U.S. Constitution for federal laws. For state laws, the power of the government must be clear in both the U.S. Constitution and the Georgia Constitution.

3. The statute must not exceed the constitutional limits on the power of the government to act. That is, a statute is unconstitutional and can be declared unenforceable if it goes beyond what the

constitution says the government can do. Both constitutions apply to a state law.

To see how this works, let's test four laws. Two are passed by Congress, two by the Georgia General Assembly.

CASE OF THE FOUR LAWS

CASE STUDY

1. Congress passes a law that requires all children to attend public schools.

2. Congress passes a law creating a new branch of the armed forces for defense of space. The law says only native-born Americans can be in this new branch.

3. The Georgia General Assembly passes a law making driving fast on state roads a crime.

4. The Georgia General Assembly passes a law creating a new municipality (city).

Assume that all four laws meet the first condition. In other words, the first two laws were adopted in accordance with methods set forth in the U.S. Constitution. The last two were adopted in accordance with methods set forth in the Georgia Constitution. Figure 2-3 is a very simple diagram of how laws are passed in Georgia. The procedures for enacting federal statutes are similar.

What Laws Can Congress Make?

The U.S. Constitution gives Congress power to enact laws on specific subjects, including powers to tax, regulate interstate commerce, establish post offices, declare war, and raise and support armed forces. Furthermore, to carry out all its

FIGURE 2-3

How a Bill Becomes a Law in the Georgia General Assembly

The Bill is...	The Committee considers the bill and...	The House considers the bill and...
• introduced in either the Senate or House • numbered • sent to Committee	• recommends, • recommends with changes, • rejects, or • holds bill	• debates bill • may amend bill • votes on bill

if recommended

if passed

Bill goes to the other house

The Other House...	The bill becomes a statute...
• puts bill through a similar process as the first house • passes the bill unchanged*	• if governor signs, or does not disapprove (veto) within 40 days after end of legislative session • if General Assembly overrides veto with a two-thirds majority vote

The bill goes to the governor

*Both houses must agree on a bill to complete passage. If they can't agree, a Conference Committee may be set up with representatives of both houses to resolve disagreements.

---

powers as outlined in the Constitution, Congress has the right to pass other laws considered "necessary and proper." This "elastic clause" in the Constitution gives Congress the power to enact laws on many more subjects than appear to be specifically covered by the Constitution. However, Congress lacks authority in other areas. It is not authorized to—and, therefore, it cannot—establish schools in local areas. It cannot adopt laws defining crimes within the boundaries of a particular state.

The lawmaking power of Congress has been extended, however, because the federal courts have broadly interpreted the powers given to Congress. For example, Congress has the power to regulate commerce among the states and with foreign nations. The U.S. Supreme Court's broad interpretation of "interstate commerce" provided the constitutional basis for laws requiring businesses engaged in interstate commerce not to discriminate on the basis of color, race, or national origin.

Although Congress cannot force states to adopt certain laws, it can establish conditions or incentives that make it in a state's best interest to do so. For example, Congress wanted to reduce the deaths and injuries caused by drunk driving by making 21 the legal age for drinking alcoholic beverages. It passed a law that gave the states two years to set a drinking age of 21 or else the states could lose federal highway funds. Georgia was one of the states that changed its drinking age law. If it had not, it could have lost $15 million in funds in 1986 alone. By making this requirement the condition of funding, Congress in essence set drinking age limits in the states.

CASE OF THE FOUR LAWS, *continued*

Has Congress been given the power to pass laws 1 and 2?

1. The Constitution does not give Congress the power to pass laws regarding public education provided by the states. Law 1 would not be valid.

CASE STUDY

Sources of Law 13

2. Congress has the power to declare war and to maintain an army and navy. These powers have been interpreted to extend to other armed forces like the air force. Undoubtedly, Congress would have the power to create this new defense-of-space branch.

What Laws Can the General Assembly Make?

The U.S. Constitution gives to the states all powers not specifically delegated to the federal government or prohibited by the U.S. Constitution. The Georgia Constitution gives the state government general powers, including "police powers." The General Assembly therefore has the power to act to ensure public health and safety and to maintain the well-being of members of society.

Defined in general terms, police powers underlie the authority behind many state and local government actions and laws. These actions range from setting up schools and colleges to maintaining police forces. Other examples include providing programs for people who cannot care for themselves and regulating service providers like physicians or taxi drivers. Police powers also are the authority for some restrictions on constitutional rights.

In the Case of the Four Laws, the Georgia General Assembly does have the power to pass laws 3 and 4. Its power to pass laws on these matters comes from the state constitution.

Limits on Lawmaking Powers

To be valid, a statute must not exceed the limits on the government's power. The freedoms given by the Constitution are such limits. American governments must have strong reasons to restrict freedoms such as speech or religion. The requirement under the law not to have life, liberty, or property taken without due process of law is also a limit, as is the need to provide equal protection under the law.

Will the laws in the Case of the Four Laws meet the test of validity?

CASE OF THE FOUR LAWS, *concluded*

1. The federal law requiring attendance in school has already been declared invalid.

2. The fact that only native-born Americans can participate in the defense-of-space branch makes this law invalid. It discriminates against Americans who are not native born. The law violates the constitutional right to "equal protection under the law."

3. One aspect of due process of law is that laws must not be so vague that enforcing them fairly would be impossible. What does "driving fast" mean? One person might say 50 miles per hour. Another might say 70 miles per hour. The law does not state what is meant. Because it is vague, this law would violate due process of law. It would be invalid.

4. This law does not exceed the limits on the power of state government. It would be valid.

City and County Ordinances

The relationship between local governments and the state differs from that between a state and the national government. The federal government was formed by a union of the states. Local governments (like cities and counties) are creations of the state.

Counties are political subdivisions of the state. The Georgia Constitution gives the governing body of each county power to adopt laws "relating to its property, affairs, and local government for which no provision has been made by general law and which is not inconsistent with the Constitution."

The state constitution also allows for creating "municipal corporations," which are cities. Cities are created by written documents called charters. Like any law, charters must be passed by the General Assembly. The charter becomes the city's "constitution." It sets forth the city government's powers and limits. It also gives proce-

FIGURE 2-4

Local Government Services

The Georgia Constitution authorizes cities and counties to enact laws to provide services such as

- fire and police protection,
- garbage collection and disposal,
- street and road construction and maintenance,
- parks and recreational areas,
- public transportation, and
- libraries.

dures for electing officials, collecting taxes, and enacting city laws.

City and county laws are called ordinances. Georgia's laws and constitution are quite specific about the kind of ordinances counties and cities can and cannot enact. For example, neither cities nor counties may pass laws establishing crimes and their punishments. Such authority is generally reserved for the state legislature. Figure 2-4 lists the kinds of laws that cities and counties may pass.

In general, the process for enacting ordinances is simpler than that for enacting federal and state laws. One reason is that in cities and counties laws usually have to be voted on by only one body of lawmakers. Also, local lawmaking bodies are usually smaller. For example, Georgia county commissions range from 1 to 11 members. Compare that with 56 members of Georgia's Senate and 180 of its House of Representatives. Compare those numbers with the 100-member U.S. Senate and 435-member House.

Codes

For the most part, laws at all levels of government are "codified"; that is, they are organized by subject matter in books or electronically. This organization makes it easy to find the laws on any particular topic because they are grouped together.

Statutes adopted by the Congress are set forth in the United States Code. Statutes of the General Assembly are organized in the Official Code of Georgia. Local ordinances are also codified. They may be organized by subject matter into separate publications such as the building code, zoning ordinance, and health and sanitation code.

Only the Facts

1. How many constitutions has the United States had? How many has Georgia had?
2. What are the conditions of a valid law?
3. How has the power of Congress to make laws been extended?
4. Are the following statements true or false? If false, correct the statement.
   a. Police powers are used by state and local governments only to catch criminals.
   b. A code is an organization of a government's laws by subject matter.
   c. A Georgia county's "constitution" is its charter.

Think About

1. "It is good that the U.S. Constitution contains the elastic clause that expands lawmaking power." Explain why you agree or disagree.
2. On the basis of what you know, does Congress or the General Assembly seem to have more limits on its power? Why?

Source 3—Administrative Laws

A third source of law consists of the rules and regulations of government agencies. For the most part, these agencies are part of the executive branch of government. Their laws are called administrative law. The rules and regulations of government agencies affect issues such as how water is purified and how schools are operated.

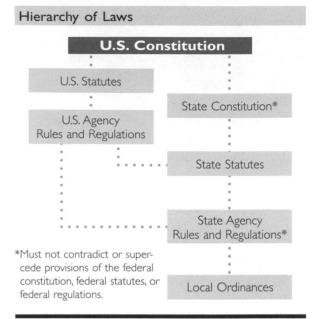

FIGURE 2-5

Major Georgia State Agencies

- Department of Administrative Services
- Department of Agriculture
- Department of Community Affairs
- Department of Corrections
- Department of Education
- Department of Human Resources
- Department of Labor
- Department of Natural Resources
- Department of Public Safety
- Department of Revenue
- Department of Transportation

FIGURE 2-6

Hierarchy of Laws

*Must not contradict or supercede provisions of the federal constitution, federal statutes, or federal regulations.

Each agency gets its rule-making power from the law that established it. For example, federal law establishing the U.S. Internal Revenue Service (IRS) gives it responsibility for collecting federal income tax. The IRS is given power to establish forms, rules, and regulations that every citizen must follow.

In the same way, state laws may establish and give rule-making power to state agencies. Figure 2-5 lists some of Georgia's major state agencies. Local government ordinances may also establish agencies, such as police or recreation departments. These local agencies are also given rule-making powers that cannot be exceeded. Just as laws passed by Congress or the General Assembly must be consistent with the authority given them by the U.S. and Georgia constitutions, agency rules and regulations must be consistent with the authority given the agency.

Source 4—Case Law

The final source of law, case law, is the result of the interpretation of statutes. The authority to interpret statutes rests with the judicial branch. (Chapter 3 clarifies the authority of the court system.) For example, a state may enact a law that makes loitering a crime, but the law may not clearly define what loitering is. If a judge subsequently decides that a person who was waiting for a friend on the sidewalk for two hours is loitering, the judge has added new meaning to the law, or "interpreted" it.

Tracking Down Sources

As you can see, there are many sources of law. There are the federal and state constitutions. There are federal, state, and local lawmaking bodies. There are federal, state, and local government agencies. Then there are the laws made by courts.

There is a hierarchy (ranking) of laws (see figure 2-6), with the U.S. Constitution at the top. Lower-ranking laws must conform to those above them. Relationships between laws are not always obvious, however. For instance, rules made by state agencies may be limited not just by state law but also by the rules of federal agencies that provide funding. For example, school lunch programs are federally funded, as are programs for teacher training, student loans, and development of classroom materials. Such program funding has increased the influence of federal laws and agencies on education. (Figure 2-7 lists some of the rules regulating schools.)

1. Name three sources of law.
2. What are the legal sources of state agency laws?

T h i n k   A b o u t

1. Give a few reasons why the legislative branch of government delegates some of its rule-making power to agencies in the executive branch.

CHANGING LAWS

Laws are made by people. Constitutions—and the government—rest on the power given by the people. There are three points to bear in mind about how ordinary people can affect laws.

Point 1: To work, laws must reflect the values of most of the people they govern. To illustrate, consider what happened in the United States some years ago. A number of people strongly believed that drinking alcoholic beverages was wrong. As a result of their efforts, an amendment to the U.S. Constitution forbidding the sale of alcoholic beverages was passed in 1920. However, it proved very difficult to enforce this law. Many Americans wanted to be able to buy alcoholic beverages. Violations of the law were com-monplace. Finally, in 1933, the amendment was repealed. In effect, so many Americans wanted to drink alcoholic beverages that the law was unenforceable.

Point 2: People's values and ways of life change. To work, laws must be able to accommodate such changes. It is easy to see how developments in technology affect laws. The coming of the automobile resulted in a network of paved roads. It also resulted in new laws and regulations. Existing laws regarding horse traffic became useless. New ones regulating drivers, use of roads, sale of cars, and other laws were needed and enacted.

Slavery is perhaps the best example of the effect of changing values on laws within our country. In the early years of this nation, the holding of other human beings as slaves was an accepted practice. Laws supported the holding of slaves. Then values changed. More and more people felt that slavery was wrong. In 1863, the Emancipation Proclamation heralded the end of the right to own slaves. The Thirteenth Amendment, passed in 1865, prohibited slavery. It is easy to understand why laws upholding slavery would not be acceptable in today's America.

Can you think of any recent laws that reflect changes in attitudes and values? One example would be the laws protecting the environment. People have become increasingly aware of the dangers of polluting the air and water. They understand the effects of creating unmanage-

---

FIGURE 2-7

Who Makes School Laws?

Can you guess the sources of the rules and regulations listed below? Does their authority come from the federal or state constitutions? statutes? agency rules?

a. Certification of teachers
b. Number of days in school year
c. Number of course hours needed to graduate from high school
d. Assignment of students to schools
e. Racial integration of schools
f. Dress requirements such as shoes, no halters

g. Regulations on free lunches
h. Smoking regulations
i. Days of attendance necessary to pass
j. Prohibition against talking out of turn in class
k. Penalties for being tardy
l. Calendar dates of each school year
m. Pupil ages for required school attendance

able amounts of garbage. They have also come to realize that the natural heritage of animals, plants, and scenic and wilderness areas could be destroyed if they are not protected.

In general, laws are slow to reflect changes in the values and customs of society. However, there are examples of how laws reflect rapidly changing values, such as those you may read about in the media concerning technology.

Point 3: In a democracy, people like you and me can work to get laws changed or added. One way we do this is by lobbying our elected representatives.

Constitutional Law

In any government, it is important that laws be adaptable to change. At the same time, a framework of principles is necessary to give laws consistency and continuity. Like a house, laws must have a foundation. The U.S. Constitution serves as the framework for federal law, and state constitutions underlie state law. In general, constitutions cannot easily be changed. However, it is possible to make changes to constitutions through the use of amendments.

The methods for amending the constitutions of Georgia and the United States are shown in figure 2-8.

As you can see, it is easier to change the Georgia Constitution. The U.S. Constitution has not been amended easily. There have been only 26 amendments in its history. One of these, prohibiting the sale of alcoholic beverages, was repealed.

If it is so difficult to change the U.S. Constitution, how has it accommodated more than 200 years of change? In effect, it has done so because its provisions have been interpreted and reinterpreted by court decisions. (This point is further discussed in chapter 3.)

Statutes and Ordinances

Statutes (and ordinances) are changed in the same way they are made (see figure 2-3). They can be amended or repealed (that is, canceled) by new laws.

The founders of our government intended for statutory law to be the most responsive to the will of the people and to changes. That is why lawmakers at each level of government are

---

FIGURE 2-8

Amending Constitutions

	①	②	③
GEORGIA			
	Amendment is proposed in the General Assembly.	Amendment is approved by a two-thirds vote in House and Senate.	Amendment is approved by majority of voters at next general election.
UNITED STATES			
	Amendment may be proposed by Congress *or* Two-thirds of state legislatures may ask Congress to call a Constitutional Convention to propose an amendment. (This procedure has never been used.)	Amendment is approved by a two-thirds vote in House and Senate.	Amendment must be approved by three-fourths of state legislatures or three-fourths of state conventions called to vote on it. (State conventions have only been called once.)

elected and not appointed. Elected representatives are expected to want to know the opinions of those they represent. How else can they represent them? Indeed, if they are not sensitive to the will of the people, they may not be reelected.

How can you let your senator, councilmember, and other representatives know how you feel about the law? You can phone, write, or visit them. You can join with others who share your feelings to work for or against passage of a particular law. When election time comes around, you can campaign, and—once you turn 18 and are eligible to vote—you can vote for candidates who support your views.

Administrative Law

Within the powers and limits set by constitutions and statutory laws, agencies can set up rules as needed. They can also adapt them as situations change.

However, many people complain that agency laws are not very responsive to public opinion or the needs of those they regulate. In fact, what can a person do to get an agency rule changed?

Some agencies have procedures that allow public review of their regulations before they are passed. Both the federal Environmental Protection Agency and state Environmental Protection Division have such review procedures. Before either adopts a regulation, it publishes the text to allow interested citizens to comment on the regulations. The agency may then make adjustments as needed.

What can a single person do to change an existing agency rule? Think about the following situation: A school principal objects to a rule of the state board of education requiring all new teachers to take extra courses for maintaining their certification. The principal feels it is unfair to the new teachers. What can she do?

She could disobey the rule. However, this response would probably only lead to trouble for her and others. She could present her arguments against the requirement to the board. If others felt the same way, they could join her in protesting the rule.

If no action resulted from a protest to the state board, the principal could consult a lawyer about court action. The court would not be concerned about whether the principal or others liked the regulation. The court would consider whether the regulation was valid. What if the regulation discriminated against certain teachers? The court might then find it invalid.

Only the Facts

1. How do the procedures for amending the U.S. and Georgia constitutions differ?

2. Why might statutory law be considered more responsive than administrative law to people's opinions?

Think About

1. What happens when governments pass laws that go against the will of many people? How do governments respond to resistance?

2. To illustrate how changes in technology have impacted lawmaking, list a few laws that regulate the use of technology.

3. "The U.S. Constitution should be amended to allow citizens to vote directly on amendments." Prepare arguments for or against the statement.

SUMMING UP

Where do laws come from? This chapter has looked at how we, the people, are the basic source of authority for all our laws. The national and state constitutions, which form the framework of our laws, have been discussed, as have statute making and ordinance making. Agencies are yet another source of law. The one source of law that has not yet been examined is the law established by courts within the judicial system. It is the subject of chapter 3.

 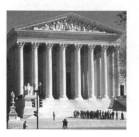 

3 Courts

There are several reasons why, at some point in your life, you may have an experience with a court:

- You may be called to serve on a jury.
- You may testify in court about some event that you saw.
- You might be involved in a divorce—your own or someone else's.
- You may commit a crime or be accused of committing one.
- You might be sued for a tort (that is, a wrongful act) as the result of an auto accident.
- You may sue someone for breaking a contract.
- You may have to probate a family member's will.
- You might adopt a child.

This chapter discusses what courts do, the different kinds of courts, and their respective responsibilities. It also examines how courts make law and how laws made by courts are responsive to change.

WHAT IS A COURT?

The judicial system is one part of the government. It is composed of various types of courts and is the branch of government responsible for interpreting laws. There are thousands of courts in the United States. Until the new constitution took effect in 1983, the state of Georgia had approximately 2,470 courts. Now, with a somewhat streamlined court system, Georgia has approximately 1,100 courts.

The basic function of all courts is essentially the same: to declare, determine, and (if necessary) enforce people's rights and duties under the law. To enforce what they decide, the courts can impose consequences on those who do not comply with their decisions. However, there are limits on what cases each court can hear or decide. The four examples that follow illustrate the different kinds of courts and the cases they hear.

FOUR CASES IN SEARCH OF A COURT

1. Danny lives in Brooks County. He buys a used auto from Edgar in Valdosta (Lowndes County). The car breaks down. Danny is sure the contract he signed when he bought the car covers the repair. Edgar disagrees. Danny has the car repaired by Reliable Rick. Danny says he will take Edgar to court if he will not pay Rick's $150 bill.

2. Janet is not hired by the Giant Gadget Company in Cobb County. (The company sells its gadgets throughout the United States.) The man selected for the job is much less qualified than Janet. Janet feels that she was discriminated against because she is a woman. She feels that she has been denied equal protection under the law. The company denies the charge. Janet decides to take her case to court.

3. Stan, a Savannah resident, is accused of mailing out ads about a fake get-rich-quick scheme that urges people to send in a $100 deposit. Stan is arrested in Brunswick, Georgia. He is charged with defrauding people of money but denies the charge.

4. During an attempted robbery at a grocery store in Hartwell, Georgia, a man is killed. Dot is arrested but denies having committed the crime. She lives in Elberton, Georgia, but is arrested in Anderson, South Carolina.

DISAGREEMENTS: CIVIL OR CRIMINAL

When courts are asked to decide legal rights and duties, usually it is to settle a dispute. All the imaginary cases involve disputes. Danny says

The basic function of all courts is essentially to declare, determine, and enforce people's rights and duties under the law.

Edgar should pay for the car repairs. Edgar says he has no legal duty to do so. Janet says the Giant Gadget Company discriminated against her. The company says it did not. The government says Stan and Dot committed crimes. They say they are innocent.

However, not all settlements of legal rights and duties involve disputes. When parents go to court to adopt a child, there is no dispute to resolve. The court simply sets out the legal relationship between the adoptive parents and the child. It states their legal rights and duties to each other.

Disputes can concern civil or criminal law. Sometimes they involve both. Disputes not involving crimes are in the realm of civil law. Criminal law concerns acts that are declared crimes by the government. Which law is involved will affect the procedures that must be followed. It will also determine whether the dispute will be tried in civil or criminal court.

When a court does hear a dispute, it is first considered in a trial court. Courts are either trial or appellate courts. Appellate courts review the decisions of trial courts and determine if the law was applied properly. The four cases in the examples will be initiated in trial courts, but it must first be determined whether they will be civil or criminal cases.

Civil Law

In a civil case, the parties use the court system to decide a private argument between them. The party initiating the civil case is called the plaintiff. The party who is sued is called the defendant. The plaintiff files with the proper court a document called a complaint stating that the defendant either

1. owes the plaintiff some legal obligation, such as money, or
2. has violated some legal right of the plaintiff. An example would be the right not to have one's property damaged, as can happen in an auto accident.

When a civil case is titled, the name of the plaintiff comes first. Case 1 is a civil case. Danny is suing Edgar for damages. Danny is the plaintiff, and Edgar is the defendant. The case would be titled *Danny Edwards v. Edgar Daniels*.

Case 2 is also a civil case. Janet Jones is the plaintiff. The Giant Gadget Company is the defendant. How would this case be titled? (Chapters 4–12 concern matters that come under the civil law.)

Criminal Law

When a crime is committed, it is considered a "wrong" against society. The person accused of the crime is prosecuted by the government. The government's laws establish what crimes are. Therefore, in criminal cases, one party is always a government. Cases titled *U.S. v. Jones* or *Georgia v. Jones*, for example, would undoubtedly be criminal cases. (Remember that in the commission of a crime, a private person may also be harmed. In that case, the victim can also bring a private civil action against the accused for the harm suffered.)

To initiate most criminal cases, a prosecutor acting on behalf of the government files a charge in the proper court. The charge states that the defendant (that is, the person charged) has committed some act considered to be a crime under the law. If federal laws are violated, the prosecutor working for the federal government will prosecute the case. If state laws are broken, a prosecutor working for the state government will prosecute the case.

Only the state and federal governments can enact criminal laws and prosecute those accused of breaking them. City and county governments can, however, enact ordinances and prosecute any violation of them. Ordinances may regulate activities in places such as city streets or county parks.

CASE STUDY

FOUR CASES IN SEARCH OF A COURT, *continued*

Both case 3 and case 4 come under criminal law. In case 3, Stan Smith is accused of committing a crime. He will be the defendant. Dot Doe will be the defendant in case 4. The cases cannot be given titles yet because it has not been determined which government will prosecute the cases. In case 3, will it be the federal or state government? In case 4, will it be the government of South Carolina or Georgia? The answers will depend on which government has jurisdiction.

THE QUESTION OF JURISDICTION

Each court has the authority to hear certain cases. The legal rights and duties that a court can decide and enforce are determined by that court's jurisdiction. Jurisdiction is the power and authority of a court to hear and decide a case. There are two general types of jurisdiction: subject matter and personal.

Subject Matter Jurisdiction

A court must have the authority to enforce the kinds of laws (or legal rights and duties) that are involved in the dispute. This authority, called subject matter jurisdiction, is defined by the law creating the court.

SITUATION 1 Cary robbed a U.S. mail truck in Gilmer County, Georgia. She is arrested in Cherokee County, Georgia.

Which county court would have jurisdiction?

To answer the question, keep in mind that federal courts are created by federal laws. State courts are established by state laws. Usually, the jurisdictions of local government courts are also defined by state laws.

A person breaking a federal law—such as smuggling drugs into the country from a foreign state—would be tried in federal court. In general, federal courts hear disputes arising under federal laws. A person breaking a Georgia law can only be tried for it in a Georgia court. The same would be true for other states as well. A federal court or a court in another state would not have subject matter jurisdiction over the case.

An exception to this general rule can occur when a state civil statute is violated. Such a violation may fall within the federal court's supplemental jurisdiction. If so, the case would then be tried in federal court.

Robbing the mail is a federal crime. The federal district court would therefore have subject matter jurisdiction in situation 1.

The law establishing a court may be quite specific as to its powers. Consider the following situation:

SITUATION 2 A state law requires that all cities must have "town courts." These courts can only try civil cases involving claims of less than $5,000.

Would the town court have subject matter jurisdiction in the following cases?

    (a) A robbery of $500 worth of goods?
    (b) An insurance claim dispute of $10,000?
    (c) A claim of damages for $500?

This court is called a court of limited jurisdiction, and it would have only subject matter jurisdiction in case (c). Case (a) is a criminal case, and case (b) involves too much money. This court has the power to hear only specific types of cases. (Note the courts in figure 3-1 that have limited jurisdiction.)

Some courts do not have limits on the types of cases they can enforce. These courts are called courts of general jurisdiction.

For some kinds of cases, however, laws give subject matter jurisdiction to more than one court. There are many examples. In Georgia, cases that involve claims for damages can be heard by the superior state or magistrates court, depending on the amount of the claim. Federal court rulings have held that cases concerning violations of federal equal employment opportunity law may be heard in state as well as federal courts. In such instances, these courts are said to have concurrent jurisdiction.

CASE STUDY

FOUR CASES IN SEARCH OF A COURT: SUBJECT MATTER JURISDICTION

1. The dispute about the car repair bill comes under state law. Therefore, it will be tried in a Georgia court. The amount of money involved in such cases often determines which court will have jurisdiction.

2. Janet is claiming a violation of her rights under the U.S. Constitution. Although they may be tried in state courts, such cases are usually tried in federal courts The federal court is the court Janet will use.

3. Using the mail to defraud is a federal crime. Stan will be prosecuted in a federal court. The case would be titled *United States v. Stan Smith*. In a criminal case, the name of the prosecuting party—which is always a government—comes first.

4. Dot's crime was committed in Georgia, so the Georgia courts have jurisdiction. South Carolina would be asked to return Dot to Georgia to stand trial. The case would be titled *Georgia v. Dot Doe*.

Figure 3-1

Georgia Court System

APPELLATE COURTS

SUPREME COURT—7 justices

Exclusive appellate jurisdiction in cases involving constitutional issues, construction of treaties, contested elections, felonies for which death penalty can be imposed, titles to land, wills, *habeas corpus*, equity, divorces and alimony, and extraordinary remedies. Also consider certified questions and certiorari from Court of Appeals.

COURT OF APPEALS—12 judges

Appellate jurisdiction in cases in which the state supreme court does not have exclusive jurisdiction.

TRIAL COURTS

SUPERIOR COURTS*—49 circuits

Trial jurisdiction: general, exclusive in felonies, divorces, titles to land, and equity cases.

Appellate jurisdiction: over probate, magistrate, and municipal courts.

STATE COURTS—70 courts

Criminal jurisdiction: misdemeanors; felony pretrial proceedings; and traffic offenses.

Civil: cases in which superior court does not have exclusive jurisdiction.

JUVENILE COURTS*—159 courts

Jurisdiction over children under 17 years old said to be delinquent, unruly, or charged with traffic offenses; under 18 said to be deprived.

PROBATE COURTS*—159 courts

Exclusive jurisdiction in probating wills, administering estates, appointing guardians, and involuntary hospitalization of incapacitated individuals. May also issue marriage licenses, supervise elections, try traffic and hunting and fishing violations, preside over criminal pretrial proceedings, etc. May also handle miscellaneous misdemeanors.

MAGISTRATE COURTS*—159 courts

Criminal jurisdiction: pretrial proceedings, warrants, bail, county ordinance, miscellaneous misdemeanors, and bad check violations

Civil: small claims under $15,000; summons.

MUNICIPAL "CITY" COURTS

Called municipal, mayor's, city council, or police courts. Jurisdiction in traffic violations, city ordinance violations, and criminal preliminaries (such as warrants). Can also handle miscellaneous misdemeanors such as possession of marijuana (less than one ounce) and shoplifting.

*Each county has one of these courts.

Personal Jurisdiction

A court must also have power (or authority) to act with respect to the parties before it. This authority is called personal jurisdiction. Two elements must be met for a court to have personal jurisdiction over the parties.

First, there must be a reasonable relationship between the court and the parties. The relationship is often a matter of place and location. In civil cases, the court in the county in which the defendant lives is usually where the case will be heard. Sometimes, the defendant lives outside the state but has enough contacts within the state to come under what is called the "long-arm" statute. The civil case would therefore be heard in the county in which the problem took place.

To understand how the long-arm statute works, suppose several Georgians were injured by a faulty product made in California. Under the long-arm statute, they might be able to sue the California manufacturer in a Georgia court. It would depend on how much contact the manufacturer had with the state. Without the long-arm statute, the Georgians might have to sue in California.

The following situation illustrates what happens in a criminal case.

SITUATION 3 Rob Berry, who lives in Muscogee County, Georgia, holds up a jewelry store in Twiggs County. He is later arrested in Greene County, Georgia.

Would the court in Muscogee, Twiggs, or Greene County have jurisdiction?

In criminal cases, the court of the county in which the crime was committed has personal jurisdiction over the person arrested. So, in situation 3, the Twiggs County court would have jurisdiction.

The second element of personal jurisdiction is the court must notify defendants of the civil claims or criminal charges against them to give them the opportunity to protect their rights. A defendant must be notified enough in advance to

The U.S. Supreme Court is the highest court in the land. What is its jurisdiction?

allow time to prepare adequately for the defense of the case. Notice can be waived (or given up), but the waiver can only be done willingly and with full understanding of the consequences.

FOUR CASES IN SEARCH OF A COURT: PERSONAL JURISDICTION

CASE STUDY

1. In a civil case, with both parties in Georgia, the case would be initiated in the county of the defendant. The case of *Danny Edwards v. Edgar Daniels* would therefore be initiated in a court of Lowndes County.

2. Janet's case would be tried in the federal district court. Most likely, she would use the court in the district in which the defendant, Giant Gadget Company, is located. In this particular case, a Georgia court might also hear the trial. The court would be in Cobb County.

3. Stan Smith's crime was committed in Savannah. It would be tried in the federal district court that has jurisdiction in Savannah.

4. Dot's crime was committed in Hart County. It was not committed in South Carolina or Elberton. The case would be tried in the appropriate court in Hart County.

Only the Facts

1. What is the main function of the courts?
2. In which kind of case—civil or criminal—is a government always a party?
3. What is the role of an appellate court? of a trial court?
4. Match the words to definitions of kinds of jurisdiction.
   1. limited
   2. personal
   3. concurrent
   4. subject matter
   (a) authority of the court to act with respect to the parties before it
   (b) the court's authority to enforce the particular kinds of laws involved in the controversy
   (c) authority to hear only specific kinds of cases
   (d) authority of more than one court to hear specific kinds of cases

Think About

1. What would be the advantages (or disadvantages) if counties rather than states had the power to declare acts as crimes?
2. Why do you think it is necessary for a court to have personal jurisdiction in a case?

THE GEORGIA AND FEDERAL COURT SYSTEMS

Georgia Courts

Even though the Georgia court system was simplified when the 1983 constitution took effect, it is still fairly complicated (see figure 3-1).

Trial Courts

Georgia has a number of courts that have what is called original jurisdiction. Courts that have original jurisdiction are the first to hear and decide a case. They are called trial courts.

The superior court is the main trial court in Georgia. Similar courts in other states may have different names. They may be called circuit courts or district courts. Superior courts are courts of general jurisdiction. They have exclusive jurisdiction over felonies (that is, the more serious crimes under Georgia law) and in certain areas of civil law. The superior courts are divided into 49 circuits, or geographic areas. In circuits that include more than one county, the superior court holds sessions in each county at least once each year. The court takes on the name of the county in which it holds sessions. In other words, when the Superior Court of the Pataula Circuit is holding sessions in Early County, it is known as the Superior Court of Early County. That is why each county is said to have a superior court.

Only 70 counties have state courts. State courts were created to lessen the caseload in superior courts. They have jurisdiction over misdemeanors (which are less serious crimes than felonies) and many civil disputes.

Each county has a probate court. These courts are among the oldest courts in Georgia. In earlier days, the judges were called county ordinaries. All probate courts have jurisdiction to probate wills (that is, to establish a will as genuine and valid). Other powers vary. Some, for example, serve as traffic courts.

Each county also has a juvenile court. In 2002, there were 120 judges serving the 159 counties. The state funds one full-time judge for every four superior court judges in a circuit. They hear matters involving children (discussed more fully in chapters 9 and 18).

The 1983 Georgia Constitution required each county to have a magistrate court by 1985. These courts replaced a variety of other courts (such as small claims courts, justice of the peace courts, etc.). They have jurisdiction over a variety of matters, including issuing warrants and hearing cases in which relatively small amounts of money are in dispute. A case involving one person suing another for damages to his or her car resulting from an accident is an example. In some cities, there are also municipal and special courts that do not come under the state system.

Appellate Courts

Like most states, Georgia has two appellate courts: the Georgia Supreme Court and the Georgia Court of Appeals. As appellate courts, they have the power to review and revise the judicial actions of lower courts.

The Georgia Supreme Court is the highest court in the state. It hears cases in which it has exclusive appellate jurisdiction. The intermediate appellate court, the Georgia Court of Appeals, hears appeals in all cases except those reserved exclusively for the supreme court. The supreme court may also hear appeals from the losing party in a decision originally appealed to the Georgia Court of Appeals. However, the supreme court can decide whether or not it wishes to review these cases. The supreme court usually reviews only two kinds of cases. One kind involves important legal principles. The other kind concerns cases in which the court thinks a great injustice might have occurred.

Superior courts also have appellate powers. They can review cases from the lower courts of limited jurisdiction. However, an appeal to the superior court differs somewhat from an appeal to the two higher appellate courts because, in some cases, additional evidence may be presented during an appeal at the superior court level. No new evidence is permitted in the higher appellate courts. In fact, at the superior court level an appeal can become a whole new trial of the case. This trial is called a trial *de novo*.

Federal Courts

The federal court system (figure 3-2) is somewhat similar to the Georgia court system. There are a number of trial courts and two appellate courts.

FIGURE 3-2

Basic Federal Court System

Supreme Court of United States

(1 chief justice, 8 associate justices)

- Tries lawsuits between states
- Reviews decisions of federal courts of appeal
- Reviews decisions of states' highest appellate courts if there is a question of federal or constitutional law

U.S. Courts of Appeals

(12 circuits, 3–15 judges in each)

- Hear appeals from U.S. district, territorial, and tax courts
- Review decisions of federal administrative agencies

U.S. District Courts

(1–4 districts in each state, 1–27 judges in each district)

- Hear criminal cases under federal law
- Hear civil cases under federal law or between citizens of two states in which the matter at issue is more than $50,000
- Hear bankruptcy cases

The system divides the country into 12 circuits. Each circuit consists of specified states and territories, except for the District of Columbia (Washington, D.C.), which is a circuit unto itself (see figure 3-3). Each circuit has a court of appeals. This court hears appeals from the district courts in the circuit.

Each state is divided into districts. There are one to four districts per state. Georgia has three districts: Northern, Middle, and Southern. Each district has a trial court. District trial courts are the principal trial courts of the federal system. They are courts of general jurisdiction. However, there are some limitations. For instance, in a civil case, the matter at issue must involve $50,000 or more for a district court to hear it.

The federal system has a number of trial and appellate courts with limited and exclusive juris-

Figure 3-3

Federal Courts: U.S. Circuits and Georgia Districts

The Eleventh Circuit Court of Appeals includes Alabama, Georgia, and Florida. Georgia is divided into three districts, each with a trial court.

peals. Generally, these appeals involve substantial questions of federal constitutional law. However, the Supreme Court can decide whether to review decisions of the court of appeals.

CASE STUDY

FOUR CASES IN SEARCH OF A COURT, *concluded*

The four cases are assigned to specific courts.

1. The case of *Danny Edwards v. Edgar Daniels* would be heard by the Magistrate Court of Lowndes County—the county in which Edgar lives. It could be heard by the county's superior court or state court, provided Lowndes County has a state court. However, a trial in those courts would be more expensive. The cost would not be justified by the amount of damages involved.

2. The case of *Janet Jones v. Giant Gadget Company* would be tried by the Federal District Court of Georgia's Northern District. If the Georgia courts were to be used, the case would be tried in the state or superior court in Cobb County.

3. The case of *United States v. Stan Smith* would come under the jurisdiction of the Federal District Court in Georgia's Southern District.

4. The case of *Georgia v. Dot Doe* would be tried by the Northern Circuit Superior Court, which serves Hart County.

dictions. These courts include the U.S. Court of Claims, the Tax Court of the United States, and the U.S. Court of International Trade (whose appeals go first to the U.S. Court of Customs and Patent Appeals). In addition, there are military courts. Military court decisions are appealed to the U.S. Court of Military Appeals, which has final jurisdiction. Bankruptcy courts are also a special type of court in the federal system. Bankruptcy cases are initiated in these courts, and appeals relating to them are conducted in the U.S. District Court.

The U.S. Supreme Court, unlike the Georgia Supreme Court, can act as a trial court. It can hear certain cases for the first time. For example, the Supreme Court would hear controversies between state governments, such as boundary disputes.

Like the Georgia Supreme Court, the U.S. Supreme Court hears only certain types of ap-

Only the Facts

1. Identify the following Georgia courts as appellate or trial courts: (a) superior court, (b) magistrate court, (c) supreme court, (d) state court, (e) court of appeals.

2. In the federal system, what is the principal trial court? What is the highest court in the United States?

3. What courts would have jurisdiction over the following kinds of court proceedings?

(a) a divorce case

(b) a traffic violation

(c) a claim of $500 for the breaking of a contract

(d) a claim of $17,000 for the breaking of a contract

(e) a suit claiming violation of constitutional rights

(f) the disposition of an estate under a will of a Georgia resident

(g) smuggling of goods across the U.S. border

(h) a boundary dispute between Texas and Oklahoma

(i) violating a city ordinance

(j) shoplifting by a 15-year-old student

JUDGES, JUSTICES, AND JURIES

Expressions such as "the court hears a case" or "the court decides" refer to the judges or justices in the court who hear and decide on the cases. Lawyers often refer to "the court" when they are speaking to the judge.

A trial court judge controls the conduct of the trial and ensures fairness to all parties. A judge decides questions of law. If there is no jury, the judge also decides questions about the facts in a case.

The right to trial by jury is a cherished part of our system of justice. Both the state and federal courts have two kinds of juries: grand juries and trial juries (also called petit or traverse juries). The grand jury indicts (or formally accuses) persons suspected of committing felonies. Trial juries decide the facts in criminal or civil trials.

Many courts have more than one judge or justice. Usually, only one judge hears each case at the trial court level. The Fulton County Superior Court has 19 judges, for example, but they preside individually over the cases brought before the court.

On the other hand, appellate cases are usually heard by several (sometimes all) judges of the court. The number of judges in a particular case depends on the laws governing the court as well as the type of case that is being heard.

To decide a case in an appellate court, usually a majority of the judges must agree on a decision. Although there can be only one decision, there may be a variety of opinions about that decision (see figure 3-4).

In the federal court system, almost all judges are appointed for life, as required by the U.S. Constitution. In the Georgia court system, however, almost all judges are elected (rather than appointed) for set terms. These terms are six years for appellate judges and four years for trial court judges. Juvenile court judges and some magistrate court judges are appointed to terms of similar length.

HOW COURTS "MAKE" LAWS

Courts interpret the law by explaining or clarifying what the law means. A court might interpret

---

FIGURE 3-4

Opinions of Justices

Supreme Court justices usually write opinions on major decisions. On one case, there may be several opinions given. They may support or disagree with the decision.

Opinions . . .

Agree with decision

- Majority opinion—Explanation of the decision, written by one judge and signed by each judge agreeing with the majority.

- Concurring opinion—Written by judge(s) agreeing with decision but disagreeing with reasons in the majority opinion. Opinion expresses what the writer feels are better reasons.

Disagree with decision

- Dissenting opinion—Written by judge(s) disagreeing with decision. Opinion explains why the writer thinks the decision should have been different.

law from a constitution, a statute, or an agency regulation. Consider the following situation:

> **SITUATION 4** The Georgia General Assembly passes a law that says carrying a concealed handgun is a crime. Tammy is charged with this crime. She was carrying a gun in a small cloth purse. During the trial, her lawyer claims the gun was not concealed. He introduces witnesses who testify that the outline of the gun was clearly visible within the purse. Therefore, her lawyer says Tammy should not be declared guilty.

In this case, the court must decide how broadly the word "concealed" should be defined. In making a decision, the judge might look for information to indicate what the legislature was thinking when the statute was written. Did it mean that the gun had to be outside any container? The judge would look to see if there were similar cases and how they were decided. He or she would carefully examine the evidence.

Suppose the court decided that Tammy was innocent. It would then say that the gun was not "concealed" by the purse. The decision would alter the definition of "concealed" in the law. In effect, it would redefine the law to say that a gun is not concealed if its outline is visible.

Suppose the court decides that Tammy is guilty. This decision also would change the definition of "concealed" in the law. It would indicate that guns in handbags are concealed, even if their shapes are visible.

Courts also make laws when they determine the validity of laws. Determining the validity of a law means considering whether it was properly enacted and if it is within the powers and limits of the government.

Court (or judicial) interpretations of powers and limits may change. For example, in the 1960s there were many concerns about the rights of persons accused of crimes. In 1963, the Supreme Court decided that a person accused of a felony was entitled to be represented in court by an attorney. This requirement then became part of the right to due process of law (that is, fair treat-

ment). Before 1963, it had not been part of that right. Can you see how this decision gave new meaning to the law concerning due process?

Common Law

So far, we have been talking about court cases involving laws made by constitutions, legislatures, or agencies. What happens when courts must decide on legal rights and duties without any written law to govern the situation?

Before the United States existed, the main source of law in England was common law. Common law can be defined as the legal rights and duties that courts declare exist in particular situations in the absence of statutes. Other courts then apply the court rulings from previous cases to current cases involving similar situations in order to resolve them.

The American system of justice originated from English common law. Much of that law has been enacted into statutes and codified, or gathered together into subject matter areas and published in books of laws, or codes.

However, some types of laws have not been enacted into statutes. Laws of torts (that is, wrongful acts that harm a person or property) and contracts are examples. The courts continuously interpret, renew, and create common law in these areas.

Reasoning by Analogy

When they consider a case, judges determine the legal rights and obligations of the parties involved. They first look for an applicable rule of law in constitutions, statutes, and agency rules. They also find out what other courts have decided in similar situations.

This method of decision making—looking to see what has happened in similar situations—is called reasoning by analogy. Reasoning by analogy is based on the idea that if two or more things agree with each other in some ways, they will probably agree in others. In other words,

Problem J is solved by Solution K.
Problem F is just like Problem J.

Reasoning by analogy suggests that Solution K should fit Problem F.

Such reasoning by analogy has become the basic tool of court decision making because it reflects the court's concern with consistency. Court decisions need to have some degree of consistency so that people will know what their legal duties are. Courts therefore rely on previously decided cases (or precedent) to form opinions in current cases.

To see how this reasoning works, read the following case:

CASE OF THE SMASHED GRAPES

Carlos was walking past the fruit bins in a grocery store. Several loose grapes had fallen to the floor and had been smashed by people passing by. Noticing a friend, Carlos turned and waved. Unfortunately, Carlos was stepping on the smashed grapes at the time. He slipped. As he fell, he grabbed the arm of the nearest person, an elderly lady. She also fell, and she broke her wrist.

The elderly lady sues the grocery store to pay her damages for her injury. She feels that the injury was the result of the store's failure to pick up the grapes. The judge of this case must decide if the grocery store should be responsible for the damages to the elderly lady. The judge will need to know what other courts have decided in similar cases.

One previous case is that of the Slippery Spot. In the Slippery Spot case, Joan Brown was hurrying across the dining area of a restaurant. Joan slipped on a spot left by a platter of buttered spaghetti spilled earlier. In falling, she knocked the tray of a waiter. The waiter was carrying a dish of lasagna. It slipped off the tray onto Mr. Wilson, damaging his suit.

In that case, the judge said that the restaurant had a legal duty to maintain a safe environment for its customers. Therefore, it had a legal duty to clean up the slippery spot caused by the spilled spaghetti. Cleaning the spot was necessary to prevent someone from falling. Because

it had not cleaned up the spot, the restaurant was held responsible for any damages caused by its failure to do so. It had to pay the damages caused by Joan's slipping and falling—including the damage to Mr. Wilson's suit.

The judge in the Case of the Smashed Grapes will decide if the same rule of law should be applied. The judge's first question will be whether the facts in the Smashed Grapes case are similar to those in the Slippery Spot case. Does the grocery store, too, have a legal duty to maintain a safe environment for its customers? If so, doesn't it have to clean up grapes that have fallen to the floor? Doesn't it need to prevent people from slipping and hurting themselves?

The facts in the two cases appear to be similar. Therefore, the judge in the Smashed Grapes case may decide that the same rule of law should be applied.

Precedents

As has been mentioned, courts often rely on previously decided cases (or precedent) to form opinions in current cases. A judge making use of the Slippery Spot case in resolving the Smashed Grapes case would refer to it as a precedent. The principle whereby a previous decision is applied to other cases in which the facts are similar is called *stare decisis* (pronounced "starry-di-sigh-sis"), a well-known principle of law. A court may decide that the facts differ from those in an earlier case, however. Then, the court is not required to follow the first case. Before deliberately breaking with consistency, a court must be very sure there is a substantial difference in the facts of the case.

CASE OF THE SMASHED GRAPES,
continued

In the Slippery Spot case, the spot had been left on the floor a long time. Both the waiter and restaurant manager had time to notice it. They had time to clean it up. The situation appears to be similar in the Smashed Grapes case. However, suppose that the grapes had just fallen onto the floor before Carlos stepped on them or Carlos knocked the grapes to the floor accidentally.

A judge depends on reasoning by analogy in deciding questions of law.

In both these situations, no grocery store employee would have had a reasonable chance to discover that the grapes were a potential problem. Therefore, the facts of the case would differ from those in the Slippery Spot case. The judge may feel that the same rule does not apply and that a grocery store should be given a reasonable opportunity to discover such a danger. The judge may decide that the grocery store should not be held liable for any damages caused by a situation it did not have time to remedy.

What if there are no decisions in cases similar to the one at hand? In other words, what if there is no applicable rule of law—no precedent—to follow? Then a court must fashion a new rule that it feels will provide a just result in the case before it.

The decision not to hold the grocery store liable in the Smashed Grapes case could therefore create a new rule of law. If the ruling were appealed, it would be reviewed by an appellate court in Georgia. If the court were to uphold the decision, it would likely become a precedent for Georgia courts. Even if it were not reviewed

by an appellate court, the decision might still be considered a persuasive precedent by another trial court in Georgia.

What if the ruling was reviewed by the U.S. Supreme Court and the court concurred with the decision? The ruling would set a precedent that would have to be considered by federal courts and courts in other states.

Equity

Infrequently, a court faces a situation in which applying an established rule of law would have an unwanted or unjust result. The power of the court not to apply a rule in a special situation is called equity.

To illustrate, suppose you have contracted to buy an antique car—a 1920 Model T. You have put some money down for the car. However, when you come to collect the car, the seller has sold it to someone else for more money. You don't want your down payment back: you want the car.

Typically, you would be entitled to get your money back. To get the car itself, however, you might bring a suit in equity. Suits in equity concern wanting to stop some action or wanting some specified performance, as in this example. In this case, you want the court to "order" the seller to sell you the car.

Only the Facts

1. Define common law.
2. What change is necessary to make the following an example of reasoning by analogy?
   Problem A is solved by Solution C. Problem B is the same as Problem A. Solution D should fit Problem B.
3. What is a precedent?

Think About

1. Why is consistency important in all law?

CHANGING COURT-MADE LAW

The Effects of Change

Courts, in general, are cautious about change. In making decisions, they usually look to what has gone before. They look to precedents. Usually, courts reject precedents only for strong reasons.

On the other hand, each court decision adds new meaning to existing laws because the law is interpreted anew in each case. In this way, court-made laws—and laws in general—are constantly being redefined and changed.

The following situation illustrates how court interpretations have accommodated changes in technology:

> **SITUATION 5** Genetic engineers in the 4891 Company have altered apple tree genes to create a new form. This "new" apple tree can produce three harvests of apples each year. The 4891 Company would like to legally protect this new form of life.

Can it do so?

The U.S. Constitution gives Congress the power to make laws regarding patents. Patent and trademark laws were originally passed to protect machines or other identifiable inventions. The U.S. Supreme Court has found that new forms of life are similar to other inventions. Therefore, new forms of life, like the apple tree, could be patented.

Similarly, court interpretations have modified laws in response to changes in values as mentioned in chapter 2. A good example is the landmark U.S. Supreme Court decision in 1954, *Brown v. Topeka Board of Education*.[1] In effect, it said that racially segregated schools are not equal. They do not provide all children with "equal protection of the law." Many years earlier, courts looking at the same issue had held that such schools could be "separate but equal." The 1954 decision reflected the changed attitudes of many people.

Using the Courts to Bring about Change

For people in many situations, the courts offer the most effective way of trying to change existing laws. In fact, the courts may seem the only protection against the power of government and society. People can initiate suits to stop harmful actions of the government or others or because they think their rights are being violated or that a government act violates existing laws. However, people are not allowed to use courts to change laws unless there is a real controversy. There must be some actual harm or a threat of an immediate harm that, once done, could not be remedied.

Sometimes—to bring about change—people deliberately break the law. For example, as a form of protest against segregation in the 1960s, African-American demonstrators broke laws designed to segregate races by eating at "whites-only" lunch counters in restaurants and using the whites-only section of buses. They intended to call the courts' attention to violations of equal protection. By breaking existing laws, people risked punishment, but they felt that the risk was worth it.

It should be kept in mind, however, that court rulings—even landmark decisions—do not create immediate changes. Sometimes it takes years—even decades—for changes to follow court decisions, as in the court decision concerning the racial desegregation of schools.

Only the Facts

1. When can people use the courts to bring about a change?

Think About

1. On the basis of what you've learned in chapters 2 and 3, how do you think you could be most effective in getting a law changed? Consider how you would act to bring about change in each type of law (such as constitutional, statutory, administrative, and case law).

ALTERNATIVE DISPUTE RESOLUTION

When parties are in a dispute, they may be tempted to take their case to court. However, there are alternatives to going to court that are quicker, less expensive, and more confidential than a public trial. Some of the advantages and disadvantages of the different forms of alternative dispute resolution (ADR) are discussed below.

What Is ADR?

The most common forms of settling disputes peacefully without going to court are negotiation, mediation, and arbitration. In negotiation, each disputing party, or someone acting for each party (such as an attorney), talks directly with the other party or attorney to reach a settlement. This method has been used for centuries, but it sometimes breaks down, and no settlement is reached.

In mediation, one or more persons (or mediators) help the disputing parties reach an agreement on how to handle their problem. The mediator does not judge or take sides; he or she merely guides the parties to a settlement that is agreeable to both sides. As in negotiation, the final decision is voluntary. Both sides must agree for it to be legally binding.

In arbitration, one or more persons (or arbitrators) hear the arguments and facts of both sides. Then they make a decision as to what to do. Arbitration is like a private trial but less formal. Unlike a mediator, an arbitrator does judge and take sides. Unlike a trial, arbitration does not usually include all of the detailed, complex rules of a court. As in mediation, the disputants must agree to enter into the process for it to be legal. However, in arbitration, the disputants agree in advance to be bound by whatever decision the arbitrator reaches. This way, they can't back out afterwards.

ADR is still very new and continues to develop in different forms and combinations. These hybrids can be created to satisfy the disputing parties. For example, "med-arb" combines mediation with arbitration. First, a mediator tries to get the disputing parties to reach an agreement of their own choosing. If they don't come to an agreement, another arbitrator steps in and arbitrates a decision.

Why Use ADR?

The best method of ADR, or even the decision to use one at all, depends on the circumstances and parties in each case. ADR does not solve all problems. In fact, its use is not permitted in some cases. Here are some of the advantages and disadvantages of ADR:

- No jury: ADR eliminates the worry of what a jury might decide. However, a party who wants a jury of peers to judge a case would have to seek a court trial instead.

- Decision making by experts: Some cases can be very complex. In ADR, the disputing parties may be able to pick a mediator, arbitrator, or evaluator who is knowledgeable in the particular field that the case involves.

- Confidentiality: While most court proceedings are open to the public, most ADR proceedings are private. Confidentiality may be an important consideration for the parties.

- Finality: Most ADR proceedings end with a decision or settlement agreement that is binding on all parties. Court trials, on the other hand, can be followed by years of appeals. A party wanting the right to appeal would probably choose to use the court system.

- Timeliness: ADR is usually, but not always, faster than the court system. Courts can be heavily backlogged with cases.

- Costs: ADR is often less expensive than the court system. It is faster and has fewer appeals. The use of fewer documents in the process also cuts time and costs. However, keeping costs down also depends on how the process is set up and customized. ADR does have some costs that courts do not. For instance, disputing parties pay for the ADR service provider. In the court system, the parties do not pay for the judge or for court administrative services. (These costs are paid by tax dollars.)

- Adversarial climate: Supporters of ADR argue that it encourages less angry interaction between parties. Opponents say that atmosphere and interaction really depend on the disputing parties.

- Venting: Often all that disputing parties really need is to vent their frustrations to an impartial third party. In these cases, mediation and other ADR forms may be more efficient than going to court.

When to use ADR, and which form to use, is a very personal decision. Would ADR be appropriate in the following situations?

SITUATION 6 Jim was fired from his job and claims he wasn't given proper notice. He also feels that he is entitled to severance and back pay equal to $2,000. His employer, Wall-Ton Cement Manufacturers, says that it is not legally required to give him notice. There was no written contract. Further, his severance and back pay were used to cover the repair bill for a machine he broke at work.

SITUATION 7 Wylie bought a package of fireworks from ACME Explosives Inc. He was seriously injured by an explosion when he used them. Wylie claims that his injuries were caused by a defect in the product. ACME asserts that Wylie used the fireworks improperly; that is, not in the manner as clearly stated in a warning label. Wylie's injuries include total and permanent blindness. ACME is concerned that if it pays Wylie anything, others will also seek payments and the company would be forced to recall its product.

SITUATION 8 Wanda and Betty have been neighbors for years. Betty has a teenage son who recently started riding his dirt bike at night in the open field next door. Wanda and her husband, Fred, have complained to Betty that the noise is distracting and annoying. Betty has asked her son to stop. At the same time, she has also told Wanda and Fred that the field is not theirs. She also points out that the biking is not that loud and it does not occur late at night. Wanda is considering calling the police or suing in court.

SITUATION 9 Amy and Sarah are high school juniors. They have been friends since the fourth grade, but lately their relationship has become strained. First, Amy made the cheerleading squad and Sarah didn't. Then, Sarah started dating Nick, whom Amy had a crush on. In fact, she had hoped Nick would ask her to the prom this year. Last week, Amy couldn't find one of her textbooks and accused Sarah of stealing it. The girls had a loud argument in the hallway in front of their lockers and were sent to the principal's office.

ADR could be used in all four situations if all the parties agreed to try it. It would be very appropriate for situations 6 and 8. The injuries in both are minor, but the cost of suing would be high. Mediation would be a very good alternative in situation 8. Wanda and Betty have been neighbors for years and will likely remain so. Mediation generally helps people stay in their former personal and business relationships after a dispute is resolved, largely because the disputing parties themselves help reach the decision.

Situation 7 may not be best solved by ADR because the injury and issues are so great. On the other hand, ADR might offer a more private setting than would an open court. Also, costs would probably be lower for all parties.

Situation 9 is unique in that no lawsuit might even be possible. What exactly would a lawsuit solve? The problems that Amy and Sarah are having go a lot deeper than the textbook incident. ADR includes peer mediation, and many schools have set up such programs. In this form of mediation, disputes between students are handled by fellow classmates. The student mediators have been trained by teachers and others who understand ADR techniques. Do you think "venting" by Sarah and Amy in such a setting would help?

Where Are ADR Sessions Held?

Where disputing parties go to use these alternatives to court depends on the case. For example, say the dispute is the result of a broken contract. The contract may have an ADR clause specifying how the problem will be resolved and by whom.

On the other hand, a great number of judicial systems now offer ADR programs. The programs have been set up and are supported by the government. In systems that have these programs, judges may urge the parties to try ADR before going to trial. The cost of these programs can be very low, even free. If these two avenues are not available and both parties want to try ADR, they will have to agree on a particular ADR provider.

Only the Facts

1. True or false: ADR is always better than suing in court. Why or why not?

2. List the advantages and disadvantages of ADR. Give one example in which ADR would probably be a good idea and another in which it probably would not.

3. What is the difference between mediation and arbitration?

Think About

1. Does the existence of ADR suggest that the court system is not working? Explain your answer.

2. Would a peer mediation program in your school be helpful? Why or why not? Who among you would be a good mediator?

SUMMING UP

This chapter has discussed the many different kinds of courts—civil and criminal, trial and appellate, state and federal—and how they make and interpret laws based on analogy and precedent. Although Georgia streamlined its court system during the 1980s, some people feel that still more changes should be made to improve our courts and system of justice. For one thing, courts labor under huge caseloads, causing great delays. Could many disputes be settled in other ways, such as ADR? Does the system allow too many appeals? These are questions to consider in the chapters ahead.

The next part of the book explains how laws affect your everyday life. These laws have to do with working, buying, borrowing, and driving. They concern your family and your home. How the courts interpret these laws and enforce rights and duties in different areas of law will be the focus of later chapters.

Note

1. 374 U.S. 483 (1954).

PART 2 CIVIL LAW

4 Contracts and Consumers

SITUATION 1 Tim, 15, thrusts a piece of paper under the nose of 13-year-old Billy Joe. "It's a contract," he says. "Sign it." The paper says, "I, Billy Joe, promise Tim the answers he needs for the math exam. In exchange, Tim will not beat up Billy Joe on the way home ever again." Billy Joe is scared. He takes the paper and scrawls his name quickly.

Is this a contract?

The first part of this chapter is about contracts. Contracts are legally binding agreements used in borrowing money, obtaining housing, and getting a job. In short, contracts are basic to living in our society. The second part of the chapter is about consumer law. Consumer law governs the spending of money for personal, family, and household purposes. It covers purchases as major as a car and as minor as a piece of gum.

CONTRACTS

The right to enter into contracts is an important legal right. A contract is an agreement between two or more people requiring each person to do something specific. This agreement may also require a person to refrain from doing something that he or she has a right to do. Contracts have four essential ingredients. To have a legal contract, there must be (1) a mutual agreement or "meeting of the minds," (2) two or more parties capable of contracting or reaching an agreement, (3) an agreement in which all parties have to carry out some obligation, and (4) a lawful purpose.

LAW TALK

caveat emptor

consideration

consumer

contract

duress

fraud

unconscionable

warranty

Requirements for a Contract

A Meeting of the Minds

Basic to a contract is a "meeting of the minds." The parties have to understand and express to each other what is expected of each of them. For instance, in a situation in which something is being bought and sold, both the buyer and the seller have to agree on what is being bought and sold and the price of what is being bought and sold. The process of making a contract usually begins with one party making an offer. The other party may accept the offer, reject the offer, or make a counteroffer. Making a counteroffer is negotiating.

To create a contract, one person must accept another person's offer or counteroffer. A legally binding contract is formed once an offer or counteroffer is accepted. An offer or counteroffer can only be accepted by the person to whom it is made.

The meeting of the minds necessary for a contract can only occur when the agreement is freely entered into by both parties. If one party is coerced into signing, then their minds have not met. The legal term for being coerced into entering a contract is "duress." Under Georgia law, duress is defined as imprisonment, threats, or other acts by which the free will of a party is restrained and his or her consent induced. For example, what if a salesperson has "pressured" you into signing a contract to buy a motorcycle? Could you get out of the contract? Maybe, but if you took the motorcycle home and used it, probably not. Your use of the motorcycle would reinforce your acceptance of the contract.

Parties Capable of Contracting

The expression "parties capable of contracting" has a very specific legal meaning. To have a contract, the minds of the parties must meet. For minds to meet, each party must understand what is taking place.

The law regards certain groups of people as incapable of understanding agreements. The mentally incompetent, for example, are considered unable to make a valid contract. The courts could void a contract signed by a mentally incompetent person.

Young people are also considered incapable of understanding enough about contract obligations to be bound by what they sign. In Georgia, the legal age of majority (the age at which a person is considered to be an adult in contractual situations) is 18 years. Youths under 18 (that is, minors) may not legally enter into contracts.

> **SITUATION 2** Jane Junior, 17, lied about her age when she contracted to buy a used car from Marty. She agreed to pay off the car over the year. But when Jane lost her job, she was no longer able to make the payments required under the contract. Marty wants Jane to pay the money or return the car.
>
> Is the contract valid, since Jane was under age? Can Marty recover his money?

The law does not allow persons under 18 to enter into contracts. However, the age requirement does not mean that persons can lie about their ages to sign contracts and retain the benefits without paying for them. In Georgia, to get out of a contract, a minor usually must return the benefits, if possible. Jane would probably have to return the car.

One kind of minor can enter into contracts under Georgia law. Someone under 18 who is not supported by his or her parents can be legally classified as an emancipated minor. An emancipated minor may enter into contracts (in certain limited situations) for necessities (that is, food, clothing, shelter, and education).

An Agreement with Obligations

Suppose Steve says to Rick, "I will give you my horse next Tuesday." Rick says, "I agree." Would this be a contract? No, it is a proposal to make a gift. In a contract agreement, both parties—not just one—must have some type of obligation. They must each make some promise to the other. These mutual obligations are called consideration. Without each party agreeing to obligations, no contract exists.

SITUATION 3 Mr. Venerable wrote a letter to Yolanda that said, "If you will drive me to the grocery store every Friday afternoon to shop, I will leave you $10,000 in my will."

Would this be an enforceable contract?

It probably would. The driving may not be worth $10,000. Nonetheless, it is a consideration, however small, for the $10,000 bequest.

In rare cases, a great variance in obligations may be used as evidence to void a contract. If the terms of the contract are so one-sided that it is obvious that no sane or reasonable person would agree to them and no honest person would take advantage of those terms, the contract is said to be unconscionable. An unconscionable contract will not be enforced by the courts. For example, suppose Mr. Venerable had offered Yolanda $10,000 to drive him one afternoon only and she had agreed. Then the contract could be voidable. That would be particularly true if there were also a great difference between the mental abilities of the two parties. For instance, if Mr. Venerable had Alzheimer's disease and Yolanda was known to have taken advantage of people, the contract could be voidable.

The consideration does not have to be of equal value on both sides, and it does not have to be money. It can be a concrete object or an action. It can be a promise to do something that someone is not already required to do, or it can be a promise to keep from doing an activity that someone has a legal right to do. What if John promises to give Richard $100 if Richard does not smoke cigarettes for a year? Their agreement would be enforceable.

It is not essential to a contract that the mutual obligations be carried out at the same time. One person may perform his or her obligation immediately. The other person may carry out the obligation at some time in the future.

It is possible to have a contract in which both persons agree to perform in the future. An example would be a contract in which an author agrees to write a textbook and a publisher agrees to publish it and pay the author $5,000 when it is done.

A Legal Purpose

Having a legal purpose is as important to a contract as having a meeting of the minds, legally capable parties, and mutual obligations. However, unless prohibited by law, almost any purpose is permissible in our free society. A contract cannot be enforced by law unless its purpose is legally permissible.

SITUATION 4 Jake and Terry write out a contract. In it, Jake says he will pay Terry $100 if the University of Georgia is number one in the football rankings at the end of the season. Terry says he will pay Jake $100 if it is not. The team does not make the top spot. Terry refuses to pay.

Can Jake take him to court to get his money?

SITUATION 5 Fred wants to sell some land to the city for a park. He will sell it for a dollar if use of the park is restricted to white people only.

Would a contract between the city and Fred be legal?

Jake and Terry (situation 4) have a gambling contract. It would be illegal and not enforceable by the courts. A contract to break a law—whether it involves gambling, beating someone up, or buying illegal drugs—does not have a legal purpose. It cannot be enforced. Further, being party to a contract to break a law can land a person in jail.

Just because a contract does not break a criminal law doesn't mean that it has a legal purpose. A contract that doesn't comply with a civil statute or that violates constitutional, statutory, administrative, or case law also is illegal. For that reason, the contract imposing racial discrimination (situation 5) would be illegal and unenforceable. Governments cannot violate the constitutional rights of individuals to equal protection under the law.

Spoken and Written Contracts

Contracts may be oral (that is, spoken) or written. However, spoken contracts are difficult to enforce in court because they are difficult to prove. Certain types of contracts must be in writing in order to be enforceable. For example, a promise to pay someone else's debt must be in writing. So must a contract to buy or sell real estate. Any agreement that cannot be fully carried out by both parties within one year must also be written.

Courts will presume that each party to a written contract has read the contract and understands it. It is difficult to convince a court that a person did not understand the terms of the contract. To the courts, the signing of a contract means that there has been a meeting of the minds. Therefore, it is very important to understand the terms of a contract before signing it. However, sometimes state or federal laws will protect a consumer even if that consumer has signed a contract. (See "Voiding a Contract: Fraud" later in this chapter.)

Unfortunately, people often sign contracts without reading them for any number of reasons. For one thing, the wording in contracts can be difficult to understand (see figure 4-1). There are currently efforts to have contracts written in plain English.

If you don't understand a contract, ask someone you trust to explain it to you. Figure 4-2 gives other guidelines to use when entering into a contract.

Enforcing Contracts

To be found enforceable, a contract must have the four essential ingredients. In addition, the court must also find that there was no legal justi-

fication for one of the parties not to carry out his or her contract obligation. If the four ingredients are in place and there is no legal justification for not complying with the contract, a lawsuit can be made successfully against the party breaking the contract.

If the party attempting to prove the contract succeeds, the court will make a decision (or judgment) in favor of that party. This decision says that the other party must pay a certain amount of money for breaching (or breaking) the contract. The winning party then has the right to collect the money from the party that is sued.

FIGURE 4-1

Contract Language vs. Plain English

Contract Language: Each of us hereby both individually and severally waives any or all benefit or relief from homestead exemption and all other exemptions or moratoriums to which the signers or any of them may be entitled under the laws of this or any other state, now in force, or hereafter to be passed as against this debt or any renewal thereof.

> *Plain English Meaning*: If I don't pay, you can come and take even the personal belongings that state law would allow me to keep.

. . . .

Contract Language: Upon default, the creditor may retain the collateral as his property or may sell or otherwise dispose of the collateral pursuant to the (state) Uniform Commercial Code, whereupon debtor shall be liable for and shall pay any deficiency on demand.

> *Plain English Meaning*: If I fail to make a payment, you can repossess and try to sell what I bought from you. If you don't get the full purchase price back, I'll still owe you the difference between the sale proceeds and the full purchase price. (For example, if you take back a perfectly good $500 TV set and can get only $150 for it, I lose the TV and still owe you $350.)

Source: Adapted from *Georgia: A Consumer's Guide*. Atlanta: Governor's Office of Consumer Affairs.

Note: This kind of language is often found in contracts between borrowers and lenders. These contracts are discussed in chapter 5.

FIGURE 4-2

When You Enter a Written Contract

- Read and understand the contract before signing it.
- Don't sign any contract that has unfilled blanks.
- Don't sign a contract if the signature line is on a page by itself.
- Be sure what you are buying or what you have been promised is clearly written. The contract should include information on the quality of goods, terms of services, repair or replacement guarantees, all charges, etc.
- Check on provisions for canceling the contract.
- Make sure any changes in the contract are initialed and dated by you and the other party.
- Make sure your copy of the contract is identical to the other party's copy.
- Keep the contract in a safe place.

What if the sued party does not willingly honor the court's order to pay? Then a court officer (for example, a sheriff) may be ordered to seize the money of the party breaking the contract and deliver it to the other party. The officer also has the power in most cases, to seize property of the contract-breaker. The property may be sold to obtain money to pay the civil judgment.

Sometimes, however, the judgment comes in the form of an order for "specific performance," which means that a party is obligated by contract to do something other than to pay money. Then the court may order the person to do whatever is required. For instance, if you made a contract to buy a one-of-a-kind baseball card of a famous player but the seller changes his or her mind, you might be able to get specific performance in the form of receiving the card itself rather than the value of the card. If a person refuses to do what the court orders, he or she could be jailed for contempt of court. However, in the United States, people cannot be jailed for being unable to pay money they owe.

Many people mistakenly believe that there is a right to cancel most consumer contracts within three days of entering into them. Only certain kinds of contracts are required by law to have a cancellation period. Examples include door-to-door sales and sales of services.

Voiding a Contract: Fraud

When one person tries to mislead another, the parties will not be expecting the same things from their contract. Such attempts to deceive are sometimes considered to be fraud.

Fraud can prevent a meeting of the minds. Therefore, a contract often can be legally voided for reasons of fraud. To void a contract for fraud, it must be shown that the party attempting to prove fraud relied on the other party's fraudulent statements. It must also be shown that these statements were crucial to the bargain. In other words, the bargain never would have been made if the fraudulent statements had not been made. A person selling a car who claims that it has 100,000 miles when it really has 200,000 would be an example of fraud. Would the following situations be examples of fraud?

SITUATION 6 A man wants to buy a used car. The salesperson says it has only been driven by a "little old lady." Later, the buyer learns that the car was owned and driven by a middle-aged businessman.

SITUATION 7 An auto dealer advertises a new line of cars as "super steeds." In fact, billboards around town say they start up like "race horses bursting from the gate." A buyer of one of the cars becomes angry when the car doesn't seem to perform as described.

SITUATION 8 Another auto dealer advertises the same new line of cars as having 350-horsepower engines. A buyer of one of the cars is suspicious of the claim. He discovers the car's engine is 250 horsepower.

Both situations 6 and 7 would not be considered fraud. In situation 6, the identity of the previous driver would probably not be regarded as crucial to the bargain. After all, which is really important—who drove the car, or how much it was actually driven? The buyer should have asked how many miles the car had been driven.

Matters of opinion generally are not considered facts by the court. What is the speed of "super steeds" in regard to cars (situation 7)? It would certainly be a matter of opinion on which minds might not meet. Such claims are quite common in advertising. They are referred to as puffery. Puffery is not illegal. It is assumed that consumers will be wary enough not to be misled by such exaggerations.

Value is also regarded by the courts as a matter of opinion. Suppose you buy a guitar for $100. You are later told it is worth only $50. You would not be able to sue on the basis of being defrauded.

On the other hand, the advertisement in situation 8 involves information crucial to the bargain. It does not just involve an opinion. Either an engine has 350 horsepower or it does not—a fact that would have to be considered crucial to the purchase of the car. The dealer's statement in situation 8 would involve fraud or breach of other state law.

O n l y   t h e   F a c t s

1. What are the four ingredients of a contract?
2. What is meant by a "meeting of the minds"?
3. What kinds of contracts must be in writing?
4. How does the state enforce contracts?
5. Give an example of fraud.

T h i n k   A b o u t

1. At what age do you think people should be able to enter into contracts? Defend your answer.
2. Unless it can be proved that there was no meeting of the minds between parties, a contract can be legally upheld even if one party did not understand it before signing. What reforms might you recommend to protect contract signers?

SUMMING UP CONTRACTS

At this point, you can easily explain why situation 1 at the beginning of this chapter is not an enforceable contract. The parties are minors, one party was under duress, the obligations are vague, and it has illegal purposes. Beating up someone is a crime called battery.

Subsequent chapters discuss different kinds of contracts, including those basic to consumer law and borrowing money. Borrowing money usually involves a contract between a lender and a borrower. Renting a home involves a contract between a landlord and a tenant. Jobs are usually contractual arrangements. Owning a car can involve a contract between an automobile dealer and a buyer. It also involves a contract between an insurance company and an insured person.

CONSUMER LAW

Long before there was any law protecting consumers, the doctrine of *caveat emptor* ("let the buyer beware") prevailed. In other words, the best protection for a consumer is to be very careful:

- Be careful about the person or firm selling the goods or services.
- Be careful about the quality of goods or services.
- Be careful about the price and terms of payment.

In this century, the first major bill to protect consumers was called the Pure Food and Drug Act. Passed by Congress in 1906, it prohibited the mislabeling of the contents of food, liquor, and medicine containers. About this time, many states, including Georgia, also passed laws to protect the public against unwholesome food and harmful ingredients in drugs. Since then, numerous consumer-protection laws have been passed.

Why has there been an increase in consumer laws? One reason is that we live in an age of mass production. Buyers and makers of goods usually don't know each other. When people bought shoes from the village cobbler, they could complain when the shoes were not well made. Now people buy shoes made in other states or countries. Getting satisfaction for poorly made shoes or other products can be almost impossible.

This disconnection between buyers and sellers means also that more and more goods travel through interstate commerce. Regulating interstate commerce is one of the powers given by the Constitution to Congress. This power has enabled Congress to pass consumer-protection laws.

In the U.S. economy, most dealings between consumers and sellers or lenders are relatively free of government control. Generally, laws regulating sellers or lenders are passed only when the practices of sellers have seemed deceptive, harsh, unfair, or misleading. Some fields of consumer law have required more regulation than others. They are discussed in this chapter and in chapter 5.

Regulating Product Quality (Warranties)

When you buy something at a store—be it a stereo cassette or a tennis racket—you expect that it will work. You also expect it to last for some period of time. What if it doesn't? What rights do you have as a buyer?

Warranties are a consumer's major safeguard of product quality. A warranty is the seller's legal promise or guarantee as to the quality of the goods. There are two kinds of warranties: implied (or statutory) and express (or contractual).

Implied (Statutory) Warranties

Implied (or statutory) warranties are imposed on products by law. Nearly every state in the United States has adopted a set of laws called the Uniform Commercial Code (UCC). Among these laws is a law providing that goods purchased from a merchant are assumed to have certain warranties. A merchant deals in goods of a particular kind. A large store like Wal-Mart is a merchant of many different kinds of goods. These warranties are said to be implied because they do not have to be formally stated by the merchant.

However, implied warranties can be waived (or given up) by the consumer.

There are three implied, or statutory, warranties: (1) warranty of merchantability, (2) warranty of fitness, and (3) warranty of title.

Warranty of merchantability. Merchantable goods are goods that are fit to be sold. The warranty of merchantability means that the goods are fit for the ordinary purpose for which such goods are sold. It can also mean they are as described on the package or label and that the goods are of fair or average quality. However, it is not a guarantee that the goods are of superior or outstanding quality. Does this warranty exist in the following situation?

SITUATION 9 Betty buys an electric fan. She takes it home, and it doesn't work. Clerks at the store refuse to take it back or exchange it. They say they never guaranteed the fan would work. There is no bill of sale beyond a cash register receipt.

Does the store have any obligation?

The warranty of merchantability exists whether or not the seller states it in words. In situation 9, there is no evidence that Betty waived any part of this warranty. Therefore, the store has a legal duty to sell her a fan that works. The result might be different if Betty found that the fan was not as quiet as she might have liked. In that case, the warranty might not apply.

Warranty of fitness.

SITUATION 10 Mr. Green needs something to kill a specific weed that is attacking his crop of beans. He asks the farm supply store owner what he would recommend. The store owner says he has just the thing. Mr. Green buys a large amount of the chemical recommended. It doesn't work.

Has the warranty been broken?

If the seller knows that the goods are to be used for a particular purpose, there is also an implied warranty that the goods are fit for that purpose. This assumption is particularly true if the buyer is relying on the judgment of the seller in selecting the goods. This warranty would apply in situation 10.

Warranty of title.

SITUATION 11 At Will's garage sale, Carol buys a handsome television set. When she takes it home, Ann, Will's cousin, appears at her door. Ann says that the television is hers and that Will had no right to sell it. She shows Carol her bill of sale. Carol calls Will. He admits the television was not his but refuses to return Carol's money.

What are Carol's legal rights?

The implied warranty of title means that a buyer has the right to assume, unless told otherwise, that a seller owns the property he or she is selling. It means the seller has the right to sell it. Buyers also can assume that they will be the sole owners of whatever they buy, unless told otherwise. In situation 11, Carol would have a legal right to the return of her money.

Waiving implied warranties.

SITUATION 12 Gerry decides to buy a used car from Tom. She looks it over carefully and test-drives it. The car seems okay to her. When she gives Tom the check, Tom gives her a bill of sale. It states that the car is sold "as is." Gerry signs the bill. A few days later, the transmission goes out on the car.

Can Gerry get any money back from Tom?

The implied warranties of merchantability and of fitness for a particular purpose may be waived by the buyer. Often, this waiver occurs when goods are accepted "as is," "in present condition," or words to that effect. To be effective,

The "as is" sign on this truck tells the buyer that there will be no refunds or exchanges.

these types of phrases must be prominent and conspicuous.

Used cars are frequently sold "as is," which means that the seller does not warrant their condition. If they break down, the loss is the responsibility of the buyer. By signing a bill of sale that stated that the car was being sold as is, Gerry (in situation 12) gave up the implied warranties of merchantability and fitness. She therefore probably cannot recover her money from Tom.

SITUATION 13 Wanda buys a dress at a shop. A sign over the cash register reads "No Refunds or Exchanges." When she gets home, she notices a bad stain in the skirt. She had not seen it when she hastily tried on the dress.

Can she get her money back?

A store that does not give refunds or exchanges is, in effect, selling goods "as is." It is making its customers give up the warranties of merchantability and fitness. However, customers must know about the policy. To be valid, the policy may have to be in writing and conspicuous to the buyer. In situation 13, the store policy was clearly posted on signs. For these reasons, Wanda probably would not be able to get her money back.

Express (Contractual) Warranties

Express (or contractual) warranties are created by certain actions of the seller or manufacturer. You are probably most familiar with written warranties that accompany goods. These warranties usually make some guarantee about the material, workmanship, and performance of a product. They usually state what the manufacturer or seller will do if a product does not perform well.

Express warranties can also be created by the seller by

1. making a specific promise or affirming a fact. Suppose a saleswoman says the store will make any necessary repairs on a computer free of charge for a year. She is creating an express warranty.

2. a written description of the goods. If a mail order catalog describes a tent as waterproof, an express warranty is created.

3. showing a sample or model to the buyer. In doing so, the seller is promising that the item actually sold to the buyer will be like the model shown prior to the sale. Suppose a shop owner demonstrates a color television, and you buy an identical model. You should expect it to perform the same way. The owner has created an express warranty.

An express warranty may also take the form of a bill of sale that a buyer must sign. However, the bill of sale may limit or disclaim the seller's responsibility for defects in the product. It may ask the buyer to give up implied or even express warranties. Be sure to read documents you are required to sign at the time of a purchase.

Warranties can be full or limited. A full warranty assures the buyer that the goods are totally free from defects at the time of the sale. It may include an obligation that the seller repair the goods within some time limit if they do not work properly.

SITUATION 14 Selina buys a sewing machine. With it is a written statement that the machine has a full warranty. The next week, the machine's motor breaks down. Selina takes it back to the store. The manager tells her the full warranty is only on the paint on the cabinet. He says that the warranty on the working parts is limited to labor only. She will have to pay $250 for a new motor, but labor will be free.

Can she sue? On what basis?

In the case of products that have more than one part, some parts may be under full warranty; other parts may be under limited warranty. A limited or partial warranty is, as the name implies, something less than a full warranty. Whether Selina can sue would depend on what the written statement actually says. Like other contracts, warranties should be read carefully. You should note that "full" warranties are the exception rather than the rule.

If a Warranty Is Broken

What can you do if a seller doesn't meet a warranty? Figure 4-3 gives guidelines for complaints about warranties and other consumer problems. However, an important law passed in 1975, the Magnuson-Moss Warranty Act, provides additional protection. The act requires that written warranties be clearly expressed so that consumers know what they are getting. It covers the different aspects of warranties such as materials, workmanship, performance, and actions that will be taken if a product does not work well. The act says that if a seller gives an express warranty, the consumer cannot lose any implied warranties.

Under the Magnuson-Moss Warranty Act, a seller who violates the terms of a warranty or service contract can be sued by a purchaser with a claim of more than $25.

Regulating Product Safety

The regulation of product safety is similar to that of product quality. However, the protections of the consumer from unsafe products are broader and cannot be so easily waived. The area of state law governing product safety is known as Products Liability Law. Products liability is part of a larger body of law called torts, which deals with the rights of individuals to recover damages for personal injuries. This aspect of tort law puts responsibilities for product safety on the maker and seller; both can be held liable for damages.

Under Georgia law, manufacturers of goods are strictly liable for injuries caused by their defective products. Defective products are not safe for their intended use, either because of a problem with their design or because of a defect resulting from the manufacturing process. Strict liability means that it is not necessary to show that the manufacturer was negligent or careless in failing to discover that its product was defective. The idea behind strict liability is that manufacturers who put goods on the market are in a better position than individual consumers to pay the costs of injuries that their products cause.

Strict liability also gives manufacturers an added incentive to produce safe products. Any person injured by the use of a defective product may sue the manufacturer under the law of strict liability, even if that person was not the original buyer of the product. The principle of strict liability differs from the protection provided by warranties, which usually only protect the buyer of the product. Georgia law also requires manufacturers and sellers of consumer goods to provide adequate warnings about the dangers associated with their products. Manufacturers and sellers may be liable if they fail to do so.

In addition, because of concerns about safety, a number of federal laws set standards for product safety (see figure 4-4). There are also numerous agencies that work to protect consumer safety. The oldest federal agency is the federal Food and Drug Administration (FDA). It reviews all drugs for safety, effectiveness, and correct labeling. If it is claimed that a food has nutritional value, then its package must be labeled. It must state the product's name, manufacturer, weight, and ingredients. The FDA is also responsible for cosmetic safety. It does not test cosmetics, but it does act on consumer complaints.

The Consumer Product Safety Commission can issue safety warnings about unsafe products. It can also prohibit the sale of dangerous ones.

The National Highway Traffic Safety Administration establishes and enforces safety standards for autos, trucks, buses, bicycles, and motorcycles. The agency also investigates complaints about the safety of motor vehicles. It can require a manufacturer to recall all models with safety defects and repair them at no cost to the consumer.

In 1990, Georgia enacted a "lemon" law. This law says that if a dealer has tried unsuccessfully a specified number of times to solve a problem with a new car that does not work satisfactorily (a "lemon"), the owner is entitled to a replacement or refund.

FIGURE 4-3

If You Have a Complaint

Identify the problem.

Shoddy or broken merchandise? False advertising? Worthless guarantee?

Decide what you want.

Refund? Payment for damages? Repairs? Replacement?

Prepare your complaint.

Photocopy records of your purchase. Keep original records yourself. Make notes of talks about the problem with company representatives.

Present your complaint.

First to the salesperson who sold you the goods. If that person does not help you, go to the manager. If the manager is uncooperative, take the matter to the company president. If the problem is with a national company, write a letter. Include full information, such as what you bought (enclose copies of documents concerning the purchase), when and where you bought it, what the problem is, and what you want done about it. Provide a time limit for action. Keep a copy of your letter.

Seek outside help.

If you still get no satisfaction, explain your problem to a consumer help agency. Legal action should be your last recourse.

FIGURE 4-4

Examples of Federal Laws Concerned with Product Safety

1906	Pure Food and Drug Act	Prohibits mislabeling of food, liquor, and medicine containers.
1907	Agricultural Meat Inspection Act	Requires regulation and inspection of meat-packing plants engaged in interstate commerce. Extended to plants doing in-state business in 1967.
1938	Food, Drug, and Cosmetic Act	Strengthens 1906 act and adds requirements for advertising and labeling cosmetics.
1953	Flammable Fabrics Act and later amendments	Allow banning of sale of flame-prone clothes and household furnishings.
1960	Hazardous Substances Labeling Act and later amendments	Set labeling requirements for hazardous (poisonous, corrosive, and flammable) products.
1966	National Traffic and Motor Vehicle Safety Act	Sets safety standards for design of motor vehicles and requires certain lifesaving equipment in motor vehicles.
1966 1970	Child Protection Act Child Protection and Toy Safety Act	Allow banning of products dangerous to health and safety of children.
1968	Radiation Control for Health and Safety Act	Sets standards for certain electronic products and limits on radiation emission by products such as color TVs and microwave ovens.

The state has another role in regulating product safety. The Georgia Department of Agriculture is responsible for ensuring the quality and safety of agricultural products bought and sold in the state. It administers inspections of meat, poultry, and milk. The department is also concerned with proper packaging and labeling and with the accuracy of commercial scales.

Only the Facts

1. Define the following:
   a. full warranty
   b. limited warranty
   c. express warranty
   d. implied warranty
2. List and define three types of implied warranties.
3. If you buy something that is labeled or tagged "as is," what are you waiving?
4. Give two examples of how a seller can create an express warranty.
5. What is strict liability?
6. Identify one federal and one state agency concerned with product safety.

Think About

1. Explain why the disconnection between manufacturer and buyer has increased the need for consumer laws. Identify and discuss other reasons for the increase in these laws.
2. Since early history, governments have been concerned with standardizing weights and measures. Explain why standardization is of such basic importance to consumers.
3. Should someone under age 18 be allowed by law to "waive" warranties? Explain your answer.

Regulating Unfair Sales Practices

Claims and Advertising

SITUATION 15 A newspaper ad reads,

SPECIAL BUY

Athlete's Own Exercise Apparatus. Good quality. One device develops muscle strength of skiers, cyclists, football players, and weight lifters. $75.

Fred arrives at the store 10 minutes after it opens. He finds that the advertised model has been sold out. However, the salesman is eager to show him several other models. He says they are much better, but they are three times the price.

SITUATION 16 While walking down the street, Joan sees a large sign on a furniture store window that says,

GOING OUT OF BUSINESS SALE

Come in today. All prices slashed 50%.

Inside she finds the dining room set of her dreams. Taking advantage of the bargain, she buys the set. However, three months later she sees the same set for less at a department store. Furthermore, the furniture store where she bought her set has not gone out of business.

The examples show two unfair and deceptive sales practices.

Unfair sales practices have existed for as long as people have been buying and selling goods. Careful shopping continues to be the best protection against being stung by such practices. A wise consumer will follow the rule of *caveat emptor* (let the buyer beware).

Do consumers like those in situations 15 and 16 have any legal recourse? Legislation in the twentieth century made these practices illegal as well as unethical. In 1914, Congress established the Federal Trade Commission (FTC) and prohibited unfair and deceptive sales practices. It gave the FTC power to issue rules and regulations governing certain transactions. Although the FTC can sue companies, consumers cannot use its provisions as the basis of a lawsuit. Therefore, most legal actions against unfair and deceptive practices depend on state laws and must be made in state courts.

Most states have passed such laws. They are nicknamed "little FTC acts." In Georgia, such an act was passed in 1975, the Georgia Fair Business Practices Act. This act established the Governor's Office of Consumer Affairs. Its staff is responsible for enforcing the Fair Business Practices Act and is trained to help consumers resolve conflicts with sellers.

The act defines certain sales practices as unfair and deceptive. It gives the administrator of the Governor's Office of Consumer Affairs power to define other practices as unfair.

Some practices that are considered "unfair" or "deceptive" in Georgia follow:

1. Representing that goods are made (or services performed) by someone other than the person actually making the goods (or performing the services). An example of this deceptive practice would be putting a designer label on a nondesigner garment.

2. Misleading buyers as to the geographic origin of goods and services. For example, labeling an American cheese with a label written in French—to deceive buyers as to the source.

3. Representing that goods or services are sponsored or approved by a person or group when they are not. An example would be claiming that a certain brand of tennis racket is used by a tennis star, but it isn't.

4. Representing that a person has credentials that he or she does not have. A violation would be stating that auto repairs were made by licensed mechanics, but they weren't.

5. Representing goods as new when they are, in fact, used.

6. Advertising goods or services with the intent not to sell them as advertised. In

situation 15, the store didn't want to sell the advertised exerciser. Instead, it used the ad to lure customers in and then sell them something more expensive. This illegal practice is called "bait and switch."

7. Advertising goods or services with the intent not to supply enough to meet a reasonable public demand (unless the advertisement states a limited quantity). This deceptive practice was used in situation 15.

8. Lying about the reasons for price reductions (situation 16).

9. Advertising that products or services have uses, benefits, or qualities that they do not possess.

10. Falsely representing guarantees. For example, saying that a product has a three-year warranty when a critical part of it, like a car engine, does not.

The Governor's Office of Consumer Affairs is responsible for enforcing other consumer protection statutes. For example, the office enforces the "lemon" law discussed earlier. In addition, the office is responsible for enforcing the Georgia No Call Law, which went into effect in January 1999. The No Call Law is designed to help people avoid unwanted calls from telemarketers. With some limited exceptions, the law prevents telemarketers from selling goods, products, and services to consumers by calling the residential phone numbers of individuals who have put their names on the Georgia No Call List. The Governor's Office of Consumer Affairs enforces the No Call Law, and another state agency, the Public Service Commission, maintains the list. The other duties of the Public Service Commission are discussed below.

Suppose that you are stung by an unfair business practice. What can you do? You can contact the Governor's Office of Consumer Affairs. You may need to send a letter explaining the problem and copies of all relevant documents such as ads, canceled checks, and contracts to the office. The

state can then investigate, and if appropriate, take action to stop the violation. Alternatively, you can sue the business. In order to sue, you must first give the seller 30 days' notice. If the company corrects the problem within that period, the problem is considered resolved.

When You Don't Buy in Stores

SITUATION 17 A door-to-door salesman convinced the Smittens to buy $500 worth of encyclopedias. The Smittens signed a contract. Later, they realized they could not afford the books.

Since they had signed the contract, what could they do?

Breaches of warranties and misleading advertising are not the only sales practices that can harm the consumer. People are sometimes pressured into buying goods or services that they don't want or can't afford. In 1974, the Federal Trade Commission established a Door-to-Door Trade Regulations Rule to protect consumers. This rule has been adopted for Georgia by the Governor's Office of Consumer Affairs. It gives the buyer the right to cancel the contract within three days of signing it. Furthermore, three duties are required of the seller:

- The seller must give the purchaser a copy of the contract or sales receipt, which must state the name and address of the seller.

- The contract must tell the buyer of this right to cancel and how to cancel.

- The seller is to leave two cancellation forms with the purchaser. If the seller does not, a letter of cancellation may be sent instead.

The rule covers most sales that are not made at a seller's place of business. However, it does not apply to sales made entirely by phone or mail or to sales of goods costing less than $25. Nor does it cover sales of real estate, insurance, securities, or emergency home repairs. However, it should protect the Smittens in situation 17.

Knowing a seller's permanent place of business also can provide a buyer with some protection. Recognizing this protection, Georgia passed a "Transient Merchants" law in 1980. The law requires a seller without a permanent place of business to obtain a license in any county in which he or she wishes to sell.

FTC rules and the U.S. Postal Service protect buyers when goods are bought or received by mail. For example, if you receive goods that you have not requested through the mail, you do not have to pay for them.

Only the Facts

1. Complete the sentences: The Governor's Office of Consumer Affairs is a state agency whose staff helps _____ _____ .

   The Federal Trade Commission makes rules governing _____ _____ .

2. Describe three illegal sales practices.

3. What is a disadvantage to buying goods somewhere other than in a store?

Think About

1. Is three days long enough to cancel a contract? Consider this question from the standpoints of sellers and buyers.

2. What other deceptive sales practices do you think should be illegal?

Regulating Specialized Services

As consumers, we buy services as well as goods. Sometimes, as in a restaurant, we buy both at the same time.

Laws also regulate the sale of services. In fact, some types of services require regulation by special government agencies. These services include public utilities (which furnish electricity, gas, and telephone service). Various personal services (building, medical, cosmetic services) are also regulated by state laws and/or boards.

Public Utility Services

In the United States, electricity, gas, and phone services are usually provided by privately owned companies that are regulated by the government in order to control costs for consumers. In Georgia, the sale of electricity, gas, or telephone service by any privately owned public utility company is regulated by the Public Service Commission (PSC). Formerly, the PSC also regulated both the conditions and the price of the service. It also determined what geographic area each utility company could serve.

Regulation was considered necessary because the utilities were essentially allowed to have monopolies within their areas of service. When there is a monopoly, consumers are not able to shop around for the best deal in utility services as they might another item, such as a car. Because there was no marketplace competition to hold down prices, governments regulated the rates.

In 1997 and 1998, the State of Georgia passed laws to deregulate the sale of natural gas and local telephone service. Although these services were regulated to prevent price abuses by companies that monopolized these industries, prices had remained high. The purpose of deregulation was to decrease price and increase quality by encouraging competition. Although the electricity industry is not deregulated, some states are considering electricity deregulation in the future.

Although pricing is no longer controlled in these industries, Georgia's Public Service Commission still oversees the provision of telephone, electricity, and gas service in the state. The commission is charged with the responsibility of preventing the loss of these vital services and abuses by the companies that provide the services.

Utilities are not always provided by private companies. In other countries, utilities and some transportation systems are government owned. Today, approximately 70 percent of Georgia's land area is served by electric companies owned

Changes in electric rates must be approved by Georgia's Public Service Commission. Why do you think this approval is required?

Insurance Services

Suppose you see a magazine ad for low-rate auto insurance for young drivers. How could you judge if the company is reliable? One way would be to find out if the company is licensed by the state to do business in Georgia.

Insurance companies in Georgia are licensed and regulated by the Insurance Commissioner. The commissioner is elected every four years by state voters. One purpose of insurance regulation is to make sure that rates and policy provisions are fair. The commissioner can regulate the rates that are charged to the public. The commissioner can also issue rules and regulations prohibiting unfair or deceptive practices.

What happens if claims are not paid promptly? Georgia law allows penalties to be assessed against the company. The commissioner can revoke licenses to sell insurance if regulations are not followed.

Personal Services

As a consumer, you purchase personal services as well as products. You pay people to check your teeth. You may pay people to fix your bicycle or cut your hair or teach you to swim.

Some of the services you purchase are provided by professionals. The term "professional" is hard to define. It usually implies that those performing the service have had special training. Some people think primarily of law and medicine when they think of the professions. However, many other personal service occupations require specialized skills and training.

How well a person can perform his or her service is important to you. If you hire someone to set your broken arm or cut your hair, you want to be sure that person knows how to do it. How can you be sure?

For some services, Georgia's state government gives some protection. When training is necessary to perform a service, the state government may create a board to set standards and qualifications. This board usually licenses, or certifies, those who will practice the service. Boards may take away licenses if standards are not met.

by cities or by cooperatives (that is, groups of users). However, private companies provide electricity to most people in the state. They serve all the major cities.

Federal as well as state regulations affect public utilities. For example, federal regulations control the prices charged for electricity sold by one electric system to another. The federal government also regulates telecommunications services, including long distance and cable service. In 1996, the federal government deregulated long distance telephone and cable rates for the same reason that Georgia did: to encourage competition and, as a result, lower prices.

Although pricing is no longer controlled, the Federal Communications Commission continues to regulate the operations of telecommunications companies to prevent abuses. For example, when long-distance services were first deregulated, some newcomers to the industry engaged in a practice called "slamming," in which they would switch customers over to their service and charge them fees without their consent. Companies that engage in this practice are subject to stiff penalties.

They can also initiate court action against anyone who practices a certified profession in the state without a license. Because citizens place so much trust in licensed professionals, a board may also suspend or even revoke a license if an individual is convicted of a drug-related offense.

Some of the state's current licensing and examining boards are listed in figure 4-5. This list does not show all of the organizations that regulate service providers in Georgia. For example, lawyers must be admitted to the State Bar in order to practice. Teachers must be certified to teach in the public school system. City and county governments may also regulate those in certain occupations, including plumbers, electricians, and taxicab drivers.

Professional licensing, or certification, means that the person has met certain qualifications of education and experience and observes certain standards of the profession. However, certification gives no guarantee of outcome. To illustrate, consider whether the Georgia boards that license barbers and cosmetologists could act on any of the following complaints:

SITUATION 18

a. Tom complains that the barber was incompetent. He says he did a terrible job cutting his hair. The barber does not have a license.

b. Susie complains that her hair was damaged by the hairdresser. A dye was left on it for too long.

c. Teresa complains that the beauty shop was filthy. She claims that the curlers were grimy, the combs were not clean, and the floor was not swept.

d. Hank complains about the outrageous prices of his barber.

The Georgia boards of barbers and cosmetologists will handle complaints about a person practicing without a license in situation 18a. They will handle complaints about unsanitary conditions within a shop in situation 18c. However, they will not act on complaints about fees or damage to hair in situations 18d and 18b.

Some types of personal services receive more consumer complaints than do others. Private vocational schools are an example of a service that varies widely in terms of quality.

FIGURE 4-5

Licensing and Examining Boards

- Accountancy, State Board of
- Athletic Trainers, Georgia Board of
- Auctioneers Commission, Georgia
- Barbers, State Board of
- Chiropractic Examiners, Georgia Board of
- Construction Industry Licensing Board, State
- Cosmetology, State Board of
- Dentistry, Georgia Board of
- Funeral Service, State Board of
- Geologists, State Board of Registration for Professional
- Landscape Architects, Georgia Board of
- Librarians, State Board for the Certification of
- Licensed Practical Nurses, Georgia Board of Examiners of

- Medical Examiners, Composite State Board of
- Nursing Home Administrators, State Board of
- Opticians, State Board of Dispensing
- Pharmacy, State Board of
- Physical Therapy, State Board of
- Private Detective and Security Agencies, Georgia Board of
- Psychologists, State Board of Examiners of
- Real Estate Commission, Georgia
- Structural Pest Control Commission, State
- Used Motor Vehicle Dealers and Used Motor Vehicle Parts Dealers, State Board of Registration of
- Veterinary Medicine, State Board of
- Water Well Standards Advisory Council, State

SITUATION 19 Sara sees an ad in the newspaper for a vocational school. It offers a six-week course in modeling. It guarantees work to students who complete the course. Sara pays $1,200 for the course. After finishing, she is given a list of possible employers. That is her only assistance in getting a job.

SITUATION 20 Greg is talked into signing a contract to go to a computer programming school. Before the school begins, he gets a job with a company that will provide the same training.

Can he get a refund of his fees?

In Georgia, private vocational schools are called proprietary schools. The Georgia Board of Education issues guidelines and standards for these schools. In order to be approved, a school must meet the minimum requirements set by the Nonpublic Postsecondary Educational Institutions Act of 1990. Approval does not, however, indicate the quality of education offered.

Georgia guidelines require proprietary schools to have job placement services. However, differences in student skills make guaranties impossible. Sara (situation 19) could consult with an attorney as to whether she has grounds for a case as a victim of false advertising. It would have been better, however, if she'd done some checking before enrolling. See figure 4-6 for some questions you should ask before signing a contract with a vocational school.

What about being released from a contract with a proprietary school? The state guidelines for these schools say that you can cancel and get a refund of part or all of your tuition. The amount refunded varies according to when you cancel. In situation 20, Greg should be able to receive some refund.

Repairs and Liens

Repair services (for cars and homes, for example) are major targets of consumer complaints. Repair

---

FIGURE 4-6

Shopping for a Private Vocational School

1. Check employment opportunities in the field. Inquire at a Georgia Department of Labor Job Services Center.

2. Resist signing a contract until you have checked out the school.

3. Question companies with whom you might want to work. Would they hire a graduate of this school? Do they prefer to give on-the-job training?

4. What is the school's placement record? How many of its graduates were placed in jobs by the school?

5. Try to talk with graduates. Were they happy with the school? Did they find a job? (Ask the school for a list of recent graduates.)

6. Compare prices of comparable courses in public schools or junior colleges.

7. Ask if the school is accredited. Find out what this accreditation means.

8. Ask if a diploma or certification is given after finishing the course. Find out what that means.

---

services are not well regulated by law. The law presumes only that the services will be in keeping with the average standards of the trade (unless the contract specifies exactly the standards to be applied).

The best insurance for consumers is to know the person or business doing the repairs. Check out their business reputation. Be sure that they have a permanent location. Then you can reach somebody if anything goes wrong.

SITUATION 21 Eric takes his car to Willie's garage for repair. When he comes to pick it up, he sees that Willie is charging him for replacing the carburetor. When he looks under the hood, the carburetor looks unchanged. Willie cannot show him the old carburetor. Eric says he will not pay the bill. Willie says he'll keep the car until he does. He says it is his legal right to do so.

What can Eric do?

The best way to ensure reliable repair services is to know the person or business doing the repairs.

Only the Facts

1. List and give examples of three kinds of specialized services.
2. What is the function of a licensing and examining board?
3. What is a mechanic's lien?

Think About

1. Provide arguments for and against regulating public utilities.
2. To protect consumers, what regulations should be established for auto or house repairs?
3. Regulation of personal services is more a function of state than federal government. Why do you think that is so?

Georgia has a mechanic's lien law. A lien is a charge on property for some debt for work performed. It can be made through a court when a person shows the authorization of another party (the debtor) to perform some work. Under this law, Willie's shop could keep Eric's car until he pays for the repair.

Alternatively, Willie's shop could return the car and file a lien at the county courthouse. A lien would mean that Eric wouldn't have a clear title to the car and would therefore have trouble selling it. If Willie keeps the car, Eric could make a written demand that the mechanic release the car to him. The mechanic would have to do so within 10 days. If the mechanic filed a lien, he would have to seek legal action within 30 days. A court hearing would then be held, and Eric could present his side of the case. The judge would decide if Eric should pay the bill.

SUMMING UP

Consumer law is a very broad subject. It covers all kinds of purchases of goods and services for personal, family, and household use. Both federal and state laws are involved, and federal and state governments have set up regulatory agencies to protect the interests of the buyer. This chapter has explained some of the legal rights and duties of buyers and sellers. The general law prohibits only the worst types of abuses, however. The burden is on the consumer to look out for his or her own interests.

5 Borrowing

O ften people do not have enough available cash to pay for something they need or want. What do they do then? What can the following people do?

- Bart's dental bill will be more than $1,000—more money than he has in savings.
- Jane wants to fly to Los Angeles for her sister's wedding, but she doesn't have enough cash for the ticket.
- Walter needs a car to get to his new job—but he can't save money until he begins working.

They may have to do without the items. Or they may borrow money to buy them. In other words, they may obtain some form of credit.

What is credit? A credit transaction happens when one party provides services, goods, or money to another party based on the second person's promise to pay later. The person who has extended the credit is the creditor. The second person, who is obligated to pay back the debt, is the debtor. John borrows $10 from his father with a promise to repay it in a week. In this situation, his father is the creditor, and John is the debtor.

Credit plays a major role in today's economy. Large businesses, such as auto manufacturers, borrow millions of dollars. Governments borrow money. Individuals use credit when they get loans from banks and use credit cards. In fact, more people use credit now than ever before.

This chapter is about laws relating to consumer credit. Consumer credit is obtained primarily for family, personal, or household purposes. Sources of consumer credit include not only parents, brothers and sisters, or friends but also banks, credit unions, loan companies, and credit cards.

CREDIT BASICS

It is important to understand that credit is not free. One reason is that when a creditor extends credit to a debtor, he or she gives up use of that money for a period of time. The creditor then does not have it to spend or invest. For example, if you lend a friend $100 for three months, you will not have that cash available to buy a bicycle you've been wanting when it goes on sale. Nor will you be earning interest on the money you loaned.

A second reason why credit is not free is that it involves the creditor taking a risk. What if the debtor does not repay the debt? Creditors generally want some compensation for taking that risk. For these reasons, creditors require that debtors give them some compensation. Usually, but not always, this compensation takes the form of interest. Interest is generally a percentage of the amount of the debt (see figure 5-1).

Arrangements involving credit are called credit transactions. Keep in mind that credit transactions are contracts. The general laws affecting contracts (discussed in chapter 4) also apply to these transactions.

Loans and Credit Sales

Two types of credit are loans and credit sales. Banks, companies, and individuals lend money with the expectation that the borrower will pay it back with interest over a period of time. In a credit sale, a buyer purchases goods or services with the expectation of paying the purchase price plus interest in installments over a period of time. The following situation illustrates loans and credit.

SITUATION 1 Donna finds a car she wants at Al's automobile lot. She can pay him $1,000. Unfortunately, she is $500 short of the purchase price. Al says, "Don't worry, my finance company will lend you the $500. You don't have to pay it all now."

Q Is this a loan or a credit sale?

FIGURE 5-1

Cost of Credit

A shopper buys a stereo for $1,000 on January 1.	$1,000.00
The interest is 18 percent per year.	× .18
In interest alone, the shopper would pay $180 for the year (if he or she did not pay any of the original amount).	$180.00

The example in situation 1 would be a loan. The dealer's finance company (like a bank) will lend the money. In this case, the dealer (Al) will be paid the full sales price immediately. Donna will borrow $500 from the finance company and pay that to Al along with the $1,000 she already has. Her debt will then be the money borrowed ($500) to pay for the car plus interest charged by the finance company.

On the other hand, Al might have said he would let Donna pay him the amount she owed for the car over time. Donna might then make six payments of $100 each during the year. Why would she pay him the extra $100? That amount is the interest that compensates Al for the delay in payment. This transaction would be a credit sale.

The distinction between a loan and credit sale is important because in most states, including Georgia, laws governing consumer credit vary according to which type of credit is extended.

Secured and Unsecured Credit

Credit may be classified as secured or unsecured, depending on what actions the creditor may take if the debtor does not repay the debt. Unsecured credit means that the creditor relies solely on the debtor's promise to repay the debt. If the debtor does not keep this promise, the creditor can sue the debtor to recover the money. However, suing a debtor who does not have the money to repay a debt is not very effective. An unsecured loan is therefore usually made only when there is little doubt that the debtor can repay it. For example, a large corporation might borrow relatively small amounts of money from a bank on an unsecured basis.

If a creditor thinks that there is a risk that repayment will not be made, he or she may require the debtor to sign a contract. This contract states that the creditor can take one or more items of the debtor's property if the debtor does not pay off the debt. This property is called collateral. When collateral is involved, credit is said to be "secured." With automobile loans, the collateral is usually the automobile itself. With bank loans, it may be a savings account.

For example, suppose you need a loan to buy a used car. You are in school and have only a part-time job. The dealer may feel unsure about your ability to pay. In this case, the dealer may require that you give him or her a security interest in the auto. A security interest is the right to repossess (or reclaim) the auto if you do not pay the debt. The dealer could then resell the car to get the money you owed. The car thus becomes collateral for the debt. You can still drive it, but the creditor has the right to take it back from you if you do not pay your debt.

A good example of a secured debt occurs when something is pawned. A person brings the pawnbroker some item of value (for example, a ring). He or she borrows money against its value. The property is left with the pawnbroker until the debt is repaid. If it is not repaid, the pawnbroker sells the property to recover the money.

Another way to get secured credit is to use a third party. This person promises to repay the debt if the debtor fails to pay. The third-party promise to repay the debt is called a guaranty; the third party becomes the guarantor. A used car dealer who is unsure about a person's ability to pay the purchase price of a car may require a third party to be involved. This third party could be a relative who works full time and agrees to pay the debt. The creditor might even require both a guaranty from the relative and a security interest in the car. A creditor can also ask for a security interest in collateral belonging to the third-party guarantor.

Money borrowed by pawning an item of value must be repaid, or the pawnbroker will sell the item.

Open-End Credit and Credit Cards

A debtor might enter into only one credit transaction with a creditor, which could be a loan or a credit sale. The single transaction is referred to as a closed-end credit transaction.

In contrast, a debtor can enter into a series of credit transactions with the same creditor over a period of time. This arrangement is known as open-end credit. For example, Hal wants to furnish his home with all new furniture but cannot afford to buy it all at once. He buys a sofa from E-Z Furniture on credit. Before the sofa is paid off, he buys a bed from E-Z Furniture on credit. Shortly after that, he buys a dresser, also on credit. In this situation, E-Z Furniture is extending Hal additional credit on a number of purchases. Therefore, the two have an open-end credit relationship. This kind of credit is also called revolving credit.

A consumer must be very careful with open-end or revolving credit relationships. The creditor in this kind of relationship may require the debtor to give a securing interest in all of the items that the debtor buys during that relationship. What if the debtor fails to make a payment on any one item in this open-credit arrangement? The creditor may have the right to repossess every single item—including items for which the purchase price was paid in full. Courts are very skeptical of these kinds of deals. They may even declare the contract void if the creditor has taken unfair advantage of the debtor (see situation 7).

Credit card purchases are another example of open credit. Goods can be bought at any time with the card. However, the credit card holder receives only one bill (or statement) for each month's purchases.

If a credit card provides open-end credit, can you spend as much as you wish? No. Credit card issuers assign a limit to the credit that each card-holder can obtain. Once that limit is reached, the issuer will refuse to approve any further purchases or cash advances.

Are credit cards free? No. The issuer may impose several different types of charges. These charges may include

- an annual card fee. Some banks charge such fees for cards. Department stores and gasoline companies usually do not.
- a monthly finance charge. This charge generally is a percentage of the amount owed. Some credit card issuers allow the consumer to avoid this charge by paying all the money owed within a specified time after receiving the monthly statement. Usually this grace period is about 30 days. Other issuers charge from the date of purchase.
- a cash advance charge. This charge is a fee for obtaining cash from bank machines by using a card or cash advance checks.
- a late payment fee.
- an over-limit charge.

State laws regulate the types and amount of charges that may be collected on credit cards. In Georgia, this law is called the Credit Card and Credit Card Bank Act. It provides for the organization of credit card banks in Georgia. It also allows lenders to impose various charges and fees on credit card accounts. Monthly statements show these fees and list all transactions on the cardholder's account during the month. These statements should be read carefully.

Credit cards—what kind of credit do they represent?

Suppose you discover a charge that you did not authorize or some other mistake on your monthly statement. You should notify the card issuer promptly. The Fair Credit Billing Act requires the cardholder to notify the card issuer in writing within 60 days after the issuer sends the first bill on which an error appears. Cardholders do not have to pay the questioned amount while the error is being investigated, but they must pay the parts of the bill that are not in question.

Only the Facts

1. Explain the differences between a loan and a credit sale, open- and closed-end credit, and secured and unsecured credit.

2. In the following example, identify the creditor, debtor, debt, guarantor, and collateral:

   Barbara, a high school senior, wants to buy a used car from Ed for $2,000. Barbara wants to pay $100 down and then pay $100 per month for 20 months. Ed will agree if Uncle Fred will promise to pay Ed should Barbara be unable to do so. Barbara must also agree to give the car back to Ed if both she and Uncle Fred cannot pay.

3. Which of the following charges are you likely to see on a credit card bill?
   a. late payment fee
   b. annual fee
   c. collateral charge
   d. over-limit charge
   e. open-end fee

Think About

1. Why do you think there has been considerable legislation on consumer credit in the last 10 to 20 years?

OBTAINING CREDIT

Suppose you're out of school and have a new job and your own place to live. You need a lot of things: furniture, a better car, appliances. You think about borrowing some money but have never tried to obtain credit. You would like answers to a few questions:

1. Where should you look for credit?
2. How likely are you to get credit?
3. How much does credit cost?
4. What should you look for in the contract?
5. What will happen if you can't meet the credit payments?

Regarding the first question, there are a number of choices. Many factors must be considered: How much money do you want? What is it for? How good a credit risk are you? Figure 5-2 offers information on places that give credit. The remaining sections in this chapter introduce some of the laws establishing rights that protect debtors and creditors and help answer the other questions.

FIGURE 5-2

Sources of Consumer Credit

Source	Form of Credit	Typical Cost of Credit	Who Can Get Loans	Notes
Banks	Loans	Fairly low	Safe credit risks	Often have minimum amount, for example, $500 for loans
	Home mortgages	Varies		
	Credit cards	Moderate, regulated by law		
Savings and loan associations	Loans	Fairly low	Safe credit risks	Provide banklike services
	Home mortgages	Varies		
	Credit cards	Moderate, regulated by law		
Credit unions	Loans	Low	Members—but risk is factor	Often have maximum amount
Finance companies/small loan companies	Loans	Varies, moderate to high	Will take greater credit risks	Usually have a maximum amount, for example, $3,000
Merchants	Credit sales	Moderate	Varies—greater risks than banks	Only useful for goods
	Credit cards	Moderate, regulated by law	Fairly safe credit risks	
Pawnbrokers	Small loans	High, varying	Only loan money on collateral	

Investigating Credit Applicants

Borrowers can choose where to apply for credit. Before deciding whether or not to give credit, however, a creditor will want to know how likely it is that the borrower will pay back the money on time. To decide, the creditor will need certain information.

The application used to obtain credit asks about the borrower's job, other sources of income, and debt. In asking these questions, the creditor is trying to determine what kind of risk the borrower will be. The creditor knows that people who are good credit risks have steady jobs and records of paying back previous debts. If the borrower is a good risk, not only will it be easier for him or her to get credit, but the interest will be less. Figure 5-3 gives some suggestions about how to become a good credit risk.

In addition, many creditors pay a credit bureau to investigate applicants. There are thousands of credit bureaus throughout the country. Financial and personal information about consumers is stored in bureau computers. The information is available to other bureaus and creditors and often to employers and insurers.

If there is anything undesirable in the report of the credit bureau, the creditor may decide not to give credit to the consumer. Clearly, a person's credit standing can be damaged by an unfavorable report. What if the report were misleading, inaccurate, or out of date?

In 1970, Congress passed the Fair Credit Reporting Act to protect credit seekers. Under the act, if you are denied credit, insurance, or employment on the basis of a credit report, you have the right to

- know the name and address of the agency giving the report.
- know what is in the report, even though you can't see or handle it.
- know the sources of the factual information contained in the report.
- request reinvestigation and correction if the information is inaccurate or incomplete.

FIGURE 5-3

How to Become a Good Credit Risk

- Build a good employment record.
- Open a savings or checking account.
- Buy something on credit, such as an inexpensive item at a department store, on a three- to four-month time plan. Pay it back promptly.
- Don't borrow more than you can pay back.

- formally object to information you believe to be wrong.
- request that corrections be sent to businesses that had previously received incorrect information.

There is no cost for information in your file if you request it within 60 days of a denial of credit.

It is important to know these rights regarding credit reports. The law gives the Federal Trade Commission the power to act against credit-reporting agencies that violate its provisions. Also, an individual can sue for damages.

Protection from Discrimination

Other laws protect people seeking credit. In 1974, Congress passed the Equal Credit Opportunity Act prohibiting creditors from discriminating against credit applicants on the basis of gender, marital status, age, race, color, religion, national origin, or receipt of public assistance income. This law also prohibits creditors from requiring answers to questions along these lines unless they bear directly on income. Under this law, creditors must give applicants reasons for being denied credit. A 1975 Georgia law also allows a person to take legal action and ask for damages if he or she is discriminated against.

Note that these federal and state laws do not guarantee anyone credit. Nor do they keep creditors from using income, expenses, debts, and reliability to determine whether they should give someone credit. However, they do make discrimination on certain grounds illegal.

Do you think the following denials of credit requests would be legal?

> **SITUATION 2** Dee applies for a loan. Most of her income comes from alimony from a first marriage. The bank learns that her former husband lost his job several weeks ago. It turns down her request.

> **SITUATION 3** Steve applies for a loan to buy a motorcycle. He is 16, but he has a good job after school. His loan is turned down.

> **SITUATION 4** Most of Carrie's income comes from public assistance. She needs a small loan for a few months—to pay a dental bill. The loan company turns her down.

Credit cannot be denied to a person on the basis of marital status. However, what if a person is dependent on income from a spouse or ex-spouse? Then the inability to repay the loan would be affected by that spouse's financial condition. In situation 2, the refusal to give Dee a loan does not discriminate because it is based on the limits of her income and on her ability to repay.

Federal law forbids discrimination in credit transactions on the basis of age. Minors, however, cannot enter into binding contracts. So in situation 3, the rejection of Steve's application would be legal.

In situation 4, Carrie may have been discriminated against because her income comes from public assistance. For the lending agency to refuse a loan solely on these grounds would be illegal.

How Much Does Credit Cost?

Finding Out the Costs

Before signing a contract, you should know how much credit is going to cost you. The cost of credit is referred to as interest. Interest rates can vary significantly depending on the source of the credit because they are affected by the national and local economies. They depend on how much of a credit risk the debtor is and the purpose of the loan. For example, for many years, students have been able to get government-guaranteed loans for their college education at rates lower than are available for other purposes.

Shop around. Find out which lender will charge you less (see figure 5-4). Be aware that a debtor may have to pay other charges besides interest. There may be

- a late charge if payment becomes past due.

FIGURE 5-4

Which Television Should Greg Buy?

An ad in the window of **Best Bargain Store** promises a price of $125 down and $25 a month for 20 months.	At Best Bargain Store, Greg's total cost will be $625 ($125 plus $25 x 20).
At **Save Here Department Store,** the same model is $500. Greg has a charge account at the store. He considers using his account to buy the set at a rate of $25 per month plus the 1.5 percent interest on the unpaid balance.	At Save Here Department Store, if Greg pays the $25 per month plus the interest, the cost would be about $571.30. Interest is figured per month by multiplying .015 by the balance of $500 that is unpaid. Greg's monthly payments would begin at $32.13 and decrease to $25.
At **Family Savings,** the set is also $500. Using his car for collateral, Greg could get a loan to buy the TV. The loan department suggests he take the loan for 20 months. Interest will be 1.5 percent on the unpaid balance plus finance charges of $1.43 per month.	Loan payments to buy the TV at Family Savings would be $30 per month. This amount includes repayment of the principal ($25 a month), interest averaged over 20 months ($3.57 per month), and the finance charge ($1.43 per month). Total cost would be $600.

- a service charge to cover the creditor's costs of sending bills, record keeping, etc.
- a charge for insuring the purchased item against theft or damage or to guarantee payment if the buyer should die during the term of the contract.

All of these types of charges taken together are generally called finance charges.

Truth in Lending Laws

The Truth in Lending Act helps consumers figure out the costs of credit. The act requires certain legal duties of creditors. When making a credit transaction, they must show the finance charges and the rate of interest. The rate must always be expressed in the same way (as an annual percentage rate) so that customers can compare it with the rates of other lenders.

Also, the creditor must inform the consumer of the rules and charges for late payments. Certain terms of the contract also are required to be clearly visible. If creditors don't do these things, they can be sued.

In 1988, Congress amended the Truth in Lending Act with the Fair Credit and Charge Card Disclosure Act. This act requires stricter credit disclosures in open-end credit or charge card applications or advertisements. The purpose of the act is to help the borrower more easily compare the costs of credit and make an informed decision before entering into a credit arrangement. Most of the required information that must be provided is shown in figure 5-5.

FIGURE 5-5

What Your Credit Card Application Must Tell You	
Annual percentage rate for purchases	Percent fixed rate or a variable rate
Variable rate information	Your annual percentage rate may vary. The rate is determined by various factors.
Grace period for repayment of balances for purchases	You have a certain amount of time (usually a number of days) to repay your balance for purchases before a finance charge will be imposed. or You have no grace period in which to repay your balance for purchases before a finance charge will be imposed.
Method of computing the balance for purchases	Average daily balance (including new purchases) or Average daily balance (excluding new purchases) or Other method (explain)
Annual fees	Annual membership fee: $ _____ per year or Other type of fee: $ _____ per year
Minimum finance charge	Amount varies.
Transaction fee for purchases	($ _____) (_____ percent of amount of purchases) Calculated as purchase amount times a percentage of the purchase price
Transaction fee for cash advances and fees for paying late or exceeding the credit limit	Transaction fee for cash advances: ($ _____) or (_____ percent of amount advanced) Late payment fee: ($ _____) or (_____ percent of amount advanced) Over-the-credit-limit fee: $ _____

Regulating Credit Costs

Interest rates are largely governed by state laws. However, in some areas, such as loans for homes, federal laws override state laws.

Georgia and most states limit the maximum amount charged for interest or other finance charges. These laws are known as usury laws. The government imposes upper limits on the interest that can be charged to consumers. In Georgia, charging more than 5 percent per month in interest on a consumer loan is a misdemeanor crime. (There are usually no legal limits on the interest rates charged to businesses.) A creditor whose finance charges exceed these limits is guilty of making a usurious loan. The creditor can be sued for usury in a civil court. In Georgia, if the suit is won, the debtor can recover all the interest that he or she had paid.

Only the Facts

1. What is the purpose of the Fair Credit Reporting Act?

2. Creditors can deny credit on which of the following bases? (a) income, (b) religion, (c) receipt of public assistance, (d) gender, (e) reliability?

3. ABC Small Loans charges John Doe $250 for a six-month loan of $500. It does not tell John what annual percentage rate he will pay on this loan. What law has been violated? What is the purpose of this law?

4. ABC charges a consumer 72 percent per year on a loan. A state law provides that no more than 60 percent per year may be charged. What kind of law is ABC violating?

COLLECTING DEBTS

Understand Your Contract

When borrowers cannot or do not make a payment on a loan, they are considered to be in default. Sometimes the situation they find themselves in seems unfair. Consider the situations that follow. Are they fair? Are they legal?

> **SITUATION 5** Brad buys a used auto for $1,000. He is to make a $200 down payment and four annual payments of $200 plus interest. The first year, he pays the $200 plus interest. During the next year, he loses his job. He cannot make the next payment. The dealer demands that he pay the $600 plus interest immediately.

In most credit agreements, when one payment is missed, all remaining payments are accelerated so that the rest of the debt becomes immediately due. It must be paid in full. In situation 5, the dealer is legally within his rights in demanding immediate payment from Brad. Brad agreed to this condition in the credit contract.

> **SITUATION 6** Sara is paying on a loan for a television at the rate of $25 per month. When she is ready to make her last payment, she discovers that the contract states she will pay $200, not $25. If she cannot make this payment, then the company will repossess her television.

Would this action be legal?

One practice that has caused debtors problems is the "balloon" payment. In this credit agreement, the last payment is much larger than the others. (The sudden increase in size is the reason for the term balloon.) Sometimes this payment is so large that an unwary debtor cannot pay it, and he or she defaults on the loan—which is what could happen to Sara in situation 6. Although some states outlaw balloon payments, they are legal in Georgia.

SITUATION 7 The Folleys bought furniture for their living room on credit. Later, they bought dining room furniture from the same dealer using an add-on installment plan. They paid the full amount of the living room set in a timely manner, but then they missed a payment. The creditor came to repossess not only the dining room furniture but also the living room set.

Was this action legal?

Add-on installment plans (situation 7) are also legal. Both sets of furniture could be repossessed, but only if the Folleys agreed to such a plan when they signed the contract, and the creditor obtained a security interest in each set of furniture. Debtors should be aware of what they are agreeing to in a contract.

All of these situations illustrate the importance of reading and understanding a credit contract before signing it.

How Creditors Can Collect Debts

Borrowing money carries the moral and legal responsibility of paying it back. Most people are careful to pay their debts. They consider it the right thing to do. They also know that they may need to borrow money again and want to be able to do so at as little cost as possible. Also, they want to avoid what can happen to people who don't pay their debts.

When a debtor is in default, the creditor has a legal right to collect the money owed. After all, in a credit contract, the debtor has taken on a duty to repay the debt, which can be enforced by courts.

SITUATION 8 Della owes money on her television set. When she misses a payment, she begins to get a series of phone calls reminding her to pay. The first call is polite, but the rest are abusive.

Are the calls legal?

The creditor—or an agency hired to collect on the debt—can try to persuade the debtor to make the payment. This action is legal unless it becomes harassment. The federal Fair Debt Collection Practices Act protects consumers from unscrupulous debt collection practices. For example, it limits how many times and for what reasons the creditor can call the debtor. It limits who else the creditor can call. It also limits what the creditor can do if the debtor says that the debt is not going to be repaid.

Under the act, collectors cannot abuse persons by threats of violence or illegal actions. They cannot say a person will be imprisoned for not paying debts, for example. It is also illegal to misrepresent facts. A debt collector cannot imply that he or she represents the federal or state government.

The Fair Debt Collection Practices Act would protect Della (situation 8) against the harassment described. What can she do? She can call a local consumer agency to report the creditor's harassment, or she can contact the phone company.

SITUATION 9 In situation 5, Brad could not pay the remaining $600 on his used auto. The auto was collateral on the loan. The dealer saw the auto parked downtown and repossessed it.

Is this action legal?

A creditor may take collateral, sell it, and use the money from the sale to pay the debt due. Repossession is usually carried out by the creditor without help from the courts or any state authority. Although this "self-help" repossession is legal in most states, the creditor must be sure that no law is being broken. A creditor may not break down a garage door to reclaim an automobile pledged as collateral for a loan, but a creditor may take the car from the debtor if the debtor leaves the car parked on a public street. (The law does not regard taking the car as stealing if the creditor already has been given the right to repossess the car.) The dealer in situation 9 is within the law to take Brad's car. However, Brad must have agreed in the contract to repossession if he couldn't pay his debt.

SITUATION 10 Brad's repossessed auto is not worth as much as it was a year ago. When the dealer sells it, it brings only $400. The dealer then goes to court to sue for the rest of the money. The court supports his claim. The dealer arranges to take some of Brad's weekly salary until the debt is paid.

Is this action legal?

Many people mistakenly believe that if a car is purchased with credit and the debt is not re-paid, the worst that can happen is that the car will be repossessed. However, even though the creditor can legally collect only the amount owed plus the cost of credit, there are several ways to recover debt, whether dealing with a car or some other item.

Suppose the creditor is a bank in Georgia. A debtor defaults on a bank loan, but the debtor has money on deposit in the bank. The law allows the bank to take this money to pay off the amount owed. This action is called setoff.

A creditor can take a debtor to court for default. As in any court proceeding, the defendant (that is, the debtor) must be notified in advance. The defendant can present his or her case at the hearing.

If the court rules that the debtor must repay the creditor, various debt-collecting measures are possible. The creditor may have the debtor's wages garnished, meaning that the creditor may demand that the debtor's employer pay a portion of the debtor's wages to the creditor. This arrangement would continue until the debt is paid off. This action was taken against Brad in situation 10.

Yet another action can be taken, as the following situation illustrates:

SITUATION 11 Sid has a string of bad luck. After taking out a loan of $3,000 to cover a series of debts, he loses his job. He cannot make the payments. The creditor obtains a judgment from the court saying that Sid must pay.

Can Sid's equipment that he uses for work be sold to pay the debt?

Sid's equipment could be sold, but only under certain circumstances. Following the judgment of the court in favor of the creditor, the creditor may then ask the court to order an attachment. The property is then taken (or "attached") by the court and sold, with the proceeds used to pay the judgment against the debtor, who is Sid.

However, attachment can be used to collect a debt only if the debtor lives—or is moving his or her property—outside the state that issues the order of attachment. Alternatively, attachment can be used if the debtor cannot be found after the required official attempts.

Protection for Consumers

In the last 25 years, protecting the consumer in credit transactions has been a major concern of federal and Georgia lawmakers. In fact, consumer credit is one of the most highly regulated consumer areas. Some of the acts passed by Congress have already been mentioned.

At the state level, the Uniform Commercial Code adopted in most states is an attempt to protect the debtor from certain acts and practices of creditors. For instance, suppose your car has been repossessed and is to be sold to pay your debt. You are anxious that the car be sold for as much as possible so that the debt will be fully paid. The Georgia code usually requires the creditor to notify the debtor of the time and place of sale. This notice gives you a chance to be at the sale. By then, you may have the money to bid on your car, or you can encourage others to bid so that the final sale price will cover the debt. Also, Georgia has passed the Georgia Fair Lending Act, which prohibits abusive home loan practices.

Some of the oldest forms of credit protection legislation are the federal bankruptcy laws. These laws allow debtors who are unable to pay their debts as they come due to hold off their creditors. They can either write off or repay their debts under court supervision.

There are two types of bankruptcy petitions, Chapter 7 and Chapter 13, for individuals. Chapter 7 is known as straight bankruptcy. In a Chapter 7, the debtor declares that he or she cannot pay his or her debts as they come due. If this declaration is accepted by the court, most unsecured debts such as credit cards are canceled. Also, debtors generally must surrender some unsecured assets to the court, which are sold and the sale proceeds used to pay creditors. On the other hand, certain debts such as taxes and student loans cannot be canceled. It is hard for a debtor to get credit after a Chapter 7 bankruptcy. The bankruptcy will remain in his or her credit history for 10 years.

A Chapter 13 bankruptcy allows the debtor to arrange to repay as much of his or her debt as possible under court supervision. A Chapter 13 bankruptcy makes it easier to reestablish credit. It also allows the debtor to cancel certain unpaid debts that can't be canceled under Chapter 7.

Recent changes in federal bankruptcy laws have made filing a Chapter 13 more attractive. It is now easier for the debtor to keep a home and certain other assets. Under Chapter 7 bankruptcy, however, it is now harder for a debtor to avoid certain payments, including alimony and child support and bills for luxury goods bought before the bankruptcy petition was filed. It has become less attractive.

Filing for bankruptcy should be a solution of last resort. Persons who have declared bankruptcy can legally be denied credit. For this and other reasons, informal solutions to overindebtedness should be looked at first.

There are credit counseling services, such as the Consumer Credit Counseling Service, in your community. These services provide advice about managing debt. Be cautious, however, about private moneylenders who call themselves credit counselors. Usually, they suggest replacing several small loans with one large loan. This practice can be desirable, but private moneylenders often are more interested in making loans than in solving credit problems.

Only the Facts

1. What is an acceleration clause? balloon clause? add-on installment clause?
2. How do repossession and attachment differ?
3. What is the purpose of the Fair Debt Collection Practices Act?
4. Imagine that you are a creditor and that one of your debtors has missed a payment. The loan was for a car, and the car is collateral. Prepare a list of steps you would take to try to collect your debt.
5. How does bankruptcy protect the debtor?

SUMMING UP

This chapter has presented some basics on how credit works in Georgia and the United States. It has focused on the legal rights given to borrowers and creditors. In regard to borrowing, it is important to remember that a credit agreement is a contract: when you borrow money, you have a legal duty to pay it back. If you don't, the creditor can make use of the power of the state to enforce the contract. Your best protection against problems from borrowing is to be wise about credit. Don't overborrow. Shop around for credit. Know your legal rights. And, once you've borrowed, realize you have a legal obligation to meet your payments.

6 Housing

S ooner or later, you will be choosing your own place to live. First, you may be deciding whether to rent a room or an apartment. Later, you may be thinking about buying land, a condominium, or a house. Whether you buy or rent, you are going to have to act in accordance with the federal, state, and local laws governing what is called real property. For your own protection, you should know as much as possible about these laws.

WHAT IS REAL PROPERTY?

Generally, the law divides property into two broad categories: (1) real property and (2) personal property. The distinction between real property and personal property is important because different laws apply to different types of property.

Real property consists of land and things attached to it, such as houses, barns, or crops. There are various types of ownership interests in real property. An interest might be rights to the minerals under the surface of the land, or it could be a right to use (but not own) a house. It could be outright ownership of land. Real property is often referred to as real estate.

Personal property consists of everything else, tangible and intangible. Something that is tangible can be perceived, particularly by touch. Your car, your watch, your clothes, and even your dog are all examples of tangible personal property.

Intangible property is harder to define. It can be shares of stock in a company. It can be the good will that a person builds up in a business. It can be a copyright or contract right. It can be your ability to perform a service.

LAW TALK

deed

environmental regulation

fixture

lease

mortgage

personal property

real property

tenant

title

zoning regulations

When an item of personal property becomes so attached to land as to be considered permanent, it becomes real property. This type of property is commonly known as a fixture. On the other hand, if an item is separated from the land, it becomes personal property. For example, a mobile home would generally be considered personal property while sitting on a sales lot. However, once it is purchased and set up, it would be considered real property.

In the chapter on consumer law (chapter 4), you read about some of the laws governing the buying and selling of personal property. This chapter focuses on laws governing the rental, sale, and use of real property.

Only the Facts

1. Give examples of real property, personal property, and intangible property.
2. Which of the following would be a fixture? a tractor? a pond? a ceiling fan? Explain your answer.

RENTING REAL PROPERTY

Probably you will rent or lease an apartment or house before you think about buying one, and it is important to know your rights and responsibilities under a lease.

When you find a place to rent that meets your needs, you'll enter into an agreement or contract with the owner of the property. This contract is called a lease. It establishes the relationship of landlord and tenant. The landlord is the person who is leasing the property to the renter. Usually, the landlord owns the property. The party who leases the property and agrees to pay the rent to the landlord is the tenant.

Note that the person who shows you the place you are going to rent may not be the landlord. He or she may be the manager of the rental property. A Georgia law requires that a tenant be given—in writing—the names and addresses of the landlord (or appointed agent) and the manager of the rental property in case the tenant needs to contact the landlord or manager regarding a problem with the property.

The Lease Agreement

It is a good practice to enter into a written lease because the rights and duties of the tenant and landlord are then clear in case of a dispute. Under the laws of most states, lease agreements for a term greater than one year must be in writing. Keep in mind, however, that a nonwritten lease for less than a year is still binding, so it is important to know its terms.

The lease generally states when the tenant is to assume possession of the premises (that is, the property). It may also state how long the tenant's possession will be. This time period is known as the term of the lease. Leases also state the amount of rent that the tenant must pay to the landlord for use of the property. They state when rent is due and sometimes allow for an extra charge for paying rent after it is due. Restrictions on use are also covered. Pets, for example, may not be allowed. The lease also covers responsibilities regarding maintenance, damages, and repairs.

Read a lease very carefully before signing it (see figure 6-1 for points to check). You may ask the landlord to remove, add, or change terms in a lease. If you have found defects in the place you want to rent, be sure to discuss them. Know how they will be dealt with before signing the lease or putting down a security deposit. If you do not understand the provisions in the lease, ask someone you can rely on to explain them.

Types of Tenancies

All leases are not alike. Different types of leases create different types of tenancies, or terms of possession. Tenancies are generally classified by the term of the lease. The most common types of tenancies are periodic and at-will.

A periodic tenancy is for a definite term or length of time, usually one year or longer. This type of tenancy ends without notice on the last

FIGURE 6-1

Checklist for Renters

Before entering into a tenant-landlord agreement, it is important to know the following:

✓ Is a lease required? If so, what are its terms? What kind of tenancy is established?

✓ What is the rent? When must it be paid? Does it cover any of the utilities?

✓ Will any of the conditions of the lease affect the right to quiet enjoyment of the property?

✓ What is the current condition of the place?

- Does everything operate as it should? Check the lights, windows, plumbing, kitchen fixtures, doors.

- Is it in good repair? Does it need painting? Are there signs of roof leaks, cracks in walls, etc.?

- Is the property well maintained?

- Is it secure? Consider lighting of grounds, locks, and windows.

- Are there signs of rodents or insects?

✓ Make notes of any defects. Some landlords have check sheets for that purpose.

✓ What obligations are there for taking care of the property? What are the obligations of the landlord?

✓ Is a security deposit required?

---

day of the term specified in the lease. However, many leases allow tenants to extend or renew these tenancies.

What if the tenant wants to move before the end of the lease?

SITUATION 1 Roland and Rebecca rent an apartment for a year. Six months later, Roland is transferred to another city.

Can they sublet (that is, can they rent it to someone else for the duration of the lease)? If they leave the place vacant, must they pay rent to the landlady?

If their lease agreement permits it, the couple can sublet the apartment, which means they can find someone to move into their apartment and assume their lease. They will, however, still be responsible for the rent being paid. If there is no provision to sublet, the landlady could but is not obligated to release Roland and Rebecca from their lease. If she will not, they may be liable for the rent until the lease ends or until the apartment is rented. In Georgia, as in many other states, a landlord who leases residential property is generally required to try to rent to another tenant. (The same is not true for commercial property, however.) In the case of U.S. military employees, a 1990 Georgia law limits the rent liability of these tenants if they move before a lease ends because of military orders.

A tenancy-at-will is one in which a landlord leases property to a tenant for an indefinite term or time period. In such a lease, either the landlord or the tenant may end the tenancy at any time, with proper notice.

SITUATION 2 Sally rents an apartment for an indefinite term. One day, her landlady tells her she must be out of the apartment in three days.

Is this demand legal?

Georgia and other states require both landlord and tenant to give notice to the other a specified number of days before ending a tenancy-at-will. In Georgia, 60 days' notice from the landlord and 30 days' notice from the tenant are required. The landlady could not therefore make this demand of Sally.

What happens if a tenant stays in possession after the lease expires? This situation is called a tenancy-at-sufferance. In this case, a tenant's right to occupy depends on the landlord. The landlord could start eviction proceedings against the tenant, agree to another tenancy under the exact terms and conditions as the lease that ended, or allow a tenancy on any other terms.

Paying the Rent

A lease usually specifies what the amount of rent will be. It also states when rent must be paid and what might happen if it is not paid. Once tenants start using their leased premises, they must pay rent to the landlord in accordance with the terms of the lease.

Consider the following situation:

SITUATION 3 Tammie's rented apartment is destroyed by fire. At the beginning of the next month, her landlord notifies her that her rent is due.

Must she pay it?

The obligation to pay rent continues through the period of the lease. It does not end even if the premises are ruined (situation 3). The obligation to pay rent in such a situation would end only if it were provided for in the lease. Make sure such an "escape" clause is in any lease you sign. However, if the lease has no escape clause, the tenant can also stop paying rent and vacate the premises after going through a process called "constructive eviction" (discussed later in this chapter).

SITUATION 4 Tim signs a lease renting an apartment for a year. It states that the rent is $350 per month. Three months into the year, he receives a notice that the landlord is raising the rent to $375.

Is this legal?

It is not, unless such raises are allowed in the lease. Check to see if the landlord can raise the rent during the lease term. The lease may provide for raising rent to cover increases in utility costs (such as heating, water, or electricity) when such costs are included in the rent. Be sure also to find out which utilities the rent covers—if any.

The terms differ for renting residential and commercial property.

SITUATION 5 Harold and Honey didn't pay their rent as due on June 1—the first time they were late. On June 3, their landlady sent them a notice to move out. They say they should have more time to pay.

Do they have legal rights?

If a tenant fails to pay rent as agreed in the lease, the landlord may have the right to dispossess (that is, move out or evict) the tenant. Many leases allow a grace period of a few days from the day rent is due. During this time, the tenant may pay the rent and not be evicted. In situation 5, if the couple's lease contained such a grace period clause, they would have the time specified in the lease to pay their rent without being subject to eviction.

A landlord can dispossess a tenant the very first time the rent is not paid on time, but some landlords are willing to give people a second and even a third chance. A landlord who repeatedly accepts late rent may give up the right to evict tenants who do not pay rent on time because continually accepting late payments in effect alters the terms of the contract.

Although a landlord has the right to dispossess someone for not paying the rent, he or she cannot just throw a tenant off the premises. Nor can a landlord try to force tenants out by shutting off heat in winter. A landlord must follow the legal procedure for eviction.

The Eviction Process

SITUATION 6 Sam and Sadie have not paid their rent for three months. One day, they come home to find they have been evicted by the landlord and his brothers. Their furniture, clothes, and possessions are on the sidewalk.

Can the landlord legally take such action?

The process of dispossessing a tenant is carefully controlled by law. In Georgia, a landlord can begin the process in a superior, state, or magistrate court. Landlords usually prefer magistrate courts because costs are lower and attorneys are not needed.

After the landlord files the eviction claim with the court, the court issues a summons. The tenant must respond within seven days. If the tenant fails to respond, the judge usually decides in favor of the landlord. The judge then issues an order allowing the marshal or sheriff to evict the tenant.

If the tenant responds to the summons within the time allowed, the court schedules a hearing. The hearing gives the tenant a chance to present arguments or defenses against the accusations of the landlord. Suppose the tenant has not paid the rent. First the landlord must prove that the rent was not paid on time. Then, the tenant may raise any defenses or claims. A successful defense might be that the landlord did not keep the premises in good repair or that the landlord failed to provide proper heating or cooling or adequate water. It is not required for the parties to have attorneys at eviction hearings, but having an attorney can be very useful if the issue is difficult to prove.

If, after the hearing, the judge decides that the landlord does have the right to dispossess the tenant, then the judge will order the tenant to leave the premises. The tenant may have to pay any rent due and court costs. If the tenant refuses to leave, the sheriff can physically remove the tenant and all of his or her possessions. If the judge rules for the tenant, the tenant may stay on the premises. The landlord may be liable for damages caused by wrongful conduct.

In situation 6, there is no evidence that the landlord made use of the court process. He thus denied the couple their right to due process of law. Further, actual physical eviction must be carried out by a sheriff or deputy sheriff under court order. Landlords cannot take such action themselves. The legal procedure required to dispossess tenants was developed to protect the rights of tenants. Such protection was needed because of past abuses by landlords eager to replace low-paying or problem-causing tenants.

Under Georgia law, landlords can also try to collect rent payments through distress warrants. Under this procedure, if the judge's ruling is for the landlord, a tenant's possessions can be sold to cover the rent due.

Only the Facts

1. Are the following statements true or false?
   a. A tenant rents property to a landlord.
   b. All leases must be written.
   c. A tenant-at-will rents for an indefinite period.
   d. It is not important to read leases carefully.
   e. Eviction hearings are held in probate courts.
   f. Landlords cannot personally dispossess tenants after an eviction hearing.
2. Describe the steps in the eviction process.

Think About

1. Explain how a lease meets the requirements of a contract.

2. As a renter, what kind of tenancy would seem most advantageous to you and why? Which would seem to have the least advantages?

3. The eviction process is a way of legally settling a dispute. How does it protect the landlord? the tenant? Are there other, peaceful ways to settle disputes between landlords and tenants?

Right to Quiet Enjoyment

Just as a tenant has an obligation to pay rent, the landlord also has legal duties (see figure 6-2 for duties and rights of landlords and tenants). One landlord duty is to allow the tenant "quiet enjoyment" of the premises. Would the events in the next situations violate quiet enjoyment?

SITUATION 7 New renters moved into the apartment above Tom and Tilly. They play their stereo loudly until early in the morning and frequently have loud parties. Tom is exhausted. He must be at work at 6:00 a.m. Tom and Tilly complain to the landlady.

 hat is her obligation?

SITUATION 8 Tracy is having a fancy luncheon. The landlord bursts in with a pest control operator who has come to spray the apartment for insects. Tracy's guests are upset. Tracy is very embarrassed.

 as the landlord within his rights?

The courts have said that a tenant in an apartment building cannot interfere with the quiet enjoyment of another tenant. In situation 7, the landlady should tell the neighbors that they must allow Tom and Tilly a quiet time to sleep.

Leases frequently give landlords the right of access for repairs, inspections, and rent collections. The right to privacy, however, is another part of enjoyment. In general, a landlord cannot enter a tenant's apartment without the tenant's permission (situation 8). Tracy has the right to ask her landlord to return at another time to spray for bugs. Since no emergency was involved, he should have asked Tracy to allow him to enter her apartment.

A landlord's rules and regulations for use of the property may be written in the lease. Such rules can affect enjoyment of the property. They

FIGURE 6-2

Rental Rights and Responsibilities

Tenant Rights	Landlord Rights
Use, possess, and control premises	Have rent paid on time
Have quiet enjoyment of premises	Have premises returned in good condition at end of lease
Expect repairs within a reasonable time	Keep a security deposit for unpaid rent or property damage
Be protected from eviction except by legal process	Legally evict a tenant who doesn't pay rent, respect lease terms, or vacate when lease is over

Tenant Responsibilities	Landlord Responsibilities
Pay rent on time	Keep premises in good repair
Obey terms of lease	Obey terms of lease
Take reasonable care of premises	See that premises meet housing codes
Pay for damages beyond normal wear and tear	Ensure quiet enjoyment of premises

may determine where a tenant can keep a bicycle or when a laundry facility can be used. They may determine whether a tenant can nail or tape posters to walls. They may prohibit pets. Be sure to read these rules before signing a lease.

Repair and Care

Landlords have obligations to make repairs. They must maintain the safe conditions of the rental unit. Tenants also have responsibilities to care for the property they rent. Sometimes written leases clearly state the repair duties of the landlord and the tenant. Other times they do not.

As a general rule, a tenant does not have to repair or replace items broken by ordinary wear and tear. Nor is a tenant obliged to repair damages caused by fire or other casualties. However, repair of damage (beyond normal wear and tear) caused by the tenants, their families, or their guests is the responsibility of the tenant.

There may be defects in the premises known to the landlord but unknown to the tenant when he or she takes possession. The landlord must repair such defects. Sometimes the defects are obvious to both parties when they sign the lease. The landlord has a duty to repair any unsafe conditions that violate housing codes or other laws.

In each of the following situations, who do you think would be responsible for the repairs?

> **SITUATION 9** Tina is showering in her apartment one morning. All the water pressure is suddenly lost. She discovers a hole in the rusted water pipe and reports the problem to her landlord. He tells Tina to get it fixed herself.

> **SITUATION 10** During a fierce storm, the branch of a falling tree smashes Cheryl's bedroom window. Her table by the window is damaged by the rain.

> **SITUATION 11** Before renting to Toby, the landlord shows him a defective gas heater in the bedroom. Toby agrees to rent the unit "as is."

In situation 9, the landlord would have to repair the damages. A rusted water pipe would be considered ordinary wear and tear. Tina would not have to make the repair or pay for it. In situation 10, the landlord would be obligated to repair the premises, but Cheryl would have to pay for repairing her own table. In situation 11, Toby knew of the problem before he rented the apartment. However, to make the residence safe, the landlord would have an obligation to repair a potentially dangerous defect, such as the gas heater.

A landlord is not obliged to inspect leased property to discover defects that arise during a tenancy. The landlord's duty is to repair such defects during the tenancy only when told about them.

What Can the Tenant Do?

What can a tenant do if a landlord fails to repair the premises when obligated to do so? Some communities have associations that help settle landlord-tenant disputes. Private tenant organizations also can be helpful. These organizations may represent an apartment complex or group of homes. What if no such organizations exist?

> **SITUATION 12** Ted has repeatedly asked his landlord to repair the plumbing. For some time there has been no hot water. He also wants the cracks in the walls plastered. The landlord has not done anything. Ted's friends give him different advice.
>
> a. Report the landlord for violating the housing code.
> b. Make the repairs and ask the landlord for reimbursement.
> c. Withhold rent until the repairs are made.
> d. Sue the landlord.
> e. Break the lease and move.

Legally, Ted could pursue some of these options. However, he should consult an attorney before proceeding with any action, except for the first option. Ted has every right to report the landlord to the government office in charge of housing code violations. Many Georgia cities and counties have enacted housing codes that regulate the condition of houses and apartments after they are built. These codes help to ensure that people's homes and neighborhoods are safe to live in. They spell out the requirements for rental property.

The appropriate authority can require and force a landlord to comply with the housing code. It can also impose a fine or other sanctions on a landlord (see figure 6-3). However, in order for the housing authority to correct the problem, the tenant must first notify it of the problem. Tenants are often reluctant to do so.

Landlords may also be held liable for any injuries sustained by tenants as a result of housing code violations. Let's look again at the example of Ted. What if the housing code required hot water to make an apartment habitable, and Ted got pneumonia from being able to take only cold showers? Ted could sue the landlord for violating a duty created by the applicable housing code provision.

Option 12b is for Ted to make the repairs himself and to then ask the landlord for repayment. What if the landlord fails to repay Ted for his repair expenses? Ted may deduct reasonable costs of the repairs from the next month's rent.

Ted can also refuse to pay rent. He can wait for the landlord to sue for the unpaid rent. What if his claims for damage for failure to repair are more than the landlord's rent claims? Ted may then stay in possession and receive the excess money. What if the rent claims exceed Ted's claims for damages? In that case, he would be liable for the excess rent. Also, Ted can continue to pay rent and sue the landlord for damages caused by the failure to repair.

SITUATION 13 Tina is bathing her child in the bathroom of her apartment. Suddenly the floor next to the tub collapses. Tina sues the owner and manager of her apartment for the injuries she sustained when this happened.

What types of damages may Tina receive?

As an injured party, Tina could receive compensatory damages. These awards are made to pay the party for loss or injury in two ways. First, they repay any out-of-pocket loss such as medical bills and/or lost wages. Second, compensatory damages are paid for pain and suffering. Tina could receive punitive damages, too. Punitive damages are intended to punish a defendant and to deter him or her from acting in a similar

FIGURE 6-3

How Housing Codes Are Enforced

COMPLAINT

Housing Inspection

Violation of Housing Code Found

Violation Notice Mailed

30 days

Reinspection

If after three notices and inspections within a 120-day period the violation has not been corrected, then

Informal Hearing

with owner, housing inspector, head of city inspection department, and city attorney to work out problem

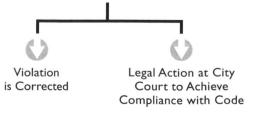

Violation is Corrected

Legal Action at City Court to Achieve Compliance with Code

way in the future. They are only awarded if the defendant's conduct is especially bad. For example, if the landlord knew the floor was about to cave in and did nothing, Tina might receive a punitive damage award.

Generally, a landlord's failure to fulfill his or her duty to repair the premises does not necessarily mean a tenant can terminate the lease. But what if the defect is so severe that the premises cannot be lived in safely? Unless the property can be restored to a fit condition by ordinary repairs, the tenant may legally break the lease. This process is known as constructive eviction. To use it, Ted should declare the apartment unsuitable to live in; he should have evidence to prove in court why it is unsuitable; and, if the apartment is truly unsuitable, Ted should vacate the premises. If he continued to live there, it could be argued that the apartment is suitable for human habitation.

Security Deposits

In Georgia as in other states, a landlord may require that a tenant pay a security deposit before the tenant takes possession of the leased property. The security deposit can be used to compensate the landlord for damages beyond normal wear and tear caused by tenants or their guests. The landlord may also keep the deposit if the tenant fails to pay rent or moves out before the lease ends.

The law pertaining to security deposits is very strict. Landlords who fail to meet the requirements can forfeit any right to keep the deposit and/or to sue the tenant for property damages.

Special provisions of Georgia law apply to landlords who own more than 10 rental units or who employ a rental management company. They must inspect their property before and after each tenant occupies it. After each inspection, they must present the tenant with a list of damages to the premises. The tenant has the right to inspect the premises and to agree or disagree with the landlord's list.

Within a month of the time a tenant leaves the property (or at the end of a lease), a landlord holding a security deposit must do one of two things. He must return the security deposit or explain in writing why any of it has been kept. None of the security deposit may be kept to cover normal wear and tear. If any of the security deposit is withheld improperly, the landlord may be liable to the tenant for an amount three times that withheld, as well as attorney's fees.

The question of what is normal wear and tear is not always clear. To illustrate, look at the damages in situation 14. Consider them from the point of view of landlord and tenant. Would they be normal wear and tear?

SITUATION 14

a. Stains on a carpet.
b. Living room walls painted in zigzag black and pink stripes.
c. Nail holes for hanging pictures throughout the house.
d. A missing chandelier.
e. A filthy apartment. Decaying food and trash throughout.

Worn places on floors, nail holes for pictures, and occasional stains could all be considered normal wear and tear. However, tenants do not have the right to remove permanent fixtures, and landlords can expect premises to be left relatively clean. Depending on the terms of the lease, redecorating and putting nails in walls to hang pictures, as in options 14b and 14c, may be prohibited.

Public Housing

Various governmental programs exist to help people with low incomes obtain adequate housing. One major program established by federal law uses tax monies to build low-income housing that is owned and managed by a city or county housing authority.

Public housing is not available to everyone. Generally, participants must be families or elderly, handicapped, or disabled persons. They must not receive more than the maximum income set by law.

In public housing, the government often pays part or all of the monthly rent. Typically, tenants pay 30 percent of their monthly net income toward rent, and the federal government pays the rest. Local housing authorities regularly examine the incomes of all tenants and adjust the rents as tenants' incomes change. They may also evict families whose incomes have risen above the limit allowed, if alternative private housing is available.

Eligible tenants cannot be evicted from public housing except for good cause. Good cause includes a serious or repeated violation of the lease. Examples would be using illegal drugs in or near a public housing project or not paying rent.

Only the Facts

1. What are the responsibilities of a tenant in renting property? What are the responsibilities of a landlord?
2. Explain what kind of damages a tenant is responsible for. What kind is the landlord's responsibility?
3. Name three actions a tenant might take if a landlord does not make necessary repairs.
4. What is a security deposit?

Think About

1. Why is it so important for a tenant to read a lease carefully?
2. It has been said that leases are written to protect the landlord's interests. Why would this statement be true? Who needs the most protection—the landlord or the tenant?
3. Should landlords be responsible for the safety of their tenants in regard to crime? Consider this question from both the tenant's and landlord's viewpoint. What precautions should be the landlord's responsibility regarding grounds? common areas like hallways? doors and locks? lighting? burglar alarms? security guards?

BUYING REAL PROPERTY

What to Buy?

Homer and Helen have been married for about five years. They have rented several apartments. They would like a home of their own.

What kind of property should they buy? For Homer and Helen, a big factor is cost. They have saved about $6,500 for a down payment. They know that banks are unlikely to give a home loan for more than two and a half to three times the purchaser's annual salary. Their combined income is $41,000 a year.

Homer and Helen have dreamed of a house with a yard, but they wonder if they could better afford a mobile home or a condominium. They do not know very much about condominium ownership.

A condominium (or "condo") is an individually owned dwelling unit in a complex of such units. Each condo owner owns a share of the common property of the complex. Common property might be a laundry, swimming pool, or landscaped grounds. The condo owner pays a monthly maintenance fee to care for this property.

Georgia law requires that two documents be prepared for each condo development. One document is the bylaws of the owners' association. This document is needed for various reasons, including the fact that there are multiple owners in one complex, all of whom have rights and responsibilities associated with the common property. The other document is the master deed. Both should be read carefully so that purchasers know what to expect. Otherwise, a new condo owner might be surprised to learn that there are certain regulations regarding property use, such as that owners cannot keep pets or play loud music late at night.

Homer and Helen also look into buying a mobile home. When they have finished their investigations, they discuss what they should do. Should they buy now or continue to rent? What are the advantages and disadvantages of the different kinds of homes? They make a chart similar to that in figure 6-4.

FIGURE 6-4

To Buy or Not to Buy?

	Cost	Investment Value	Maintenance Cost	Maintenance Time	Control over Use of Property	Privacy	Ease of Relocating and Resale	Other Factors
Private House?	highest	probably greatest	a lot	a lot	greatest; limited by local government and neighborhood regulations	greatest	could be difficult	
Condo?	medium	good	some; could increase	very little	some; limited by condo association rules	varies	could be difficult	may have recreational facilities
Mobile Home?	low	poor because of depreciation	some	some	some; limited by local government regulations and mobile home park rules	varies	desired location could be difficult; resale would vary	vulnerable to winds
Rental?	low to medium	none (except that because there is no down payment the money could be invested elsewhere)	very little	very little	least	varies	easiest to relocate	may have recreational facilities

Homer and Helen decide they really want a house with a yard. Helen wants to garden, and Homer would like to have a dog. They decide to try to find a house they can afford.

Looking for a House

Selecting a home typically involves a real estate broker or agent. The broker brings the purchaser and seller together to negotiate the sale. Generally, the real estate broker is paid by the seller through a brokerage commission. In Georgia, this commission typically equals 6 to 7 percent of the total purchase price of the home.

A local real estate agent helps Homer and Helen look for houses. Finally, they find a house they like at a price they can afford. It is a small, white frame house with three bedrooms and one and a half bathrooms. There are large oak trees in the yard. The house is in a neighborhood convenient to their jobs. All of the houses in the neighborhood look well cared for.

There are several steps the couple must follow to get the house:

I Inspecting the Property

A friend advises them that before making an offer for the house, they should

- inspect it very carefully, inside and out.
- look for signs of breaks and leaks, wear and tear.
- have it inspected for termites.
- ask the age of the roof and the heating system.
- be certain of the boundaries.

- find out about easements and zoning regulations.
- find out if things that are not fixtures (such as a refrigerator or porch swing) go with the house.

As a result of the inspection, Homer and Helen discover that some of the plumbing is in need of repair. The seller agrees to have the repairs done.

2 Signing the Purchase Contract

Homer and Helen make an offer for the house, which the seller accepts. The realtor prepares a contract for the transaction.

A written contract for buying real property is required by law. The contract makes the sale enforceable should there be a legal dispute. The contract should include all the terms of the sale. Usual terms of a contract include

- description of the property, including all fixtures to be retained by the seller.
- official location of the property.
- purchase price.
- sale costs for buyer and seller.
- commission for real estate agent.
- actions seller must make (such as repairs).
- amount and conditions for earnest money.

3 Depositing Earnest Money

Earnest money essentially is a good faith deposit paid to the seller upon the signing of the contract. It is applied toward the total purchase price when the sale is closed. What if the actual sale does not occur for reasons that are not the fault of either the purchaser or the seller? Usually the earnest money is then refunded to the purchaser. It is important that there be a contract clause that makes earnest money refundable. If the contract is breached (or broken) by the purchaser, he or she usually forfeits the earnest money. The seller keeps it as payment of any damages caused by the purchaser's breach.

Home buyers may finance their purchase with a mortgage loan. What percentage of their income should their monthly payments be?

4 Obtaining Funding

Like most people, Homer and Helen do not have enough money to pay the entire price of a home. They must therefore shop for a loan.

Loans for homes are called mortgage loans. They are one kind of credit. Mortgage loans are secured loans (see the discussion in chapter 5). The property (that is, the house and the land it is built on) becomes the collateral needed to secure the loan.

As a general rule, a mortgage loan is taken out for a long period of time, typically 15 to 30 years. The homeowner borrows a specific amount of money for this time period. The amount borrowed is known as the principal. The period of years for which the loan is made is known as the term of the loan. The principal is paid back over the term of the loan at a particular rate of interest. The length of the term influences the amount of monthly payments. Homer and Helen know that these payments shouldn't be more than 20 to 25 percent of their income.

Through most of the years of payment, a high percentage of the monthly payment goes to pay the interest rather than the principal amount of the loan. Suppose Homer and Helen obtain a 30-year loan of $75,000 on the house at 8 percent. Of the first monthly payment of $550.32, $500.00 would be interest. Truth in Lending laws require that borrowers be informed of these figures prior to taking the loan.

In the past, most mortgage loans were at fixed interest rates; that is, the monthly payments were the same over the term of the loan. Recent years have been less stable economically. Lenders have found this kind of mortgage lending unprofitable. They have created new types of mortgages with adjustable and variable interest rates. This variety of mortgages makes home-loan shopping more complex.

Most home loans come from banks and savings and loan associations. Several federal government aid programs assist buyers in getting loans. The Federal Housing Administration (FHA) and Veterans Administration (VA) both insure home loans. This insurance encourages banks to lend to people whose loans they might not otherwise approve. FHA and VA loans allow lower down payments and usually have lower interest rates. VA loans are only available to veterans of the armed forces.

The Georgia Residential Finance Authority offers low-interest mortgage loans for eligible low- and moderate-income borrowers. However, there are geographical as well as income restrictions. In addition, persons convicted of certain illegal drug activities are not eligible to participate in the program.

5 Checking the Title

Besides trying to arrange for financing the house by obtaining a mortgage loan, Homer and Helen hire an attorney to examine the title of the property they are buying. A title is one's right to ownership of a particular piece of real property. The title examination (or search) is critical for the homebuyer. It is important to know that the seller is the sole and rightful owner of the property and that there are no problems with the title.

Building a home involves certain legal considerations, such as the builder's contract and local building codes.

A title search involves tracing the chain of ownership of the property. In Georgia, the search covers 50 years. The searcher looks to see that no one else besides the seller has any claim or right to the property.

The searcher also looks to see that there are no defects in the seller's title. A defect in the title might be taxes owed on the property. Another defect might be the right of other people to use part of the property as a driveway. In other words, a title defect concerns anything that might interfere with the purchaser's use and enjoyment of the property.

6 Closing the Sale

Homer and Helen have arranged a loan with a local lending company, and the title search shows that the seller has a clear title to the property. It is time for the closing, or settlement of the sale.

Federal law requires that the buyers be notified of the closing costs at least 24 hours before the closing. These costs may include fees for the loan application, property appraisal, title search, attorney's fees, and title insurance. (Title insurance protects a buyer against any claim overlooked in the search.) Generally, the buyer must be prepared to pay these fees and the agreed-upon down payment on the house. The lender pays the remainder of the cost of the house. The seller will pay the real estate agent's fee and title transfer. At the closing, the documents are signed that complete the sale.

7 Recording the Documents

The document that represents the passing of ownership from the seller to the purchaser is the deed. The deed states that for a particular sum of money, the seller grants (or conveys) to the purchaser the property described. Once the deed is signed by the seller and handed to the purchaser, the purchaser becomes the owner of the property.

When the purchaser finances the property with a mortgage, another document is required. This document is known in Georgia as a deed to secure debt. This deed establishes the new buyer's property as collateral for the loan. The deed to secure debt is executed (or signed) by the purchaser and given to the lender.

After the sale is closed, the signed documents must be recorded at the local courthouse. By recording each real property sale, land records can be safely and centrally maintained.

Now, at last, Homer and Helen own their home.

If You Can't Repay the Loan

If a mortgage loan is not repaid as agreed, the mortgage lender may obtain the collateral and sell it to satisfy the debt. This process is known as foreclosure.

Suppose Bill buys a house. Several years later, he loses his job. His wife's salary is low. They miss several payments on their house. Shortly thereafter, Bill receives a notice from the bank stating that an ad will be placed in the county newspaper announcing that the house is to be sold at foreclosure. The sale will occur on the courthouse steps on the first Tuesday of the month.

As in other legal processes, notification is very important. It gives Bill time to try to get some money to make the payments or satisfy the bank. It gives him time to find out if he has any grounds for legal action to prevent foreclosure.

If Bill does nothing, the house may be sold at public outcry (that is, at a public sale). A person buying the house would pay an amount equal to the unpaid principal on Bill's loan, plus interest and debt collection costs. In this scenario, Bill and his family would lose their home and the money invested in it.

Note that property can also be seized and sold at public sale by a county government to meet unpaid property tax debts. Delinquent taxpayers (that is, those who fail to pay the tax assessed on their house) must also be notified before the sale.

Once you decide to buy a home, it is important to be aware of the legal steps and the financial demands of purchasing it. A lack of knowledge can result in financial loss and hardship.

O n l y   t h e   F a c t s

1. How does ownership of a condominium differ from that of a private home?

2. List steps in buying a house.

3. Explain the reason for a title search.

4. Correct any errors in the following statements.

   a. At a closing, the purchase agreement is signed.

   b. The process by which a landlord obtains the collateral of a tenant and sells it to pay the debt is called foreclosure.

   c. A deed is a document representing the passing of property ownership from the seller to the buyer.

   d. A mortgage is not a form of credit.

1. Review the requirements for a contract. Explain how a house purchase agreement meets these requirements.

2. Explain how the rights of a seller, buyer, and lender in a sale of real property are protected.

3. Look back at chapter 4. How does the advice to buyers of personal property apply to buyers of real property?

USING REAL PROPERTY

You will recall that Homer and Helen recently bought a house. Can they use it in whatever way they wish? Suppose they want to use part of it for a beauty shop? Suppose they want to raise chickens in the backyard or build a greenhouse? Can they do these things? After all, one of the reasons for buying a house is to be able to use it as you wish.

Over time—particularly as populations have increased—people have found it necessary to regulate the use of real property. Limits on use of property often reflect the line between the rights of the individual and the rights of others (see figure 6-5). Some of the reasons are to make certain that

- a noisy or smelly factory can't locate next to your house.
- you have parks and woods to play in.
- you have water and air that is clean and safe.
- your new house won't fall down because of faulty construction.
- you can live wherever you want, regardless of your race or national origin.

These needs have resulted in various local, state, and federal laws. Laws regulating or influencing land and property use include (1) zoning regulations, (2) subdivision covenants, (3) ease-

---

FIGURE 6-5

Whose Side of the Fence Are You On?

Whose rights should prevail? Can you suggest any general rule for judging these disputes? Where do one person's rights end and another's begin? Would these problems arise in a society with fewer people spread farther apart?

Resident Says	Neighbor Says
I'm paying money to rent this apartment. I should be able to do what I want in it. I need the cash I get from building and selling cabinets. Sometimes I have to work late to finish an order.	Listen, I pay rent, too! I can't get any rest. I can't even enjoy a quiet evening at home. My neighbor is always hammering or running that noisy power saw. Sometimes the noise doesn't stop until midnight.
All my life, I've wanted to own a house with a little land around it. My dream was to raise some chickens and keep a few goats.	I'm sorry, but the rules of this subdivision are clear: No chickens, no goats. Besides, they are noisy and smelly. I don't want to live beside a barnyard.
I don't understand: What's wrong with having a business in my house? I own the place. And this is just a small ice cream shop. It gives the neighborhood teens a wholesome place to go.	What's wrong with it? This is a neighborhood zoned for single family homes. If I had wanted to buy a house next to a noisy restaurant, I wouldn't be living here. Look at the cars parked all over the lawns. You should see the trash the kids throw out.
Why can't I dump the wastes from my plant into the river? I pay taxes like everyone else. Why should I get stuck paying for fancy filters? Mind you, I'm talking about a very small amount of waste.	Hey, my kids swim in that river. I want it to be safe for them. One of my pals likes to fish there. Some communities even get their drinking water from it.

---

ments, which relate to the use of one person's land by another, (4) building and housing codes, (5) environmental regulations, and (6) antidiscrimination laws. As you read about these laws, think about why they are needed.

Zoning Regulations

Zoning regulations are city and county laws that limit the purposes for which property owners can use their land and property. They may also restrict the height and size of buildings on pieces of land.

Why are there zoning regulations? Imagine what would happen if people could use their land for any purpose, without regard for others. You could wake up one day to find your house in the middle of a dump or surrounded by paper mills. Zoning laws prevent these scenarios and promote organized land use.

Generally speaking, zoning regulations function as follows. A county or city first makes a master zoning plan. In the case of a city, the master plan is actually a large map that divides the city into areas. Each area has a particular zoning designation (see figure 6-6). For example, the city outskirts may be largely rural. They may be zoned A-1 (small agricultural). The use of the property would be confined to small farms. More central areas of the city may be zoned R-1 for single-family residences or R-5 for multifamily residences. Other areas may be zoned C-1 for commercial or industrial uses. In addition to land-use limitations in a particular zone, there would be various building size, height, and use restrictions.

Sometimes property owners try to get an area rezoned to a different designation so that it can be used for purposes other than those

---

FIGURE 6-6

Part of a Zoning Map

Several of the following types of zoned areas can be found on the portion of a zoning map, at right.

R-1	Single Family Residential
R-2	Single Family Residential
R-3	Single Family Residential
R-4	One and Two Family Residential
R-5	Multifamily Residential
L-B	Local Business
G-B	General Business
C-B-D	Central Business District
0-1	Office-Institutional
M-1	Limited Industrial
M-2	General Industrial
GD-300	Planned Commercial
GD-400	Planned Residential Area
GD-500	Planned Office-Institutional
R-5H	High-Rise Multifamily Residential
O-I-B	Office Institutional Business

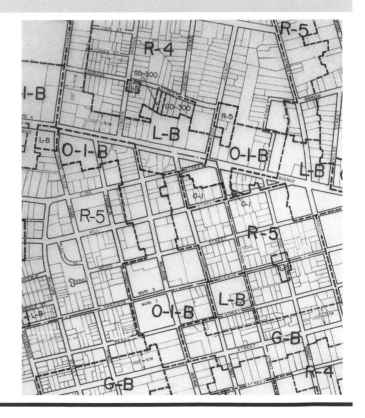

allowed under the current zoning plan. Other times, they may ask for a zoning variance for part of an area. A variance is similar to an exception to a rule. It allows part of an area to be used in a way that is not generally allowed under the zoning plan. Typically the people affected will have strong feelings for or against proposed rezoning or requests for variance. For instance, they may not want apartments in their neighborhood of single-family houses. They may object to a store selling liquor near a school or church. In your local media, you may find news of people supporting or protesting zoning actions.

Subdivision Covenants

Subdivision covenants also regulate the use of land and property. These covenants often are found in organized residential subdivisions or neighborhoods. They form a kind of compact among property owners and sometimes property developers. Although similar to zoning regulations, they are private restrictions on land use. The restrictions are not imposed by government laws. Their legal force would be like those of a contract.

A main purpose of covenants is to keep neighborhoods attractive and pleasant. They may require all residences to be a minimum size or restrict the use of certain materials or colors on exterior buildings, for example.

Easements

When a property owner does not have access to a public road, legal permission may be needed to cross a neighbor's property in order to gain access. In such a situation, the neighbor may grant permission in the form of a legal document similar to a deed that is recorded at the courthouse. The document, together with the rights it grants, is called an easement. Easements may also be granted in situations in which adjoining property owners share a common driveway. Furthermore, utility companies must obtain easements for their power or phone lines.

Building Codes

Permits are required for construction in communities because local governments have building codes as well as housing codes (discussed earlier in this chapter). Building codes are laws that specify certain standards for constructing, altering, and repairing buildings. Their purpose is to see that buildings are soundly constructed of proper materials. They also ensure that electrical, plumbing, heating, and air conditioning fixtures are appropriate and properly installed.

Before building, construction plans must be submitted to the city or county's inspection department. They are checked to see if the standards will be met. If so, a permit is issued. Inspections are made during construction to be sure that work is carried out according to plans.

Environmental Regulations

Pollution has increased. Garbage is becoming unmanageable. Resources such as water are becoming more limited. Natural areas such as parks, woods, and wetlands are threatened by development. Not surprisingly, laws must be passed to protect the environment. Many of these laws directly affect real property ownership.

Some laws are intended to improve air quality. An example is a local ordinance that prohibits burning out-of-doors. Other laws and regulations concern water. For purer water, a 1990 Georgia law requires stricter control of sewage treatment facilities and sewage discharge. Also, buildings built after 1990 are required to have toilets and showerheads that save water. To protect plants, animals, and water, government agencies regulate the use of farm chemicals. They also monitor uses of land where endangered species live.

The issue of environmental regulation generally has to do with the public good versus the right to private use of property. This controversy has become more significant with increases in population, zoning concerns, and environmental regulations protecting land, air, and water.

Antidiscrimination Laws

The Federal Fair Housing Act forbids discrimination because of race, color, sex, national origin, handicap, or familial status. (Familial status is another way of saying families with children.) Generally the act covers the sale, rental, or advertising of dwellings. It applies to landlords who own more than three rental units or who advertise their units.

In 1990, Georgia passed a fair housing law similar to the Federal Fair Housing Act. It also prohibits discrimination in making appraisals or loans for purchasing, constructing, or repairing residential property.

When someone believes they have been discriminated against, they can file complaints under either the federal or state fair housing laws. (Federal complaints are filed with an agency of the U.S. Department of Housing and Urban Development. A complaint about a violation of state law would be made to the Fair Housing Division of the state Office of Fair Employment Practices.) Alternatively, the person could take the claim to court.

Only the Facts

1. Define the following: (a) zoning master plan, (b) variance, (c) subdivision covenant, (d) easement, (e) building code.
2. What is the basic difference between a housing code and a building code?
3. Name a law that helps prevent discrimination in housing. What rights are protected by the law?

Think About

1. Many environmental regulations affect uses of property. In what ways does the need to protect the environment relate to growing population?
2. Rights of property owners are restricted by some of the laws regulating land use. What, if any, benefits do the property owners gain from these laws?

SUMMING UP

During your life, you will probably be involved more than once in renting and/or buying a place to live. It is important to be aware of your financial limits and to understand the legal duties and rights of the leases or contracts you sign.

Enjoying your property may also depend upon knowing your rights and responsibilities in using it. Limits on use of property often reflect a balance between the rights of various people (including landlords and tenants, homebuyers and sellers, and neighbors). When people lived farther apart, their rights to use property didn't conflict as much as they do today. Many of our laws governing use of property reflect population growth. Almost every prediction points to increases in populations and decreases in available land. How do you think these changes will affect laws concerning real property?

7 On the Job

In the spring, thousands of high school students look for jobs. Some are looking for permanent, full-time work. Most seek summer jobs. You may be among them.

When you go for a job interview, do you know what questions you should ask to be sure of your legal rights and duties in that position? Do you know what laws will affect you after you are hired? This chapter offers you such information.

GETTING A JOB

The Job as a Contract

To begin with, it is important to know that when a person works for another person, the two have a contract. At its simplest, one person promises to pay a certain price for the services of the other person. The other agrees to work at the stated price. This contract relationship for work is, typically, an employer-employee relationship. The person offering the opportunity to work is the employer. The person working is the employee.

Although the employment relationship is a contractual one, most employment relationships are "at will, " meaning that the job is for an indefinite term. As such, it can be terminated by either the employee or the employer at any time with or without notice and with or without "cause," or reason for doing so.

You may recall that in a contract there must be a meeting of the minds. Each side must be clear about what the terms of the contract are. For this reason, when you apply for a job, you should find out what your duties will be for the job. Ask what your hours will be. Note any special requirements for clothing or personal equipment.

LAW TALK

affirmative action

benefit

equal employment opportunity

labor union

pension

Social Security

status category

unemployment compensation

workers' compensation

You should also learn what the duties of your employer will be. What salary will you earn? What benefits are being offered? Knowing the terms of an employment contract is important to liking and keeping a job. Ask questions if the employer doesn't provide the information. Figure 7-1 gives some guidelines.

Employee Selection

During an interview, you as the applicant are learning about the job and trying to make a good impression. At the same time, the interviewer is trying to decide if you are the right person for the job. Are there any laws that affect the interview and whether or not you get the job?

Age—The Law for Minors

If you are a minor, your age may affect your chance of being hired for a job. Child labor laws were developed in the 19th and 20th centuries to prevent abuses relating to how many hours per day children worked and the conditions under which they worked. Today, state and federal laws prohibit most work for young children and allow limited work for older ones. In Georgia, children under 18 years old may work, subject to certain rules (see figure 7-2).

Equal Employment Opportunity

SITUATION 1 The personnel manager of a local plant of the National Motor Co. Inc. reads through his notes on applicants for a job as foreman:

Paul Dworski—20 years' experience, good references, white, aged 45, male.

Harvey Lincoln—5 years' experience, great references, African American, aged 25, male.

Joan Finch—10 years' experience, good references, white, aged 32, female.

Ed Winston—4 years' experience, fair references, white, aged 25, male.

FIGURE 7-1

What You Should Find Out about a Job

During a job interview, you will be asked many questions about yourself. It is also a good time to ask questions about the job. Before taking a job, be sure you can answer these questions.

1. **What will my duties be?**

   Ask as many questions as needed to be clear about your duties. Note that although jobs may have the same title, the duties may differ from employer to employer. (For example, some jobs require a secretary to do bookkeeping, and others do not.) Find out if there is a written job description that you can read. Large companies generally provide these.

2. **What is the rate of pay?**

3. **What are the hours of work?**

   a. At what time of day will I begin and end work? (In professional, career-track jobs in which a salary is paid, you may be expected to work as long as needed to do a job well.)

   b. Will I work Monday through Friday or another schedule? Will the schedule vary?

   c. If the job pays by the hour, what is the overtime policy?

   d. If this is temporary or summer work, when does the job begin, and when does it end?

4. **What clothing or equipment is needed?**

   a. Do I need my own car for sales or deliveries?

   b. Do I need to supply my own tools, such as hammers?

   c. Are special clothes, such as uniforms, required? Who supplies them?

   d. If street clothes are worn, should they be professional or casual?

5. **What are the fringe benefits?**

   Benefits may include vacations, pensions, sick leave, coffee breaks, holidays, insurance, etc. Ask about them at the end of the interview. Employers are not impressed with someone whose first question is, "When can I leave for my vacation?"

6. **What are the opportunities for promotion?**

   This question is appropriate for full-time, permanent work.

The personnel manager thinks there is only one candidate for the job. He feels the position should go to a younger white man. He offers the position to Winston. Is this decision fair? Is it legal?

Starting in the 1960s, laws were passed in the United States to prevent unfair hiring decisions based on employers' personal preferences. Under President Lyndon B. Johnson, the Civil Rights Act of 1964 was passed prohibiting hiring, promoting or demoting, or firing an individual on the basis of race, sex, color, religion, or national origin. Businesses that engage in interstate commerce and that have at least 15 employees were made subject to this law. In 1972, amendments extended the coverage to government employers. They also added enforcement powers. The Civil Rights Act of 1991 added new remedies for violations of Title VII and provided for jury trials. The Civil Rights Act also created the Equal Employment Opportunity Commission to enforce Title VII. This commission can take action on charges of discrimination made by an individual or a group of individuals or based on its own investigations.

The Civil Rights Act was followed by other federal laws. The Age Discrimination in Employment Act of 1967 prohibits putting older workers (age 40 or above) at a disadvantage with respect to employment opportunities. The Rehabilitation Act of 1973 makes it illegal for some employers to deny people jobs (for which they are otherwise qualified) because of physical, mental, or emotional handicaps. The act applies to employers who do work for or receive funds from the federal government.

What kinds of handicaps does the Rehabilitation Act cover? Would the handicap described in the following situation apply?

> **SITUATION 2** A school teacher was fired because she had tuberculosis, a contagious disease. She sued, saying that her dismissal violated the Rehabilitation Act. At issue was the question of whether a contagious disease was a handicap under the act.

In 1988, the U.S. Supreme Court ruled that a teacher could not be fired solely because of having a contagious disease that his or her employer feared might be spread. In the ruling, the Court

FIGURE 7-2

Georgia Work Laws for Minors		
Age	**Work Allowed**	**Hours**
Under 12	Only farming and domestic service or within limits of law for parent(s) or guardian(s). Also acting in movies or as photo model if workplace is approved by state Secretary of Labor.	
12–15	In nonhazardous employment with work permit.*	On school days, 4 hours per day maximum; nonschool days, 8-hour limit. Limit of 40 hours per week all year. Also, can only work between 6 a.m. and 9 p.m., except for newspaper delivery (must be 15 years old), which can start at 5 a.m.
16–18	With a permit,* any work except serving alcoholic beverages.	May not work during class hours if enrolled in school.

*Work permits are issued by schools.

The Americans with Disabilities Act extended protection for qualified disabled persons in the work place.

extended the definition of handicapped in this act to include persons with infectious diseases. What if the teacher did pose a risk to students? That question, the Court felt, should be decided locally, as a matter of meeting the general qualifications of the job.

Congress later amended the Rehabilitation Act to clarify that point. Now, an individual with a contagious disease who does not pose a direct threat to others and who is able to perform his or her job is covered under the Rehabilitation Act.

The Americans with Disabilities Act (ADA) extended protection for qualified disabled persons. Unlike the Rehabilitation Act, it is not limited only to employees who do work for or receive funds from the federal government. It applies to employers, government agencies, and labor unions that have more than 15 employees.

The ADA requires employers to make reasonable accommodations for qualified applicants and employees with a disability if the accommodations will help the applicant or employee perform the essential functions of a particular position. Such accommodation must not cause undue hardship to the company, however, nor can it create a direct threat to the health and welfare of other employees or the public.

What is a "reasonable accommodation"? It might be making facilities accessible, buying special equipment, reassigning the employee, providing the employee with a leave of absence, or modifying policies. It could mean providing qualified readers or interpreters. What is "undue hardship" to the company? The courts look at the employer's budget, the number of employees, and the number and cost of facilities. The nature and cost of the accommodation itself are also weighed.

The ADA covers individuals who test positive for HIV (Human Immunodeficiency Virus). However, in 1994, a federal district court in Philadelphia dismissed the claims of an HIV-positive surgeon who brought suit under the ADA and the Rehabilitation Act. The court found that the surgeon posed "a significant risk" and a "direct threat" to the health of patients who undergo surgical procedures. As a result, the surgeon was not protected by these acts. The ADA also protects employees from discrimination based on their association with an individual with a disability. For instance, an employer is prohibited from terminating an employee because the employee associates with an individual who has AIDS (Acquired Immune Deficiency Syndrome).

All of the people covered by these acts are in "status categories." People are in status categories because of events beyond their control; for example, a person cannot "control" his or her age or ethnic origin. Exclusion on the basis of status categories is called discrimination. It is illegal. Courts look closely at the rules and practices of employers that are said to discriminate. One thing they consider is how related these rules and practices are to performing the job. For example, a company might have a rule that all electrical engineers must have college degrees. This requirement might be said to discriminate against African Americans because fewer blacks than whites have college degrees. However, the rule is clearly relevant to the job. Therefore, a court would allow such a rule to stand.

How do you think the court ruled in the real case described in situation 3?[1]

> **SITUATION 3** Sprogis, a flight attendant, was discharged by United Airlines after being married. She sued because male flight attendants could be married and keep their jobs. United Airlines claimed that their rule had a reasonable basis. It said husbands of female attendants would complain about the hours. The airline claimed that male passengers preferred single flight attendants.

The court ruled in favor of Sprogis. The company had clearly set up a rule discriminating on the basis of sex. The court also said that marital status was not relevant to the job. Generally, courts have found discrimination on the basis of marital status to be illegal unless it is somehow relevant to the job.

Affirmative Action

Affirmative action is a process to correct inequalities in employment that have typically occurred in the past. That is, affirmative action provides opportunities to those who have previously been denied opportunities. It has been used mostly with government employers and employers that have federal contracts (that is, those who do work for or receive funds from the federal government). However, other employers often have voluntary affirmative action programs.

Courts sometimes order affirmative action to correct past discrimination. Suppose a large company has only a few women employees. That company could be required by the court to advertise job openings so that more women can compete for jobs. Or it could be required to hire enough women to match the percentage of females in the general population.

Situation 4, a real-life example of affirmative action under the Civil Rights Act, illustrates further:

> **SITUATION 4** A trucking company in Atlanta had two types of drivers: over-the-road and in-town. Over-the-road drivers carried truckloads of goods from Atlanta to Houston, Texas, and back. In-town drivers made local deliveries. Over-the-road drivers started at a lower rate of pay than did the in-town drivers. After a few years of experience, the over-the-road drivers made more money. Only white men were hired as over-the-road drivers. Most of the in-town drivers were African American. After complaints arose, the Equal Employment Opportunity Commission told the company to make some black drivers over-the-road drivers. The company refused.

Eventually, the U.S. Supreme Court[2] made the company transfer some blacks to the over-the-road group. The company also had to hire new drivers to balance the ratio of blacks and whites in both groups of drivers. Several black drivers had been denied the chance to become over-the-road drivers. The employer was also required to pay them the higher wages they would have received. Because the union was responsible as well, it had to pay some lost wages. The contract between the union and the company had to be rewritten to prevent future discrimination.

Keep in mind that affirmative action was designed to help offset unfair treatment of women and minority workers in the workforce. How, then, does affirmative action apply in situation 5?[3]

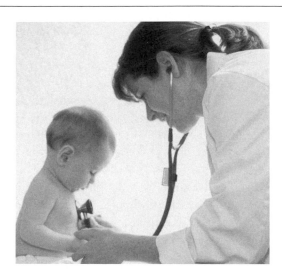
Reflecting society's changing values, recent laws have extended job opportunities for women and minorities.

SITUATION 5 Allan Bakke, a white male, applied to medical school and was not accepted. The school had an affirmative action policy that reserved a certain number of places for minority applicants. Several minority students with lower qualifications were accepted over Mr. Bakke. He sued on the basis of what has been called reverse discrimination.

In 1978, the Supreme Court found that Mr. Bakke's equal protection rights had been violated.

When workers are laid off, the Supreme Court has in several cases protected the seniority rights of workers (that is, those who have been working for a company the longest) over those hired under affirmative action. In a 1988 decision, the Court majority said that taking away jobs can seriously disrupt lives. Such action puts "the entire burden of achieving racial equality on particular individuals." The Court felt that the burden was too great.

Affirmative action has been controversial. Those in favor of the policy say that lack of an affirmative action policy will lead to continued discrimination. Opponents argue the unfairness of reverse discrimination. Affirmative action has also been threatened by increasing political pressure to limit or abolish it. The outcome of this controversy is unclear, but we can expect to see changes in the area of affirmative action in the future.

Although the Supreme Court has continued to uphold affirmative action hiring plans, many of its decisions have weakened affirmative action. For example, the Court has put more of the burden of proving on-the-job discrimination on minorities and women. In 1989, the Court overturned an affirmative action plan favoring minority contractors in Richmond, Virginia. Similarly, the Georgia Supreme Court soon after rejected an Atlanta ordinance that favored minority and women contractors. These decisions have made claims of violation of affirmative action more difficult to prove.

Drug Testing and Privacy

Requiring tests for substance abuse as a condition of hiring or continued employment is also controversial. Opponents argue that drug testing without suspicion of wrongdoing violates an important constitutional right. The Fourth Amendment provides protection against government search and seizures without reasonable suspicion of wrongdoing. Drug testing is a type of search. In determining whether to test for drugs, the courts must balance conflicting interests. Should testing take place only if there is a reasonable suspicion of drug use? Which is most important: preserving a constitutional right or efforts to limit drug use?

In general, testing by private employers is legal because the Constitution applies only to government action. However, drug testing is a subject for mandatory negotiation in union contracts. As of 1990, the Supreme Court had generally approved testing by public employers of employees in jobs in which there was a compelling interest in public safety. For example, it had upheld testing of railroad employees involved in accidents that resulted in fatalities. It had also upheld testing of U.S. Treasury Department employees seeking positions in which they would carry firearms or act to control drugs. Random testing of justice department workers, railroad employees, and truck drivers, on the other hand, has not been upheld.

In 1990, Georgia laws authorized random testing of employees in high-risk jobs, and a 1995 Georgia law now requires drug testing for certain state positions. It also mandates that applicants for those positions submit to drug testing as a prerequisite to employment.

O n l y   t h e   F a c t s

1. Laws regulating work for children affect which of the following: hours? conditions of work? wages? insurance?

2. Could a national corporation deny work to people simply because they are (a) Methodists? (b) Japanese Americans? (c) grandfathers? (d) waitresses? or because (e) they have a history of heart disease? Explain your answers.

3. How does equal employment opportunity relate to affirmative action?

T h i n k   A b o u t

1. State your feelings about affirmative action from the points of view of (a) an employer ordered by the courts to practice it; (b) an African American who in the past has been refused jobs because of race; (c) a woman aged 45 who lost a promotion to a less-qualified male; (d) a white male who was turned down for a job although he was as well qualified as the woman who received it.

2. Give arguments for and against random drug testing of employees.

YOUR RIGHTS AND DUTIES ON THE JOB

Contract Rights

Employment contracts are usually oral (that is, spoken). The employer says, "You're hired." You, as the employee, say, "I accept." Be sure, though, that you understand all of the terms of the contract before you agree. Figure 7-3 gives you a general idea of what your basic duties under the contract will be. It also shows what you can expect from your employer. An employer's policy manual may define employee rights and duties when no written contract exists.

Written contracts occur in two general areas:

1. First, if there is a union, then the union and the company have a written contract. This is called a collective bargaining agreement. It will govern the wages, hours, and conditions of employment. Most of the information about the job will be in the agreement.

2. Written contracts are also common in the "personal services" area. Salespersons, teachers, professional sports players, and others have written contracts. These contracts should be read carefully. If confused, the applicant should hire a lawyer to explain what the contract states.

FIGURE 7-3

Basics of an Unwritten Job Contract

As your employee, I agree to follow instructions, obey the rules of your workplace, and carry out the tasks assigned. I understand that I may be fired if I don't fulfill these promises or for any other reasons that are not discriminatory.

Signed: _____

As your employer, I will give directions, set the hours of work, and provide a safe workplace with most of the necessary tools. I promise to pay you the agreed-upon wages and give you the benefits specified. If these expectations aren't met, you have the right to take legal action and/or leave the job.

Signed: _____

Contracts are enforceable in a court of law. An employee or an employer can become involved in a lawsuit if he or she is not careful to respect the rights, terms, and conditions that are spelled out in a contract.

As an employee, you have rights given by the employer through a contract—regardless of whether the contract is oral or written or whether it is an individual contract with the employer or a union contract. You also have the rights given by the laws of the United States and state of Georgia. If the statutory law or the contract provides for a right, then an employee has that right. Otherwise, the right does not exist in Georgia.

> **SITUATION 6** Carolyn didn't pay much attention to the description of benefits when hired by her current employer. Now, she has worked for a year. She would like a paid vacation. The manager tells her that the firm doesn't give vacations. "That's not fair," Carolyn says. "Everyone gets vacations. It's a law."
>
> Is she right?

Neither federal nor state law requires employers to provide vacations, breaks, or pensions. Nor do statutes require them to provide health insurance or paid sick leave. If your employer has no vacation policy, then you do not have the right to a vacation. If your employer-employee contract does not give paid sick leave, then you are not entitled to be paid for those days you are sick and cannot work. Most employers give these benefits, however, because they could not keep employees if they did not. If they do provide them, the law does require that benefits be provided without discrimination.

Statutory Rights

Not all rights and benefits for employees depend on contracts. Some are provided by state and federal laws. You have already read about some of these laws, like the Civil Rights Act of 1964. This section describes some others.

Rights Concerning Hours and Wages

Minimum wage. The Fair Labor Standards Act was passed by Congress in 1938. Among other things, it requires most employers to pay minimum wages to employees. It also sets minimum rates for overtime pay and pay scales for students working in the summer. As of September 1997, the minimum wage was set at $5.15 an hour; most companies cannot pay less. However, the 1996 amendments to the Fair Labor Standards Act permit employers to pay a person under 20 years of age an "opportunity wage" of not less than $4.25 per hour during the person's first 90 days of employment.

Employment law can often be seen as a response to contemporary problems or needs. The minimum wage law was passed during the Great Depression. At that time, many people needed jobs. Because so many people were desperate for any kind of work, some employers paid people as little money as possible. The minimum wage law was passed to ensure that a person would be paid at least enough money to live on.

Are all employees today protected by the minimum wage law?

> **SITUATION 7** Dini is offered a job as waitress at $2.13 per hour plus tips. She is puzzled. She thought the minimum wage was over $4.
>
> Why is she being offered less?

There are many exceptions to the minimum wage law. People who work for tips, such as waitstaff (situation 7), are not covered to the same extent as employees who work for wages only. Businesses with less than $500,000 in average dollar volume of sales or receipts per year are not covered by the minimum wage laws. Professional people—such as doctors, lawyers, dentists, and architects—are also exempt from these laws.

Not everyone favors a minimum wage law. Those opposed to it say that it decreases the number of available jobs. Businesses simply hire fewer employees. What do you think?

Standard workweek. The Fair Labor Standards Act also sets 40 hours per week as a standard workweek. It requires employers to pay an overtime premium (that is, higher wages) for all hours worked over 40 hours in a week to certain employees who are paid by the hour. (An exception is agricultural workers who do not necessarily work standard hours.) Most salaried employees, though, are not paid for overtime.

The rights and obligations of the employer and the employee are generally the same for part-time and full-time work. (Part-time work is less than 40 hours a week.) However, temporary part-time employees or those who work less than 20 hours a week usually are not eligible for benefits. Further, part-time employees do not receive overtime wages unless they work more than 40 hours a week.

In situation 8, does it appear that Hal and John are being paid as they should be under the act?

SITUATION 8

a. John works for a company full time at $6.00 an hour. His boss asks him to work an extra eight hours one week at the same rate of pay.

b. Hal works for the same company 20 hours a week at $5.15 an hour. The boss asks him to work an extra 30 hours a week for the next three weeks. The boss doesn't mention extra pay.

In situation 8, both Hal and John should receive overtime wages: John for 8 hours, and Hal for a total of 30. If the company will not pay them, they should talk to a representative of the federal Department of Labor (see figure 7-4). The department can sue an employer on behalf of eligible workers who are not paid the minimum wage or overtime wages.

Equal pay for equal work. The question of equal pay for equal work is also regulated by law.

FIGURE 7-4

Georgia Department of Labor

• This state department is in charge of federal and state programs that concern job opportunities, job training, and unemployment compensation. It has local offices in most Georgia cities. Visit an office for information about jobs in your area. You can also find out about job training programs such as the federal Job Corps for persons 16 to 22 years old and the state's Job Training Partnership program.

• The department also enforces state laws regarding management/labor relations, wages, workers' compensation, health and safety in the workplace, and pensions.

SITUATION 9 Val, a single woman, and Reed, a married man with a child, are hired as librarians in a large city library. They both have master's degrees in library science and will have exactly the same duties. Each has two years of part-time experience. Reed's salary is $24,000 a year. Val's is $18,000.

Is this difference in pay legal?

The federal Equal Pay Act (1973) requires that men and women receive equal pay for substantially the same work. Val's salary (situation 9) appears to be discriminatory and illegal. Other federal acts have extended the requirement for equal pay to other groups likely to face discrimination.

A related question for courts is that of comparable worth of jobs. Women contend that jobs that traditionally have been held by women (such as nursing, teaching, and child-care jobs) offer less pay than do jobs held by men. Yet jobs that women traditionally have held may demand more skill or training. And isn't the work of a nurse as important to society as that of a corrections officer? Why then would these jobs have different rates of pay? What do you think?

Rights Regarding Harassment

What if employees constantly ridicule another worker because of his or her religion? The courts have held that under the Civil Rights Act, employees have a right to workplaces in which they are not treated badly by fellow employees because of religion, race, or other factors. Similarly, employees have the right not to experience unwanted pressures of a sexual nature.

Sexual harassment can be suggestive remarks or unwanted advances. The Supreme Court recently clarified grounds for successful harassment lawsuits. A victim must only show that discriminatory behavior in the workplace creates an environment that is objectively hostile and abusive to a reasonable person as well as to him- or herself. This definition includes behavior that detracts from the victim's job or discourages the victim from staying in the job or advancing in his or her career. The employer can be sued.

Right to a Safe Working Environment

As an employee, you also have the right as much as possible to a safe workplace. The Occupational Safety and Health Act (1970) enables the government to set health and safety standards for employees in interstate commerce. To carry out the standards, the law created the Occupational Safety and Health Administration (OSHA). If an employee believes that a workplace is unsafe, OSHA will inspect it. If the inspector finds unsafe conditions, improvements will be required.

OSHA has required that hand and foot guards, railings, better lighting, and many other safety devices be installed in workplaces. OSHA has also required that many hazardous substances be labeled. Examples of other OSHA-required safety measures are in figure 7-5.

A Georgia law—the Public Employee Hazardous Chemical Protection and Right to Know Act—provides further protection. It requires that employees be informed of the hazards of chemicals produced or used in their workplaces. Employers must label dangerous chemicals and also provide safety information through written matter and training programs. Employees also have the right to inform their physicians about the hazardous chemicals to which they are exposed.

The Georgia Department of Labor is responsible for inspecting and certifying elevators and other potentially dangerous equipment, including boilers and amusement park rides.

FIGURE 7-5

Examples of Occupational Safety and Health Act (OSHA) Requirements

OSHA Requirement	Purpose
Fans/Ventilators	To prevent workers from inhaling fumes
Special clothing	To prevent workers from absorbing chemicals through skin
Protective eyeglasses	To protect against flying debris or caustic substances
Alarm signals	To notify workers of leaks of dangerous substances
Showers after work	To prevent workers from carrying dangerous substances on their bodies outside the workplace
Health screening, such as chest x-rays	To detect any problems early enough for effective treatment

Right to Join a Labor Union

After you begin work, you'll make friends at the job. Some of your fellow employees may have common desires, suggestions, and complaints about work. You may decide to form a committee to talk to the employer about those matters. You may think that the employer will pay more attention to 10 or 20 employees than to 1 employee. In effect, labor unions evolved in this way to combat low wages, long working hours, and unacceptable working conditions.

Today, there are two main types of unions. First there are those whose members are in the same craft or profession. Examples would be unions of musicians or of electricians. The second type of union is that of people in the same industry. United Auto Workers is an example.

Contracts between employers and unions are called collective bargaining agreements. These agreements set pay scales, hours of work, and general working conditions in the workplace. The union represents all the employees as a group when it signs the contract with the employer.

In the United States, thousands of collective bargaining agreements govern millions of workers. Most of these contracts are the result of give-and-take (that is, negotiations) between unions and employers. For example, a union may want a pay raise of 75 cents per hour. The employer may want to be able to switch people to weekend work when necessary. Union leaders and company heads talk about what they want. They try to reach a compromise. In this example, the company may pay a 65 cents per hour raise. The union may agree to increased weekend work. Each issue is settled in this fashion.

If the parties cannot agree, the company and the union can use economic force against each other. The employer can "lock out" the employees. The employees can go on strike. In a lockout, the employer closes the factory until the union and the company come to some agreement. In a strike, the union says it will not work without a satisfactory contract. The workers refuse to go to work. They may form a picket line in front of the plant to discourage all workers and delivery persons from entering.

In a strike, employees refuse to work.

Whether a strike or a lockout, the economic forces are the same. The company loses the money it could have made. The employees do not get their paychecks. Generally, things are settled and a contract is signed. Actually, strikes and lockouts are infrequent. Most collective bargaining agreements are made without any lost work.

SITUATION 10 Jerry applies for a job at a food-processing plant. He has had similar jobs and is an excellent worker. However, he is known to be an active union member who has helped to organize other unions. Plant management labels him a troublemaker and refuses to hire him.

Is this decision legal?

The Labor-Management Relations Act of 1947 (referred to as the Taft-Hartley Act) makes it illegal for an employer to discriminate against employees because the employee is for or against the union. Say someone is fired for these reasons. The employer or the union, whichever is responsible for the firing, is then liable for that person's lost pay. It is illegal for a firm not to hire someone because he or she is a union member or organizer (situation 10).

The Labor-Management Relations Act governs private companies and their unions. It does not regulate public employers. In Georgia, for instance, state law forbids the state or a public school system from having a binding collective agreement with a union.

> **SITUATION 11** Ron takes a job with a factory that has a strong union. He needs the work but does not favor unions and does not want to pay the dues.

Q Does he have to join and pay dues?

It depends on where he lives. In most states, the union and the company can make contracts requiring employees to pay union dues. The idea is that because everyone benefits from the union—usually by getting a bigger paycheck—then everyone should support the union. In a minority of states, laws forbid such collective bargaining agreements. These laws are called right-to-work laws. The idea behind these laws is that no one should be forced to be a member or financial supporter of an organization.

Georgia is a right-to-work state. That is, it is not legal for an employer and a union to have a contract that requires each employee to join the union. Nor can the contract require an employee to pay dues to the union. Some states, on the other hand, are non-right-to-work states. In those states, a collective bargaining agreement exists between a company and a union, which means that employees could be fired for not joining the union or paying union dues. If Ron's factory (situation 11) is located in a non-right-to-work state, he could be fired.

O n l y   t h e   F a c t s

1. In an employer-employee contract, what are the basic obligations of the employer? What are the obligations of the employee?

2. In which situations are employment contracts usually in writing?

3. Which of the following rights are required of most employers by statutory law? (a) equal pay for equal work (b) health insurance (c) pensions (d) safe working conditions (e) minimum wage (f) freedom from sexual harassment (g) vacations

4. What is a collective bargaining agreement?

T h i n k   A b o u t

1. In 1996, Congress passed a law allowing employers to pay a person under 20 years of age an "opportunity wage" (not less than $4.25 per hour during the first 90 days of employment). Explain why you agree or disagree with this change in the law.

2. Give one argument for or against a right-to-work law.

3. What issues regarding employer-employee-government relations are represented in the following statement?

   "This is my business. I should be responsible for the safety of my employees. If people don't like conditions, they can quit. Why should the government stick its nose into my affairs?"

4. Are labor unions still necessary to ensure adequate working conditions? Defend your answer.

ENDING A JOB

If You're Fired or Laid Off or If You Quit

> **SITUATION 12** Kent gets really mad at his supervisor. The guy's on his case again—this time for not putting a fitting in correctly. Kent finally shouts, "I quit." He walks off the job.

Q Can he legally end an employment contract like this?

SITUATION 13 Sales are so slow that a company decides it must fire 100 employees. It fires only Mexican Americans.

Would they have grounds for a suit?

SITUATION 14 The superintendent of the county school system fires a highly respected English teacher. The teacher's principal says that the teacher is impossible to get along with.

Does the teacher have any protection against this firing?

Unless stated in the contract or by law, either side may end an employment relationship whenever either wishes. The employer is free to fire an employee. The employee is free to quit.

In situation 12, Kent could quit—but he would forfeit his right to unemployment compensation. Also, it is considered proper to give employers enough notice so that they can hire someone else. This notification may even be required by the contract.

Employers are free to end employment relationships at any time. However, the firings in situation 13 appear to discriminate against Mexican Americans. Unless these employees can prove discrimination, however, they may not be able to do anything about their situation.

In some jobs, especially government jobs, employees have a right to a hearing if they are fired, demoted, or punished. In situation 14, the teacher may be able to have a hearing and successfully argue her case. With a private company, there is no automatic right to a hearing. Such a right might be provided by the company or a union contract.

Employers can lay off employees when there is no more work available. Layoffs are usually temporary. In order to stay in business, employers have the right to lay off as many employees as may be necessary. However, a 1988 law, the

Worker Adjustment and Retraining Notification Act, generally requires employers to give 60 days' notice of layoffs and plant closings affecting more than 50 employees during a 30-day period.

If laid off—and in most states, if fired without a good reason—an employee can apply for unemployment compensation. In Georgia, the state Department of Labor runs the unemployment compensation program. The purpose of the program is to help offset a person's lack of a paycheck while looking for another job. However, this support usually lasts only 6 to 12 months.

If You're Sick or Injured

SITUATION 15 A crew member laying a sewer line was badly injured when he was hit by a pipe carried by a crane. For years, he has been unable to walk.

What recourse does he have?

SITUATION 16 For years, a factory worker has been spraying chemicals onto wooden parts as they passed by on an assembly line. She becomes ill and is diagnosed with cancer. It is learned that the chemicals she worked with caused the cancer.

Can she seek legal help?

When an employee becomes injured or sick or is killed at work, workers' compensation ("comp") programs go into effect. Although state governments run these programs, they are funded by individual employers. In Georgia, workers' comp is operated by the State Board of Workers' Compensation.

The employee in situation 15 must prove to the board that he has a work-related injury or illness. If the board awards compensation, his employer must make payments to him, usually a small amount of money over a period of years. Employers may buy insurance to cover these costs.

The amount paid is based on a schedule (or list) of benefits in the state law. For example, a certain amount may be awarded for loss of a hand; another amount for loss of an eye. What if the employee in situation 15 were permanently disabled and unable to work again? He might be able to retire on a disability pension.

Compensation might not be given if the illness or injury is not listed on the state schedule of benefits. In that case, the employee in situation 16 might have to prove in court that her illness was work-related. More and more employees who are endangered by exposure to poisonous substances are suing employers for damages.

Federal law does not provide for sick leave as such. However, the 1993 Family and Medical Leave Act (FMLA) provides for leaves of absence in four situations:

1. upon the birth of a child (for both male and female employees);
2. upon the adoption of a child;
3. in order to care for a spouse, child, or parent suffering from a serious health condition; and
4. when the employee has a serious health condition that makes him or her unable to perform the job.

The FMLA requires employers of 50 or more people to provide up to 12 weeks of unpaid leave within a 12-month period to employees who require or request a leave of absence in one of these situations. When the employee returns, the company in most instances must return the employee to the same (or equivalent) job without a reduction in pay or benefits. Either the employer or the employee can substitute any collected paid vacation or personal days for any part of the 12 weeks of FMLA leave. In the case of leave for serious health conditions, the employer may substitute any collected sick leave and vacation or personal days for part of the 12-week leave.

When You Retire

If you have not yet started full-time work, retirement seems very, very far away. However, if you have worked, some of your money may have gone into the federal government's Social Security program. The Social Security program provides income to retired persons.

Like other job-related laws, those concerned with retirement reflect changes in society. Traditionally, in many places (including the United States), children or relatives cared for the elderly. However, family patterns change. Today, most employees expect to support themselves on pensions from their former employers and/or Social Security.

What Is a Pension?

A pension is a plan for paying a person after retirement. The funds for pension plans may be contributed by both employer and employee, or

After retirement, people still need food, housing, clothing. Where does the money come from?

funds may come from the employer only. Employers are not required to provide pensions, however.

The amount of the pension is usually based on the worker's income and length of service with the employer. Generally, the higher-paid employee with the greater length of service will receive the larger pension.

Problems in private pension programs led to the Employee Retirement Income Security Act (ERISA) of 1974. One problem was that employees had to work for a company for as many as 20 years before having rights to pension benefits. However, many Americans change jobs frequently. ERISA required that rights to a pension be guaranteed (or vested) after shorter periods of time, generally five years.

Another problem was that employers would fire workers to avoid paying a pension. If an employee can prove this practice, then under ERISA, the court could order the company to pay. The person might also be able to sue the company for age discrimination.

Social Security

Social Security is similar to a pension plan. Contributions to Social Security are deducted from workers' paychecks. All who contribute to the system during their working years are eligible for Social Security.

Social Security is different from welfare. Most of those who receive Social Security have contributed to the program while employed. Contributors receive benefits regardless of their level of income. A citizen receiving welfare, on the other hand, must be at or below poverty level.

The Social Security Act was passed in 1935 during the Great Depression, when Franklin D. Roosevelt was president. Many Americans had lost their jobs and had no pensions or savings to support themselves. The purpose of the law was to have some income available for older persons when they retire. Today, for many people, Social Security provides most or all of their retirement income. The program has been expanded by Congress through the years to include as-sistance to widows and children, disability for injured workers, and other benefits.

The Social Security program is controversial. One reason is its cost. In 1983, in an effort to prevent the program from running out of money, Congress raised the age level for receiving retirement benefits from 65 to 67. However, these laws did not resolve the problem or the controversy. Currently, some workers wonder if they will receive social security benefits at all when they retire. You will hear more about this issue in the future.

Only the Facts

1. Explain the difference between workers' compensation and unemployment compensation.
2. What is a pension?
3. What is the purpose of the Social Security program?

Think About

1. Imagine that you are a legislator and that you must vote on a bill requiring that all businesses with five or more employees provide a pension plan for employees. List reasons for approving the bill and reasons for voting against it. Then decide how you would vote.

SUMMING UP

Your rights and duties in any job will be defined in your agreement with your employer. Certain rights, however, have been established by state and federal laws. These laws tend to protect the rights of the employee rather than the employer. Most of these laws were—and are—controversial. For example, people continue to argue about the need for a minimum wage and a standard workweek. There is also considerable disagreement about continuing affirmative action efforts.

In the area of employment law, it is easy to see how government actions result from social concerns and economic conditions. Look closely at current conditions and social attitudes. For example, if unemployment is very high, it is likely that government actions will be taken to relieve this problem. As the percentage of older Americans in the population increases, the government can be expected to give more attention to pension and retirement laws.

Notes

1. *Sprogis v. United Airlines, Inc.*, 444 F. 2d 1194 (7th Cir. 1971).
2. *Franks v. Bowman Transportation Co.*, 424 U.S. 747 (1976).
3. *University of California Regents v. Bakke*, 438 U.S. 265 (1978).

8 Marriage

The next two chapters are about family law. This chapter deals with the legal relationship between husbands and wives. It is about marriage and ending marriages legally. Chapter 9 explains the effect of law on children and their parents.

Some of the laws affecting marriage and family life are very old. Some are very new. Like other laws, they reflect changing patterns and values in our society. Note in this chapter how laws have been affected by the changing role of women in society. Also note how changing attitudes about divorce have affected the law.

GETTING MARRIED

A friend says to you, "Gene and I want to get married. Do you know what we have to do? What does the state of Georgia require?" Would you know how to answer?

How is being married different from living together? Marriage is a legally enforceable contract between two people promising to be husband and wife. Two people who live together may agree to split the cost of food. They may even purchase property together. However, in Georgia, they have no special legal rights unless they are married.

In Georgia, to have a valid marriage, the two people must

- be legally competent to contract marriage.
- agree to be husband and wife.
- consummate the marriage (according to the legal definition).

Requirements for Marriage

Who Is Legally Competent to Marry?

Could the following persons legally get married in Georgia?

a. Terry, whose divorce isn't final, to Wendy?
b. Tom to his widowed daughter-in-law, Judy?
c. Maria to her stepson, Jeff?
d. Ken and Susan, who are first cousins?
e. June, who is 16, to Bob, who is 17?

Some people are not allowed, by law, to marry. For example, in Georgia, a person must be mentally competent to marry, meaning he or she must be capable of understanding the idea of marriage. Also, a person who is already married to someone else cannot legally marry. In Georgia and elsewhere, a married person who marries again without a divorce is guilty of bigamy, a crime. If the new spouse knows about the bigamy, he or she is guilty of the crime of marrying a bigamist. Terry (in example a) couldn't marry Wendy until his divorce is final.

Two people who are closely related by blood or marriage cannot marry. For example, the law forbids a man to marry his daughter, his stepdaughter, his sister, his aunt, his niece, his mother, or his grandmother. Likewise, a woman cannot marry her corresponding relatives.

These relationships within which marriage is forbidden are known as the degrees of consanguinity. They are set forth in the Official Code of Georgia Annotated §19-3-3. Laws on incest are a direct result of these degrees. If you marry (or have sexual relations) with anyone within these prohibited degrees, you commit incest and may be criminally prosecuted.

In examples b and c, the couples could not marry. The couple in example d could marry. Georgia permits marriages between first cousins. Most states, however, do not permit such a marriage.

Governments also set minimum ages for a legal marriage. To marry in Georgia, you must be at least 16 years old. If you are under the age

A probate court judge issues marriage licenses in Georgia.

of 18, you cannot get a marriage license without parental consent. June and Bob would need parental consent (example e).

Persons under the age of 16 may marry if there is proof that the female is pregnant or that they are the parents of a living child. However, the county probate court is required to notify the parents of anyone under age 18 who is applying for a marriage license.

Ability to Contract Marriage

The first requirement for a valid marriage is the ability (or capacity) of the parties to contract. Ordinarily, an adult has the capacity to enter a contract. There are occasions, however, when an adult lacks the capacity necessary to enter the marriage contract. For example, if an adult has been declared incompetent by a court, he or she lacks the capacity to contract. A married person also lacks the capacity to enter a (second) contract of marriage.

The Marriage Contract

Another requirement for a valid marriage is that the two persons verbally agree to be husband and wife at the present time. There is no legal marriage if the persons agree to be married in the future. The agreement to marry can be a spoken one. What of the agreements in the following situations? Would the marriages be valid?

SITUATION 1 Sam gets Mildred so drunk that she goes through their marriage ceremony unaware of what is occurring.

SITUATION 2 Holly and Lester decide to get married for a joke—thinking they can quickly get out of it.

Georgia law says that to create a contract of marriage, the parties' consent must be voluntary. No fraud can be practiced upon either one. A marriage in which one party was tricked or defrauded may be voided (or set aside) by court action. Mildred (situation 1) may be able to get the marriage voided because Sam "tricked" her into it by getting her drunk. Similarly, duress that prevents voluntary consent may allow one of the parties (the victim of duress) to set aside the marriage. Duress is any unlawful threat to make another person do something against his or her will. A threat at gunpoint is an example of duress.

Although not true of contracts generally, a marriage contract has been held valid even though it was made in jest. The courts' view has been that there is no way to prove objectively that the parties were acting in a "spirit of fun and jest." How could witnesses know or testify to the parties' true feelings? For this reason, Holly and Lester (situation 2) would have to get a divorce to end their marriage.

Note that in a marriage ceremony the law's concern is with the basic agreement to marry. Promises—such as those to love, honor, and obey—are personal rather than legal commitments.

Consummating the Marriage

Consummation is the third requirement for a valid marriage. The legal definition varies according to the type of marriage. In a ceremonial marriage, consummation may be achieved by obtaining a license to marry and having a ceremony performed by an authorized person. Consumma-

tion may also be accomplished when the man and woman, using words of present tense, agree to marry—but only if they are in a state that recognizes what is called common law marriage. Sexual intercourse is not required to consummate a valid ceremonial marriage.

Kinds of Marriage

Ceremonial Marriage

Marriages begin with a formal marriage ceremony, which may be a religious ceremony or a civil ceremony performed by a judge.

Before a formal marriage ceremony can be performed, the couple must get a marriage license. This license may be obtained from the courthouse in the county in which the marriage will take place or in any county, provided that one of the applicants is a state resident. If the marriage is to be performed in a state other than Georgia, the requirements of that state must be followed in order to have a valid marriage. Laws on marriage and marriage licenses vary from state to state. In Georgia, marriage licenses are issued by judges of the probate courts (see figure 8-1).

Before receiving the license, couples must take a blood test for certain diseases, including syphilis, sickle cell anemia, and rubella (or German measles). The blood tests can be given by the county board of health. Even with a formal ceremony, license, and blood test, however, a marriage is not valid unless the three requirements mentioned earlier are met.

Common Law Marriage

A common law marriage is a marriage formed without a formal ceremony. Although formerly recognized in Georgia, in 1996 the state legislature did away with this form of marriage. However, all of the states, including Georgia, recognize a common law marriage that was properly created in another state that permits such marriages. Furthermore, Georgia recognizes any common law marriage that was valid in Georgia prior to the enactment of the 1996 law.

FIGURE 8-1

Application for Marriage License

County of _____ County No. _____

Please type or neatly print (USING BLACK INK) all the information below.

GROOM'S INFORMATION	BRIDE'S INFORMATION

1. _____
   (First, middle, last name)

2. _____
   Current address

   _____
   City and county

   _____
   State and zip code

   _____
   Daytime phone number

3. _____
   Age   Date of birth   Race

4. _____
   Birthplace (city or county and state)

5. **Are you blood related? Yes ____ No ____**

6. _____
   Occupation or name of company

7. _____
   Last name you will use after marriage

8.a. Number of previous marriages _____

8.b. If previously married, how was it dissolved?
     (circle) Death   Divorce   Annulment

8.c. Upon what grounds? _____

8.d. When and where? _____

9. **Is there any legal impediment? Yes ____ No ____**

10. _____
    Father's first, middle, and last name

11. _____
    Father's birthplace (city/county and state)

12. _____
    Mother's first, middle, and maiden name

13. _____
    Mother's birthplace

14. _____
    Parent's current residence (city and state)

15. _____
    Date of contemplated marriage

BRIDE'S INFORMATION:

_____
(First, middle, last name)

_____
Current address

_____
City and county

_____
State and zip code

_____
Daytime phone number

_____
Age   Date of birth   Race

_____
Birthplace (city or county and state)

_____
Occupation or name of company

_____
Last name you will use after marriage

Number of previous marriages _____

If previously married, how was it dissolved?
(circle) Death   Divorce   Annulment

Upon what grounds? _____

When and where? _____

Is there any legal impediment? Yes ____ No ____

_____
Father's first, middle, and last name

_____
Father's birthplace (city/county and state)

_____
Mother's first, middle, and maiden name

_____
Mother's birthplace

_____
Parent's current residence (city and state)

_____
City or county where marriage will take place

I HEREBY CERTIFY THAT THE FOREGOING ANSWERS WERE MADE UNDER OATH AND SUBSCRIBED BEFORE ME BY BOTH OF THE CONTRACTING PARTIES. I FURTHER CERTIFY THAT I HAVE RECEIVED THE DHR AIDS BROCHURE AND LIST OF TEST SITES.

_____   _____
APPLICANT (groom)   APPLICANT (bride)

THIS _____ DAY OF _____ , _____

Signature of Probate Clerk _____   Permanent Address: _____

Living Together

What if a couple lives together—with no intent to marry? In other states, such as California and New York, people have attempted to create a new kind of legal relationship called contract cohabitation. This type of relationship allows two unmarried people to enter into a contract respecting the arrangement of them living together without being married. The Georgia courts have refused to recognize such contracts. According to Georgia law, such contracts are illegal because they involve sexual relations between two people who are not married.

Only the Facts

1. In Georgia, what are the three requirements for a valid marriage?

2. How does a common law marriage differ from a ceremonial marriage? What common law marriages does Georgia recognize? Why does Georgia law not recognize contract cohabitation?

3. How old must you be to be married in Georgia? For what ages is parental consent required?

Think About

1. Marriage is regarded as a legal contract. Compare the requirements for a marriage with those for a contract. How do they differ, if at all?

2. Should an AIDS test be required for a marriage license? Explain.

3. Why do you think the law prohibits some people from marrying? Consider prohibitions regarding bigamy, family relationships, and age.

4. Explain why the state prefers ceremonial to common law marriages.

BEING MARRIED

Prenuptial Agreements

Can any rights and duties be settled before marriage? Consider situation 3.

> **SITUATION 3** Darrell and Marcia are considering marriage. Marcia is supporting herself as a sales clerk. Darrell has some valuable property and expects to inherit more. He knows marriages don't always work out. He wants Marcia to agree to give up her rights to alimony (support) payments or to any division of property if they divorce. Marcia insists that he agree to pay her $50,000 if they divorce, in return for her agreement to give up her rights.

Would such an agreement be fair? Would the courts accept it as valid?

Couples sometimes make prenuptial agreements such as that described in situation 3 before they get married. Such agreements settle the rights each will have if they get divorced.

In 1982, the state supreme court said that prenuptial agreements would be recognized in Georgia. The court set up three guidelines for judges to use in deciding whether to enforce a prenuptial agreement. A judge is to consider the following questions:

1. Was the agreement obtained through fraud, duress, or mistake? Were important facts regarding the financial conditions of the parties not disclosed or misrepresented?

2. Is the agreement unconscionable? In other words, is it so one-sided that one party will get a great deal and the other practically nothing?

3. Have the facts and circumstances changed since the agreement? Would it now be unfair or unreasonable?

If any of these conditions are true, the agreement might not be recognized. Using these questions as guidelines, consider whether Marcia and Darrell's agreement in situation 3 would be valid.

Legal Rights and Duties

SITUATION 4 At 3 p.m. on a Saturday, Sara Gomez and Bobby Joe Whitson were single. At 4 p.m. of the same day, they are married.

What does the change mean for them in terms of legal rights and duties?

A marriage creates certain legal rights and duties between two people. Some rights and duties occur right away. For example, upon being married, either spouse has the right in Georgia to give up his or her own surname (family name) and take that of the other. A partner can keep his or her own surname, or a partner can use both surnames with a hyphen. In other words, Sara could be Sara Gomez, Sara Whitson, Sara Gomez-Whitson, or Sara Whitson-Gomez. Sara and Bobby can also call themselves Sara and Bobby Gomez-Whitson or Sara and Bobby Whitson-Gomez.

Generally, a couple cannot sue each other in Georgia once they are married. Exceptions to this law cover special situations, including divorce, child support, legal separation, and abuse. Suppose Sara were injured in an auto accident. Even though Bobby Joe was driving and responsible for the accident, she could not sue him for damages.

The couple may make use of a new tax status. Sara and Bobby Joe can file joint income tax returns for the year in which they were married and thereafter.

Suppose Bobby committed a crime and Sara witnessed it? Could Sara be forced to testify against Bobby? What if Bobby came home and told Sara what he had done? Would that change your answer? What if the crime took place before the marriage and the trial after the marriage? Can Sara be made to testify to what she saw or heard before the marriage?

The answer is "no" to all of the above questions. Spouses cannot be forced to testify against each other in a criminal case, unless the crime (such as abuse) is against the person of a minor child.

In Georgia, a wife and husband have rights to inherit from each other if one spouse dies intestate (that is, without a will). If divorced, spouses may have rights to alimony (or payments of support) from each other. Each also has a right to an equitable division of the property accumulated together during the marriage.

Individual Responsibilities

Under Georgia law, each spouse is an individual able to assume legal rights and duties. Therefore, each can enter into contracts by him- or herself or together (individually or jointly). Each can sue others and be sued by others.

SITUATION 5 Rose buys living room furniture in her married name, Mrs. Larry Jones. Her husband, Larry, however, insists that they cannot afford the furniture. He refuses to pay the charges.

Must he pay?

Before April 1, 1979, in Georgia, a husband was legally responsible for any debts or purchases his wife made for "necessaries" (that is, food, clothes, medical services, and shelter). For example, if his wife signed a contract to lease an apartment, he might be responsible for the rent. He would be responsible even though he never signed the contract.

In 1979, the U.S. Supreme Court decided a very important case, *Orr v. Orr*.[1] The Supreme Court held that it is unconstitutional to put the burden of support on the man in marriages or divorces. It said such laws discriminate against men. One of the results of the decision is that the Georgia legislature repealed the state law that made a husband automatically responsible for his wife's debts. Now neither husband nor wife is automatically responsible for the debts of the other. In situation 5, Larry would not have to pay Rose's debt unless he also signed the contract making himself liable for the debt. Payment for the furniture is Rose's obligation because she purchased it.

Creditors often protect themselves by requiring both spouses to sign credit card applications or leases. Such a requirement makes each spouse responsible for purchases or contracts made by each other.

The Right Not to Be Abused

The government favors and encourages the institution of marriage. It encourages marriages by interfering in them as little as possible. No laws specify proper marital behavior. No laws, for example, state how a couple should divide the household chores. No law states how many children a couple should have, if any.

However, Americans have pushed governments to "interfere" in one aspect of family life: violence to and between family members. Beginning in the 1970s, increased awareness about domestic violence or abuse of children, spouses, and (more recently) the elderly resulted in legal protection for these victims. The need to protect these groups from abuse and neglect outweighs policies of not interfering in family life.

In 1981, the Georgia legislature established court relief for "family violence." It gave the superior court authority to act to protect victims. The Family Violence Act applies to family members, former spouses, foster families, and other persons living in the same household. It also protects persons who are parents of the same child (regardless of whether they were ever married). Those persons who formerly lived in the same household are also protected. The court can

- direct a person to stop committing such acts.
- exclude the person committing the violence from the household.
- require the abusive party to provide alternative housing for a spouse and children.
- remove minor children temporarily from parental custody.
- award support for children and/or a spouse.

Another recognized offense against family members is sexual battery. A 1990 law defines

Domestic violence is a subject of recent laws reflecting current conditions.

this offense as the touching of another person's intimate body part(s) without that person's consent. It also prohibits this act within or outside the family.

Only the Facts

1. Give three examples of legal rights and duties created by marriage.
2. What is the significance of the Supreme Court decision in *Orr v. Orr*?

Think About

1. Consider this statement: "A man's home is his castle. What he does at home is his business, even if he may be abusing his wife. She can always leave him, can't she? The government has no right to interfere." How might you argue against the statement?

ENDING MARRIAGES

Sometimes marriages don't work out. Others may be void (that is, the marriage is said never to have existed because one of the parties lacked the capacity to enter into a marriage). One or both partners may not want to live together anymore. They may want to end the marriage. Because marriages are legal contracts, the law requires that they be dissolved by the court. A partner who simply walks out on a spouse deserts the other spouse. In Georgia, to walk out on children or a pregnant wife is abandonment and a crime. Leaving a spouse and children does not eliminate the legal duty to support them. Further, neither spouse can remarry legally until the former marriage is legally ended.

Annulments

What happens if the requirements for a valid marriage are not met? What if after you were married, you discovered that your partner was not eligible to contract a valid marriage? Or what if your new spouse has tricked you into marriage?

SITUATION 6 Deanna has just learned that her new husband Philip was never divorced from his first wife.

What can she do?

One way to end a marriage is to annul it. An annulment is a declaration by a court that a marriage never existed: It was never a valid marriage in the first place. When one of the parties to a marriage is ineligible to enter into a marriage contract under state law, the marriage can be annulled. However, an annulment will not be granted if a child or children have been born or are to be born as a result of the marriage.

In situation 6, Philip is still married. Therefore, his marriage with Deanna is automatically void and may be annulled.

SITUATION 7 Joan and Wayne were married in a religious ceremony. They were married because Joan told Wayne she was pregnant. Wayne now learns that Joan had lied. He would like out of the marriage.

What can he do?

Suppose a person is tricked or forced into marriage. Or suppose one of the parties is insane. In these cases, the marriage is voidable but not automatically void. If no annulment is sought and granted, the marriage remains valid.

Situation 7 is an example of a voidable marriage. Wayne can go to court and obtain an annulment because Joan lied to him. Suppose, however, Joan was really expecting a child. Wayne would not be able to get an annulment. He could, however, obtain a divorce.

SITUATION 8 Gary, 17, and Sandra, 16, get married without parental consent.

Can their parents have the marriage annulled?

A marriage of persons under 18 who have married without parental consent can be voided as long as there is no child or child-to-be. A third party, such as a parent, can legally act to void the marriage. However, suppose one or both partners to a marriage were underage when they married, but they have continued living together until they are both 18. Then, under Georgia law, the marriage would be considered valid.

Legal Separation or Divorce?

Marriages can be ended in several ways under Georgia law. You have just read about the conditions under which marriages can be annulled. In addition, both legal separations and divorces are valid in Georgia and in other states.

How does a legal separation differ from divorce?

Unlike divorce, a legal separation doesn't end a marriage. It provides a legal way to settle some of the issues that arise when spouses decide to separate. For example, when couples separate, one or the other might need financial support. If there are children, custody, visitation, and support must be decided. A legal separation must, like a divorce, be granted by a court. When it grants a legal separation, the court also resolves or helps to resolve the other issues. Acceptable grounds or reasons are similar to those for divorce (see figure 8-2).

Legal separation is useful when spouses wish to separate but not end the marriage. It is useful for people who do not want to divorce for religious reasons. Or it may be used if one spouse does not want to deprive the other of insurance or pension benefits that person might lose in a divorce.

A divorce is a declaration by a court that a marriage contract is broken and has ended. The divorce occurs on the day the divorce decree is granted by the judge and filed at the courthouse. After the divorce, the two people are legally "single." They can remarry. This new status may affect their lives in many ways.

Divorce

Grounds for Divorce

CASE OF LINDA SMITH V. PETER SMITH

Linda, 45, and Peter, 48, have been married for 25 years. They have three children—Hazel, 14, Bobby, 16, and Charles, 18. Charles is a freshman at Georgia Tech.

Linda taught school before Charles was born. She worked while Peter got his master's degree. Linda has been a housewife and mother for 18 years.

Peter was a senior vice president in a local company, making $90,000 per year. He quit his job to start his own computer consulting firm. He expects to make $50,000 his first year. Peter has moved into an apartment.

Linda goes to see a lawyer, who explains what the grounds for divorce are in Georgia.

Grounds for divorce are the reasons the court will accept as valid for ending a marriage. The grounds have changed and will continue to do so as society changes. For example, there used to be 12 grounds for divorce in Georgia (figure 8-2). All of these were "fault" grounds, meaning that, to get a divorce, one spouse had to prove that the other was at fault in causing the marriage to break down.

FIGURE 8-2

Fault Grounds for Divorce in Georgia

Apply at Time of Marriage

1. Partners closely related by blood or marriage
2. Mental incapacity
3. Impotency
4. Force, menace, duress, or fraud in obtaining the marriage
5. Pregnancy of the wife (by another man) which was unknown to the husband

Apply after Marriage

6. Adultery by either of the parties
7. Willful and continued desertion by either of the parties for the term of one year
8. The sentence of either party to two or more years of prison for an offense involving moral turpitude (such as murder, involuntary manslaughter, rape, embezzlement)
9. Habitual intoxication; drunkenness
10. Cruel treatment
11. Incurable mental illness
12. Habitual drug addiction

However, often people do not feel fault is the reason for the divorce, or—even if fault exists—they do not want to make such accusations in public. In 1973, the legislature passed a law creating another ground for divorce known as the no-fault ground. This ground means that the marriage is irretrievably broken. It is called the no-fault ground because neither party has to prove the other at fault. The court is interested only in whether the marriage contract is irretrievably broken and that there is no hope of reconciliation.

Although fault need not be proved in Georgia, both spouses can still make accusations of each other. Each party can testify about the conduct of the other. Evidence of wrongdoing is relevant to alimony and the division of marital property. However, it does not affect the amount of child support granted.

Filing and Notification

CASE OF SMITH V. SMITH, *continued*

After talking to her lawyer, Linda Smith files for divorce. She asks for a no-fault divorce. Her lawyer tells her the suit will be filed in the Superior Court of Bibb County, the county in which Peter lives.

After the petition for divorce is filed, Peter is notified by the court. He hires his own lawyer, Justin Jones. In most cases, it is important that the parties have different lawyers. If a lawyer represents both parties, the lawyer is acting more like a judge than an advocate for one client.

Peter will not contest the divorce. He agrees that the marriage is irretrievably broken.

A divorce must be filed in the proper court. In Georgia, superior courts have exclusive subject matter jurisdiction in divorce proceedings (see chapter 3). The rules governing personal jurisdiction of courts in divorce cases are very specific. For example, all states require some residency before allowing a person to seek a divorce. A person must have lived in Georgia for at least six months before filing for divorce in the state. Further, the lawsuit must be filed in the county in which the defendant, or the person being sued, lives.

In Georgia, a divorce cannot be granted for at least 30 days after the defendant is legally notified of the divorce. The date of notification is therefore very important. In no instance will the court grant a divorce automatically. The person who filed the lawsuit must ask the court for the divorce decree after the waiting period has passed.

The waiting period can be seen as a cooling-off period or a time for possible reconciliation. It is also a time for both partners to settle matters to their satisfaction before the divorce is final. In Georgia, all support, custody, and property division issues must be settled either by agreement of the parties or by trial before the divorce is granted.

Note that Georgia gives divorcing parties the right to a jury trial. Both parties must waive this right for a judge to try the case.

Determining Personal Rights and Obligations

As you will see, many things have to be settled in a divorce.

1. Child custody
2. Visitation rights
3. Child support
4. Alimony
5. Division of property
6. Division of debts

In a divorce, one parent usually is given physical custody of the child or children, meaning that the children live with that parent and visit with the other parent. That other parent has visitation rights. Sometimes, legal custody of the child or children is joint between both parents. In that case, the children live part-time with each parent. (Custody is discussed further in chapter 9.)

CASE OF SMITH V. SMITH, *continued*

Peter and Linda agree that Linda should have custody of the children.

Peter wants to see them regularly. Linda agrees to the visitation rights he wants. As you read this section, think about how you might advise that other matters be settled between Peter and Linda. Prepare to make some recommendations for settling their affairs.

Alimony

One important financial question is that of alimony for a dependent spouse. Alimony is a right of one spouse to receive financial support from the other spouse, if there is a need for such support. It is not, however, a guaranteed right of either party.

In the past, the wife was the receiving party and the husband was the paying party. This arrangement is no longer the case necessarily. In

1979, in *Orr v. Orr*, the U.S. Supreme Court said that laws that gave only the wife the right to support payments discriminated against men. The laws were, therefore, unconstitutional.

Even a dependent spouse is not always entitled to alimony. For example, a spouse who commits adultery or abandons the other will probably not receive alimony.

An important consideration when alimony is awarded is how much to pay. In 1981, the Georgia legislature established new factors for determining the amount of alimony to be awarded to a dependent spouse. Basically, the amount of alimony payments reflects the need of one party for support and the ability of the other to pay.

Linda's and Peter's assets and liabilities are shown in figure 8-3. Should Linda receive alimony? How much?

Child Support

A second important issue is child support. It is generally paid in Georgia until a child becomes self-supporting, marries, or reaches the age of 18. However, Georgia law provides that a parent may be required to support a child enrolled in a secondary school until the child reaches the age of 20. Child support is a right that belongs to the child, not the parent. Parents cannot agree between themselves that it will not be paid.

Generally the parent without custody pays child support. The parent with whom the child lives receives child support as trustee for the child, which means that the money is to be used for the benefit of the child. The amount of child support depends on the needs of the individual child and the incomes of each parent. The usual "needs" of children include adequate food, shelter, clothes, and medical and dental care. However, support can include unusual needs, such as special education, private school tuition, or even a car.

Georgia has child support guidelines that became effective in July 1989. These guidelines outline a percentage of the payor's gross income that must be paid for each child (see figure 8-4). The guidelines may be adjusted for special circumstances, however. Any child support amount that is less than what the guidelines establish must be approved by the judge.

FIGURE 8-3

Assets and Liabilities of Linda and Peter Smith

Assets	Liabilities
House: Current worth $150,000. If sold, they would receive about $81,000 ($150,000 less mortgage and $9,000 real estate agent commission on sale).	Mortgage: $60,000
Cars: 1995 Honda Civic sedan; 1999 Nissan Frontier pickup (titles in Peter's name); 2003 Toyota Prius hybrid automobile (in both names, driven by Charles)	Auto loan on Nissan truck in Peter's name: $5,000 still due
Furniture, linens, and kitchen housewares	Business start-up loan in Peter's name: $50,000
Ski boat: Current value $8,000 (registered in both names)	Credit cards: $3,500 in debts
Retirement: Because he left the company for which he worked, Peter will receive a lump sum pension plan payment of $150,000 that must be placed in an Individual Retirement Account to avoid taxes.	
$100,000 life insurance on Peter: Cash value—$15,000	
Money Market Account—$25,000, titled in both names but originally a gift from Linda's parents to Linda	

FIGURE 8-4

Child Support Guidelines

Number of Children	Percentage Range of Gross Income
1	17 to 23
2	23 to 28
3	25 to 32
4	29 to 35
5 or more	31 to 37

Division of Property

Another important issue is the division of the couple's property. In December 1980, the Georgia Supreme Court decided the case of *Stokes v. Stokes,*[2] one of the most important cases in Georgia family law. It concerned the property rights of the parties in a divorce action. The court held that the judge or jury should divide the couple's marital property (that is, any property acquired during the marriage) equitably between the husband and wife, but each could retain any property that he or she owned prior to the marriage. It didn't matter in whose name or names the marital property was listed.

Certain types of property have been designated by the courts as nonmarital. Examples are any property that a person owned before a marriage or received by gift or inheritance during the marriage.

Some important guidelines have come from this case. They are generally followed by Georgia courts in dividing property in divorce or legal separation cases. A judge or jury is to

- assign each spouse's property to that spouse, including the property and assets each owned prior to the marriage or property personally inherited or given to the party during the marriage.

- equitably divide between the parties the real and personal property and assets acquired during the marriage, without considering in whose name the title is (as with a deed to a house or a certificate of title to a car).

FIGURE 8-5

The Smiths' Monthly Budgets

Peter

Food	$ 200
Apartment Rent	$ 600
Utilities	$ 150
Clothes	$ 25
Gas Auto Repairs	$ 90
Installment Payments	$ 200
Medical Bills	$ 20
Haircuts	$ 30
Laundry and Dry Cleaning	$ 20
Recreation	$ 100
Total	$1,435

Linda

Food	$ 400
House Mortgage	$ 800
Utilities	$ 250
Clothes	$ 100
Gasoline and Auto Repairs	$ 150
(Proposed) Car Payment	$ 250
Medical and Dental Bills	$ 75
School Expenses	$ 35
Pets	$ 35
Haircuts	$ 60
Recreation	$ 250
Miscellaneous	$ 200
College Expense	$ 200
Total	$2,805

To divide marital property, the judge or jury considers

1. the length of the marriage and any earlier marriage of either party;
2. the age, health, occupation, vocational skills, and employability of each party;
3. the service contributed by each spouse to the family unit;
4. the amount and sources of income, property, debts, liabilities, and needs of each of the parties;
5. debts against the property;

6. whether the division is instead of, or in addition to, alimony; and

7. the opportunity of each spouse to earn money or acquire property in the future.

Division of Debts

Another financial issue involves debts that must be paid. The court may divide the responsibility for the debts, or it may order one or the other spouse to pay all debts.

Other Financial Matters

Before getting a divorce, a couple should make a monthly budget showing the amount of money each needs to live. They should also list their assets and their debts. Superior courts have certain budget forms called financial needs affidavits on which this information must be written.

What if financial matters cannot be settled by an agreement? The couple will then need to have a trial by either a judge or a jury. Actually, only a small percentage of divorce cases go to trial in Georgia.

CASE OF SMITH V. SMITH, *continued*

The Smiths cannot agree on how their financial affairs should be settled. Pretend you are the judge who must decide for them. Review the case. Look at Linda and Peter Smiths' assets and liabilities (figure 8-3). Look at their budgets (figure 8-5). Note that the budgets total $4,240. After taxes, Peter's monthly pay is $3,250. Before he quit his job, it was $5,500.

Think about your initial recommendations for alimony, child support, and division of property and debts. Here are some of the issues on which Linda and Peter disagree:

• Peter gets angry when Linda's lawyer asks him for $1,000 a month in alimony and another $1,000 each month for child support Peter thinks Linda should go to work. Linda says that it will take at least two years for her to get her master's degree in education. She cannot find a decent job otherwise. What do you think?

• Peter wants to sell the house immediately and divide the proceeds equally. Linda wants to keep the house for the children and herself. She would like to sell it when Hazel (now 14) goes to college. She wants 75 percent of the cash proceeds from the eventual house sale. She also wants half of Peter's retirement benefits. She believes she will need the money more than Peter will. What do you think?

• Peter thinks Linda should pay half the credit card debt. After all, the purchases were for her and the children. Linda's lawyer says the credit cards were in Peter's name, so he is responsible. What do you think is fair?

• Peter wants the motor boat. Linda never uses it. She thinks they should sell the boat and pay off some of the debts. She wants Peter to buy her a new car. Peter says she can use the gift from her parents to get a new car. What would you do with the boat? Should Linda get a new car? Who pays for it?

Now you must determine how the Smiths' property and debts should be divided. You need to recommend how much alimony and child support Peter should pay. Then you must decide, in light of this, how you would adjust the proposed budgets to fit the reality of Peter's current salary. Should Peter agree to pay for Charles and the other children to go to college? Should he go back to his old job if he can?

Settlements

In many divorces, the parties settle all the issues by a written agreement, which is reviewed by the court. The court can change the agreement if it is very unfair to one party or to the children. Usually, a court will change an agreement only if the child's or children's best interests are not met. Courts are most concerned about the welfare of the children.

Suppose it was agreed that Peter would pay Linda $1,000 each month in child support and alimony. Then Peter's business fails two years later, or Linda gets a job paying $1,500 a month, or either of them remarries. Can any changes be made in the settlement?

Very often, the financial circumstances of the mother, father, or both change over the years after the divorce is final. The changes may mean that the alimony or child support needs to be modified.

Support provisions can be changed only once every two years. Any alterations must be based on a substantial change, upward or downward, in the financial condition of either spouse. Alimony can be modified when the spouse receiving the alimony lives continuously and openly in a sexual relationship. The relationship can be either heterosexual or homosexual.

At the time of divorce, parties can agree to waive or give up their future rights to change the amount of alimony. Such a waiver is probably unwise. Unexpected changes may occur in the future. In general, the right to alimony ends when the receiving spouse remarries.

Since 1986, changes in child support may also be modified by the court when a substantial change in the financial condition of either parent or the needs of the child occurs. Parents cannot waive the right to modify child support because it is a right that belongs to the child or children.

O n l y   t h e   F a c t s

1. How does separation differ from divorce?
2. Define (a) no-fault divorce; (b) alimony; (c) child support; (d) marital property.
3. Name some of the effects of the Supreme Court decision in *Orr v. Orr.*

T h i n k   A b o u t

1. If you had been in the legislature, why might you have voted for the law establishing no-fault divorce?
2. Why do you think there is a six-month residency requirement for filing a divorce? Why is there not one for obtaining a marriage license?
3. Should both men and women be entitled to alimony? Should anyone be entitled to it?
4. Do you think it is fair that neither parent can be forced to provide support for a child who has reached the age of 18 (or 20 if the child is in secondary school)? List reasons for and against support of this law.
5. Would your decision about division of property change if Peter was divorcing Linda because she had been unfaithful?

SUMMING UP

This chapter has shown that, for the most part, the government favors marriage and families and tries not to legislate on these matters. When the law does interfere in family life, it is often to ensure that children are cared for or to protect the basic rights of individuals. Recent laws about family violence demonstrate how the courts must often choose between interfering and not interfering. In these laws, the government chooses to protect the individual over not interfering in family life. Do you agree with this preference?

Notes

1. 440 U.S. 268 (1979).
2. 246 Ga. 765 (1980).

9 Children

Have you ever thought about how laws affect your relationships with others? With your friends, for example, or with your parents? This chapter looks at the relationship between parents and children. What do you think your legal rights and duties are toward your parents? What are your parents' rights and duties toward you?

Protecting children is in the broad interest of societies and governments. Governments believe that children need support until they reach a certain age. In Georgia, that age is generally 18. Parents are responsible for their children unless a court takes away their rights to their children either temporarily or permanently. The court must then find someone else to care for the children.

RIGHTS OF CHILDREN

When a child enters into a family, the husband and wife assume new legal rights and duties. These duties continue until

- the child reaches the age of majority or adulthood (18 years old in Georgia or 20 if the child is enrolled in secondary school),
- the child gets married, or
- the child becomes an emancipated minor, meaning that the court declares that the child can survive independently apart from his or her parents.

The Right to Support

The Georgia Code requires each parent to provide for the maintenance, protection, and education of his or her child until the child reaches the age of majority or age 20 if the child is enrolled in a secondary school. Before 1979, only fathers had a legal duty to support their children. The case of *Orr v. Orr* (discussed in chapter 8) extended this duty to mothers.

Parents must provide children with the necessities: food, clothing, housing, and medical care. Moreover, they have an obligation to supervise their children and to provide proper parental care and control for their physical, mental, and emotional health and moral development. They also have an obligation to see that children go to school at least as long as the law requires (in Georgia, the age of 16).

The parents in the following situations all claim that because of circumstances, they no longer have to support their children. Are they right?

SITUATION 1 Pat is a widow, and her job keeps her on the road. She has therefore arranged for her daughter, Ginger, seven, to live with her sister. Her sister has several children. Ginger is just one more to feed. Pat figures she doesn't need to pay her sister any money for Ginger's support. She needs all the money she makes anyway.

SITUATION 2 Lewis, five, is a troubled child. He was born out of wedlock. Both of his parents have their own separate families. He lives with his mother, Aline. His father, Woody, is supposed to pay child support but rarely does.

Q Should Woody feel responsible for his son? Why or why not?

SITUATION 3 Jesse is divorced and lives far away from his former wife and two young children. He knows they're getting by. Besides, he wants to remarry and needs his entire salary. He stops sending child support payments.

As long as parents have parental rights to their children, they have a legal duty to support them financially. The parents' obligation holds true even if the children do not live in their homes. If a child lives with a relative, the relative could sue for the child's support from a living parent. In situation 1, Pat's sister could sue her for Ginger's support.

The legal duty of support extends to both parents of illegitimate children. In situation 2, the father has a legal duty to pay support. An illegitimate child is one whose parents were not married to each other when the child was born and do not later marry. Georgia statutes now refer to illegitimate children as children born out of wedlock. Note that the law favors the legitimation of children. It assumes that it is in the best interest of the children. For this reason, Georgia law recognizes the children of a bigamous marriage as legitimate. Further, a child can be legitimated if a father legally recognizes a child as his by marrying the mother or by filing a petition in superior court for a legitimation order.

What if, in situation 2, Woody denied that he was Lewis's father? Is there anything that Aline could do? When it is not certain who the father of a child is, the mother, the alleged father, the child, or the child's custodian may ask the superior court to determine paternity. In such a case, the court may require the parties involved to take a human leucocyte antigen (HLA) blood test. Such tests are considered to be reliable in determining fatherhood. Additional scientific tests to establish paternity can be ordered by the court. One of these tests is a deoxyribonucleic acid (DNA) probe. If the DNA test establishes a 97 percent or greater probability that the man in question is the father, then he is presumed to be the father unless he can prove through other evidence that he is not. If it were proved that Woody is Lewis's father, the court would require him to support Lewis.

In a divorce, the settlement for child support is a court order, and the court will strictly enforce it. In situation 3, Jesse could be held in contempt of court for failing to pay support. He could be put in jail for failing to pay child support or be charged with abandonment.

The court may also garnish the wages of the parent who has failed to pay. That is, the court can order the parent's employer to deduct a certain amount from each paycheck and send it to the other parent. A garnishment is usually initiated by the parent who is supposed to receive the support.

Another way in which the courts enforce child support payments is called an income deduction order. Child support is automatically withheld from the paycheck of the parent who is ordered to pay the child support. This money is sent directly to the other parent.

Sometimes the court orders a father to pay child support into the registry of the county court. The registrar then pays the mother the child support, taking a small percentage as a fee.

Recent state and federal laws have strengthened the enforcement of child support. For example, federal laws help locate fathers who have abandoned their children. Fathers can be found through social security numbers and by other legal means. It is becoming more difficult to avoid child support obligations.

What if a parent cannot financially support the children? Families that cannot provide for children under age 18 may be eligible for financial assistance through Aid to Families with Dependent Children (AFDC). This federal program is administered in Georgia through the county Department of Family and Children Services (DFCS) (see figure 9-1).

Other government aid may be available for people with low incomes. Examples are Medicaid and food stamps (which provide partial payment of health care and grocery bills). Public assistance is not a gift, however. Consider the following situation.

SITUATION 4 Burt walked out on his wife, Karen, and three young children. Karen was not able to get a job that paid enough to support herself and the children, so she obtained aid through AFDC. Two years later, Burt was located in a neighboring state. He had a good job.

Was Burt liable for past support of the children?

FIGURE 9-1

Department of Family and Children Services (DFCS)

The Department of Family and Children Services (DFCS) is part of Georgia's Department of Human Resources. Each county has a DFCS office. Each provides a variety of social services, including foster care for abused and neglected children and adoption placements. Child protection services include investigation of reported child abuse. DFCS also offers services such as home management aid, family planning, and employment counseling. DFCS administers welfare and assistance programs such as food stamps and Aid to Families with Dependent Children (AFDC).

Georgia's Child Support Recovery Act (1973) says the "payment of public assistance to or on behalf of a child creates a debt due . . . the state by the parent or parents responsible for the support of the child." The act enables DFCS to be reimbursed by the parent who should have been paying child support. In situation 4, Burt would be liable for present and past support, meaning that DFCS could get its money back by garnishing Burt's wages. Burt could be charged with the crime of child abandonment.

The Right Not to Be Abused

SITUATION 5 Sometimes Ollie, age 12, misses school. His pal, Matt, assumed that Ollie was sickly. One day Ollie tells Matt that when his mother gets mad at him she locks him in his room, sometimes without food. He shows Matt bruises on his hands from pounding on the door. Matt knows that Ollie is always truthful.

What should Matt do?

Children have the right not to be abused. The law protects them from physical abuse (situation 5) and emotional abuse by parents or other people. Parents have the duty to protect their children from abuse by others.

You have learned about the 1981 Georgia law providing court protection against family violence. However, victims of family violence are often afraid to report abuse. Also, friends, neighbors, or teachers often hesitate to get involved.

Georgia law requires those working in many professions to report suspected child abuse. These professions include doctors and nurses; school teachers, administrators, and guidance counselors; social workers; child care and child-counseling personnel; and law enforcement officers. It is a crime for these people to deliberately fail to report suspected abuse. The law does not require other people, such as neighbors, to report suspected child abuse. However, to encourage them to do so, the law protects well-intentioned people who report child abuse from being sued for slander.

Whom should you call in your county to report child abuse? The county DFCS office should be contacted. Look under entries for your county in the phone book. Child abuse can also be reported to a juvenile court service worker, the police, or the district attorney.

Children also have the right not to be neglected by their parents. A parent must provide adequate food, clothing, and shelter for his or her child. Adequate means just that. It does not mean designer clothes or everything else that a child ever wanted. A child who does not receive adequate food, clothing, and shelter may be determined by the court to be deprived. Neglect can also be reported to DFCS, which can help the family obtain necessary food, clothing, and shelter.

RIGHTS OF PARENTS

Along with their responsibilities to their children, parents have some rights provided by the law. Parents have considerable power over the lives of their minor children. They can require obedience from them. Generally, they have the right to represent them in court. However, in cases in which the parent is the victim of a crime and he or she alleges that it was committed by the child, the parent cannot represent the child. In this case, the court must appoint an attorney to represent the child's interest. Parents also have the right to control the personal property of their children.

SITUATION 6 Sandra works every day after school washing dishes in a restaurant. Her mother insists that she contribute 75 percent of what she makes to the family.

Is this demand legal? Is it fair?

Legally, both parents of a child are entitled to the services and earnings of the child. If the mother and father are divorced, the parent who has physical custody is legally entitled to the child's services and earnings. Most parents, however, allow children to keep their earnings.

Parents have the right to require that minor children live with them and obey their reasonable and lawful commands. Under Georgia law, parents also have the right to administer reasonable discipline. This discipline can be "in the form of corporal (physical) punishment, restraint, or detention."

The key word in the paragraph above is reasonable. Is it reasonable for a parent to command a child to clean up his or her room or take out the garbage? Would it be reasonable for a parent to order a child to hold up a bank or stay in a closet for a week? Unless the child were physically unable to do the tasks, the courts would likely consider the first two commands quite reasonable. The third demand (that a child do something illegal) would not be reasonable. The fourth would be considered abusive.

SITUATION 7 Cindy's parents are having trouble with her. Cindy, who is 14, leaves the house at night without permission. She sometimes doesn't get back until after midnight. She misses school half the time. Her father and mother are worried and no longer know what to do.

What are their choices? Can the courts enforce obedience to parents?

Can a parent legally require a child to clean his or her room?

FIGURE 9-2

What Is an Unruly Child?

"Unruly child" means a child who

a. while subject to compulsory school attendance is habitually and without justification truant from school; or

b. is habitually disobedient of the reasonable and lawful commands of his/her parent, guardian, or other custodian and is ungovernable; or

c. has committed an offense applicable only to a child; or

d. without just cause and without the consent of his/her parent or legal custodian deserts his/her home or place of abode; or

e. wanders or loiters about the streets of any city or in or about any highway or any public place, between the hours of 12:00 midnight and 5:00 a.m.; or

f. disobeys the terms of supervision contained in a court order that has been directed to the child, who has been adjudicated unruly; or

g. patronizes any bar where alcoholic beverages are being sold unaccompanied by his/her parents, guardian, or custodian or possesses alcoholic beverages; and

h. in any of the foregoing is in need of supervision, treatment, or rehabilitation; or

i. has committed a delinquent act and is in need of supervision but not of treatment or rehabilitation.

Source: Adapted from Official Code of Georgia Annotated §15-11-2.

A child who will not obey his or her parents or go to school is considered unruly. Figure 9-2 lists behaviors considered by Georgia law to be unruly. There are many ways in which parents can deal with unruly children. To avoid involvement with the court, Cindy's parents and Cindy might obtain counseling or participate in some form of family therapy. Cindy's parents might send her to a school specializing in problem children.

What if the problems continue? Then Cindy's parents could sign a juvenile court petition charging Cindy with ungovernable or unruly behavior.

If approved by an intake officer, Cindy's case would be reviewed by the court. A judge might exercise one of several alternatives. The judge could have Cindy and her parents enter into a contract outlining their rights and obligations. The contract might describe certain behaviors required of Cindy as well as her parents. If either Cindy or her parents failed to comply with the contract, they could be held in contempt of court.

Another court option might be to place Cindy on probation. She would have to meet certain requirements (for example, attend school daily and take particular classes) to avoid further discipline from the court. If necessary, the court could assign Cindy temporarily to a group home or other place for children having similar problems.

Only the Facts

1. When do children become legally independent of their parents?

2. What are the legal obligations of parents to their children?

3. What are the obligations of citizens in reporting child abuse?

4. Name at least two rights of parents.

5. List several behaviors of a child that the law terms as unruly.

Think About

1. It is the responsibility of the government to care for members of our society (young or old) who can't care for themselves and whose families can't or won't. Give reasons for and against this statement.

2. In the People's Republic of China, people are required by law to support their elderly parents if such help is needed. Discuss whether such a law should be enacted in this country.

3. Give reasons why parents should be entitled to the earnings of their children. Can you think of arguments against this right?

WHO WILL TAKE CARE OF THE CHILDREN?

Usually, it is expected that children will be cared for by their parents. But what happens when a marriage ends and the parents—or court—must decide who gets the children? Typically, one parent (historically, the mother) is awarded physical custody. The child then lives with this parent, who makes most of the day-to-day decisions affecting the child's life. The other parent (or the noncustodial parent) usually has the right to visit with the child. This visit might take place at his or her separate home. This parent is usually obligated to pay support for the child.

A concept that is becoming more popular in Georgia is joint custody, a situation in which parents share custody of their children. In practice, the mother might keep the children on weekdays and the father on weekends and holidays. In some cases, the children might live with each parent on alternating weeks. Divorced parents who can cooperate well together have chosen this type of custody for the children.

Parents themselves can enter into an agreement regarding custody. It will be effective unless the judge decides otherwise. If parents cannot agree, the judge makes the decision. This decision may be difficult. Both spouses may be able to provide a wholesome environment for the child, but the judge must decide which home would be better.

Whatever type of custody is chosen, it may not be a permanent decision. In Georgia, either parent may file an action to amend the terms of a custodial arrangement whenever he or she feels a change should be made. For the court to approve the petition, the parent must show a substantial change in circumstances affecting the welfare and best interest of the child.

Based on this standard, do you think the following situations justify changes in custody?

SITUATION 8 Dorothy Jones remarries. She asks the court to change the custody of her two children from her former husband to herself. She says that she will now be able to stay at home with them. She says she can give them better care than he can.

SITUATION 9 Ken and Susan have been brought up as Methodists, the religion of their mother. When custody is given to their father, he begins taking them to his Jewish synagogue. Since the father is bringing them up in a different faith, the mother thinks he should be denied custody.

In general, grounds for change of custody have to be very substantial. Remarriage has not in itself been considered by the courts to be sufficient reason for a change of custody. A court might not see the change in situation 8 as great enough to justify moving the children from a stable environment, nor in situation 9 is the mother likely to be given custody. Georgia courts have generally held that the parent with custody is entitled to bring up the children in his or her faith. What seems to be in the best interest of the children is the chief guideline for the judge.

In a joint custody arrangement, the children may live with their mother during the week and with their father on weekends and holidays.

What Will Happen to Me?

Children whose parents are divorcing will probably wonder if they have a voice in who gets custody. Before the age of 14, children may or may not be consulted about their wishes. Upon reaching 14, a child has the legal right to choose which parent he or she wishes to be the custodial parent. The court must accept the child's choice unless the other parent proves that the chosen parent is unfit.

In some disputes over custody, the court will appoint a lawyer to represent the children. Appointed only for the court action, this lawyer is called a guardian *ad litem*. This lawyer talks to the children and other people involved in their lives, including parents, teachers, and counselors. The lawyer presents the court evidence of what will be in the children's best interest and makes a recommendation for custody.

Georgia law provides that the divorced parent without custody has a "natural right of access" to the child, or visitation rights. These rights may be denied only under exceptional circumstances. An agreement about visitation rights must be made at the time of the divorce settlement. If the parents cannot agree, the court

decides for them. The agreement can later be modified. A guardian *ad litem* may also give the court a recommendation regarding visitation.

SITUATION 10 Mike's mother and stepfather are getting divorced. His mother will have custody of Mike. Mike enjoys doing things with his stepfather. Mike's stepfather would like to visit with Mike after the divorce.

Will he be allowed to do so?

It would be up to Mike's mother as to whether Mike and his stepfather could continue to do things together. Under Georgia law, stepparents, grandparents, and foster parents do not have visitation rights. Do you think they should have such rights?

A child whose parent remarries becomes a stepchild of the new spouse. The new spouse becomes the child's stepfather or stepmother. In some instances, the new spouse may decide to adopt the stepchild. In most cases, both natural (or biological) parents must consent to the adoption.

Uniform Child Custody Jurisdiction Act

Sometimes custody decisions cause a great deal of bitterness. Some parents actually kidnap their own children from their former spouses. Georgia and other states have passed a Uniform Child Custody Jurisdiction Act that helps the courts of different states cooperate in enforcing child custody orders. Another problem that this law attempts to resolve is illustrated in situation 11.

> **SITUATION 11** Sharon's parents have been separated for over a year, although they have never filed for a divorce. Sharon and her mother have always lived in Georgia. Sharon's father recently moved to Kentucky. Sharon visits her father in Kentucky. While she is there, her father files for divorce in Kentucky. He asks the court to award him custody of Sharon. When Sharon's mother learns about this situation, she immediately files for divorce in Georgia. She asks the Georgia court to award Sharon's custody to her.

What if each court awards custody of Sharon to a different parent?

The Uniform Child Custody Jurisdiction Act is intended to prevent contradictory custody orders. Under this act, the court in the state in which Sharon has been living for at least six months would ordinarily have jurisdiction to determine her custody.

A parent filing an action to gain custody of a child must tell the court where the child has been living for the last five years. The parent must also tell the court if there have been any other legal actions involving the custody of the child. In situations in which more than one case is pending in different states at the same time, the judges are supposed to communicate with each other to resolve any disputes.

In situation 11, Sharon's father would have to tell the Kentucky court that Sharon had been living in Georgia. Sharon's mother would have to tell the Georgia court about the case that was pending in Kentucky. The judges in both states would contact each other. They would prob-ably decide that the Georgia court should determine who is to have custody of Sharon because Georgia is the state in which Sharon has been living.

When Parents Can't Meet Responsibilities

What happens when parents can't or don't take care of their children? As you have learned, there is some financial aid for parents who can't afford to support their children. But what if a parent is too ill to care for a child, refuses to provide proper care for a child, or cannot break a pattern of severely abusing a child?

A child who is neglected or abused is, by law, a deprived child. If a child is found to be deprived by the juvenile court, he or she may be removed temporarily or permanently from the parent's home. The juvenile court might place the child in the temporary legal custody of the county DFCS. DFCS can place deprived children in emergency care facilities, group homes, or with relatives.

Sometimes, DFCS places the children under the care of foster parents. Foster parents are temporary parents licensed by the state or designated by the court to care for children. They may be relatives of the child. Often foster parents are simply a couple who wish to help such children.

If necessary, the juvenile court can terminate all of a parent's rights regarding a child. It can do so if the parent has completely abandoned or severely neglected or abused the child. Abandoning a child means the parent has failed to pay child support or to communicate with the child for over a year.

Termination of a parent's rights means much more than taking the custody of a child away from a parent. After termination, the parent will have no further right to see the child or to inherit from the child, nor will the child have the right to inherit from the parent. The child may be adopted without the biological parent's knowledge or consent.

Understandably, courts are extremely reluctant to take these measures. The bias of the law supports parents caring for their own children. Termination will not be permitted without a full investigation and court hearing. The child must be represented by a lawyer at the hearing. The parent may choose to be represented at the hearing.

Under what conditions do you think the juvenile court should completely terminate the rights of a parent to a child? If a parent is mentally ill? very poor and uneducated? without a home? What should be the general rule?

The Supreme Court of Georgia has said that parental rights can only be terminated under certain circumstances:

- There is the present (not past) inability of a parent to care for the child.
- The deprivation is likely to continue.
- The continued deprivation is likely to cause serious physical, mental, emotional, or moral harm to the child.

The court must also find that it is in the child's best interest that parental rights be terminated.

When parents' rights to their children are ended, the court must appoint a guardian for the children. Guardians, under Georgia law, are persons responsible for minor children or others who cannot care for themselves. (Natural parents are called natural guardians.) Usually, a temporary guardian is named. A permanent home and guardian are then found. The permanent home might be with a relative or with permanent foster parents. If the child is adopted, the adoptive parents become the guardians.

When Children Are Adopted

Sometimes parents voluntarily give up, or surrender, their rights to their children. For example, a woman may have a child she does not want to keep or feels unable to provide for. She may then decide to put it up for adoption.

The Adoption Process

An adoption is a legal process in which one or both parents (the adoptive parents) are legally substituted for the biological parents. When a child is adopted, the rights and duties of the biological parents end. There are no visitation rights for biological parents unless the adoptive parents allow visitation by the biological parents. A situation in which the biological parents may visit the child is known as an open adoption. An adopted child will not inherit from the biological mother and father unless he or she is named in a will.

CASE STUDY

CASE OF THE WANTED/ UNWANTED CHILD

Lisa is going to have a baby. She is still in school and has no income. She is not married and knows that she cannot support the child.

Chuck is the father. He is about seven years older than Lisa. Chuck plays the drums with a struggling country western band. He's broke most of the time. He thinks Lisa should have an abortion. However, Lisa carries the baby to term. After it is born, she decides to put it up for adoption.

Lisa is advised to notify either the state Department of Human Resources or a licensed child-placing agency. She is told the mother and the father of the child (the biological parents) must consent to the adoption unless one or both cannot be found. To start adoption proceedings, she and the child's father must fill out and sign a form titled "Surrender of Parental Rights: Final Release for Adoption."

After these surrender forms are signed, parents have 10 days to withdraw their surrender of rights to the baby. This 10-day period is a cooling-off period during which parents may change their minds. After this period, it is very difficult to withdraw the surrender.

Parents also surrender their rights to children if they abandon them. Abandonment means deserting a child—that is, physically moving apart from the child—with the intent of ending the parental relationship. In adoption proceedings, the father sometimes cannot be located. Such abandonment may result in the forfeiture of his natural parental rights. Legal abandonment occurs when a parent fails to pay child support, communicate with the child, or visit with the child for over a year.

After a petition for adoption is filed, the Department of Human Resources investigates this case to attempt to verify the information in the petition. The legal procedure for an adoption takes at least three months.

Rights of Natural Parents

This couple adopted their baby through proper court procedures. Do they have any rights as adoptive parents?

CASE STUDY

CASE OF THE WANTED/ UNWANTED CHILD, *concluded*

Lisa's baby is adopted by Andy and Gretchen. Andy manages a large grocery store. Gretchen teaches preschool children. They have not been able to have any children. They adopted the baby through proper court procedures.

However, Lisa lied when she filled out the surrender forms for adoption. She said she did not know where the father could be found. She said she was not even sure of his name. Because he wanted her to have an abortion, she didn't think Chuck would care. Chuck was never notified about the adoption proceedings.

Six months after the baby's birth, Chuck learns about the adoption proceedings. His country western group is making it big. He has a new girlfriend. They plan to get married soon. He'd like to have his child. He files a motion to set aside the adoption. He claims, as the child's natural father, he was not given proper legal notice of the adoption. Nor was his written consent obtained. He wants custody of his child.

In general, courts favor natural parents in deciding cases involving adoption laws. In 1978, a Georgia statute put much more importance on the rights of the natural parents of a child who is placed for adoption.

A father has legal parental rights whether or not he is married to the mother. A biological father must be given the opportunity to care for and know his child. The 1990 Adoption Act specifies how the father of a child born out of wedlock is to preserve his right to object to the adoption of the child and seek custody. If, as in the case of Lisa, the mother knows who the father is, she must, by law, reveal his identity and location. The father must be given personal written notice of the adoption proceedings, if possible. Otherwise, an attempt must be made to notify him through a notice in a newspaper.

The natural father has a right to ask the court for custody of the child if he has made any efforts to support the child in the past or to develop a relationship with the child. Recently, the Georgia Supreme Court ruled that the father must be given an opportunity to explain his reasons for not doing either before an adoption can be allowed over his objections.

If you were the judge in this case, what would you do? What are Chuck's rights as the natural parent? Should Andy and Gretchen have any rights as adoptive parents? What is in the best interest of the child?

Who Can Adopt?

Any adult person—whether married or not—may petition the court to adopt a child if he or she

- is at least 25 years old or is married and living with his or her spouse;
- is 10 years older than the child;
- has lived in Georgia for six months before filing the petition; and
- is financially, mentally, and physically able to have permanent custody of the child.

If the person is married, the petition must be filed by both spouses unless the adoption is requested by a stepparent. Persons who want to adopt children can apply to the state Department of Human Resources or a licensed child-placing agency. Agencies may have their own rules about the kind of parents who may adopt a particular child. They may want the adoptive parents to have a background as similar as possible to the child's biological parents. Georgia, however, has no laws about matching backgrounds of children and adoptive parents. For example, biracial adoptions are legal in Georgia.

Who Can Be Adopted?

SITUATION 12 Tom's parents were divorced when he was 10. He was put in his mother's custody. When he was 13, his mother remarried. Now he is 17, and his stepfather would like to formally adopt him.

Who must consent to the adoption?

Many stepparents adopt stepchildren. Tom's stepfather can petition the court to do so. If the natural parent or parents of the child are living and have not abandoned the child, their consent must be obtained. Children older than 14 years (as Tom is) must also give their consent. A person can be adopted at any age. At 21, a person can be adopted with his or her own consent alone.

If parents have had their parental rights terminated by the court or they are dead, their children may be adopted. In this case, whoever had custody of the child would have to give consent.

Adoption Records

According to law, the records of an adoption proceeding must be sealed, or closed. Some adopted children want to look into these records to find out who their biological parents are. Sometimes biological parents wonder what happens to their children. Courts have only reluctantly allowed records to be seen. Georgia law provides a procedure for obtaining these records. A parent or child may list his or her name with the state registry. This listing makes it easier for either party to find the other if they choose to.

Recently, more adoptions have become open, meaning that the biological and the adoptive parents know who each other are. Depending on the degree of openness of the adoption, the biological parents may communicate with or even visit with the child. Or the adoptive parents may send pictures of the child to the biological parents. Even in an open adoption, though, the biological parents have no legal rights to visitation. Neither may they ask the court to enforce visitation.

Only the Facts

1. In Georgia, who decides in a divorce case who will have custody of the children? What is the main guideline for the decision?
2. Match the following:
   1. guardian   3. adoptive parent
   2. foster parent   4. natural parent
   a. person licensed by the state or appointed by the court to temporarily care for children
   b. biological parent
   c. parent legally substituted for biological parent
   d. person appointed by the court to be legally responsible for minor children
3. Describe someone who would, according to the law, be a deprived child.
4. What requirements are there for a person who wants to adopt a child in Georgia?

1. At what age do you think a child should be able to choose which parent should have custody of him or her after a divorce?

2. Who should have visitation rights to children after divorce? Consider aunts and uncles, foster parents, stepparents, and grandparents.

3. Rachel, 22, was adopted. She wants to know her roots—that is, to know the names of her biological parents. Should the adoption proceedings be opened to give her the information? Why or why not?

4. John is filing for custody of his son Paul. Paul, at six, has been in an adoptive home since he was three months old; he doesn't know any other parents. John argues that he was lied to and didn't even know until last year that he had a son. He argues that Paul is his son and he has the right to raise him. Paul's adoptive parents are very upset. They love Paul and don't want him to be taken away to live with a man who is a total stranger to him. What do you think is in Paul's best interests?

DEATH IN THE FAMILY

Care of the Children

If one parent of a child is dead, generally the other parent will have custody. Who takes care of the children if both parents die? The answer depends on whether or not the parents have left a will. A will is a written document witnessed by others. It states how a person's property is to be divided after he or she dies. The writer can also direct who should take care of his or her children. Without a will, the courts and state laws decide who gets what a person owns and who cares for their children.

Parents may name a person in their will to be responsible for their minor children. This person is called a testamentary guardian, "the guardian of the child's physical person." Testamentary guardianship is a form of child custody. If the person named in the will refuses or is not available to act in that capacity, the court may appoint someone else.

The court may also appoint a guardian of the child's property. A guardian of the property has the duty to use the child's property only for the benefit of the child. Also, the guardian must report about the property management to the county probate court. In Georgia, both the probate and juvenile courts have the authority to appoint guardians when a child has no surviving parents.

Inheriting Family Property

Without a Will

Consider the following situations:

SITUATION 13 George wanted his wife (by a second marriage) to inherit his house. He often said he wanted his two children (by his first marriage) to inherit the family business. He did not make a will.

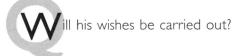

Will his wishes be carried out?

SITUATION 14 Carolyn was an illegitimate child. For much of her life, she lived with an aunt. As an adult, Carolyn made considerable money in real estate. She never married. Carolyn is killed in an accident. She did not make a will, but she did tell her lawyer she wanted most of her estate to go to her aunt when she died. However, her mother claims it all.

Will the court award the estate to Carolyn's mother?

If a person dies without a will, the person is said to have died intestate. Certain rules of inheritance known as intestacy laws apply. In effect, the legislature writes the deceased person's will because the person's property will be distributed according to the intestacy laws. Following are some of Georgia's rules of inheritance that apply when a person dies intestate:

- If the person has no children, the spouse who survives will inherit the entire estate.

- If there are one or two children, the spouse and those children shall have an equal share of the estate. If there are more than two children, the spouse receives one-third of the estate and the children divide the remaining two-thirds.

- If an unmarried and childless person dies without a will, that person's father and mother inherit equal portions.

- If there is no mother or father, the order of inheritance is the brother(s) or sister(s) of the person who dies or their descendants. If there are no brothers or sisters or descendants of brothers or sisters, the grandparents of the person who dies, the person's aunts and uncles, and the person's cousins inherit—in that order. If there are no relatives, then the state will assume ownership of all property.

In Georgia, children born out of wedlock have been granted the same rights of inheritance from mothers as children born within a marriage. Also, mothers can now inherit from their children who have been born out of wedlock just as they can from children born within a marriage. However, the father of a child born out of wedlock cannot inherit from his child unless he has been established as the father in one of several ways as specified by Georgia law. Likewise, a child born out of wedlock cannot inherit from his or her father except under certain circumstances. Inheritance is allowed if there is strong evidence of paternity and if the father treated the child as his own. The child may also inherit if genetic testing shows a 97-percent probability of paternity and the paternity is not successfully rebutted by other evidence.

What would happen in situations 13 and 14? In situation 13, all the property would be divided equally among the spouse and the two children. Everything—house and business—may have to be sold in order to divide it. In situation 14, Carolyn's mother will inherit Carolyn's entire estate.

About Wills

Making a Will

It is best to have a will prepared by a lawyer. In order to be enforced, a will must be made properly. It is required that a will be dated, and the signature must be properly witnessed by at least two people (three in some states) who do not inherit under the will. There are additional requirements.

If a person who has a valid will marries or has a child, the will is automatically void, with one exception. It is valid if it contains a paragraph saying that the will was made in contemplation of the upcoming change. Otherwise, after the change occurs, a new will is needed. Divorces are treated differently. If the party with the will divorces, the will remains valid. However, by law the ex-spouse does not receive any benefits.

It is wise to periodically review any will to be sure it is up to date. State laws may change. The family membership or property holdings may change.

Conditions of Wills

SITUATION 15 In his will, Arthur leaves all his money and property to the church. He leaves his wife and children nothing.

Is this arrangement legal?

In Georgia, a will maker is not required to leave any property to a spouse or children. In other states, the spouse and children are automatically entitled to a specified amount. However, in Georgia, a person can disinherit the entire family with a valid will, which is what Arthur did in situation 15. All of his property goes to the church.

Although a person can disinherit his or her family, he or she cannot deprive them entirely. Whether a parent or spouse dies with or without a will, a spouse and dependent children in Georgia have a statutory right to support, although the support can be relatively modest.

Only the Facts

1. How do a testamentary guardian and a guardian of the property differ?
2. What are intestacy laws?
3. Give several reasons for regularly updating a will.

Think About

1. Why do you think a will must be witnessed by people who do not inherit under the will?
2. Some people object to a person's being able to practically disinherit a spouse and/or children. How might you write a law to be more protective of their interests?

SUMMING UP

In this and the previous chapter, you've learned about the laws affecting the relationships of wives and husbands and children and parents. Most of these laws and government actions are directed toward protecting family members and nurturing the family, although the definition of what constitutes a family is changing. In the past, the "extended" family included grandparents, uncles and aunts, and cousins to whom there were strong emotional and economic ties. The modern-day family consists primarily of parents and children, and it is increasingly divided from within by divorce. The family unit will likely continue to reflect changes in society, and laws will in turn continue to adapt to those changes.

 **When You Harm Others**

Protecting citizens from harmful acts is basic to an orderly society. To protect citizens, governments pass laws making wrongful acts crimes. A crime can be described as a wrongful act that injures or interferes with the interest of society (crimes in Georgia are listed in figure 15-1).

However, many acts that result in harm to others are not crimes. Accidentally hitting another car with your own is not a crime, even though it could cause harm. It is a tort. Generally speaking, a tort is a wrongful act that injures or interferes with an individual's person or property. A tort can be intentional or unintentional (negligence), or it can be a tort of strict liability.

TORTS AND CRIMES

Consider these three events:

1. Mary sells heroin to Jack.
2. Steve, not looking where he is going, knocks Mrs. Frayle down.
3. During an argument, Linda slaps Beth in the face.

Which do you think would be a crime? Which a tort? Understanding the difference between crimes and torts is important because the law treats them in different ways (see figure 10-1).

The state has made selling heroin (event 1) a crime. Mary would be prosecuted for this crime in a criminal proceeding by a district attorney representing the people of the state. If found guilty, Mary could be fined and sent to jail. The victim of a crime is not a party to the legal action. Jack would not be suing Mary. Rather, he would be one of several witnesses for the state in the case against her in court.

FIGURE 10-1

How to Tell a Crime from a Tort

	Definition	Court Proceeding	Accused	Victim	Charges Brought by	If Defendant Loses
Tort	A wrongful act that injures or interferes with another's person or property	Civil	Defendant	Plaintiff	Plaintiff	Defendant pays damages to plaintiff.
Crime	A wrongful act that the state or federal government has identified as a crime	Criminal	Defendant	The person hurt and the State of Georgia or other governmental entity	Government	Defendant is punished. May serve a sentence. Fine may be paid to government; possible restitution is made to victim.

Tort cases are heard in civil proceedings. The legal process is quite different from criminal proceedings. The civil process provides a legal means for victims of harmful acts to be compensated for the harm done to them. Event 2 is a tort. Mrs. Frayle has been injured by Steve's act. In order to recover money for the harm or damage she has suffered, the civil process requires that Mrs. Frayle sue Steve. Furthermore, she must bear the cost in terms of time, energy, and money for doing so.

In such a legal action, the victim of the tort is usually called the plaintiff. The plaintiff begins a court action against the alleged (or supposed) wrongdoer, usually called the defendant or tortfeasor. In event 2, Mrs. Frayle would be the plaintiff. Steve would be the defendant.

To win a tort case, the plaintiff must prove two things: (1) the defendant committed the tort and (2) as a result of the tort, the plaintiff or the plaintiff's property was injured. If a plaintiff (like Mrs. Frayle) can prove both, she is entitled to recover money damages from the defendant to compensate for the injury. The defendant (Steve) is liable, which means he is responsible for paying the damages.

The same act may be both a crime and a tort. Event 3 is an example of an act that is both a crime and a tort. Linda may face a criminal ac-

tion by the state and a civil action by Beth, the individual who was injured.

Why are two different legal actions against one wrongful act possible? In effect, criminal law provides a way of punishing people who commit crimes. It acts to protect all citizens from such wrongdoing. Criminal law is not concerned with the individual victim. The law of torts, on the other hand, provides a way to compensate victims of wrongful acts.

In reality, victims of crimes like burglary, rape, and armed robbery rarely sue the wrongdoers, primarily for practical reasons. For instance, if the wrongdoer has no money or property from which to collect, a lawsuit would accomplish nothing.

Only the Facts

1. What is a tort? How does it differ from a crime?

Think About

1. What advantages are there to a victim of an act that is both a crime and a tort to having it prosecuted as a crime? to initiating a civil suit as a tort?

INTENTIONAL TORTS

An intentional tort is a deliberate act of a person that causes injury to another's person or property. It is this type of conduct that may be a crime and a tort. As you read, consider what legal rights and duties are defined by these intentional torts. For example, in the first tort discussed, you have a legal duty not to harm another through assault. Similarly, you have a legal right to protection from assault. You also have a legal right to payment for damages from the person who harms you.

Intentional Torts: The Person

There are seven basic intentional torts that relate to injury to the person: assault, battery, wrongful death, false imprisonment, defamation, malicious prosecution, and intentional infliction of emotional distress.

Assault

An assault may be defined as a threat of bodily harm. The person who is threatening must appear able to carry out that threat. An assault may also be an attempt at bodily harm; no physical touching or injury need occur. There need only be an act that creates a reasonable apprehension (or expectation of harm) in the victim.

Which of the following situations, then, would be an assault?

> **SITUATION 1** Waiting for the school bus, Cal says to Paul, "I am going to shoot you right now." Paul does not see a weapon.

> **SITUATION 2** Mel pulls a knife from his pocket. He says to Bill, "I'm going to cut you."

In situation 1, no assault has taken place, even though there was a threat of bodily harm. There is nothing to indicate that Cal had the ability at that time to carry out the threat. However, an assault has occurred in situation 2. There, both the threat of harm and the apparent ability to carry out the threat are present.

Battery

Battery is the intentional touching of one person by another without consent (or permission). The law assumes that every person has a right to be free from unwanted, intentional physical contact by other people. For the purpose of this tort, the law also considers that any clothing a person wears or objects that person holds are part of the person.

Every touching of a person, however, is not necessarily battery. In our sometimes crowded world, a certain amount of physical contact between people can't be avoided. Consent is presumed in many situations.

Which of the following would be an example of battery?

> **SITUATION 3** Susie suddenly grabs a pencil out of Tom's hand. She does not touch Tom.

> **SITUATION 4** Tom is angry. He throws a heavy book at Susie. It hits her arm.

> **SITUATION 5** Jack is standing in front of Alice on an elevator when it stops on Alice's floor. While getting out of the elevator, Alice pushes Jack slightly.

A bump in a crowd is probably not battery.

Battery has been committed by Susie in situation 3 because the pencil is considered to be part of the "person" of Tom. In situation 4, Tom has committed battery. He touched the person of Susie with the book without consent. However, there is no battery in situation 5. Jack is presumed to have consented to some degree of physical contact by standing in an elevator. Such consent is presumed in most places where physical contact is likely. Examples would be football stadiums, public buses, and movie theaters.

Wrongful Death

Wrongful death, as used in the law of intentional torts, may be defined as the death of a human caused by an intentional act of another. A surviving relative of a wrongful death victim has a right to sue the person who committed the tort. The suit would be to recover money equal to the value of the victim's life. Survivors can sue even if the person responsible for the crime has not been prosecuted and found guilty in a criminal case.

> **SITUATION 6** Hilda works at a hospital. She feels sorry for Sam, who has a terminal condition and is being kept alive on a respirator. She deliberately unplugs Sam's life-support system, knowing that her action will kill Sam.

Q Would this act be the intentional tort of homicide?

Not only is the act the intentional tort of homicide, it is also a crime. Therefore, Sam's widow could sue Hilda to recover the value of Sam's life, and Hilda could be tried in a criminal proceeding.

What if Sam asked Hilda to "pull the plug" because he did not want to live the rest of his life on a respirator? The Georgia Supreme Court has held that a patient who was rational and competent to make that decision could choose to end his own life.[1] In this situation, Hilda would not be liable to the family if she pulled the plug. However, she must have acted under the authority of Sam's primary treatment physician.[2]

How can the value of a life be calculated for a lawsuit? A special scale, called an actuarial table, is used. This table predicts how long a particular person would normally live. Another scale is used to predict how much money the person would have earned.

Lawsuits based on the intentional tort of wrongful death are rare. Remedies are usually sought through the criminal justice system. Lawsuits based on "wrongful deaths" resulting from unintended actions (or negligence) are more common. An example would be a suit based on a death resulting from an auto accident. Another example would be a malpractice suit in which the careless act of a physician was said to have caused a death.

False Imprisonment

False imprisonment is the unlawful confinement to a bounded area of one person by another for any length of time whereby he or she is deprived of his or her liberty. Actual physical restraint is not necessary for the tort to occur. If the person reasonably believes that he or she is not free to leave, then a false imprisonment has occurred.

Generally, the injury resulting from false imprisonment is emotional (resulting in, for example, humiliation, fear, or embarrassment). However, physical injuries can occur from the restraint itself or when the person attempts to escape. In either case, the wrongdoer would be liable for all such injuries.

Which of the following would be false imprisonment?

> **SITUATION 7** Sid and Ralph decide that it would be fun to scare Jim by pretending to lock him in a room. They send Jim into the room to get a football. When he goes in, they slam the door behind him. They tell him the door is locked, but it isn't. An hour later they release him.

> **SITUATION 8** Frieda is locked in a ground floor room by Arnold. There is a large window in the room. Frieda opens the window and escapes safely.

Officer Jones of the city police department arrests Maria with an arrest warrant for a crime. Maria is found to be not guilty of the crime.

In situation 7, Sid and Ralph have committed the tort of false imprisonment. Jim thought he wasn't free to leave. It doesn't matter if the door wasn't locked. In situation 8, the fact that Frieda found an easy and safe manner of escape does not relieve Arnold of responsibility for imprisoning her. If she had been injured when escaping, he would be liable for the physical injury.

In situation 9, there has not been false imprisonment. The arrest and detention were lawful. What if the arrest had been unlawful—due, for example, to an invalid arrest warrant? The officer still would not be liable for the tort of false imprisonment. Unless their actions are purposefully unlawful, police officers generally have immunity from lawsuits when acting officially.

Defamation

Defamation may be defined as an untruthful statement made by one person to another about a third person that damages the reputation of the third person. Defamation may be written or spoken. Defamation would occur if Carol told her teacher that Larry had copied answers from her tests but he had not. It would occur if a newspaper reported to its readers that an actor was usually drunk at public occasions when the newspaper knew this statement was a lie.

Slander is spoken or oral defamation. Libel is printed defamation. In a case of slander, the victim must be able to show actual damage as a result of the false statement. There are certain situations, however, in which damages from slander are presumed. Consider, for example, statements that a person is dishonest in his profession or that a person has a socially feared disease. These statements create the presumption of emotional harm or harm to the reputation of that person.

In a case of libel, damage is presumed merely from the publication of the false statement. This distinction is based on the theory that the printed word is more harmful than the spoken word. People in the public eye have less protection against defamation than do private persons.

Truth is an absolute defense in cases involving the torts of slander and libel. In other words, if what is said is true, the person claiming that slander or libel has been committed will not prevail. Common defamatory statements can be statements that

- another person has committed a crime. ("Lucy stole my lunch money.")
- another person has committed an act that would make him or her a social outcast. ("Winston lies about everything.")
- would cause a person to suffer public ridicule in his or her business or profession. ("Dr. James is a quack.")
- would cause a person to suffer public ridicule or scorn. ("Abigail has a venereal disease.")

Based on what you have read, which of the following would be defamation?

SITUATION 10 Warren sends a note to Grace. In it he says, "You cheated on the quiz." Warren knows that what he said is not true.

SITUATION 11 Tony says to Cora, "Eric is a kleptomaniac." Tony believes what he said is true, but it is not.

SITUATION 12 Cora writes the school newspaper column. She puts what Tony said about Eric in the next issue of the paper.

SITUATION 13 Linda sees Jane steal Gloria's notebook. Linda tells Gloria in front of the whole class, "Jane is the thief; she stole your notebook." The school's reporter prints the quotation.

There has been no libel in situation 10. The statement is false and would injure Grace's reputation, but it was not published or communicated to another person. In situation 11, Eric has been slandered by Tony. He may recover damages if he can show some actual injury resulting from the slander, such as being excluded from a fraternity. Tony's lack of malice or bad intention may reduce the damages Eric would recover. However, it does not excuse the harm done to Eric.

In situation 12, Eric has been libeled by the publication of the defamatory statement. He would not have to show actual damage as he did in situation 11. The damage is presumed as a matter of law. In situation 13, Jane has neither been slandered nor libeled, even though her character and reputation have been injured. Certainly, the statement was communicated, orally and in writing, to a large number of people. However, the statement was true. Truth is an absolute defense.

While reading about defamation, you may have wondered about the First Amendment right to free speech. Doesn't this right conflict with the tort principle of defamation? If so, how is this conflict resolved? Legal scholars have debated these questions for years and continue to do so. In general, it is believed that the two principles do not conflict. Consider the reasons for both principles. On the one hand, freedom of speech is absolutely essential to maintaining a democratic society. On the other hand, a person's good name and reputation are valuable. In fact, these principles coexist by balancing a person's right to free speech against another person's right not to have his or her reputation wrongfully harmed. As such, one can say or write whatever he or she wishes about another, but not if it is false and harmful.

Malicious Prosecution

Malicious prosecution is the tort that results when law enforcement officers or prosecutors misuse the criminal justice system to falsely accuse and try an individual on charges that are fabricated. Several elements must be proved to show that this tort has occurred. Someone must have been charged and prosecuted for a crime. The prosecution must have been initiated mali-

ciously (that is, with intent to harm). There must not be any probable cause for the charge. (Probable cause is defined as enough evidence to cause a reasonable person to believe that the accused probably committed the act charged.) The accused must have suffered injuries, and he or she also must have been found not guilty.

Inflicting Emotional Distress

This tort may be defined as emotional distress deliberately inflicted on one person by another. The acts by the defendant must be extreme and outrageous. Also, they must be intended to cause emotional distress, and the plaintiff must actually suffer severe emotional distress. However, courts and juries have generally been unsympathetic to plaintiffs seeking to recover damages for this tort because it is difficult to prove the damage or injury claimed. Do you think such damages could be proved in cases like the following?

SITUATION 14 Mary is in labor and calls an ambulance to take her to the hospital to deliver her child. The ambulance arrives one hour later. The ambulance attendants refuse to take her to the hospital where her personal physician is waiting. Instead, they take her to a nearby county hospital, ignoring her protests and telling her to be quiet. Mary is so agitated, she has a very difficult delivery.

SITUATION 15 Mike and Bob think it would be funny to scare their elderly neighbor, Mrs. Jones. While she is asleep in her bedroom, they sneak to the back door and rattle the doorknob. They tap on her window shutters and make a general disturbance outside her house. Mrs. Jones is awakened and is badly frightened. When she gets up to see about the noises, she is trembling so badly that she slips and falls on the stairs.

Both situations are examples of claims of this tort that have been successful in Georgia courts. The ambulance attendants are liable for money damages to Mary. Mike and Bob are liable to Mrs. Jones for her injuries and distress.

1. Identify and define the intentional torts in the following situations:
   a. Ken, the school tough guy, says he'll beat up Zeke if he won't give Ken his lunch.
   b. Leaving a rock concert, Bob pushes into Carol, nearly knocking her down.
   c. Andy angrily accuses Harry of stealing his jacket.
   d. The school paper reports that the principal has taken bribes. This allegation turns out to be false.
   e. Laura is found to have sent Joan anonymous threats. Joan is very upset by them.

2. What is the difference between assault and battery?

3. Explain the differences between slander and libel. In which must actual damages be shown?

T h i n k   A b o u t

1. In the tort of false imprisonment, why doesn't it matter whether a person is actually constrained?

2. Explain the conflict between the principles of defamation and the right to free speech.

3. Have you ever been the victim of a tort? Have you ever committed a tort? At the time, did you know that the act was against the law?

Intentional Torts: Property

There are four basic intentional torts that relate to injury to property. They are trespass to real property, trespass to personal property, conversion of personal property, and nuisance. You will recall that real property is land and whatever is attached to or growing on it, such as houses or crops. Personal property consists of everything else, tangible or intangible (see Chapter 6 for definitions of real and personal property).

Trespass to Real Property

This tort may be defined as the unauthorized entry onto the real property of another. An example of trespass to real property would be if you deliberately rode your motorcycle through Mr. Johnson's flower beds and damaged valuable roses. You would be liable for the damages. Because such a trespass is also a crime, you could face criminal prosecution.

In every case involving civil trespass to real property, it is presumed that the trespass caused damage. In other words, the owner of the real property need not prove there was actual damage to win a lawsuit against the trespasser. In the example, Mr. Johnson would not have to prove damages. He would simply have to prove that you came onto his property without permission.

A person can be liable for trespass to another person's real property without even setting foot on it. For example, a man builds a dam on his own land, and it causes surface water to back up onto a neighbor's property. In this situation, the man who built the dam may be liable for the damages suffered by the neighbor.

In this area of torts, money for damages is sometimes not the real object of a lawsuit. The issue is more often who owns the land. Consider situation 16:

SITUATION 16 Abner and Gene are neighboring landowners. Abner puts up a fence on what he thinks is the boundary line between the two pieces of land, but the fence overlaps Gene's property by three feet.

Is this infringement a trespass to real property? What is the issue: ownership or damages?

In this kind of dispute, both the trespasser (the defendant, Abner) and the plaintiff (his neighbor, Gene) claim to own the land. The law provides a means of peaceful settlement of these types of disputes. Without such means, people

might try to solve problems inappropriately (for example, by destroying the fence). To resolve the case, the court must first determine who owns the disputed land. It must then determine whether a trespass has taken place. If Gene is found to own the land, a trespass has occurred. Gene could recover money for the loss resulting from the trespass. However, his real objective most probably is to secure the correct boundary line in order to preserve his real property. In such a case, the court could order the reestablishment of the boundary line between Gene and Abner.

Trespass to and Conversion of Personal Property

Trespass to personal property occurs when there is a temporary interference with the custody or possession of the personal property of another. For example, say Judson's neighbor "borrows" his car without Judson's knowledge. That would basically be a trespass to personal property, even if Judson didn't know the car was taken until its return. If the car was damaged, then the neighbor, the person who committed the tort, called the tortfeasor, would be liable for the damages. The amount of damages requested would be affected by inconvenience, loss of use, and loss of income to Judson.

When the interference in custody or possession is of a permanent nature, then conversion of personal property occurs. This tort depends a great deal on the intent of the defendant. Did the defendant intend to return the property? It also depends on the ability of the plaintiff to recover the property and, often, the amount of time the defendant has had the item. This tort is similar to the crime of theft by taking.

Which of the following situations do you think is a trespass to personal property? Which is a conversion of property?

SITUATION 17 Gail takes Linda's bicycle without Linda knowing it. She uses it for several hours. Then Linda sees her and takes the bicycle back. One wheel is badly damaged.

SITUATION 18 Bob "borrows" Jim's car without permission while Jim is out of town. He drives it for 2,000 miles before returning it.

In situation 17, a trespass to personal property has occurred. Gail would be liable for the damage. If there were no damage, she would be liable for use and wear and tear. In situation 18, Bob's interference with Jim's possession may have been so great that it would be a conversion of personal property. Bob might be liable to Jim for the full value of the car.

Nuisance

SITUATION 19 LMN Corporation dumps its chemical wastes into the Blue River. The wastes are not harmful, but they give off a bad smell. The smell particularly bothers the residents of Riverview Subdivision. Frequently, the smell makes it unpleasant to use their yards and enjoy their property.

SITUATION 20 Fritz and Drew are neighbors. Fritz works during the day. Drew works from 4 p.m. to midnight. When Drew gets home, he likes to work in his shop, where he designs and builds furniture. The noise from Drew' sawing and hammering night after night prevents Fritz from sleeping.

Can anything be done about these problems? These situations come under the tort of nuisance. Nuisance may be defined as anything that causes harm or inconvenience to another. It usually affects others' use or enjoyment of their property. Nuisances frequently concern noises, smells, or lights.

There are two basic types of nuisance: public and private. A public nuisance causes inconvenience or damage to the public as a whole. Situation 19 is a public nuisance. When there is a public nuisance, citizens can ask the district attorney to file a petition in the superior court to stop it, and the court can issue an injunction (an order to stop the activity).

Those who are specially damaged by the nuisance can initiate a lawsuit to recover damages as well as stop the nuisance. Rather than one person bearing the costs of a lawsuit, all those who are especially affected by the nuisance could join together in a "class action" suit against the people or group causing the nuisance. Government agencies, like the Environmental Protection Agency, can also initiate actions against public nuisances harmful to the environment.

On the other hand, a private nuisance usually damages or inconveniences a limited number of individuals (situation 20). One or all of the persons affected by a private nuisance may file a petition to stop it. They can also sue for the actual damages incurred. Further, most cities have ordinances under which citizens can ask local authorities to halt nuisances. In fact, Georgia law states that this request should be made before court action is sought.

Determining what is or isn't a private nuisance is not always easy because everyone has different tastes and tolerances for inconvenience. For example, some people might be inconvenienced by the nighttime rehearsals of a neighbor's rock band. Others might enjoy the music. To decide whether an act is a nuisance, a court uses this standard: would such an act inconvenience, offend, or damage a reasonable person? Consider situation 21:

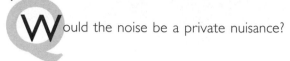

SITUATION 21 Denise, who is a very nervous person, lives on a quiet street. The owner of the neighboring lot decides to build a house. The construction noise upsets Denise so much that she has to be hospitalized.

Would the noise be a private nuisance?

Probably not because the noise would not harm an ordinary, reasonable person.

Only the Facts

1. John planted a hedge that extends two feet into his neighbor's land. The neighbor sues. What tort is involved? What might be the reason for the neighbor's lawsuit?

2. Explain why the following would be public or private nuisances: (a) a major city's airport flight path, which has many low-flying and noisy airplanes flying directly over a neighboring small town; (b) a continuously barking dog.

Think About

1. Why is time an important consideration in the difference between trespass to and a conversion of personal property? Suggest the time frame you would consider necessary for an act to constitute conversion of property in the case of a car, a canoe, and a chain saw.

2. Generally, what should private individuals do before petitioning to halt a private nuisance or suing for damages?

3. Which intentional torts to person or property do you think are also crimes? Why?

NEGLIGENCE

What if someone's person or property is harmed because of something you do or don't do unintentionally? This kind of situation is called negligence. Negligence is perhaps the most common form of tort. It is the type most likely to result in a lawsuit. Today, the most common acts of negligence occur in the operation of automobiles. To prove negligence, the plaintiff must show that the defendant had a legal duty to the plaintiff that he or she failed to perform (breach of duty). Furthermore, the plaintiff must prove that the breach of the defendant's duty was the "proximate cause" of the actual injury and damages suffered by the plaintiff (that is, what the defendant did or did not do that led to the injury or damages).

Legal Duty and Failure to Perform It

What is a legal duty that one person may have to another? A legal duty is, simply stated, that standard of care that society expects every person to exercise for the safety and convenience of others. Sometimes duties are imposed by statute. Standard of care is measured by the supposed conduct of an imaginary "reasonable and prudent

An auto accident is the most common type of tort caused by negligence.

person." A breach of duty occurs when this standard of care is not met. To illustrate, look at the two situations that follow. Did negligence result from failure to carry out legal duties?

SITUATION 22 Trudy has just waxed her kitchen floor. It is quite slippery when Ingrid comes to visit Trudy. Unaware, Ingrid walks into the kitchen. She slips and falls.

Is Trudy negligent?

SITUATION 23 Del has a pile of leaves and tree branches that he wishes to burn. Although the wind is blowing steadily, Del sets the refuse on fire. There is a utility building near the pile of refuse that belongs to Del's neighbor. The building catches fire from sparks carried by the wind and is destroyed.

Was Del negligent?

Neither Trudy nor Del exercised the ordinary care for safety that the law expects of a reasonable and prudent person. Trudy should have warned Ingrid of the slippery floor. Del shouldn't have burned trash on a windy day. Both would be liable for the damages caused by their negligence.

It should be noted that the test of negligence is not whether the defendant believes the conduct to be reasonable. It is whether a "reasonable and prudent person" would believe it to be reasonable. In a court case, the jury usually decides what the standard of care is and whether or not it has been met. Jury members must draw from their own experiences to determine what a reasonable person would do under the circumstances of the case.

The standard of care required of a defendant may be affected by who that defendant is. For example, a surgeon performing an operation is not judged by the reasonable and prudent person standard. The reasonable and prudent person is not ordinarily qualified to perform surgery.

Rather, the surgeon would be judged by a reasonable and prudent standard for a surgeon.

The standard of care required of a defendant may also depend on who the plaintiff is, particularly regarding the care a property owner owes to persons who come on to his or her property. The care will depend on whether the person is a trespasser, licensee, or invitee (see figure 10-2).

Proximate Cause and Actual Damage

The breach of duty (or failure to meet a legal responsibility) must be the proximate cause of the alleged injury in order for there to be negligence. In other words, there must be a direct link between the breach of the defendant's duty and the injury suffered by the plaintiff. The question to be asked is, "But for" the act of the defendant (that is, if it weren't for the defendant's act or failure to act), would the plaintiff have suffered the injury? Consider the following situation:

> **SITUATION 24** An elderly woman goes to the hospital with a stomachache. A nurse takes her temperature and vital signs. Suddenly, the woman collapses. One hour later, she is pronounced dead of a heart attack.

Can the hospital be sued for medical malpractice because the heart attack occurred while she was in its care?

Probably not. There must be some link between the care or lack of care and the ultimate injury (in this case, death). It would be difficult to prove that the nurse's actions somehow caused the heart attack. In other words, the proximate cause of the heart attack was not the care provided by the nurse or hospital. Therefore, the hospital would not be liable for medical malpractice.

The injury must also be foreseeable for the suit to be successful. Under the law, the performer of an act is liable for an injury only if it was a foreseeable consequence of the act. In other words, a defendant would not be held liable for a negligent act—even though it caused the injury—if no reasonable person could have foreseen such consequences. Consider the situation that follows:

> **SITUATION 25** Bill is negligently speeding down a busy street. His car collides with a pickup truck parked at the curb. The truck is loaded with dynamite for construction work. It explodes. Mary, walking on a nearby sidewalk, is seriously injured. Jane, sitting next to a window in a building a block away, is cut by flying glass. Alice, holding her baby several blocks away, is frightened by the explosion and drops the baby.

FIGURE 10-2

Duties of a Property Owner

Person Entering Property	Relationship with Owner	Duty of Owner to Person
Trespasser	Enters without owner's permission.	Not to intentionally create a hazard. Setting a booby trap for trespassers would be unlawful.
Licensee	Enters with permission for the owner's benefit, for example, a customer at a retail store.	To warn of both concealed and obvious dangers.
Invitee	Enters with permission of owner, for example, a social guest.	To warn of dangers or repair them. However, the owner is not responsible for concealed and unknown defects such as an improperly installed ceiling.

Bill's negligent act was obviously the cause in fact of all the injuries. Would he be held liable for the injuries to Mary? Jane? Alice's baby?

Bill would be legally responsible for Mary's injuries. It is foreseeable that a nearby pedestrian could be injured by an automobile collision. Bill may not be legally responsible for the injuries received by Jane and by Alice's baby. Such injuries to persons far removed from the scene of an accident would not appear foreseeable as the natural and probable consequence of the negligent act. However, that would be an issue for a jury to decide.[3]

The final element required in order for the tort of negligence to be completed is actual damage. No matter how careless a person is, if no damage or injury results from that carelessness, then no tort has been committed.

STRICT LIABILITY

SITUATION 26 The Widget Company manufactures a product that self-cleans bathtubs. Homemakers across the country buy the cleaner. Unfortunately, the Widget Cleaner leaves a slick, invisible film on the tub surface. Many people slip and fall. Over 200,000 lawsuits are initiated. The company was careful in making the product.

Is it liable?

SITUATION 27 Ron purchases a bottle of soda pop. Before he can get the top off, it explodes. The caps on these bottles are defective. The cap hits him in the eye. He has a black eye for weeks.

Can he recover damages?

Many times people are injured not through the direct action of another but by a product that has a defect in its design or manufacture. A legal action taken to recover damages for such an injury is called a product liability suit.

In Georgia, an injured person may sue the manufacturer under the doctrine of strict liability. Under this doctrine, the defendant does not have to be negligent. In other words, the plaintiff does not need to prove that the manufacturer failed to perform a legal duty or use a reasonable standard of care. The plaintiff need only show that the manufacturer marketed a product that caused injuries. Therefore, in situation 26, the company's care in making the product and lack of intent to harm would not protect the company from liability. Those injured could sue individually or together in a class action. They should be able to collect damages.

The strict liability principle recognizes the consumer's right not to be hurt by a product that is used in the manner intended. Once a product is shown to be defective, manufacturers are expected to provide notice of defect and recall the product. A person who disregards such a notice may not have a strict liability claim.

In some states, the seller can be sued under strict liability, but that is not true in Georgia. The seller is protected because it can be difficult to see the defect in a product just by looking at it. However, sellers can be found liable for negligence for failing to detect or warn of a known danger.

In situation 27, Ron clearly could sue the cap manufacturer under strict liability, but would the grocer be liable? Was he negligent? Would it make a difference if he had seen bottles with these caps explode before or if it were a new kind of soda pop that the store started carrying?

The doctrine of strict liability benefits consumers by forcing manufacturers to do more research and set higher safety standards for their products. The costs of research (and lawsuits) are passed on to consumers in the form of higher prices.

Only the Facts

1. What legal duty do people have to each other?

2. List the four criteria for a tort of negligence. Are the criteria met in the following case?

John's dog, which roams around his fenced-in yard, is known to bite. John does not warn the man coming to plant trees in the yard. When the man enters the yard, the dog bites him. As he scrambles over the fence, the man falls, breaking his arm. He sues John.

3. What must the plaintiff show in a tort of strict liability?

Think About

1. In some intentional torts, damage is presumed; it need not be proved. In a tort of negligence, damage must be proved. Why do you think the law makes this distinction?

2. How might strict liability affect the way a manufacturer designs or makes a product?

BRINGING A LAWSUIT

Who Can Be Liable?

Generally, depending on the action, a child younger than a certain age is not held legally responsible for actions that cause harm. However, Georgia law states that a child's parent may be liable to a person whose person or property is willfully injured or damaged by the child's acts. This law is intended to deter children from doing "pranks" that cause damage.

Children of young ages are also considered legally incapable of negligence (or unintended wrongful acts) in Georgia, except when a child commits a harmful act using an object intended for use by an adult. Cars, tractors, chain saws, and powerboats are examples of such objects. If a child injured someone while driving the family boat, the child would have committed a tort. The parents would be liable for damages.

Corporations, governments, and individuals can be held responsible for torts. Corporations are creations of the law. They can sue and be sued. Obviously, corporations can act only through their employees. So, if injuries result from the act of an employee on the job, the corporation may be held liable.

Governments are also creations of law. Injuries may result from the actions of government officials or employees. However, in regard to torts, governments have certain immunities, meaning they may only be held liable for certain actions (note the immunity of the police officer in situation 9).

Georgia laws passed in 1987 provided civil immunity to members, directors, trustees, and unpaid officers of nonprofit charitable or government entities if they act in good faith or within the scope of their duties. Immunity is not available for willful misconduct. Health care providers in charity cases also have immunity.

How Much Do You Ask For?

One question in a lawsuit is how much the plaintiff will ask for in terms of money damages. There are two main categories of damages: actual and punitive. Actual damages cover the injury or harm suffered. Actual damages include special or compensatory damages and general damages for pain and suffering. Special or compensatory damages repay the injured party for economic loss, including repayment for lost wages and medical bills. These damages must be proven at trial with evidence of certain factors such as days missed at work, earnings per day, amount of medical bills incurred, cost of prescriptions, and amount of damage to property. General damages are damages presumed to have been sustained in an accident. For example, if you are involved in a serious car accident, the law will presume that it caused you pain and suffering. Unlike for special damages (such as lost wages, medical bills), there is no exact amount for the jury to award.

Punitive damages are the other type of damages. They are awarded in order to punish the defendant and deter others from causing harm in similar ways. These damages are assessed when wrongdoing is aggravated by violence, oppression, malice, fraud, or "wanton or wicked" conduct by the defendant.

In the 1980s, there was some reaction to the large amounts of damages being awarded by juries to plaintiffs, particularly in medical malpractice cases. Insurance premiums were raised, and there were organized protests by the premium payers and insurance industry. This outcry in turn led to legislation being passed throughout the country. In Georgia, it resulted in the Tort Reform Act of 1987.

What were some of the reforms made to reduce the amounts of damages? Several can be illustrated by earlier situations in this chapter:

> **SITUATION 14**, *continued* Mary sues the ambulance attendants for intentional infliction of emotional distress. At the trial, they say they truly believed that Mary was scheduled to deliver at the local hospital. They thought she was confused because she was in labor. The jury members like Mary; she seems sweet. They don't like the ambulance attendants who are unshaven and sloppily dressed. The jury awards Mary $1,000 in actual damages and $1 million in punitive damages. The ambulance service's insurance does not cover punitive damages.

Before the 1987 law, Mary could have collected the million dollars. Now, however, the law puts caps on punitive damages. Further, it sets a higher standard of proof of misconduct. Mary would have to present clear and convincing evidence that the ambulance attendants showed malice, willful misconduct, or total lack of care in order for punitive damages to be awarded.

> **SITUATION 27**, *continued* Suppose others had joined Ron in his lawsuit, and the jury had awarded $200,000 in punitive damages.

Under the 1987 Georgia law, 75 percent of the damages awarded would go to the state and not to the parties. This law was passed to prevent victims from recovering a large windfall instead of an amount of damages that more closely par-allels the loss the plaintiff suffered. However, this stipulation applies only in product liability lawsuits.

These reforms have faced some legal challenges. In 1991, the Georgia Supreme Court struck down a provision allowing defendants to introduce evidence of other compensation (such as an insurance payment) for injuries except for death. The court ruled that neither the plaintiff's nor the defendant's wealth could be an issue.

Tort reform continues to be the focus of debate in Georgia and elsewhere. This debate is especially contentious in the area of medical malpractice. There are still no limits on the amount of punitive damages that can be awarded for medical malpractice claims. In some cases, this lack of limits has caused medical malpractice insurance costs to rise and, as a result, some hospitals have closed.

Defenses to Intentional Torts

Up to this point, we have discussed the kinds of torts for which a person may sue. But what happens to the person who is sued for a tort? There are three general types of defenses to torts: general denial, justification, and mitigation (to mitigate means to make something less severe).

The denial type of defense simply involves a defendant saying, "No, I didn't do what the plaintiff says I did." When this type of defense is employed, the jury must determine whether to believe the plaintiff or defendant. It then awards or denies damages accordingly.

To use the defense of justification, the defendant admits doing the acts complained of by the plaintiff but denies that the acts were wrong. For example, suppose you were being sued for battery. You might admit knocking down the plaintiff, but you deny that it was wrong because you were acting in self-defense. If the jury agreed with your defense, then the plaintiff would lose.

The third type of defense is mitigation. Defendants using this defense admit the conduct claimed by the plaintiff; that is, they admit their conduct was wrong. However, they attempt to reduce the amount of damages claimed by proving that they had no malice, bad faith, or intent to cause harm. Say you were sued by your neighbors for playing your stereo too loud every night. You might claim that you would have turned down the sound if you knew it bothered them. In other words, you would claim the harm was not intended. The success of your defense would depend on whether the jury agreed with it.

Defenses to Negligence and Strict Liability

If a person is sued for money damages arising from negligence, there are two main defenses available. These defenses may prevent the plaintiff from recovering money damages, or they may reduce the amount of money awarded for damages. These defenses are (1) assumption of the risk and (2) comparative (or contributory) negligence.

What if the defendant can show that the plaintiff knew about the danger but proceeded to act anyway? The plaintiff would not be able to recover damages for his or her injuries. This defense is called assumption of the risk. To be used, the risk must be a foreseeable one. Suppose Mitch goes to a baseball game and is hit by a ball fouled into the stands. The chance of that happening is foreseeable. He would have assumed the risk. However, what if Mitch were injured by a hitter throwing a bat into the stands after striking out? That risk might not be foreseeable. The batter may be liable.

Sometimes an injury is caused by the negligence of both parties. Figure 10-3 illustrates this kind of situation. Under the rule of comparative negligence, each party is assigned a percentage of the total negligence (100 percent). The plaintiff can only recover money damages if his or her percentage of negligence is less than 50 percent.

To determine the amount of an award at trial, the jury would first determine how much to give the plaintiff for his or her injury. The amount would then be reduced by the plaintiff's percentage of fault. In figure 10-3, let's say

---

FIGURE 10-3

Comparative Negligence: You Be the Jury

The Situation

Frank was negligent when he placed an obstruction in the street. It could be readily seen only in daylight.

After dark, Whitney rode his bicycle down the street. He had no headlight, and he was racing at top speed. He collided with the obstruction and was injured. Can Whitney recover money for his injuries?

The Law

Both Frank and Whitney are negligent. The rule of comparative negligence applies. To decide how much, if any, Whitney should recover, assign a percentage of negligence to each according to the amount of fault. Be sure the percentage totals 100.

Percentage of Negligence

Frank _____ % + Whitney _____ % = 100%

Whitney's medical expenses are $10,000. Use your percentages to determine how much, if any, Whitney would recover.

---

the jury awarded Whitney $10,000 for his injuries but found that he was 20 percent negligent. The total award would be $8,000 ($10,000 minus 20 percent).

In Georgia, the rule of comparative negligence has replaced the harsher rule of contributory negligence. However, contributory negligence is still used in other states. Under this harsher rule, the plaintiff could not recover any damages if he or she had been at all negligent.

In a strict liability case, the defendant would try to show that the product was not the cause of the damages or that there were no damages. Misuse of the product might also be claimed, although courts have said that some misuse should be anticipated.

Abusive Lawsuits

The Georgia legislature created a new tort that may be used as a defense by plaintiffs or defendants. It is a tort for abuse of the judicial process.

It occurs when a party brings a claim or asserts a defense with malice and without basis for it in law or fact.

> **SITUATION 28** Ben is driving along the highway, not paying attention. He rear-ends Kay's vehicle. She sues for damages. Ben claims he wasn't negligent and the accident was Kay's fault, even though he knows that's not true.

Ben may be liable under this legal principle. The defense he asserted had no basis in fact. What if his defense was that Kay had a legal duty to look in her rearview mirror every few seconds to avoid the possibility of Ben's negligence? That defense would have no basis in law. There is no such legal duty.

PROTECTION AGAINST LAWSUITS

How can you protect yourself from being sued for a tort? The amount of money damages asked for can be devastating—in the thousands of dollars. Your best protection is to exercise care in your daily activities. The law is not hard to follow. It simply requires a person to behave so as not to cause injury to the person or property of another.

However, you may further protect yourself from the consequences of a negligent act with insurance coverage. The two most common types are homeowner and automobile coverage. Insurance provides a fund of money to be used if a negligent act by the insured person causes damages. Most insurance policies do not provide coverage for intentional torts that result in harm to a person or property.

Only the Facts

1. What does it mean if a plaintiff is awarded actual damages?

2. Describe one defense for an intentional tort and one for an unintentional tort. Which defense might John use (see "Only the Facts" question 2, p. 142)?

3. How could Ben (situation 28) have protected himself from a lawsuit?

Think About

1. Explain why corporations should be able to sue and be sued.

2. "Punitive damages should not be granted at all." Why do you agree or disagree with this statement?

3. List and explain two reasons why there should be tort reform in the area of medical malpractice.

SUMMING UP

The law of torts provides a way of compensating people if they have been injured or their property damaged by others. It comes from common law, statutes, and court decisions. Although this chapter is based on the law of torts in Georgia, the general principles would hold true in other states.

The underlying principle of the law of torts is one of the moral bases of many societies: treat others as you would wish them to treat you. The rules of tort law are really commonsense standards of conduct. By following them, we protect our own rights and those of others.

Notes

1. *State v. McAfee*, 259 Ga. 579, 385 S.E.2d 657 (1989).

2. See O.C.G.A. §§31-32-1–31-32-12.

3. Adapted from Justice Andrews's dissenting opinion in *Palsgraf v. Long Island R.R. Co.*, 248 N.Y. 339 (1928).

11 Behind the Wheel

CASE STUDY

CASE OF THE NEW DRIVER

Tina and her older brother, Walter, are waiting in line at the Georgia State Patrol office. They and their parents have recently moved to Georgia from New York. Tina, who just turned 17, has discovered that Georgia requires that she be 18 before she can be fully licensed to drive. In the meantime, she is applying for the Class D temporary license. Walter drove her to the patrol office, but she'll get to drive on the way home.

Before you may legally operate a motor vehicle on Georgia's public highways, you must have a valid driver's license. A driver's license carries with it great responsibility. More Americans die as a result of motor vehicle accidents than any other cause. Thousands more are permanently disabled. An auto is a means of transportation. It can be a source of pleasure—but it can also be deadly. Therefore many rules and regulations govern the use of motor vehicles. This chapter looks at some of these rules and regulations. It also discusses auto insurance, what happens when there is an accident, and traffic court.

TRAFFIC SAFETY LAWS

Getting a License

Each state sets its own requirements regarding the licensing of drivers, but requirements tend to be similar among states. A motor vehicle license must be carried at all times when operating a vehicle. Failure to drive without carrying a valid license is a misdemeanor in Georgia and can result in a fine. Driving a vehicle is a privilege and not a right. Accordingly, the government has the right to take away that privilege if you disobey the laws.

LAW TALK

driver's license

driving under the influence (DUI)

liability insurance

motorist insurance

uninsured

In Georgia, licenses are classified according to the type of vehicle to be operated. The Class C driver's license is the one that most people use. Essentially, a Class C license entitles a driver to operate a car or a pickup truck. An applicant must be at least 18 years old to obtain a Class C license. There are other classes of licenses that permit drivers to operate motorcycles, buses, or larger trucks.

Any Georgia resident who is at least 15 years old may apply for an instruction (or learner's) permit to drive a Class C vehicle (that is, a car or pickup truck). The applicant for an instruction permit must pass the same exams that all other driver's license applicants must pass, except for the driving test. The instruction permit is valid for two years, and it permits the holder to drive only when accompanied by a person who is at least 21 years old and holds a valid Class C driver's license.

Georgia recently changed some of the licensing requirements for teenagers. The Teenage and Adult Driver Responsibility Act, passed in 1999 and amended in 2001, created the Class D (or intermediate) license for drivers who are at least 16 years old. Unless a teenager has a valid license from another state when he or she becomes a resident of Georgia, he or she must complete an alcohol and drug awareness course. All driver's license applicants, including teenagers seeking a Class D license, must pass tests on their understanding of traffic-control devices, traffic laws, and safe driving practices in Georgia, in addition to an on-the-road driving test.

To be eligible for the Class D license, an applicant must be at least 16 years old, have had a valid instruction permit for the previous 12 months, and have not been convicted of certain driving violations in the 12 months prior to application. Some of these offenses are violation of DUI laws, hit-and-run, drag racing, eluding a police officer, and reckless driving. A Georgia teenager who has a valid Class D license may apply for the Class C driver's license at age 18 if he or she has not been convicted of any of those same driving violations in the 12 months prior to application. Applicants for a Class C license who already hold a Class D license are exempt from the on-the-road driving test.

The Class D license puts certain restrictions on drivers. A Class D license holder may not drive between the hours of 12:00 midnight and 6:00 a.m. Furthermore, a Class D license holder may not drive when there are more than three other passengers in the car who are younger than 21 years old and who are not members of the driver's immediate family. Finally, during the six-month period immediately following the issuance of a Class D license, the holder may not drive a car or truck when any other passenger in the vehicle is not a member of the driver's immediate family. A Class D license holder can be charged with a violation of these laws only in addition to being charged with any other traffic offense.

In order for a person under 18 years old to obtain a driver's license, he or she must be enrolled in school and satisfy certain attendance requirements or be enrolled in a state-certified home schooling program. Otherwise, it must be proved that the applicant received a high school diploma, a general educational development (GED) equivalency diploma, a special diploma, or a certificate of high school completion or that there is parental permission to withdraw from school or that the applicant has left high school and enrolled in college. Applicants who are enrolled in high school cannot obtain a driver's license if they have been suspended for threatening a teacher or other school personnel or for possession or sale of drugs or alcohol on school property or possession or use of a weapon on school property.

An applicant for a Class D license must also have completed an approved driver education course and must have at least 20 hours of driving experience supervised by someone at least 21 years old, including at least six hours at night. Applicants who have not completed a driver education course must have at least 40 hours of supervised driving experience.

Licenses to operate motor vehicles are required in most foreign countries and all states.

Requirements vary from state to state. For example, some states require driving tests to be performed in traffic. In Georgia, if a road test is required, it may be taken on a driving course. The age of licensing also varies. As already discussed, in Georgia, the minimum age for a learner's permit is 15; for an intermediate license, 16; and for an unrestricted license, 18. Although requirements might differ from state to state, a Georgia license is valid in all other states, but a learner's permit may not be. A Georgia license is valid in some foreign countries but not in others.

At some time, you might move from Georgia to live in another state or country. You will then have to get a driver's license in that jurisdiction. Similarly, someone moving to Georgia from another state or country must get a Georgia driver's license. In Georgia, the license must be obtained within 30 days after moving to the state. An out-of-state student (who pays nonresident tuition) does not have to obtain a Georgia driver's license, however. The student may drive in Georgia with a valid license from his or her home state.

Regulating Vehicles and Traffic

CASE OF THE NEW DRIVER, *continued*

With her intermediate driver's license tucked in her wallet, Tina turned on the ignition of the family's car. Walter sat beside her. Halfway home, Tina stopped for a red light. After a few seconds, Walter said impatiently, "You can turn. Don't you know the rules? Don't you know that you can turn right on red if it's clear?" "There's a lot to remember," Tina said, embarrassed.

Once you have a license, you may operate motor vehicles on the public roads. However, more is required than getting behind the wheel and turning the key. Every driver must obey the laws governing the operation of motor vehicles.

The purpose of traffic laws is to provide rules that will allow the safe operation of motor vehicles on streets and highways. The basic goal

There are many rules and regulations that a new driver has to remember.

is to prevent more than one vehicle from occupying the same space at the same time. Several types of laws apply to operating motor vehicles. First, as has been discussed, there are rules and regulations that govern the licensing of vehicle operators. Second, there are regulations that require the registering and licensing of the vehicles themselves. Some states have laws requiring vehicles to be inspected every year by qualified mechanics.

In Georgia, in counties with populations greater than 200,000, cars and light trucks have to be inspected for emissions control. This requirement is part of a federal program to reduce air pollution. The required annual inspection includes air pumps, filters, catalytic converters, and the level of exhaust emissions.

Various kinds of laws concern vehicles. For example, a 1991 bill made it a misdemeanor to play a car stereo so loud it can be heard 100 feet away. Some people oppose this law. They say it limits their freedom of speech. Still another Georgia law limits the tinting of motor vehicle windows. The law was passed to make it easier for police officers to see into vehicles. It was opposed by owners who had to replace tinted windows at their own expense. Do you think that is fair?

There are also laws that regulate the actual manner of operating motor vehicles. In this state, these laws are collectively called the Uniform Rules of the Road. They are found in Title 40 of the Georgia Code. Among them are laws passed to increase the safety of drivers and passengers. In 1988, Georgia enacted a law requiring the occupant of each front seat of a passenger vehicle to wear a seat belt. A driver can be fined for failure to wear a seat belt. Georgia also has a law requiring children under four years old to be restrained in an approved car seat when riding in a motor vehicle.

Special safety regulations apply to motorcycles. Georgia law requires every motorcycle driver and passenger to wear some sort of footwear. They must also wear a safety helmet with an eye shield. Although the safety values of these requirements are generally accepted, these laws have been controversial. The issue is, should the decision to wear a helmet or seat belt be left to the individual? Or is the safety of individuals enough in the public interest for the government to require these safety precautions? What do you think?

Who Makes the Traffic Laws?

The basic rules of licensing, inspection, and operation of motor vehicles are made by state legislatures. Generally, these rules are adopted by city and county governments, and they allow city and country police officers to enforce state traffic laws. This system builds consistency into the way traffic laws are enforced across the state.

Local governments, however, may regulate speed limits on roads within their boundaries—except on interstate highways. This local control explains why one city may have a speed limit of 30 miles per hour (mph) on its streets and another city may have a 35 mph speed limit. Local governments also decide where to put traffic-regulating devices such as signs and lights.

The federal government also exerts some control, usually by setting requirements for funding. For example, to reduce gasoline usage after the petroleum shortage in the early 1970s, it required states to set a maximum speed limit of 55 mph or lose federal highway monies. A similar kind of pressure was exerted on states to change the legal drinking age to 21 years.

Effective July 1, 1996, speed limits were increased to 65 mph and 75 mph on certain highways. Which speed was allowed depended on the population in the area. Because there are now different speed limits on highways, you must pay special attention to posted signs.

State laws are not all alike, but states do try to make traffic signs and rules of the road uniform. This uniformity helps make travel from one state to another safe and easy. Among foreign countries, there are many differences in traffic regulations. For example, in England and Japan, people drive on the left-hand side of the road.

Penalties for traffic violations also differ in other countries. In many countries, the penalties for driving under the influence of alcohol or drugs are more severe than in the United States. In some countries, your auto may be impounded (or seized) if you commit a traffic violation.

Only the Facts

1. Which of the following are state requirements for Class D driver's license applicants? (a) must be at least 18 years old; (b) must pass a test on understanding of official traffic-control devices; (c) must pass a test on basic car maintenance; (d) must pass a test on knowledge of safe driving practices and Georgia's traffic laws; (e) must have taken a driver's education course and have 20 hours of supervised driving or 40 total hours of supervised driving; (f) must take an on-the-road driving test; (g) must have a high school diploma or the equivalent; (h) must have a license to drive a motorcycle; and (i) must have completed an alcohol and drug awareness course.

2. To whom does a Class D driver's license apply? What driving restrictions does this intermediate license put on teenagers?

3. What three types of laws apply to the operation of motor vehicles?

Think About

1. Licenses have to be renewed periodically. Should a person be able to get a lifetime license? Should there be a maximum as well as a minimum age?

2. "I think the law should require motorcycle drivers to wear helmets." List arguments for and against this statement.

3. Should penalties for violating the seatbelt law be more severe? If so, what should they be?

4. "Rules and regulations for operating motor vehicles should be the same in all states and countries." Explain why you agree or disagree.

WHEN THERE IS AN ACCIDENT

CASE STUDY

CASE OF THE NEW DRIVER, *continued*

Tina and Walter were on a two-lane highway near their home. Suddenly, the car in front of them slowed down almost to a stop as it began turning right. There was no signal, no brake lights. Tina was too close to stop in time.

It was not a hard crash. They were not hurt.

Tina and Walter got out of the car to survey the damage. The driver of the other car was a man about their father's age, Mr. Elder. The rear bumper of his vehicle was bent, one taillight was broken, and the trunk was sprung open. The right headlight of Tina's car was broken, and the right front fender was dented.

Walter said, "I'll go to one of these houses and call the police. Wait here, Tina, and don't move anything."

When your car hits another car, you must stop at the scene of the accident unless there is no injury and no property damage. Hit-and-run driving is a serious crime in all states. In Georgia, it can be punished by fine or imprisonment—even if you didn't cause the accident. If you panic and flee, return to the scene of the accident or report to a police station. The penalty may be reduced if you do.

In Georgia, on two-lane streets, the law requires the driver of an auto involved in a collision to stop his or her vehicle immediately. The driver should try to create the least obstruction possible for other traffic.

On expressways or multilane highways, the same rule holds if there is an injury, death, or extensive property damage. If there is not, the driver should move the vehicle to a median or safety lane. The driver should not move the vehicle, however, if it would further damage the vehicle or create a safety hazard.

In any accident, notify the police or sheriff's department at once. Tell them if an ambulance is needed. If you are in an accident and it is the other person's fault, that driver may try to persuade you that calling the police is not necessary. He or she may offer to pay for the damage and suggest that you both deal with the situation later. However, the driver may change his or her mind or give you false information. It is in your best interest to call the police and get a police report. If you should hit an unoccupied car, try to find the owner. If that's not possible, leave a note with your name and telephone number.

CASE STUDY

CASE OF THE NEW DRIVER, *continued*

While they waited, Tina and Mr. Elder swapped names, addresses, driver's license numbers, tag numbers, and the names and addresses of their insurance companies.

Soon a police officer, Patrick Rolle, arrived. After being satisfied that there were no injuries, Officer Rolle asked Tina and Mr. Elder for their driver's licenses. He also asked for proof of liability insurance coverage. While getting this information, he watched them closely. He was looking for signs that either was under the influence of alcohol or drugs.

In the 1980s, public concern about accidents and fatalities caused by drunk driving increased. As a result, Georgia, like other states, toughened its DUI (driving under the influence) laws. The legal drinking age was increased from 18 to 21 years of age. Local laws were passed banning "happy hours" or prohibiting open containers of alcoholic drinks on public streets. Lawsuit decisions made private hosts and bartenders responsible for accidents caused by persons who were unfit to drive when they left the host's home or a bar.

Anyone under 21 years old who is convicted of underage possession of alcohol while operating a motor vehicle may have his or her license suspended for 120 days. The license can be reinstated only after the person completes a DUI alcohol and drug awareness program. In addition, any person under 21 who is convicted of attempting to buy alcohol will have his or her license suspended for six months for the first offense and for one year for any subsequent convictions.

Drivers who are suspected of being under the influence of alcohol or drugs will be arrested. They will be asked to take a breath analysis or blood-alcohol test. A person can refuse. However, a refusal will result in an automatic suspension of the driver's license. On the other hand, the field sobriety tests noted in figure 11-1 are voluntary. There is no adverse consequence that directly stems from refusing to take the tests, but a refusal may be used against a person in a subsequent trial for DUI.

Under Georgia law, a person with 0.08 gram blood alcohol content is considered to be DUI without further evidence. An even lower level of 0.02 is set for drivers under the age of 21. If a person is convicted of DUI, his or her license can be suspended for up to a year for a first offense, up to three years for a second, and entirely revoked for a third. In order for a driver's license to be reinstated, the driver must complete an approved alcohol and drug course and pay a fine. Persons convicted of DUI will most likely go to jail as well. For a first offense, imprisonment could be 10 days to 12 months; for a second of-

FIGURE 11-1

If Stopped by a Police Officer

- When an officer signals you to pull over, slow down. Look for the first opportunity to pull off safely on the right side of road.
- Stay inside your car and roll down the window.
- Step outside only if asked to do so by the officer. He or she may check to see if you are under influence of drugs or alcohol.
- If the officer thinks you are under the influence of alcohol, he or she may require that you step out of your car. You may then be asked to perform field sobriety tests, including walking a line, touching your nose, and saying the alphabet. These tests are 100 percent voluntary. You may refuse to submit to them.
- Provide the officer with your license and proof of insurance when asked.
- Provide the officer with any reason for violating a traffic code after the officer explains why you were pulled over.
- Always be polite. Officers have some discretion in issuing citations.
- The officer may take your license and issue you a temporary license to ensure that you appear in court. The citation should indicate when and where your court appearance will be.
- Never try to flee when an officer attempts to pull you over. Doing so will increase penalties against you, including the possibility of license suspension. It may also result in your being charged with the crime of evading a police officer.

fense, 90 days to 12 months; and for a third offense, 120 days to 12 months. In addition, community service must be completed: 40 hours for a first offense and 30 days for any subsequent offenses. Fines are as follows: $300–$1,000 for a first offense; $600–$1,000 for a second offense, and $1,000–$5,000 for any subsequent offenses.

Being convicted of DUI can affect you in other ways, too. Your insurance rates will go up. It may also be hard to get insurance. Other costs in addition to a bail bond fee for release after arrest might include a surcharge on the fine or charges for reinstating a license, towing a car to your home, transportation while your license is suspended, and enrollment in an alcohol abuse prevention program.

CASE STUDY

CASE OF THE NEW DRIVER, *continued*

Officer Rolle asked each driver separately to explain how the collision took place. He also interviewed Walter as a witness to the accident. Then Officer Rolle studied the positions of the cars. He drew a diagram of the accident that showed the skid marks of each vehicle. He also looked at the damage done to each car.

After his investigation, he had to decide whether to charge one or both of the drivers with traffic violations. The skid marks indicated that Tina was probably going a little too fast. He charged her with operating her vehicle too fast for conditions. Officer Rolle charged Mr. Elder with making an improper turn and having defective brake lights.

Officer Rolle then issued citations to Tina and Mr. Elder. The citations directed them to appear at traffic court at a specified time and date.

After any automobile collision, each driver should report the accident to his or her automobile insurance company as soon as possible. If the accident has no investigating officer and results in injuries, death, or property damage in excess of $500, the driver must file an accident report. This report is sent to the Commissioner of Public Safety of Georgia.

O n l y   t h e   F a c t s

1. List three things a driver of a vehicle should do following an accident.
2. List three observations or items of information a police officer would make or gather at the scene of an accident.

T h i n k   A b o u t

1. Why is "hit-and-run" a serious crime?

2. What do you think penalties should be for a DUI, first offense, where there are no serious injuries or damages? for a DUI, first offense, in which several people are killed? Give reasons for your answers.

AUTO INSURANCE

CASE STUDY

CASE OF THE NEW DRIVER, *continued*

Tina's parents were glad no one was hurt, but they were not exactly pleased about the accident. They told Tina to phone the insurance company right away. They said the insurance company would need to have as much information as possible, starting with the insurance policy number.

Every person who drives a vehicle in the state of Georgia is required to have insurance on that motor vehicle. The purpose is to protect people who travel on the public roads. In this way, if they are involved in an accident, they can be compensated for their loss. Compensation includes general and special damages. Special damages include payment for medical bills, lost wages, and repair of vehicle damage. General damages include pain and suffering.

The law requires that each person carry proof of insurance and that such proof be shown upon request by presenting an insurance card that provides the name and address of the company, the policy number, and the name of the insured ("named insured"). What does it mean to be a "named insured"? In the case of Tina and Walter, Tina was driving her parents' vehicle. The name of the insured would probably be her parents, not Tina specifically. How is it that she is covered under her parents' policy? Most insurance policies cover not only the main owner or driver of the vehicle but also "insured persons," including resident relatives (relatives who live in the same household) and permissive users (those given permission to use the vehicle). For example, if Tina's mother owned the vehicle and her sister came to town and drove it, the sister would be considered a permissive user. She would, therefore, also be insured. Thus, if Tina's aunt drives negligently and causes an accident, Tina's mother's insurance company would cover her for her negligent acts. It would also pay any claims filed against her.

What about Tina? Well, Tina is certainly a resident relative because she lives with her parents. Therefore she is insured under their policy. She does not have to go out and get her own insurance policy. However, most insurance companies want to know the names of all persons who may drive the car. In all likelihood, Tina is named on her parents' policy. In some instances, the insurance company will attempt to exclude a particular person, like a teenager. It is therefore very important to read the insurance policy to see if anybody or anything in particular is excluded from coverage.

A person who purchases insurance coverage may choose, to some extent, the type of coverage and the amount of coverage he or she wants (see figure 11-2). Types of coverage include the following:

- liability—automobile insurance coverage that pays damages to other parties for injuries or property loss when the insured is at fault;
- comprehensive—automobile insurance coverage that pays for damages to the insured vehicle when the damage occurs other than by collision;
- collision—automobile insurance coverage that pays for damage resulting from collision even when the insured is at fault; and
- uninsured motorist coverage—automobile insurance coverage that protects the insured from loss in automobile accidents in which the other driver is at fault and is uninsured.

Automobile liability insurance and uninsured motorist coverage are required by law, with minimum coverage limits of $25,000. A person can have more coverage—in fact, as much coverage as he or she wants or is willing to pay for. Collision insurance is not required, and sometimes people with older vehicles choose not to purchase it. Other types of coverage may also be optional. A declaration page (part of an insurance policy) sets forth the type and the amount of coverage the person has purchased. Figure 11-3 is an example of a declaration page.

However, many people who buy insurance do not ask enough questions about it until they need to make use of it—usually, not until they get into an accident. At that time, they may discover that they don't have enough insurance, particularly in the case of uninsured motorist coverage (explained later in this section).

Liability Coverage

Liability insurance coverage extends to both property damage (vehicle and other property) and personal injury.

FIGURE 11-2

Auto Insurance

Type of Auto Insurance	Required by Georgia Law?	What Does It Protect?	Whom Does It Compensate?	Based on Fault?
Liability	yes	person and property	others	yes
Collision	no	property	self	no
Comprehensive	no	property	self	no
Uninsured motorist	yes	person and property	self and passengers	yes

Note: Georgia law requires motorcycle operators to have liability insurance. The other types of coverage are not required.

FIGURE 11-3

Automobile Declaration

INFORMATION ON COVERED VEHICLES

UNIT	ST	TER	YR	VEHICLE DESC	VIN	SYM	CLASS	DRVID
00001	GA	001	96	HONDA ACCORD	IHGBA5325GA142365	8	886110	00001

COVERAGE IS PROVIDED ONLY WHERE A LIMIT OF LIABILITY OR PREMIUM IS SHOWN

COVERAGE	LIMIT OF LIABILITY ($) PERSON	/ ACCIDENT	PREM ($) UNIT00001	DED ($)
BODILY INJURY	100,000	300,000	153	
PROPERTY DAMAGE	50,000		156	
MEDICAL PAYMENTS	5,000		42	
UNINSURED MTR – BI	100,000	300,000	98	
UNINSURED MTR – PD	50,000		6	
COMPREHENSIVE	(unlimited)		40	100
TOWING & LABOR	25		4	
EXTND TRANSPORTATION	15	450		
TOTAL UNIT PREMIUMS: (per six-month period)			499	

Note: All figures represent dollar amounts.

Personal Injury

The personal injury portion of liability coverage provides coverage when the insured person's (usually the driver's) negligence or fault causes an accident in which another party is injured. The coverage of the at-fault party (the negligent party) is made available to the victim of the accident. Figure 11-3 shows Tina's coverage. She has $100,000 liability insurance for each person but no more than $300,000 for each accident. It should be noted that a person who is injured is not limited in his or her recovery to the amount of insurance available: the injured party may also sue the at-fault party for damage over the amount of insurance available.

Property Damage

The liability coverage provided by an insurance policy pays for damage to another person's prop-

erty caused by the insured. Note that Tina's liability coverage is $50,000. In her collision, Tina also badly damaged the other car. The driver of that car can make a claim against her for the amount of damage done to the car—up to $50,000. On the other hand, say Tina drives negligently, loses control of her car, and crashes into somebody's house. That homeowner's claim against Tina would be covered under this portion of Tina's insurance policy as well.

Collision

If you have collision coverage—and many people don't—your insurance company will pay for the damage done to your own auto as a result of a collision, even if the accident is your fault. You will have to pay the amount you chose as the deductible when you took out your policy (usually $100, $250, or $500), but the insurance company will pay for the remaining amount of the loss. A deductible is defined as the amount of loss an insured person pays for him- or herself when a claim is filed against the insurance he or she has.

If you are in an accident and the other person is at fault, you have two options. You can have your insurance company pay under your policy's collision coverage, or you can try to make the at-fault party pay. You will probably be reimbursed for the loss more quickly if your own insurance company pays. If you decide to have your own insurance company pay, you will have to pay the deductible as previously discussed. However, because the accident is not your fault, at some point you most probably will be reimbursed for the deductible by the at-fault party.

Comprehensive

Another type of property damage coverage protection is called comprehensive coverage. It is provided by a person's own insurance company for his or her own vehicle. It covers damage from any cause except collision. This coverage would include damage to a person's car from fire, wind, water, or other natural causes. It would also protect the insurance holder if the auto were stolen or if a rock flying up from the roadway broke the windshield. Comprehensive coverage is not required under Georgia law. Note that in figure 11-3, the policy includes comprehensive. The insured has unlimited coverage, pays a premium of $40 every six months, and has a deductible of $100.

Uninsured Motorist Coverage

Uninsured motorist (UM) coverage is perhaps one of the most necessary types of automobile insurance. Using Tina as an example, let's say she is driving along when somebody hits her car. Tina is rushed to the hospital with a broken arm and leg, which require surgery. She has to wear a cast for three months and undergo rehabilitation for six months. Her medical bills are $60,000.

Tina doesn't have any health insurance but is covered by her mother's car insurance policy.

If you have collision coverage, your insurance company will pay for the damage done to your own auto in an accident.

However, the car insurance provides for only $5,000 in medical benefits.

Who will pay for Tina's medical bills? The person who hit her? What if that person carries only the minimum liability limit required in Georgia—$25,000? That amount certainly won't be enough to pay for Tina's medical bills. This situation is when Tina's uninsured motorist coverage comes into play. Because the person who hit her is underinsured (not enough insurance), Tina will be able to make a claim against her own insurance company. The same would be true if the person who hit her were uninsured (had no insurance at all).

How much can Tina get from her insurance company? She is eligible to receive up to the difference between her UM coverage and the liability coverage of the at-fault driver. Her UM coverage is $100,000/$300,000—in other words, her policy will pay up to $100,000 per person hurt in an accident but with a maximum of $300,000 total paid out per accident. Because the other person's liability coverage is $25,000, Tina could get up to $75,000 under her UM coverage, more than enough to pay for all of her medical bills. Of course, she can get no more than the amount needed to cover the full amount of her bills.

Most people in Georgia carry little UM coverage. Georgia law requires only $25,000 UM coverage.

If Tina had only $25,000 UM coverage, what would happen to her? She has $60,000 in medical bills, and the person who hit her can pay $25,000 under his liability policy, leaving a balance owed of $35,000. Tina's medical benefits will pay $5,000. Her balance is now $30,000. How much can she collect from her own insurance company under her UM coverage? Nothing. She can recover only the difference between her UM coverage and the at-fault party's liability amount. She has $25,000 in UM coverage; the other party has $25,000 in liability coverage. The difference between the two is zero, leaving Tina with the $30,000 balance that she'll have to figure out how to pay. As in the previous example, she could sue the person who hit her. But if the person only has $25,000 in coverage and doesn't have a good job, a house, and other property, Tina will probably never recover more than the $25,000 policy limit.

Purchasing Auto Insurance

If you own or operate an automobile, you must purchase insurance. There are many insurance companies doing business in Georgia. The rates they charge vary. The rates depend on factors such as the applicant's age, sex, marital status, and driving history. They also vary with the type of motor vehicle to be insured.

Rates for younger persons, particularly those under 21 years, are higher than for the general population. They are higher for young men than for young women; studies have shown that men in this age bracket cause more accidents than do women. There is evidence, however, that some young people are more likely than other drivers to be safe. Therefore some insurance companies reduce rates somewhat for young drivers who have, for example, taken driver's education courses or who make good grades. As long as accident statistics show young drivers cause a large proportion of accidents, the high insurance rates are likely to prevail.

The dollar amounts of coverage will also affect the rates charged. As mentioned earlier, a person may elect to have a large amount of coverage, but the insurance costs will be high, too. The type of coverage also will affect the cost. For example, a person may choose to have full coverage, including liability, collision, comprehensive, and uninsured motorist coverage. Such a policy would cost more than one with just the required liability coverage.

O n l y   t h e   F a c t s

1. What types of auto insurance are required in Georgia?
2. What types protect you against the costly effects of your own negligence?
3. What types of auto insurance cover property damage?
4. Why is it so important to have adequate uninsured motorist coverage?

T h i n k   A b o u t

1. Why do you think the state requires that people have liability but not collision insurance?
2. Should a driver pay for uninsured motorist coverage because other drivers aren't properly covered? Does that seem fair? Why or why not?

GOING TO TRAFFIC COURT

Most traffic violations are misdemeanors. Misdemeanors are less serious crimes than felonies. In Georgia, traffic misdemeanors may be handled by the county probate court, state court, magistrate court, juvenile court, or a municipal court.

Drivers younger than 16 have their cases heard in juvenile court. The driver's parents and/or any witnesses he or she wishes to call may be present. As in adult court, the police officer may give evidence. The driver (or his or her attorney) may cross-examine the witnesses. Penalties for a misdemeanor traffic offense for a juvenile may be a reprimand, suspension of driver's license, requirement to attend traffic school, and/or a fine. More serious traffic offenses are treated as delinquent acts, and the consequences can be significantly more serious.

CASE STUDY

CASE OF THE NEW DRIVER, *continued*

Tina reported to traffic court at the time indicated on her summons. She saw Mr. Elder there. The room was crowded with people charged with traffic offenses. Judge Rhodes sat at the front of the court. There was no jury.

Each case was called in turn. First, the judge called the name of the person charged with the violation. Then he gave the charge(s) against him or her. He asked if the person understood the charges.

When called, Tina pleaded not guilty to driving too fast for conditions. She told the judge the speed limit was 40 mph on the road where the accident occurred and that she was going only 35 mph.

She called Walter as a witness. Walter said that he was a passenger in the car. He said he was watching closely because Tina had just gotten her license. He confirmed that she was going 35 mph.

The judge asked Tina about weather conditions and traffic congestion at the time of the accident.

Judge Rhodes also called upon the investigating officer. Officer Rolle said the skid marks at the scene of the accident indicated that Tina was driving too fast to avoid the collision.

Many people plead guilty to traffic offenses even if they think they are innocent because the courts will often accept the testimony of the arresting officer without proof to the contrary. Without witnesses, such proof may be impossible to obtain. Admissions of guilt become part of a person's driving record.

If a person pleads or is found guilty, the penalty depends on the offense. It also depends on whether or not the person has any past criminal or traffic violation record. The judge can require a fine or levy a jail sentence. In addition, depending on the offense, the Department of Public Safety (which regulates licenses) may suspend or revoke the person's license (see figure 11-4). Some traffic court judges require guilty drivers to attend driver training classes, or they may require drug and alcohol abuse education classes. In some states, a driver does not have to appear in court if he or she pleads guilty. The driver can simply mail in the fine charged for the offense.

FIGURE 11-4

When Can a Driver's License Be Taken Away?

A driver's license will be suspended when the driver

- is convicted of a homicide while operating a vehicle.
- fraudulently applies for or uses a driver's license.
- races on the highways.
- attempts to flee by car from a police officer.
- commits a "hit-and-run" or leaves the scene of an accident.
- fails to pay for gasoline on two or more occasions.
- fails to appear in traffic court at the appointed time and date for any offense other than a parking violation.
- refuses to take a blood, breath, or chemical test to determine if he or she is driving under the influence of alcohol. (The license will be automatically suspended but will be returned if the driver is found not guilty.)
- accumulates 15 or more points (see figure 11-5) in 24 months, unless the driver takes a driver training class and reduces the number of points.
- operates a motor vehicle while under the influence of drugs or alcohol.
- is convicted of certain drug offenses even if the driver wasn't under the influence of drugs while driving.
- fails to comply with a court order mandating that he or she pay child support.
- is convicted of driving without insurance.
- is under 21 and is convicted of reckless driving (in which case, his or her license will be revoked).

Every time a driver is convicted of violating traffic laws, he or she is assigned points. These points are recorded in that person's driving record (see figure 11-5). If a driver accumulates a total of 15 or more points during any 24-month period, his or her license will be suspended or revoked. The 1997 Georgia driver responsibility legislation set stiffer penalties for young drivers. Drivers under 21 may have their licenses suspended for any of the offenses in figure 11-5 that earn four or more points, and drivers under 18 may have their licenses suspended for accumulating 4 or more points during any 12-month period.

Decisions of traffic courts can be appealed to the superior courts. Usually, however, the costs of appeal by far cancel out the possible advantages, especially where misdemeanor offenses are concerned.

CASE STUDY

CASE OF THE NEW DRIVER, *concluded*

Judge Rhodes told Tina that even though she was driving below the posted speed limit, she was still required to adjust her speed to the condition of the road. He found her guilty and fined her $20. Mr. Elder pleaded guilty to making an improper turn and having no brake lights. He was fined $15 and had three points added to his driving record.

Felony Traffic Offenses

The three most common traffic violations that can result in felony charges are vehicular homicide, serious injury by vehicle, and habitual violator. These felonies are tried in a superior court in Georgia, as are all other felonies.

Vehicular homicide involves a situation in which a person is killed by an auto. The driver at fault may have been driving under the influence of alcohol or drugs, driving recklessly, or fleeing from police officers. This offense is usually a felony and in most cases carries a penalty of 2 to 10 years in prison.

Serious injury by vehicle also occurs when a driver injures another person while violating DUI or reckless driving laws. A serious injury

---

FIGURE 11-5

Traffic Violations and Points in Georgia

- reckless driving—4 points
- unlawful passing of a school bus—6 points
- improper passing on a hill or curve—4 points
- exceeding the speed limit by more than 14 miles per hour but less than 19 miles per hour—2 points
- exceeding the speed limit by 19 or more miles per hour but less than 24 miles per hour—3 points
- exceeding the speed limit by 24 or more miles per hour but less than 34 miles per hour—4 points
- exceeding the speed limit by 34 or more miles per hour—6 points
- failure to obey a traffic control device or traffic officer—3 points
- all other moving violations—3 points
- possessing an open container of alcoholic beverage while driving—2 points

Note: Once in every five-year period, a driver can have his or her point record reduced by 7 points if he or she completes a driver education course.

---

would be loss of use of any part of the body, including brain damage. This violation of law is considered a felony and carries a penalty of 1 to 15 years in prison.

A number of acts can cause a driver to be classified as a habitual violator by the Department of Public Safety. A person is declared a habitual violator if he or she commits three offenses during a five-year period consisting of any combination of certain serious offenses or DUIs. A habitual violator may have his or her license revoked for five years. He or she can also receive one to five years in prison and/or a fine of not less than $1,000.

After being charged with a traffic violation, a driver must decide whether an attorney is needed to assist in the defense of the charge. Many persons attend traffic court on misdemeanor traffic offenses without having an attorney. However, very few attend court without an attorney when they are charged with felony traffic offenses.

Driving under the influence (DUI) is the cause of many serious traffic accidents. How has the government responded to public concern about this issue?

Only the Facts

1. What courts in Georgia can try traffic misdemeanors? What court in your community tries traffic misdemeanors?
2. Jennifer is found guilty of reckless driving four times in two years. What may happen to her?
3. What kinds of traffic offenses are felonies rather than misdemeanors?

Think About

1. If people want to plead guilty to traffic offenses, should their cases be handled outside court? State an advantage and a disadvantage.
2. Some people believe that the penalties for vehicular homicide or habitual violators are too mild. What do you think and why?
3. What do you think about the penalties given to Tina and Mr. Elder? Were they fair?

SUMMING UP

The development of the automobile has resulted in a complex network of laws. In this chapter, you have learned about the rules and regulations that govern the use of motor vehicles. You now know about the different types of driver's licenses, how traffic laws are made and enforced, what happens when there is an accident, and the various kinds of insurance and their importance. Governments in different countries and states respond differently to issues having to do with the operation of motor vehicles and driver safety. As with so many laws, those to do with the operation of motor vehicles ultimately reflect societal changes.

12 In a Lawsuit

You probably have some idea of what is involved in the criminal justice process, if only through watching television programs. But you may know less about the civil justice process, even though there are more civil than criminal law cases.

As you may recall, a main function of our courts is to settle disputes. The process of settling a dispute through court action is called litigation. This chapter is a case study of a civil law proceeding. The characters are imaginary, but the situation is based on what could take place in a real case. The main character in the case will receive an injury. She will then seek payment from the party whom she believes to be legally responsible.

Watch in this chapter for what lawyers do to prepare for a case. As the case moves toward the actual trial, note how it becomes more like verbal combat—in other words, more adversarial. Note the rules that define or limit this adversarial tendency. The rules are intended to ensure that each party will have a fair hearing. Finally, in reading this chapter, consider how the civil justice process might be streamlined.

BEGINNINGS OF THE CASE

The Accident

Mary Jones is an 18-year-old senior at Druid Valley High School in DeKalb County, Georgia. Mary is an excellent student. She also works part-time at McDougal's drive-in restaurant. It is a few blocks from her home. On the night of May 7, Mary leaves work at 11 p.m. She decides to walk home. On the way home, she begins to worry about a big test she has the next day. Mary stops at the traffic light on Druid Avenue. As soon as the light turns green, Mary begins to cross the street. A car approaches to Mary's left, coming fast, without lights. When the driver notices Mary, he slams on his brakes. The car skids into Mary. Its front bumper hits her at knee-level. She is knocked to the pavement. The car finally skids to a stop. The driver gets out to see how Mary is.

The 23-year-old driver of the car, John Smith, has had a terrible evening. He has been worrying about his job. He has just had a fight with his girlfriend. And now—this!

There is a witness to the accident. At the time of the collision, Bill Hawkeye is walking his dog. He is on the sidewalk across the street from where Mary is hit. He immediately finds a phone and calls the police. The police arrive with an emergency medical service vehicle in about five minutes. Mary is taken to a local hospital.

Meanwhile, the police question John. After the investigation, they charge John with speeding, operating his car at night without lights, and failure to obey a traffic signal.

At the hospital, Mary is found to have a badly broken leg and assorted cuts and abrasions. The leg injury keeps her in the hospital for four weeks. Mary's hospital stay and medical care cost over $20,000.

Soon after the accident, John appears in the local traffic court. John pleads guilty to the charges. The traffic court judge imposes a fine and suspends John's driver's license.

The Claim

While in the hospital, Mary is contacted by Joe Hartness. Mr. Hartness is an insurance adjuster for John's auto insurance company, Peach State. As an injured pedestrian, Mary is entitled to receive payment for certain "economic losses" from John's insurance policy. The company pays Mary's physicians and the hospital bill.

After a time, Mary returns to school, but she continues to feel considerable pain in her left leg, particularly in the knee. It makes it impossible for her to go back to work. She begins to worry about keeping up with school and about her future. She loses weight and becomes extremely nervous.

Mary contacts Mr. Hartness, the Peach State insurance adjuster, and tells him of her continuing problems. She asks whether she is entitled to any additional benefits under John's automobile insurance coverage.

Mr. Hartness tells her that Peach State has paid benefits on her behalf under its medical payments coverage. What she is asking for now, he says, are general damages for "pain and suffering." He says his company will not pay such damages to Mary unless required to do so as the result of a lawsuit.

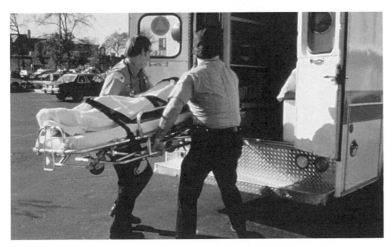

As an injured pedestrian, Mary is entitled to receive payment for her physicians and hospital bill from John's insurance policy.

Retaining a Lawyer

Mary talks to a lawyer, Fred Barr, about her case. Mr. Barr tells Mary that she is entitled to seek general and special damages from the person responsible for her injuries (John). A lawsuit can be initiated if necessary (see figure 12-1 for situations in which a lawyer may be needed). Mr. Barr explains that general damages in a personal injury action may be physical and mental pain and inability to work. Special damages are those damages that can be calculated as a result of a particular loss. For example, the wages Mary lost from work while she was in the hospital could be added and awarded as special damages.

After being retained by Mary, Mr. Barr begins to investigate the case and the surrounding circumstances. He takes written statements from the investigating police officers and the sole witness (Mr. Hawkeye). He obtains a copy of the accident report filed by the investigating officers. He also gets copies of Mary's hospital records,

Mary obtains an attorney to seek additional damages for "pain and suffering."

medical bills, and prescription receipts. From Mary's part-time employer he requests proof of her income losses during her hospitalization and recovery.

Attempt to Settle Out of Court

Mr. Barr contacts Mr. Hartness, the insurance adjuster. Mr. Barr wants to settle Mary's claim out of court, if possible. Mr. Hartness agrees to meet with Mr. Barr.

After discussing the facts of the case, the following exchange takes place.

> **Mr. Barr**: My client would be willing to accept $75,000 in settlement.
>
> **Mr. Hartness**: Based upon my company's evaluation of the case, we will offer $40,000. This is, I might add, our top offer.
>
> **Mr. Barr**: I'm sorry, I can't recommend that my client accept $40,000, although I will, of course, pass your offer along to my client. I believe that a jury would return a verdict of more than $75,000.

Unfortunately, Mr. Barr and Mr. Hartness are not able to settle Mary's case. (Neither side may offer evidence at the trial of these settlement negotiations.) Mr. Barr advises Mary to file a civil suit for damages against John. In this case, Mary Jones will be the plaintiff; John Smith, the defendant.

FIGURE 12-1

When You Need a Lawyer

Throughout this book, there are situations that show when a lawyer can be helpful. This list gives some guidelines.

In Civil Cases

- When you are sued.
- When you want to sue someone.
- When a specific right to property of some value is involved, as when buying or selling real estate.
- When you want to transfer your property to others.
- When you want to set up a business.
- When you want to end a marriage.
- When you want to protect or enforce what you consider a legal right.

In Criminal Cases

- When you are accused of a crime, especially when you may be imprisoned. You have a constitutional right to a lawyer in these cases. (If you cannot afford a lawyer, the state must provide one.)
- When you may be faced with serious consequences, such as a large fine or the loss of your driver's license.

Determining Court of Jurisdiction

Before filing (bringing) suit, the attorney must determine which court has jurisdiction over the case. You will remember that jurisdiction has two main aspects—subject matter and personal jurisdiction. That is, a court must have the authority to enforce the kinds of laws that are involved in the dispute (subject matter jurisdiction), and it must have the power to act with respect to the parties before it (personal jurisdiction).

Under Georgia law, a civil lawsuit for damages in which personal injury is involved must be brought in superior or state court. Further, Georgia law provides that the proper place of trial in a case like Mary's is the county in which the defendant resides when the lawsuit is filed. The courts in this county will have personal jurisdiction. Mr. Barr learns that John is a resident of DeKalb County, Georgia, so Mary's case is filed in the Superior Court of DeKalb County.

Think About

1. What are the advantages for each party of settling disagreements out of court?

2. Why do you think settlement negotiations are not admissible in trials?

3. Why should the court of proper venue be where the defendant—rather than the plaintiff—lives?

PLEADINGS

Complaint

To start a civil action, the plaintiff's attorney must file a complaint with the appropriate court. Filing means delivering the complaint to the court clerk. The complaint is a legal document prepared by the plaintiff or his or her attorney. It sets out, in numbered paragraph form, the plaintiff's version of the facts supporting the claim against the defendant. It indicates which court has jurisdiction. If appropriate, it names the amount of money the plaintiff is asking the defendant to pay.

Mary's complaint against John is shown in figure 12-2. It says that Mary's injuries and damages were caused by and through the negligence of

---

FIGURE 12-2

In the Superior Court for the County of Dekalb, State of Georgia

MARY JONES, Plaintiff,	vs.	JOHN SMITH, Defendant.

COMPLAINT

COMES now MARY JONES with her Complaint and for grounds thereof shows the Court the following:

I.

The Defendant, JOHN SMITH, is a resident of DeKalb County, Georgia, and whose residence address is 909 Broad Street, DeKalb County, Georgia. Said Defendant is thus subject to the jurisdiction of this Court.

2.

On or about May 7, 2003, on Decatur Road, in DeKalb County, Georgia, Defendant negligently drove his automobile against the Plaintiff, a pedestrian.

3.

As a direct and proximate result of the negligence of Defendant, Plaintiff was thrown to the ground and her leg was broken. Plaintiff suffered great pain of body and mind, and suffered a loss of income.

WHEREFORE, Plaintiff prays:

(a) That Summons and Process issue as by law provided;

(b) That she have judgment against the Defendant in the sum of one hundred and twenty-five thousand ($125,000) dollars, or whatever the jury thinks meet and proper, together with all costs of Court, and;

(c) That Plaintiff be afforded such other and further relief as may be deemed just and proper.

Fred Barr
Attorney for Plaintiff

1000 Kindler Building
Decatur, Georgia 30030
(404) 000-0000

John. To file Mary's complaint, Mr. Barr delivers it to the clerk of the Superior Court of DeKalb County (see figure 12-3 for descriptions of professionals involved in court proceedings). The clerk then assigns the case a number. This case will be number 81999.

Summons

The plaintiff in a civil case also must inform the defendant that a claim is being made against him or her. This notification is very important. The defendant is usually notified by being served (or presented with) a copy of the complaint and a paper called a summons. The summons tells the defendant that he or she has 30 days from the date of receiving the summons to respond to the claims made in the plaintiff's complaint.

In Georgia, a summons is usually hand-delivered to the defendant at his or her home. The server is usually the county sheriff or some other officer of the court. Serving is not always easy. In Mary's case, when the sheriff's deputy first went to John's home, John was not there.

The deputy returned several days later, after working hours, but John slipped out the back door. John did not want to be involved in a lawsuit. The next day, the deputy arrived as John was leaving for work and served him with the summons. (John should not intentionally avoid being served with the complaint. It is against the law to do so, and there could be serious legal consequences.)

Answer

After receiving the summons, the defendant should respond to the plaintiff's claims. The response is called the answer. The answer is a legal document that is filed with the clerk of the court. In it, the defendant admits or denies the allegations made in the complaint. The answer may also state the defendant's legal defenses to the complaint.

The defendant's answer must also set out any claims that the defendant may have against the plaintiff arising from the event that resulted in the plaintiff's action. A defendant's claim against a plaintiff is known as a counterclaim.

FIGURE 12-3

Professionals Involved in Court Proceedings

Clerks of Court

Clerks of court are appointed; however, in Georgia, the clerk of each county superior court is elected by county residents. They file legal documents and keep records on court cases, real property, voting, and other matters. Clerks of court differ from law clerks, who assist judges or lawyers by researching legal issues or drafting opinions and are law school students or recent graduates.

Sheriffs and Marshals

Sheriffs are elected by county residents; marshals are appointed. They enforce the decisions and orders of the court (in Georgia, the sheriff has this responsibility; in federal courts, the federal marshal does). They also serve (deliver) papers of the court (such as summonses), bring persons before the court, and keep order in the courtroom.

Lawyers

Lawyers are retained (hired) by parties to represent them in legal disputes. They "fight" for a party's interests in a case, give advice and counsel in legal matters, and keep parties informed about their legal rights and duties.

Bailiffs

Bailiffs help judges keep order in the court. They usher jury members in and out of the jury box and witnesses to the stand.

Court Reporters

Court reporters record the proceedings of a trial (usually by using a stenotype machine or tape recorder) and then prepare written transcripts of the proceedings.

The plaintiff's complaint and the defendant's answer are the basic pleadings in any civil case. The pleadings establish what factual and legal issues are in dispute and what must be determined in the trial. A defendant's failure to respond to the plaintiff's claims by not filing an answer is called a default. If the defendant defaults, he or she loses the case. It is therefore very important to respond when served with a complaint. The plaintiff may prevail if the defendant does not respond.

As soon as John is served the summons, he contacts Mr. Hartness, his insurance adjuster. In addition to medical payment coverage, John also has liability and collision coverage with Peach State Automobile Insurance Company. Mr. Hartness refers John's case to an attorney, Sally Bright. She will represent him in the trial.

Ms. Bright prepares an answer to the plaintiff's complaint. The answer agrees that the court has the jurisdiction to hear the case. It denies that John was negligent. It also denies that any injury to the plaintiff was directly caused by an act or failure to act on the defendant's part. No counterclaim is made.

Because the defendant denies the allegation of negligence, this matter is left for the plaintiff to prove. The plaintiff will also have to prove that John's negligence caused her injuries.

Sometimes a judge in a civil case can decide the questions of fact and law solely on the basis of the pleadings filed with the court. This decision is called judgment on the pleadings, and it is made in cases in which there is no real controversy. Suppose in his answer John had admitted to negligence and had agreed that his negligence caused Mary's injuries. Suppose he had agreed to the damages asked. Then there would be no real controversy. However, in the case of *Jones v. Smith*, the controversy is clear. The case will come to court.

Only the Facts

1. Match the following terms and definitions:
   1. summons
   2. complaint
   3. pleadings
   4. answer
   5. counterclaim
   6. default
   7. judgment on the pleadings

   a. the defendant's failure to respond to the plaintiff's complaint
   b. a document notifying the defendant of the plaintiff's suit
   c. the documents giving the claims and answers of the plaintiff and defendant
   d. a judge's decision on the case based solely on the pleadings
   e. the document setting forth the defendant's claims against the plaintiff
   f. the defendant's response to the claims of the plaintiff
   g. a document setting forth the plaintiff's claims against the defendant

Think About

1. Why do you think Mr. Barr asks for $125,000 in damages on the claim? Didn't he indicate a willingness to settle for $75,000 with the insurance company?
2. Why is a summons delivered by a court officer rather than by the plaintiff's lawyer? Why not send it in the mail?

PREPARING FOR TRIAL—DISCOVERY

Once a civil case is filed, it takes several months (sometimes over a year) for it to come to trial, particularly in the more populous counties in Georgia. The old adage that "the wheels of justice turn slowly" is very true in the civil law arena.

Attorneys have much pretrial work to do. Filing a complaint or an answer is just the beginning. Mr. Barr knows that he will have to present evidence to prove his client's claims. Ms. Bright knows she will have to discredit his evidence.

In most civil cases, the lawyers for the parties will engage in some degree of pretrial discovery. Discovery refers to a variety of techniques and procedures that the law of Georgia permits both parties in a lawsuit to use to find out about the other side's case. Discovery is used for fact gathering. It can also be important in defining the real points of controversy in a given case.

Today, quite broad and far-reaching discovery is usually permitted. Each party's attorney can develop a wealth of information about the other side's case. A main advantage is that neither attorney is likely to be surprised by the other at the trial. A disadvantage of extensive discovery is that it is time-consuming and expensive.

Interrogatories

Interrogatories are one technique of discovery. They are written questions that one party's attorney sends to another party's attorney. They must be answered in writing and under oath by the party to whom they are addressed. These answers must be filed with the clerk of the court and served to the opposing attorney within 30 days of the mailing of the interrogatories. Except in very complex cases, Georgia law limits the number of interrogatories to 50. Failure to respond can result in sanctions and penalties by the court.

In the case of *Jones v. Smith*, Ms. Bright, the defendant's attorney, begins the discovery process. She serves (mails) interrogatories to Mr. Barr. Questions in a case like this usually relate to a party's medical history, previous accidents and hospitalization, circumstances of the accident, identity of witnesses, medical expenses, and wage loss. One of the interrogatories that Ms. Bright sends to Mr. Barr follows:

> What are the names and addresses of all practitioners of the healing arts (physicians, chiropractors, osteopaths, etc.) who have examined or rendered treatment to plaintiff from the date of the incident through and including the present time? Please include in your answer the dates these doctors were seen, the reason for such visit, and the amount charged.

A party does not have an absolute right to have discovery of anything and everything. For example, suppose an attorney asked, "State whether you smoked marijuana before operating your automobile on April 3." This demand could be rejected because the U.S. Constitution protects citizens against self-incrimination. Suppose the demand was, "Please state the substance of any conversation you have had with any attorney regarding this case." This interrogatory attempts to invade another protected area: the confidential attorney-client relationship. It also could be rejected.

Request for Production of Documents

In this legal document, one attorney asks the opposing lawyer to make certain documents available for inspection and copying. This procedure is often used to "discover" medical bills, photos of accident scenes, repair bills, estimates, etc. Like the interrogatories, a "request for production" must be responded to within 30 days. Again, failure to respond to requests can result in sanctions and penalties by the court.

In the case of *Jones v. Smith*, both attorneys use this procedure. Ms Bright requests copies of medical bills. Mr. Barr requests a copy of John's insurance policy.

Deposition

Another widely used discovery tool is the deposition. A deposition is oral testimony of a plaintiff, defendant, or witness taken under oath. It is recorded by a court reporter who puts it into a printed or typed form that becomes the actual deposition. Depositions are usually much better ways to gain information than are interrogatories. Answers to interrogatories are often very short. They disclose as little information as possible. Depositions, on the other hand, allow the questioning of witnesses in person, with follow-up questions to probe for additional information.

At depositions, the opposing attorney has a right to be present to protect the interests of his or her client. He or she may examine a witness

Courts often allow the deposition of a witness to be read to the jury in open court.

being deposed by the other attorney. This questioning is known as cross-examination.

Depositions are frequently used at trials to impeach or discredit a particular witness's testimony. A deposition records and preserves the testimony of a witness. Therefore it can verify that a witness has either changed or forgotten his or her previous testimony. Using the deposition at a trial for this purpose is called impeaching a witness.

The law recognizes that it is expensive, inconvenient, and sometimes impossible for some witnesses to appear at a trial of a case. Courts often allow the deposition of a witness to be read to the jury in open court. In this way, the witness need not come to court to testify. Rather than compelling a physician to appear in court, for example, his or her deposition will be read. A deposition may also be read if a witness has died or moved outside the jurisdiction of the court.

In a personal injury case like *Jones v. Smith*, Mary's attorney takes the depositions of all the physicians who treated her. This process can be expensive. A rate of $300 per hour is not unusual for physicians giving depositions. Additionally, each side pays for a copy of the deposition, which is also costly.

Mr. Barr asks the physicians about their diagnoses and treatments. An excerpt of the deposition of one physician, Dr. Henry, follows.

Mr. Barr: Dr. Henry, did you supervise Ms. Jones's case while she was in the hospital?

Dr. Henry: Yes, she was my patient.

Mr. Barr: Do you know when she was discharged from the hospital?

After Dr. Henry gives the date, Ms. Bright cross-examines him.

Ms. Bright: Doctor, before the plaintiff was discharged from the hospital, didn't you advise her to follow up with treatment in your office?

Dr. Henry: Yes, that's correct. I did see Ms. Jones, the plaintiff, as you refer to her, as a patient in my office after her discharge from the hospital.

Ms. Bright: And you have not had occasion to see her or treat her, as a patient, in the last several months, have you?

Dr. Henry: I don't know what you mean by "several months." I did see her about four months ago. I told her to call for an appointment if she experienced further problems.

Only the Facts

1. Define the three common discovery techniques.

Think About

1. "Witnesses should not be paid for their time in giving depositions or testifying." Give arguments for or against that statement.

THE TRIAL

The trial of case no. 81999, *Mary Jones v. John Smith*, will be held in the Superior Court of DeKalb County, Georgia. Thomas Fayre will be the trial judge presiding over the case. The judge's role and authority are most important to the trial. A judge

- insists that order prevail in the courtroom and that the case be fairly tried.

- controls conduct of the trial, declaring recesses and continuances (or postponements) when necessary.

- controls introduction of evidence, determining whether it will be accepted for the jury's consideration.

- decides on motions made by the attorneys. (A motion is a request made to the judge that certain action be taken in the case.)

Questions of Law and Fact

In each legal dispute, questions of law and fact must be resolved by the court. Questions of law can only be decided by the judge. Questions of fact are decided by the judge if there is no jury. Otherwise, they are decided by the jury. What are these kinds of questions, and how do they differ?

Questions of law are about the legal principles that apply to the case. In the case of *Jones v. Smith*, Judge Fayre must resolve the questions of law. For example, knowing what the law says is necessary for an act to be considered negligent, he must decide if the allegations support a claim of negligence. If they do not, he could dismiss the case.

Questions of fact concern the facts of the case. In the case of *Jones v. Smith*, a jury will decide the questions of fact. One question will be whether John actually committed the acts alleged by Mary. Another will be whether his actions resulted in injuries to Mary.

The Jury

The right to a trial by jury in civil cases is guaranteed by the Georgia Constitution. After the case is called for trial, the first step is the selection of the jurors. In civil cases heard in state court, juries may have only six members. However, if the amount in question is more than $10,000, either party may request 12 jurors. (A superior court jury, as is the case in *Jones v. Smith*, will have 12 members.)

Juries are composed of adults (people aged 18 and over) from the entire community. No one may be unfairly excluded from jury service on the basis of race or sex. However, persons who are 70 years or older can ask to have their names removed from the list.

The list of potential jurors is compiled by a county's board of jury commissioners. The board is a body of six members appointed by a superior court judge for six years. From the list, a group of citizens is called to be available for jury duty for up to a week. They compose what are called jury panels. From each panel, juries will be selected to try individual cases.

There are 36 prospective jurors in the panel for the case of *Jones v. Smith*. Before selecting 12 for the jury, the attorneys will ask them questions. This examination is called the *voir dire*, which is French for "to see and to speak." The purpose of the *voir dire* is to select a fair and impartial jury. The attorneys, of course, will also look for jurors who might be sympathetic to their side of the case. In effect, jurors are selected through a process of elimination (figure 12-4 describes the trial process). As you read, note the two ways in which an attorney can reject a juror.

The questioning begins when Judge Fayre asks all of the prospective jurors some general qualifying questions. He asks, "Are any of you related to either Mary Jones or to John Smith? Do any of you employ Mary Jones or John Smith? Are any of you a stockholder, employee, officer, or director of Peach State Automobile Insurance Company (John's insurance company)?" All of the jurors answer "no" to the judge's questions.

If one juror had answered "yes," he or she might have been rejected for cause. Rejecting for cause is one way a juror can be dismissed. It means that there is some logical reason why that juror should not be selected. Answers to questions might reveal that the juror is related to someone in the case. Or they might show that the juror has already formed an opinion about the case.

In the *voir dire*, the attorneys question the jurors in turn. The clerk calls the name of the first prospective juror, Patrick Pierson. He stands. Mr. Barr begins the questioning.

> **Mr. Barr**: Are you presently employed, Mr. Pierson?
>
> **Mr. Pierson**: Yes, sir. I'm a plumber. I work for Watt Pipes Plumbing Company.

> **Mr. Barr**: Are you married, Mr. Pierson?
>
> **Mr. Pierson**: Yes, sir.
>
> **Mr. Barr**: Is your wife employed outside the home?
>
> **Mr. Pierson**: Yes, sir. Part-time. She's a bookkeeper.

Mr. Barr then asks if Mr. Pierson has children. Mr. Pierson says he has a boy aged 13 and a girl aged 9. Mr. Barr also asks if Mr. Pierson has served on a jury in the past. He learns that Mr. Pierson was on a criminal case—a robbery.

Ms. Bright then questions Mr. Pierson. She first determines that he has never been a party in a civil case. She then asks the following questions:

> **Ms. Bright**: Are you personally acquainted with either myself or the plaintiff's attorney, Mr. Barr?
>
> **Mr. Pierson**: No, ma'am.
>
> **Ms. Bright**: Are you personally acquainted with the plaintiff, Miss Jones, or my client, Mr. Smith?
>
> **Mr. Pierson**: No.

Attorneys can also ask questions of the panel as a whole. Ms. Bright asks all of the jurors if they, or any member of their family, have ever

During the *voir dire*, both attorneys question possible jurors to uncover any bias about the case.

FIGURE 12-4

The Trial Process in Civil (and Criminal) Cases

1. Jury selection—*voir dire*

2. Opening statements

   In civil cases, the plaintiff; in criminal cases, the prosecution

   Defense

3. Presentation of case

   Plaintiff (in civil cases, prosecution in criminal cases)—direct, cross-examination, redirect

   Defense—direct, cross-examination, redirect

4. Closing statements

   Plaintiff (in civil cases, prosecution in criminal cases)

   Defense

   Plaintiff (unless the defense presents no evidence or witnesses other than the defendant. In that case, the defendant has the option of going first and last.)

5. Jury deliberation

   Judge charges the jury

   Jury elects a foreman

   Jury deliberates

   Jury announces decision

6. Verdict (in a criminal case, sentencing follows)

---

been injured in an accident. She asks those who say "yes" if the injuries were serious. Mr. Pierson says that his wife once had minor injuries from an accident. The attorneys hope their questions will uncover any bias, prejudice, or preconceived notions on the jurors' part about the case.

After *voir dire* is completed, the attorneys proceed to select a 12-member jury. Each remaining juror will be considered individually. There will be additional dismissals as the attorneys use their peremptory strikes. With peremptory strikes, a reason for striking need not be given. Prospective jurors usually never know why they were dismissed. Usually, they are stricken because one of the attorneys feels that the prospective juror will not look favorably upon his or her client's case. However, the strikes must be used carefully. Each side has a limited number,

and the first 12 persons who are not stricken from the list of potential jurors will form the jury for the trial. The plaintiff's attorney is first to strike jurors from the panel.

Attorneys may not systematically strike jurors because of their race or their sex. The U.S. Supreme Court has found that systematically removing jurors of one racial type or sex is presumptively unfair. The opposing counsel may make a motion to the trial judge accusing the other attorney of using strikes for a discriminatory purpose. The other side must then give reasons not based on race or sex for why they used their peremptory strikes against each juror they struck.

Finally, in the trial of *Jones v. Smith*, 12 jurors (and one alternate), including Mr. Pierson, are selected. The judge instructs them to take seats in the jury box. Those jurors not accepted are excused. When the jury is seated, Judge Fayre calls for opening statements in the trial.

Opening Statements

In a civil case, the plaintiff's attorney has the right to make the first opening statement to the jury. The opening statement is not evidence, but attorneys usually tell the jury what they expect the evidence to show. A trial is an adversary proceeding, so attorneys try to make the opening statement sound as favorable as possible to their side of the case.

Mr. Barr outlines the nature of the case to the jury in his opening statement. Mr. Barr also introduces the parties in the case. He wants the jurors to be familiar with the "cast of characters" in the trial. He begins this way:

> Ladies and gentlemen of the jury, my name is Fred Barr. I represent the plaintiff in this case, Ms. Mary Jones. She has brought this case against Mr. John Smith. My client comes into court seeking money damages for injuries she sustained when she, a pedestrian, was hit and struck down by an automobile that was being driven by John Smith, the defendant in this case.

Mr. Barr goes on to tell the jury about some of the facts of the collision. Then he tells about Mary's progress after the accident. He outlines the evidence he expects to present. He asks the jury to keep an open mind. He also asks the jury to base its verdict solely on the evidence presented and the judge's instructions.

Then Ms. Bright, John's attorney, makes her opening statement. She begins,

> My name is Sally Bright, and I represent John Smith. You have two basic questions to decide: what happened on May 7, and who is responsible for the injuries claimed by Mary Jones? When you hear all the facts, you will understand why Ms. Jones is not entitled to a judgment against Mr. Smith.

She goes on to tell the jury that she believes the evidence will show that the defendant was not speeding and was not negligent. Therefore, her client is not liable to the plaintiff for any money damages.

Presenting the Evidence

After the opening statements, Judge Fayre calls upon the plaintiff's attorney, Mr. Barr, to present his evidence. Mr. Barr knows that the burden of proof is on him and his client. That is, he must present evidence to the jury proving to its satisfaction that the facts of the case support the claim against the defendant. Mr. Barr must show that his client was injured, and he must also show that these injuries were the result of the negligence of John.

Evidence is a legal term meaning a matter of fact tending to prove, or disprove, another matter of fact at issue in the case. The two principal kinds of evidence are real and testimonial evidence. Real evidence refers to physical or tangible (touchable) things or documents. Photographs of the accident scene would be real evidence. Testimonial evidence refers to evidence given by witnesses (testimony). Usually, both real and testimonial evidence are used in a case.

During a trial, one attorney may object to evidence that the opposing lawyer wishes to introduce. The judge determines whether the evidence will be admitted. In other words, the judge decides whether the jury will be allowed to hear or consider the evidence. Sometimes the judge may refuse to allow evidence that is clearly inadmissible even without an objection from the other attorney.

The rules of evidence have been developed over many years. The concept underlying these rules is this: facts that tend to help a trier of fact (the jury) arrive at the truth should be admitted as evidence. Facts that do not aid the jury in the search for truth should be rejected as irrelevant.

In Mary's case, an example of relevant evidence would be Mr. Hawkeye's testimony about what he saw of the collision. Testimony by someone else about what Mr. Hawkeye said about the accident would not be allowed. Such testimony would be hearsay evidence. Hearsay evidence is considered unreliable, and it is generally not admissible. (There are some very important exceptions to the hearsay rule, however. An example would be the statement of a dying victim identifying the murderer.)

To aid the jury, Mr. Barr has prepared a large diagram of the scene of the accident (see figure 12-5). Such a diagram is not evidence. It is to help the jury understand the physical setting of the collision. Such visual aids are often used in the trial of accident cases, if the judge permits.

For his first witness, Mr. Barr calls Mary to the witness stand for direct examination. Mary is sworn in by Mr. Barr, with the following oath: "Do you solemnly swear (or affirm) that the testimony you are about to give in the case now pending before this court shall be the truth, the whole truth, and nothing but the truth, so help you God?" Mary answers, "I do." Mr. Barr then questions Mary:

> **Mr. Barr**: Will you state your full name for the court and jury?
> **Ms. Jones**: Mary Jones.
> **Mr. Barr**: Are you the plaintiff in this case?
> **Ms. Jones**: Yes, I am.

Mr. Barr: Are you seeking damages from the defendant, Mr. Smith, in this action?

Ms. Jones: Yes.

Mr. Barr then questions her about the accident. He asks her to describe what happened "in her own words." He asks what she recalls of the defendant's driving. Mary testifies about her injuries and her medical treatment. She describes her pain, discomfort, nervousness, and loss of sleep.

Mr. Barr then asks Mary to authenticate her medical bills and prescriptions. Authentication means that she identifies these documents. Then she testifies that these bills represent actual expenses. Mr. Barr asks that these documents be entered and accepted as evidence in support of Mary's claim for damages.

Now the defense attorney has the right to cross-examine Mary about her testimony. One purpose of cross-examination is to reduce the impact of the direct examination. Alternatively, cross-examination may be used to cast doubt on the truthfulness of the witness.

In cross-examination, the attorney may ask leading questions. These are questions phrased so as to suggest the answer the questioner wants. (They cannot be used in direct examination.)

Ms. Bright: It was dark that night, wasn't it?

Ms. Jones: Yes, but not so dark that I couldn't see.

Ms. Bright: But you didn't look up and down the street for approaching traffic before crossing the street, did you?

Ms. Jones: No.

Ms. Bright leads Mary to admit that she really didn't get a look at John or his car before the impact. Mary also admits that she started to cross the street as soon as the traffic light turned green. She did not first look for oncoming vehicles.

Mr. Barr may ask additional questions of the witness as soon as the defense is finished. This procedure is referred to as the redirect. It may be used by both attorneys. Both attorneys also may recall any witness to the stand during their presentations of evidence.

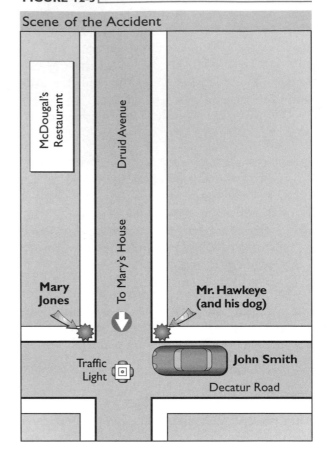

FIGURE 12-5

Scene of the Accident

McDougal's Restaurant

Druid Avenue

To Mary's House

Mary Jones

Mr. Hawkeye (and his dog)

Traffic Light

John Smith

Decatur Road

As his presentation of evidence continues, Mr. Barr reads to the jury portions of the physicians' depositions that he had taken earlier. Ms. Bright reads her cross-examination of the physicians to the jury. Judge Fayre advises the jury that the readings of the physicians' depositions are to be treated as evidence just as if the physicians were testifying in court.

Note that physicians are a kind of expert witness. Expert witnesses, because of their particular training or experience, can draw certain inferences or conclusions from the facts of a case. For example, a physician could give an opinion as to whether a collision could cause the injuries that were reported. The opinion of a nonexpert witness on the same question, however, would not be allowed.

The eyewitness to the accident, Mr. Hawkeye, is then called as a witness by Mr. Barr. The witness is sworn in. Mr. Barr begins his direct examination of the witness. He establishes that Mr. Hawkeye was near the intersection of Druid Avenue and Decatur Road in DeKalb County on the evening of the accident.

> **Mr. Barr**: At about what time were you there?
>
> **Mr. Hawkeye**: Around 11 p.m. I was walking my dog.
>
> **Mr. Barr**: Did you observe an automobile-pedestrian collision?
>
> **Mr. Hawkeye**: Yes.
>
> **Mr. Barr**: Didn't you observe the automobile traveling about 50 miles per hour?
>
> **Ms. Bright**: Your Honor, I object to the question on the grounds that Mr. Barr is asking his witness a leading question. He is, in fact, suggesting the answer he wants.
>
> **Judge Fayre**: Objection sustained.
>
> **Mr. Barr**: I'll withdraw the question.

Mr. Barr goes on to question Mr. Hawkeye about what he actually observed of the accident. He asks what Mr. Hawkeye recalls about how John was operating his automobile.

On cross-examination, Ms. Bright begins as follows:

> **Ms. Bright**: How far away were you from the collision you said you observed?
>
> **Mr. Hawkeye**: About 30 or 40 feet.
>
> **Ms. Bright**: You have no way of knowing, do you, the actual speed Mr. Smith was traveling just prior to this collision?
>
> **Mr. Hawkeye**: No.

Ms. Bright continues to cross-examine. However, she cannot discredit Mr. Hawkeye's testimony, nor can she force him to contradict any of it.

At the close of Mr. Hawkeye's testimony, the plaintiff's case is completed. Mr. Barr says, "Your Honor, the plaintiff now rests."

Motion for Directed Verdict

After the plaintiff's case is completed, Ms. Bright says,

> Your Honor, I move for a directed verdict in favor of the defendant on the grounds that the plaintiff has failed to prove each element of her case and a jury of reasonable persons could not differ in their verdict for the defendant. (In other words, based on the plaintiff's evidence, a jury must find for the defendant.)

In effect, Ms. Bright is saying that the plaintiff hasn't proved her case. She is asking the judge to dismiss the case at this point. If the judge grants the motion, then the verdict (decision) is "directed" in favor of the defendant. The case would not go to the jury. However, Judge Fayre says,

> I cannot agree with your motion. The plaintiff has made out a case in negligence so far as a question of fact for the jury. Therefore I will overrule and deny your motion at this time. You may proceed with your side of the case.

Similarly, the plaintiff's attorney may ask for a "directed verdict" in favor of the plaintiff at the close of all the evidence. A directed verdict would be requested if it appeared that reasonable jurors would agree that the plaintiff had clearly proved his or her case. Even if the directed verdict were granted, however, the jury would have to decide the issue of damages.

The Defense

The defendant's attorney, Ms. Bright, must discredit the evidence that the plaintiff has presented. Ms. Bright has a difficult tactical decision: she may call witnesses as part of the defendant's case, or she may choose not to put additional evidence before the jury. An attorney might decide to follow the second course, particularly if the new evidence would simply be a rehash of the plaintiff's evidence. Remember, the defendant's attorney has had a chance to cross-examine all of the plaintiff's witnesses. Weaknesses in the plaintiff's case can be shown through cross-examination.

Ms. Bright decides not to put up any evidence. In so doing, she will be allowed to make the opening and concluding final arguments to the jury. Usually, the plaintiff's attorney has the right both to go first and conclude in closing argument.

Closing Arguments

After all the evidence for both sides has been presented, the judge calls for the closing arguments. During this time, each attorney may argue his or her case to the jury. A closing argument is quite different from an opening statement. In the opening statement, an attorney usually outlines the entire case in a somewhat matter-of-fact manner. In closing arguments, attorneys comment directly on the evidence and witnesses. They argue the matters they feel have been proven by the evidence. They cannot, however, speak of anything that was not presented as evidence during the trial.

Ms. Bright has decided to "waive" her opening argument. She is hoping to impress the jury with her conclusion. She knows that will be the final argument the jury will hear.

Mr. Barr, in his closing argument, emphasizes that the plaintiff has proven three essential elements: (1) negligence on the part of the defendant, which was the (2) proximate cause of the (3) damages, for which the plaintiff should be compensated. He tells the jury that it cannot undo the wrong inflicted upon his client, the plaintiff. He says that the jury can do for the plaintiff what the law allows, however. That is, it can award money damages for the plaintiff's injuries.

In her closing argument, Ms. Bright states that the evidence clearly shows that the plaintiff is well recovered from any injuries she might have suffered from the accident. Even if the jury should find the defendant guilty of negligence, she says, it should award only a minimal sum for the plaintiff's general damages.

Charge to Jury

After Ms. Bright's closing argument, Judge Fayre charges the jury—that is, he instructs the jury about the law that is to be applied to the facts of the case. In a personal injury case, the judge's instructions are usually lengthy. The judge explains the law on matters such as who has the burden of proof. Judge Fayre also instructs the jury about the law of negligence, the elements of a negligence action, including proximate cause, and the law relating to damages. The judge explains the need for a unanimous verdict. "Verdict," he says to the jury, "simply means 'truth.' And that is what you must seek in your very private deliberations."

Jury Deliberations and Verdict

As soon as the jurors retire to the jury room, they elect a foreman. Mr. Pierson is selected. Then the jurors consider the questions before them. In the *Jones v. Smith* case, the jury must decide two questions: Were the plaintiff's injuries the results of John's negligence? If so, what amount of damages should the plaintiff receive? According to Georgia law, the proper measure of general damages as related to mental pain and suffering is determined by "the enlightened conscience of fair and impartial jurors."

In deliberating, jurors discuss the evidence presented. They consider the points made by the attorneys. If they have a question about the law or how it is to be applied in the case, the bailiff is notified. The bailiff informs the judge. The jury then returns to the courtroom to receive further instructions from the judge if the judge feels that it is necessary.

To aid in their deliberations, the jurors have the documentary evidence introduced during the trial with them to examine, including the medical bills and prescriptions that Mr. Barr had Mary authenticate while she was on the witness stand. This jury may have copies of the pleadings (the complaint and answer) to review. It is up to the judge as to whether to send the pleadings out with the jury.

The jurors have trouble reaching a unanimous verdict on both questions. Because the jury verdict must be unanimous, jurors on the opposing sides try to persuade the others to their viewpoint. Sometimes jurors never agree. If a unanimous verdict is impossible, a mistrial is declared by the judge. Then the case would have to be tried again before another jury.

In the *Jones v. Smith* case, the jury finally reaches a unanimous decision. The jury foreman, Mr. Pierson, calls for the bailiff. The bailiff tells the judge that the jury is ready to return to the courtroom. After both parties are present, the jury is called into the courtroom.

When the jury is again seated in the jury box, Judge Fayre asks, "Have you reached a verdict?" The jury foreman responds, "We have, your honor." The foreman hands a written verdict, signed by all the jurors, to the judge.

The judge asks the plaintiff's attorney to publish the verdict, meaning read it aloud in open court. The verdict reads, "We the jury find in favor of the Plaintiff in the sum of $75,000 on this third day of July, 1997. Signed, Patrick Pierson, foreman."

Outcome of Case

Thus, Mary has won a verdict for damages. When the plaintiff prevails (wins), the court will order whatever action is necessary to enforce the obligations of the defendant to the plaintiff. In cases such as *Jones v. Smith*, the defendant would be ordered to pay the plaintiff the amount of money that the court has declared to be due. What if the defendant does not pay? The plaintiff may then take legal action to seize property owned by the defendant that could then be sold to satisfy the defendant's obligation to the plaintiff.

In this case, the judgment will be paid by John's insurance company. It will pay up to the amount of his liability insurance coverage. However, the judgment would not be paid right away if the case were appealed by John and his attorney.

Although the jury awarded her $75,000, Mary will not receive all of that money. The fees for her attorney, which may be from 25 percent

to 40 percent of the award, will be deducted. Other legal expenses, such as costs of depositions from witnesses, will also reduce the amount Mary receives.

In other cases, the court may require the defendant to perform a particular legal duty. For instance, the defendant may be requested to deliver goods under the terms of a contract. If the defendant does not obey such an order, he or she may be held in contempt of court. In that case, the defendant would be punished by fine or jail until he or she obeys the order. Sometimes a court will simply declare the rights and duties of the parties, as in a divorce, when the judge orders that the marriage be dissolved.

Only the Facts

1. What is a *voir dire*?
2. How do the opening statements and closing arguments differ?
3. Fill in the missing word. (a) A document is _____ evidence.
   (b) The statement of a witness is _____ evidence.
4. What is the judge's charge to the jury?
5. Fill in the missing word.
   a. Prospective jurors are usually not told the reason for _____ strikes.
   b. Jurors may not be systematically be struck because of _____ or _____ .
   c. Juries decide questions of _____ ; they do not decide questions of law.
   d. _____ evidence is usually not admissible.
   e. To reach a verdict, a jury vote must be _____ .

Think About

1. Recently, in a few cases, defense attorneys have used psychological testing to evaluate potential jurors.

Psychological testing is costly. Is it fair?

2. Should a jury always have to return a unanimous verdict?

3. If you were an attorney in this case, what particular qualities might you look for in jurors? Would you accept Patrick Pierson? Why or why not?

4. Do you think Ms. Bright should have presented a defense? What evidence might she have presented?

5. Do you agree with the verdict? Why or why not?

APPEALING THE DECISION

John and his lawyer are not happy with the outcome of the case. Is there anything they can do about it? If dissatisfied with the decision, either party in a civil case (and the defendant in a criminal case) may ask for an appeal. Then a higher or appellate court will review the decision of the trial court. The higher court may uphold or overturn (that is, reverse) the trial court decision. An appeal, however, must be filed within a certain period of time after the trial court decision becomes final.

Generally, appealing parties must state why they think something was wrong with the trial court decision. These reasons are called the grounds for appeal. They must involve questions of law. An appealing party cannot argue that the trial court made the wrong decisions on the facts because the trier of fact's determination of the facts is final—a basic element of our legal system. The judge or jury is considered to be in the best position to evaluate the evidence, such as the testimony of a witness and how credible it appears to be. Only in extraordinary circumstances can the facts be reviewed.

There are, however, a number of acceptable grounds for appealing a case. The losing party may

- challenge the manner in which the trial was conducted.

- argue that the judge allowed irrelevant, prejudicial evidence to be presented.

- argue that the wrong rule of law was applied by the court in declaring the rights and duties of the parties.

- argue that no evidence was presented that supported the jury's findings.

- although it rarely occurs, show that additional evidence has been discovered after the trial that would justify reconsidering the case at the trial level. The new evidence must clearly make a difference to the outcome of the trial. Also, it has to be something that could not have been discovered before the trial.

Suppose one of the following events had occurred in relation to the trial of *Mary Jones v. John Smith*. Would it have given grounds for appeal?

1. During the trial, the only witness for Mary was a woman. She testified that her cousin saw the accident and that John was clearly at fault.

2. Travis Eller returns from a trip around the world. He did not know about the trial. He says that he saw the accident. He says that John was driving very carefully and that Mary stepped in front of the car without looking.

3. Ms. Bright knew that Mr. Hawkeye had a grudge against John for something John did to Mr. Hawkeye's cousin. However, she did not reveal this information during the trial. She knew it could discredit Mr. Hawkeye's testimony, but she feared it would reflect poorly on John's character. She considers using it in an appeal of the case.

4. In the trial, Mary and John gave their versions of what happened. That was the only evidence in the trial. The jury believed and decided in favor of Mary.

Events 1 and 2 might result in review by an appellate court. The evidence in event 1 is hearsay evidence. It would be a question of law as to whether this evidence should have been allowed. In event 2, it would seem that Ms. Bright would not have any way of knowing about the witness until after the trial.

However, the evidence in event 3 was available to Ms. Bright at the time of the trial. She knew of the bias of the witness. She chose not to present it. It would not be valid grounds for appeal. Event 4 does not present valid grounds for appeal either. The decision of the jury was based on facts, not law. An appellate court will not reconsider it.

If the appellate court rejects the request for appeal, the decision of the trial court stands. If the appellate court hears the appeal, it can decide to let the trial court's decision stand, reverse the trial court's decision, or in a civil case, ask the trial court to rehear part or all of the trial. If the case is sent back to the trial court, the parties may agree to settle out of court instead. Sometimes, the decision of an appellate court can be appealed to another appellate court (see the discussion in chapter 3).

O n l y   t h e   F a c t s

1. Are grounds for appeal based on questions of law or facts?
2. Which of the following would be grounds for appeal?
   a. irrelevant evidence presented
   b. jury seemed bored
   c. wrong rule of law applied
   d. evidence failed to support jury findings
   e. jury findings were disappointing
3. What happens if an appellate court reverses the trial court decision?

OTHER WAYS TO ACHIEVE JUSTICE

Is a court trial like that of the case of Mary Jones and John Smith the best way to achieve justice? Is it the only way to resolve disputes?

Actually, most civil cases are settled before they reach trial. Frequently, the parties negotiate a solution to their dispute. Negotiation is a bargaining process in which both parties try to work out a mutually satisfactory solution. You may recall that Mr. Barr and the insurance adjuster tried to negotiate a solution to this case.

In Georgia and throughout the United States, courts and individuals are turning more often to alternatives to the legal process to settle disputes. Generally, these new processes are referred to as alternative dispute resolution (ADR) (see chapter 3). In fact, some courts are even ordering parties to attempt to resolve their dispute using ADR before they can bring their case to trial in the courts. Most of these alternative processes are gaining popularity in this country for several reasons. They are often less expensive alternatives to litigation. They are also generally faster than litigation, and they often achieve a more fair and equitable result than litigation. You will recall that the two most common forms of ADR are arbitration and mediation.

In arbitration, disagreeing sides agree to have a neutral third party (called an arbitrator) hear their arguments and settle their dispute. Parties agree in advance as to whether they will accept the arbitrator's decision as final.

You will recall that in mediation, parties also ask someone else to help settle their dispute. However, the mediator does not make the decision; rather, he or she guides the two parties as they work out their own decision.

SUMMING UP

You have been a witness to the case of *Mary Jones v. John Smith*. You have seen the pleadings and learned how the trial preparations were handled. You have observed the trial and heard the verdict. Now look back on each of the steps. Think about each procedure in turn. Think about it in terms of these questions:

1. Is the entire process too slow and cumbersome? Could some procedures be eliminated or streamlined to speed up the flow of cases through the courts? What about pretrial discovery? *Voir dire*? Wouldn't it save the courts money to let the plaintiff notify the defendant? How important is notification to the defendant anyway?

2. How do these procedures support the right to a fair trial as guaranteed by the Constitution? How does each procedure ensure fairness? For example, do you think it is necessary to have a trial jury? (Couldn't a judge rather than a jury have decided Mary's case just as easily?) Should a unanimous decision always be required?

3. Is the adversarial system essential to justice? What kind of solution might Mr. Barr and the insurance adjuster have been able to negotiate? What might have been the outcome if the case had gone to arbitration or mediation? Might it have been fairer?

As these questions suggest, litigation provides a good but not perfect system of ensuring justice. The system has strengths as well as weaknesses. It is important to recognize both. Adaptations can be made and often are. As a citizen, you may one day be voting on amendments to the state constitution that affect the judicial process. Understanding how the process works will help you decide how to vote wisely.

PART 3 CONSTITUTIONAL PROTECTIONS

13 Rights and Responsibilities

I f somebody asked you to list your most precious possessions, what would you include? Perhaps you highly value a musical instrument, a pet, a fashionable wardrobe, a vehicle. Perhaps you would list health or talents, family or friends. Would you include your legal rights in the list?

The most important legal rights you have come from the U.S. Constitution. You probably can name a few of them. One is freedom of speech. Another is freedom of religion. These rights may seem so basic to you that you take them for granted, but they are very important, as this chapter explains.

WHAT ARE CONSTITUTIONAL RIGHTS?

We call a right "constitutional" because it is written into a constitution. There is a U.S. Constitution, and each state has its own constitution. The U.S. Constitution outlines the basic rights that can be exercised by all citizens of the United States. Each state's constitution also outlines rights for its citizens. If a state constitutional right conflicts with a U.S. Constitutional right, the U.S. right prevails. As such, the state constitutions can add rights (for example, some state constitutions provide for the right to an education even though it is not mentioned as being a right in the federal constitution), but they can't take away any U.S. Constitutional rights.

How do constitutional rights differ from other legal rights? Unlike other legal rights, constitutional rights cannot be changed by statute (a law passed by Congress or a state legislature). That is, a legislative body cannot just pass a new law that changes rights found in the U.S. Constitution or a state constitution. Rather, constitutional rights can be altered only by amending the constitution, which is a much more complex process than is the passing of a statute. Because they are not easily changed, constitutional rights have greater permanence than statutes do.

Constitutional rights protect you—from whom? Whose actions do they limit? Consider the events in situation 1:

> **SITUATION 1** You write a letter proposing a shorter school year. Three things happen:
>
> a. The local newspaper refuses to print it.
>
> b. The mayor forbids the newspaper to print your letter. He threatens to arrest the editor if the letter appears in the paper.
>
> c. Your father tells you to keep quiet. He's heard enough of your ideas on a shorter school year.

Is your constitutional right to free speech being violated by the newspaper, the mayor, or your father?

Constitutional rights are limits upon the power of a government (whether at the local, state, or federal level) to affect you in one way or another. They also limit the power of individuals acting on behalf of any government. However, constitutional rights do not apply to a private person's actions against you, nor do they apply to your actions as a private person against others.

In situation 1a, the local newspaper may refuse to print your letter. The newspaper is a private business. Its refusal would not violate your constitutional rights. Neither does your father's command violate your right to free speech (situation 1c). However, the refusal of the mayor of the city government to allow the newspaper to print your letter would be unconstitutional (situation 1b). This government action would violate the right to freedom of the press.

Up to this point, we have talked about constitutional rights. However, remember that government can also pass laws. Laws (or statutes) may put restrictions on business, protect the public, or extend rights.

Laws are written for many different purposes. Some laws protect against crimes. There are laws to protect the environment. Some laws affect business. For example, state and federal governments have passed laws that extend constitutional rights against discrimination to private companies. Private employers cannot discriminate based on race, sex, national origin, or religious beliefs. Private businesses, like restaurants, cannot refuse to serve persons because of their race.

A government must always stay within the limits of constitutional rights, even when adopting laws to extend rights. Thus a government could not adopt a law prohibiting people from saying hurtful things. Such a law would limit the constitutional right of free speech.

Only the Facts

1. What is the difference between a constitutional right and other legal rights?
2. Does the U.S. Constitution protect citizens against the actions of individuals or the government?
3. How can constitutional rights be extended to limit private activities?

Think About

1. What would happen if a right such as freedom of speech were statutory, not constitutional? Would we have more or less protection from the power of government? How difficult would it be to take away a right if it were statutory?

FREEDOM OF SPEECH

In American society, we can freely discuss government affairs. We can express controversial ideas, even unpopular ideas. We can hear and consider all points of view before we vote for political changes. This freedom of speech is the basis of democracy. Our rights to free speech and a free press are both specified in the First Amendment to the U.S. Constitution (see figure 13-1 for the Bill of Rights). They are also guaranteed by the Georgia Constitution in Article 1, section 1, paragraph 5: "No law shall be passed to curtail or restrain the freedom of speech or of the press. Every person may speak, write, and publish sentiments on all subjects but shall be responsible for the abuse of that liberty."

What Is Speech?

SITUATION 2 Expressing his anger at government failure to help the homeless, an artist paints a picture of the flag that many people consider to be offensive.

SITUATION 3 A campaign worker hands out pamphlets on a street corner.

SITUATION 4 A group of students wear white armbands to high school one day. The armbands are in memory of the school's graduates who were killed in recent wars.

What is "speech" anyway? Would the activities in these situations be speech? Would they be protected by the right to free speech?

Obviously, talking is speech. So is writing. So are pictures (situation 2) and other forms

---

FIGURE 13-1

Bill of Rights

Amendment I

Congress shall make no law respecting an establishment of religion, or prohibiting the free exercise thereof; or abridging the freedom of speech, or of the press; or the right of the people peaceably to assemble, and to petition the government for a redress of grievances.

Amendment II

A well regulated militia, being necessary to the security of a free state, the right of the people to keep and bear arms, shall not be infringed.

Amendment III

No soldier shall, in time of peace be quartered in any house, without the consent of the owner, nor in time of war, but in a manner to be prescribed by law.

Amendment IV

The right of the people to be secure in their persons, houses, papers, and effects, against unreasonable searches and seizures, shall not be violated, and no warrants shall issue, but upon probable cause, supported by oath or affirmation, and particularly describing the place to be searched, and the persons or things to be seized.

Amendment V

No person shall be held to answer for a capital, or otherwise infamous crime, unless on a presentment or indictment of a grand jury, except in cases arising in the land or naval forces, or in the militia, when in actual service in time of war or public danger; nor shall any person be subject for the same offense to be twice put in jeopardy of life or limb; nor shall be compelled in any criminal case to be a witness against himself, nor be deprived of life, liberty, or property, without due process of law; nor shall private property be taken for public use, without just compensation.

Amendment VI

In all criminal prosecutions, the accused shall enjoy the right to a speedy and public trial, by an impartial jury of the state and district wherein the crime shall have been committed, which district shall have been previously ascertained by law, and to be informed of the nature and cause of the accusation; to be confronted with the witnesses against him; to have compulsory process for obtaining witnesses in his favor, and to have the assistance of counsel for his defense.

Amendment VII

In suits at common law, where the value in controversy shall exceed twenty dollars, the right of trial by jury shall be preserved, and no fact tried by a jury, shall be otherwise reexamined in any court of the United States, than according to the rules of the common law.

Amendment VIII

Excessive bail shall not be required, nor excessive fines imposed, nor cruel and unusual punishments inflicted.

Amendment IX

The enumeration in the Constitution, of certain rights, shall not be construed to deny or disparage others retained by the people.

Amendment X

The powers not delegated to the United States by the Constitution, nor prohibited by it to the states, are reserved to the states respectively, or to the people.

---

of artistic expression. So is distributing speech (as in situation 3, for example). The right to speech also guarantees the right to read and hear speech.

Sometimes our actions speak louder than our words. Actions that we use to make a point are called symbolic speech. Symbolic speech is protected. Both situations 2 and 4 are examples of this protected form of free speech. Burning an effigy of a public figure would be protected speech. The U.S. Supreme Court has said that burning the flag is symbolic speech and is protected. This decision holds true unless the Constitution is amended or the court reverses its decision.

Can we do whatever we want in the name of symbolic speech?

SITUATION 5 Henry goes barefoot to school to symbolize his personal war against poverty. No one gets the message until he explains it, but the school principal is not impressed. The school dress code requires all students to wear shoes.

If armbands are symbolic speech, wouldn't the absence of shoes be also? Probably not, if no one understands what the action symbolizes. Are dress and hair codes constitutional? Don't they violate an individual's rights under the First Amendment? In general, the courts have said "no." They have allowed schools to have reasonable dress codes. The next sections will help you understand why dress codes have been allowed.

Limits on Free Speech

Can you say whatever you like whenever you want? Are there any limits? As with any freedom, freedom of speech carries with it a corresponding duty. You must use this freedom responsibly. You may exercise some of this responsibility yourself, apart from the requirements of laws. Think about times when you have curbed your own speech to protect yourself or others. The courts impose responsibility as well. They have justified limits on the freedoms of speech and press in cases in which speech would (1) create

a "clear and present danger" and (2) disrupt government activity.

Clear and Present Danger

The Supreme Court has held that the government may act to restrain speech that presents a clear and present danger. One classic example is that you may not yell "fire!" in a crowded theater if there is no fire. If you did, there would be needless panic. People might be injured. The need for public safety outweighs the right to free speech.

Are situations 6 and 7 examples of clear and present dangers? Should speech be limited in them?

SITUATION 6 A member of the Communist Party stands quietly on the steps of the state capitol in Atlanta. She hands out pamphlets to visitors. The pamphlets do not suggest that the current government be overthrown by force. Rather, they urge revision of the Georgia Constitution to create a communist state government.

SITUATION 7 At a protest rally outside city hall, a speaker tells the crowd to destroy the building. Many protestors are carrying bricks, and some even have guns.

The Communist Party member on the capitol steps in situation 6 does not present a clear and present danger. The government has no right to interfere with her activity. Would it make a difference if she were urging people to overthrow the state government by violent means? Her speech could be prohibited only if she were urging such violence to people capable of carrying it out in the immediate future. In situation 7, the speaker is urging violence to people who can carry it out. The speaker's words do present a clear and present danger. The right of others not to suffer harm outweighs the speaker's right to free speech.

Disruption of Government Activity

Courts also allow restraints on speech that interferes with important government activities. In the following situations, does the exercise of free speech threaten the functioning of a government activity? Do the actions justify the government's restraint of free speech?

> **SITUATION 8** At a criminal trial, a spectator talks loudly to his companion. The judge warns all spectators in the courtroom to be quiet. The visitor continues to talk loudly. Finally, the judge imposes a fine of $25 on him for disrupting the trial. The judge has him escorted from the courtroom.

> **SITUATION 9** A group of students carry large homemade posters to school. The posters protest cruel treatment of animals. Other students taunt the protestors. A fight ensues. The school bans use of all posters inside the school building.

Some government activities require more order than others. The activities of a courtroom, for example, require more order than do activities that take place at a park. For this reason, the courts have allowed governments to restrict free speech in some situations more than in others.

Situation 8 is a good example of how free speech can disrupt a government activity. In this situation, the judge and jury would have been distracted by the noise. The defendant's right to a fair trial would override the visitor's right to free speech.

In situation 9, the fight clearly disrupted the educational process. However, limiting a constitutional right to prevent interruption of a government activity, as in this situation, is a serious decision. The ban of all posters may be excessive. Certain questions arise. Were the posters the cause of the fight? Will a ban on posters prevent further disruptions?

As you can see, limits on the right to free speech represent a balance. The rights of the individual must be weighed against the rights of other individuals or society. Even though there are only two main limits on the freedom of speech (that is, speech that presents a clear and present danger and speech that interferes with important government activities), the govern-

Can you say whatever you like whenever you want? Are there any limits on free speech?

ment is still able to regulate (or restrict) speech according to certain rules.

Content-Neutral versus Viewpoint-Based Restrictions

The government can regulate free speech as long as the regulation is content neutral, meaning that it doesn't discriminate against certain viewpoints by restricting them. The government is not allowed to regulate a person's speech based only on the viewpoint expressed in that speech or activity. For example, if the city allows student organizations to hold gatherings in a local public park, then the city cannot prohibit a student organization from holding a gathering in the park just because the city does not like the viewpoint or ideas of that particular student group. On the other hand, if the city prohibits the same gathering because the number of attendees may be too large for the park to handle, then the prohibition is considered to be content neutral because it has no relation to the student organization's viewpoints or opinions. Therefore the prohibition is acceptable.

Time, Place, and Manner Restrictions

Another way the government can restrict a person's freedom of speech without violating his or her constitutional rights is with time, place, or manner restrictions. An example of this type of restriction is a law that says that no loud music may be played in a public area after 11 o'clock at night. A state or local government may justifiably restrict speech to protect citizens, to reduce crime, or to safeguard reasonable enjoyment of public areas.

Do All Kinds of Speech Have the Same Protection?

The First Amendment was written mainly to ensure the free exchange of ideas within our society, but speech has many purposes.

Commercial Speech

Speech that is intended solely to make money is called commercial speech. Commercial speech receives less protection than do other forms of speech. For instance, the government can require that commercial messages be truthful. You have encountered examples of this requirement in the chapters on consumer and credit law. The government can prohibit commercial messages related to unlawful activity. Drug dealers, for example, cannot advertise cocaine in the newspaper.

In addition to the restrictions mentioned earlier, the government can regulate commercial speech if the regulation advances a substantial interest and is not any broader than necessary. For example, the Supreme Court found that a state law that requires stores located near schools to keep all tobacco products behind the counter advances (or promotes) that state's "substantial interest" in not advertising tobacco products to young people.[1]

Slander and Libel

As you learned in chapter 10, slander or libel is speech that is not true and may injure others. Usually the injury is to a person's reputation. The First Amendment allows you to say whatever you like, but it does not protect you against liability for damages caused by slander or libel. It does not give you the right to hurt someone else.

Fighting Words

"Fighting words" are speech or expressions likely to cause an "imminent breach of the peace." That is, they incite others to violence against you or others. Like slander, fighting words are not protected by the First Amendment. However, the courts have interpreted fighting words very narrowly. Just what would constitute fighting words is unclear.

> **SITUATION 10** You are a basketball player, and your team is under a lot of pressure to win the sixth game of the season. Near the end of the first half, a player from the other team elbows you in the stomach. You double over in pain and yell, "I'm going to break your jaw!"

In this situation, you are urging violence against a person. You also have the ability to carry out the action, and your words might therefore be considered inciting. But consider another example: after the game, you hear that a team that has regularly beat your team in the state finals is winning a game in a city about 200 miles away. Most probably, it would be different if you said you were going to break the jaw of that team's coach. You do not have the present or immediate ability to carry out this action. This situation makes these words less inciting, or less likely to cause a breach of the peace.

Security of Prisons, Schools, and Military Bases

The courts have repeatedly decided cases in favor of free speech rights in situations involving students, prisoners, and military personnel. However, because of the need for security, the rights of these groups may sometimes be limited. Consider the following situation:

> **SITUATION 11** Some students at school are wearing Confederate flag T-shirts. Others are wearing shirts with "Malcolm X" printed on them. The school principal bans all T-shirts with messages on them.

The courts have said that students generally have free speech rights at school unless what they say creates a "reasonable likelihood of material and substantial disruption." What if the students get into fights about their T-shirts? Would there be a reasonable likelihood that material and substantial disruption would occur in this situation? The ban on all T-shirts with messages may be too broad. What would be a better dress code rule?

Obscenity

Should the government allow the free expression of language that deeply offends some people? Should X-rated TV programs be available to young children without government restrictions? What about music that has obscenities or Internet websites that have offensive speech? Most people, especially parents, have very strong opinions on this issue.

In majority decisions, the U.S. Supreme Court clearly has held that obscene material is not protected by the First Amendment. What the court has not done, however, is to clearly define obscene material. The Supreme Court has said that material is considered to be obscene only if three factors are present:

1. It appeals to the prurient interest. (Prurient refers to an obsessive interest in sexual matters.)
2. It depicts or describes, in an obviously offensive way, sexual conduct.
3. The work, taken as a whole, lacks "serious literary, artistic, political, or scientific value."

There are many problems with this standard. For example, people do not agree on which works have literary or artistic value. The Supreme Court has held that "contemporary community standards" are to be used to decide what is obscene.

Is this a helpful guideline? Think about how this standard would apply in Georgia. Should the standards of the entire state be used? Should each local community set its own standards? Who in the community should say what the standards are?

1. In interpreting the First Amendment, how have the courts defined speech?
2. Give an example of symbolic speech.
3. Name the two principles that can be used to justify limits on free speech.
4. What is commercial speech?
5. Which of the following would not be protected by the First Amendment? (a) obscenity, (b) slander, (c) offensive language, (d) fighting words, (e) commercial speech.

T h i n k   A b o u t

1. List some of your responsibilities in exercising your freedom of speech. Explain how the rights of others might be harmed if you did not act responsibly.
2. In which of the following government agencies should dress codes be permitted? (a) prisons, (b) military branches, (c) libraries, (d) parks, (e) schools, (f) courtrooms. Explain your reasons.
3. A law is proposed to make recording companies "rate" music, just as movies are rated, to indicate that lyrics are violent or sexually explicit. Give arguments for and against this law.
4. You are asked to appoint a committee of 15 to determine standards of obscenity for your county. What kinds of people will you ask to serve as representatives of community standards? What will be your definition of obscenity?

FREEDOM OF THE PRESS

The authors of the U.S. Constitution wanted a strong and independent press to ensure that the public would always be informed about what was happening in government and society. A free press enables people to make informed decisions on issues and candidates for office.

Not all countries guarantee the right to freedom of the press. In many countries, the newspapers and radio and television stations are owned and run by the government. What problems, if any, could arise in that situation? What might be the benefits of that system?

In the United States, anyone with the means and desire can publish a magazine or newsletter. Radio and television stations may be regulated, however, because there are a limited number of frequencies (or channels) on a radio or television set. Nevertheless, this control cannot be used to suppress information.

To have freedom, the press must have access to information and be able to present the information it obtains. As you will see, sometimes these rights conflict with others.

The right to a free press is basic to democracy.

The Right to Access

Members of the press feel that they have a right to know about government activities. However, governments may want to deny the press access to some information. When this kind of conflict occurs, courts have to decide between the public's right to know and the government's reason for withholding information. Consider the following situations.

SITUATION 12 The planning commission of Shadyside, Georgia, wants to bar the press from its monthly meeting. The commission expects to vote on the location of an airport. Town citizens have strong, varying opinions about the matter. Commissioners want to play down the conflict.

SITUATION 13 The city council of Shadyside wants to review the personnel record of the police chief and possibly discipline him. The council denies the press access to the meeting.

SITUATION 14 The national government bars reporters from observing military maneuvers in the South Pacific.

"Sunshine laws" in Georgia (and other states) require governments to hold open meetings when official actions are taken. For this reason, the press could not be denied access in situation 12. There are exceptions. One is when disciplinary actions might be taken against public employees (situation 13). In that case, the individual's right to privacy is seen as more important than the public's right to know.

At times, the federal government has denied the press access to information in the interest of national security (situation 14). Clearly, to preserve democracy, it is important to guard against too many government actions that take place in secret. Generally, however, the courts have supported the government's position on this issue.

Disclosing Sources

Another conflict occurs when the government asks reporters to reveal their sources. Sometimes, reporters are given important information by people who want to remain anonymous. These people might stop providing information if their names were made public.

This conflict usually occurs in relation to criminal trials. The Sixth Amendment of the U.S. Constitution guarantees a defendant the right to confront witnesses who give evidence against him or her. Defense lawyers may therefore insist on learning the names of sources, or prosecuting attorneys may want the names of sources to build a stronger case.

Do reporters have to reveal their sources? Traditionally, courts have held that the need for a fair trial outweighs the right to a free press in this situation. However, the courts have only insisted on learning the names of sources that are essential to a case. Georgia and most states now have "shield laws." These laws allow reporters to protect their sources in certain situations.

Even if a shield law exists, though, courts can require the disclosure of a source if it is essential to the case and cannot be obtained another way. Often, when a court insists on the disclosure of a reporter's source, the name will be revealed in the judge's chamber. In this way, the source is given as much privacy as possible.

Prior Restraint to a Free Press

SITUATION 15 Sonja is accused of murdering her nephew and niece. The bodies were disposed of in a particularly gruesome way. Day by day, the press reports on police investigations. They print details about Sonja's personal affairs. The police are convinced Sonja is guilty.

Will the press coverage prevent her from getting a fair trial?

The situation is not unusual. Defense attorneys frequently ask whether a trial can be fair when it receives a lot of publicity. The question is, does a great deal of publicity cause potential jurors to form opinions about the guilt or innocence of the defendant before a trial? The courts have decided that such publicity may prevent a fair trial. In response, the courts have issued "gag orders" to prohibit press coverage before and during trials. The problem is that gag orders amount to prior restraint of the press, which is forbidden by the Constitution as censorship before publication. Consequently, gag orders can be used only under certain circumstances.

Courts have other alternatives. For example, they can move trials to other areas. They can delay trials. They can take care in instructing jurors. They can ask jurors what they have seen in newspapers and on television about the case. They can further ask if exposure to that information has affected jurors' views.

Prior Restraint and School Newspapers

SITUATION 16 A journalism class at Hazelwood East High School in St. Louis produced a newspaper. It was paid for partly by sales and partly by the Board of Education. As was customary, the journalism teacher submitted an issue to the principal to review. The principal objected to two articles. One article was about the pregnancies of three unidentified students. The other dealt with the impact of a divorce on an identified student. The principal took out the stories.

Can the principal take such action?

In this real-life case, three student staff members sued on the basis of censorship or prior restraint. The newspaper even had a school-approved policy that upheld First Amendment rights. This case went to the U.S. Supreme Court. The school had argued that publication of the articles would imply school endorsement. Because the paper was produced in a class and mostly financed by the school system, the court's majority agreed with the school on this point. In addition, it felt that schools have the right to regulate class activities in a reasonable manner. In effect, the court provided a right for schools to exercise editorial control over student publications in such situations. However, the court said any censorship must have a valid educational purpose, and it cannot be directed at silencing a particular viewpoint.[2]

1. Why is a strong and free press important to democracy?
2. Define "gag order" and "sunshine law."

T h i n k   A b o u t

1. In which of the instances that follow would you put another right or interest over freedom of the press?
   a. tests of a controversial and expensive missile
   b. expenditures of the Central Intelligence Agency
   c. the hearing of a 14-year-old boy accused of a string of burglaries in a small community
   d. the grief of parents whose child was just killed
2. Based on what you have read in this section, list rules your school newspaper should follow. Are there subjects the paper should not cover?
3. What is the value of free speech and a free press? Why have people been willing to make great sacrifices for their freedom?

FREEDOMS OF ASSEMBLY, ASSOCIATION, AND PETITION

Freedom of Assembly

SITUATION 17 A group of parents are unhappy with a decision by the city government. Due to limited funds, the summer recreation program is being discontinued. The parents decide to object by holding a demonstration near city hall. They march to the front of the building. There they stand quietly for one hour, holding their signs and handing out leaflets.

Do you think that the parents should be permitted to demonstrate in front of city hall? Does their activity disrupt the government's activities?

Another right given to Americans is the right to assemble. However, the courts have generally said that governments may set reasonable restrictions on the time, place, and manner in which people gather. They can set these restrictions to prevent a danger to or disruption of government activity.

Any law restricting a group's freedom to assemble must be very clear and have clear guidelines that a state, police, or other enforcement agency can follow. Governments may require permits for activities such as those in situation

What if the government had the right to disperse persons who gather to protest laws?

At the state capitol, citizens express their views on a legislative issue. The constitutions of Georgia and the United States guarantee the people the right to assemble peaceably.

Freedom of Association

Closely related to freedom of speech and assembly is freedom of association. This freedom is the right of individuals to associate with others for political, social, or economic reasons. There are professional groups such as associations of teachers or musicians. There are labor unions. There are business organizations such as chambers of commerce. There are neighborhood associations. There are environmental protection organizations. There are groups sponsoring high school events. You can probably think of many more.

What would happen if the government could forbid any association it did not like? What if it could forbid associations of African Americans or Hispanics? What if the president of the United States decided to forbid all other political parties but his own? Would democracy still be possible?

Thinking about these questions will make you understand more clearly some of the reasons for the freedoms of association and assembly. These freedoms allow opportunities for exchanging and developing ideas. They allow forums in which people can discuss their problems and how to deal with them.

In addition to protecting the right to associate with whomever you want, the First Amendment also protects the right of private individuals not to associate with others. For example, private clubs or organizations may exclude individuals from membership. The government, though, does not have the right to exclude people from government participation or employment for just any reason. For example, a public school cannot admit students based solely on their race or national origin, except in very rare instances.

There are some limitations on the rights of individuals to associate. The right to associate does not extend to gathering for illegal or criminal purposes. Sometimes people form associations to object to laws or government policies. In those cases, the right to associate is especially important. As a matter of fact, the framers of the U.S. Constitution had two purposes in mind

17. However, the procedures for obtaining a permit must be clear and fairly applied. A permit cannot be denied because a group or its cause is disliked.

Furthermore, such restrictions must be reasonable. A government might prohibit demonstrations in front of a building's entrance during work hours. However, to allow demonstrations only between 2 a.m. and 3 a.m. would be unreasonable.

Suppose the parents in situation 17 decided to distribute their pamphlets door-to-door in their neighborhood. What if they wanted to drive a vehicle with a loudspeaker through the downtown area? In these instances, the right to free expression might conflict with other people's right to peace and order. Courts can prohibit groups from disrupting traffic on a freeway or littering a park, for example. Cities may require permits for door-to-door solicitors in order to protect people's privacy. However, those permit requirements cannot infringe on a person's right to religious freedom or anonymous political speech. Because of noise nuisance, the use of loudspeakers may be limited or prohibited.

when they wrote the document: (1) to establish a government and (2) to protect the people from oppression by that government. The freedoms in the Bill of Rights permit people to act to change our society without the need for violence. Without these freedoms, the Civil Rights movement, for example, might never have occurred.

During the Civil Rights movement, people protested existing laws by disobeying them. This form of protest is called civil disobedience. A person does not have the right to avoid punishment for civil disobedience. However, the government may never prevent a group of persons from associating to object to a civil law.

SITUATION 18 Alex applies for a job. The application asks if he is a member of the Communist Party. He is a member of this group—but he does not want to say so.

Do such questions limit freedom of association?

Many people fear that identifying the members of a group will lead to their harassment. However, courts have supported such disclosure if the government can show a compelling interest in identifying the group members. A compelling interest might be to prevent illegal activity.

What if Alex was applying for a job with the Department of Defense in situation 18? Would that make a difference?

Right of Petition

The right of petition to the government is expressly mentioned in the First Amendment. This right guarantees that individuals may seek access to all agencies of government, not just their elected representatives. Thus, you can call the mayor to complain about garbage collection, or you and other students can sign a letter asking the school principal to have several basketball team rallies. This right means that you can, with others, ask a court to halt the polluting of a river. The Georgia Constitution also guarantees the right to assemble and petition.

Only the Facts

1. Explain the importance of freedom of assembly and freedom of association.
2. Give two rules a government must follow if it requires a permit for a demonstration.
3. When is the right of association not protected?
4. What is the right to petition? Give an example of when it might be used.

Think About

1. "The government should be able to demand the names of members of a group opposed to paying taxes." Give reasons for and against the statement.

FREEDOM OF RELIGION

Another First Amendment freedom you have probably heard about is freedom of religion. It requires the federal government to be absolutely neutral in matters of religion. First, no law can limit an individual's right to worship according to his or her particular religious belief. Second, no law can establish or advance any religion.

In the Georgia Constitution, there are several paragraphs regarding freedom of religion:

Freedom of conscience. Each person has the natural and inalienable right to worship God, each according to the dictates of that person's own conscience; and no human authority should, in any case, control or interfere with such right of conscience.
[Article 1, section 1, paragraph 3]

Religious opinions; freedom of religion. No inhabitant of this state shall be molested in person or property or be prohibited from holding any public office or trust on account of religious opinions; but the right of freedom of religion shall not be so construed as to excuse acts of licentiousness or justify practices inconsistent with the peace and safety of the state.

[Article 1, section 1, paragraph 4]

Separation of church and state. No money shall ever be taken from the public treasury, directly or indirectly, in aid of any church, sect, cult, or religious denomination of any sectarian institution.

[Article 1, section 2, paragraph 7]

Free Exercise of Religious Beliefs

In the free exercise of religion, there are two elements. One is the freedom to believe. The other is the freedom to act in accordance with one's religious beliefs. The freedom to believe is absolute. That is, the government cannot take

The First Amendment ensures our right to worship in our own religion. Can government regulate our religious actions or activities?

any action to force an individual to believe or not to believe in a particular religious principle. In contrast, the freedom to act in accordance with one's religious beliefs is not absolute. It may be regulated by the government to a limited extent. However, a government cannot enact a law that discriminates against a particular religion.

SITUATION 19 In Massachusetts, a special committee has to approve the educational program that a private school provides to ensure that it meets the state's compulsory attendance laws. The New Life Baptist Church objects to this requirement. Its members believe it is a sin to submit their educational program to a non-religious body for approval. They request that they not be required to submit to the regulation, saying it discriminates against their religion.

Does the Massachusetts law discriminate against this religion?

The state's Court of Appeals considered the rights of parents and students to express their religious beliefs. It weighed them against the state's interest in children receiving an adequate education. The court held that the state's interest was more important.

Governments may not make individuals act against their religious beliefs. However, what about the following situation?

SITUATION 20 During World War II, several children and parents in West Virginia refused to obey a law requiring them to salute the flag in schools. They said the action was against their religion. Their beliefs forbade them to bow down to or serve "graven images."

In a landmark decision for free expression, the U.S. Supreme Court upheld the rights of the parents and children to exercise their religious beliefs.[3] In subsequent decisions, the court has held that a government may not require a public employee to swear to a belief in God. Nor can a government refuse unemployment compensation to a man fired for refusing to work on Sunday because of his religious beliefs.

Consider the events in situation 21. Is the limitation of Rhonda's rights justifiable?

SITUATION 21 Rhonda is arrested for drunk driving. The government wants to take a blood sample. She refuses. She says her religious beliefs forbid any intrusion into the body. The government takes away her driver's license.

A court would probably restore Rhonda's license to her. The government's action could only be justified if an alternative method of obtaining evidence had been offered and refused. For example, she could have been allowed to breathe into an intoximeter.

More difficult cases arise when an individual refuses medical treatment because of a religious belief. Generally, when the situation is life threatening, courts have ruled in favor of the well-being of children over the religious beliefs of the parents.

The classic example of religious activity prohibited by the government is polygamy. Polygamy occurs when a person has more than one spouse at one time. The Mormon Church once held the belief that men should have several wives (the church has since prohibited polygamy). Polygamy is now a crime in all states. The U.S. Supreme Court has held that polygamy is a punishable offense.

No Establishment of State Religion

The other aspect of freedom of religion is that the government may not take any action that establishes or promotes any religion. This "establishment clause" is the fundamental principle of separation of church and state.

Many settlers of our country felt very strongly about this principle. They came from countries where there was a state religion. Many were persecuted in their native countries for practicing other religions.

Today, government actions are continually being challenged on the grounds that they violate this separation (see figure 13-2). Govern-

FIGURE 13-2

Church Tax Exemption

Most states exempt churches from paying property taxes. Does this exemption violate the separation of church and state? Apply the three requirements to decide.

1. Does this exemption have a nonreligious purpose?
   Yes. The exemption is also given to other nonprofit organizations, such as schools and hospitals.

2. Is its main effect to advance or repress religion?
   Although the property tax exemption certainly helps church finances, advancing religion is not its main effect. Because the exemption is given to all churches, it does not advance a particular religion.

3. Does the exemption result in too much entangling of government and religion?
   Because of this exemption, the government cannot use its power to tax to regulate church activities. The main effect of the exemption is actually to increase the separation of church and state.

ment assistance to church schools in the form of busing or tuition credits has been objected to on these grounds, as has prayer in schools or in other public places.

Of course, some government and church interaction must occur. Churches need government services like fire and police protection. However, in keeping with the principle of separation of church and state, the courts have said that any law or government activity must meet three requirements:

1. It must have a nonreligious purpose;

2. Its main effect must not be to repress or advance religion; and

3. It must not result in too much entangling (or involvement) of government and religion.

Figure 13-2 shows how these criteria are applied to one activity. How would you apply this test to situation 22?

SITUATION 22 A state wanted to set up a special school district to serve the disabled students of a particular religious sect. Years earlier, the state had provided special services to disabled students in their private, single-sex religious schools. Then in 1985 the Supreme Court decided that these services were unconstitutional.

In its 1994 decision, the Supreme Court ruled against the establishment of a specific school district to serve the disabled students of one particular religious sect.[4] The Court held that this action equates to an unconstitutional establishment of religion. It would be giving the children of one religious sect special treatment for their religion. However, establishing such school districts for all students—regardless of their religion—might have been found constitutional.

SITUATION 23 Several students at Westside High School in Connecticut decided to form a Bible group. They wanted to meet after school hours on school property, but the principal refused to give them permission. He said that such a meeting would violate the establishment clause. The students protested, pointing out that the scuba and chess teams got to meet after school on school property.

What decision would you have made about this real-life situation? Should the principal have allowed the Bible group to meet after school was over? The court thought so. It said that it is one thing to coerce students into religious activity: that would be supporting establishment of religion. Permitting it on a nondiscriminatory basis, however, does not.[5]

SITUATION 24 For a long time, pregame prayers (invocations) had been delivered before Douglas County High School football games. In 1985, a student objected to these prayers. He felt they were against his religious beliefs as a Native American. The school came up with a plan for school clubs to select speakers to present the invocations, but the student wanted all pregame speeches to be nonreligious.

Do the pregame invocations meet the three requirements? The 11th Circuit Court of Appeals found that the invocations had a religious purpose.[6] In the predominantly Protestant community, the court said a main effect would be to publicly advance Protestant Christianity. The court ruled that the invocations violated the establishment clause.

A Supreme Court decision in 2000 agreed with the 11th Circuit Court of Appeals. It found that invocations prior to football games, even if they were initiated and led by students, violated the Constitution's establishment clause.[7]

O n l y   t h e   F a c t s

1. Name the two aspects of the First Amendment right of freedom of religion.

2. In keeping with the principle of separation of church and state, the courts have said that any law or government activity must meet three requirements. List them.

T h i n k   A b o u t

1. Is a court likely to find the following acts constitutional? Why or why not?
   a. a law forbidding the teaching of evolution in public schools unless "creation science" is also taught.
   b. a blind person using state funds to attend a Christian college to become a pastor. (Note that the state provides funds for the education of blind individuals.)
   c. construction of a logging road in an area held sacred by Native Americans.
   d. after-school meetings of Christian youth groups in a public school.

2. Are church and state always separate in this country? Give evidence for your opinion. Why do you think we have the concept of separation of church and state?

3. "Under no circumstances should the government be allowed to prohibit an individual's religious practices." Do you agree or disagree? Explain your reasons.

4. Do you think prayer in school is a good idea? If so, which prayer should be used? What about a moment of silence?

OTHER CONSTITUTIONAL GUARANTIES

There are other constitutional rights besides those in the First Amendment (see figure 13-1). Some are specified, such as the Second Amendment right to bear arms. Others are not specified, such as those in the Ninth and Tenth Amendments. Some have been recognized by court interpretations over the past two centuries. Freedom of association has already been discussed. Three important rights—the rights to bear arms, to privacy, and to vote—are discussed in this section.

Is There a Right to Bear Arms?

Recent controversy over laws to control ownership of handguns has focused interest on the Second Amendment. This amendment guarantees to citizens the right to bear arms. Historically, this right was to make sure that each state could maintain a "militia." Therefore the courts have said that its protection specifically relates to establishing a state militia. The amendment does not prohibit laws limiting people's right to own guns and other weapons. There is a similar provision in the Georgia Constitution that expressly authorizes the General Assembly to "prescribe the manner in which arms may be borne" (Article 1, section 1, paragraph 8).

Is There a Right to Privacy?

You will not find a specific reference to a right to privacy in the U.S. Constitution. Indeed, this right has been drawn from a number of constitutional guaranties of privacy from governmental intrusion, including the Third, Fourth, and Ninth amendments. In 1904, Georgia was the first state in the country to recognize a right to privacy.

The right to privacy affects our lives in matters beyond searches, protection of records, and drug testing. It affects our right to die rather than live in a coma. It protects reproductive and family rights. The courts have said that the government may not interfere without proper reason in matters relating to family relationships. For example, any requirements a government sets for getting married must be reasonable. Would laws such as the following be constitutional?

> **SITUATION 25** In order to obtain an abortion, a dependent unmarried minor is required by a state law to notify one parent. The requirement can be waived by the juvenile court if it is in the "best interest of the minor."

> **SITUATION 26** To control population, the state makes it a crime to have more than two children.

In protecting the rights of individuals to make choices about their families, the courts have recognized a person's right to have access to birth control. They have prohibited laws requiring that some welfare recipients be sterilized. In a controversial 1973 decision, *Roe v. Wade*, the Supreme Court recognized the right of women to an abortion.[8] (Since then, those opposed to abortions have worked hard to have this decision overturned.) On the other hand, two 1990 decisions of the U.S. Supreme Court have made constitutional a Georgia law similar to that in situation 25, even though the Georgia law limits the rights of minors with respect to abortion.[9]

Do couples have a right to decide the size of their families? Yes. The law in situation 26 would be unconstitutional. Not all countries allow their citizens such freedoms, however. The Chinese government has tried to ensure that couples have only one child. A former Romanian government used its power to force citizens to have as many children as possible.

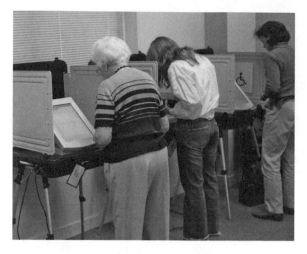

Georgia was the first state to lower the voting age from 21 to 18. The Twenty-sixth Amendment to the Constitution gave 18-year-olds across the country the right to vote.

Is There a Right to Vote?

The U.S. Constitution barely mentions the right to vote. Indeed, for much of the country's history, many people did not have that right. For over 130 years, voting was mostly limited to white males aged 21 years and older. Even their right to vote was sometimes restricted. They sometimes had to pay a special tax, called a poll tax, or pass a literacy test.

Constitutional amendments have extended the right to vote. In 1870, the Fifteenth Amendment extended voting rights to men of all races. In 1920, the Nineteenth Amendment gave women the right to vote. In 1943, Georgia became the first state to lower the voting age from 21 to 18. State officials felt that those old enough to fight in World War II were old enough to vote. In 1971, the Twenty-sixth Amendment gave 18-year-olds across the country the right to vote.

Only the Facts

1. Are the following statements true or false?

   a. The Constitution gives everyone the right to have a handgun.

   b. The Fourth Amendment specifically says that people have a "right to privacy."

   c. People have the right of access to birth control measures.

   d. Women have been able to vote since the Civil War.

   e. Georgia was the first state to change the voting age from 21 to 18.

   If the statements are false, explain what is incorrect about them.

Think About

1. Not everyone agrees with the Supreme Court's interpretation of the Second Amendment. Give a reason for disagreeing and one for agreeing.

2. Should minors have to notify a parent before they have an abortion? Give arguments for and against.

3. Should family members be able to allow withdrawal of life-giving procedures from a hopelessly comatose relative? A 1990 court decision let the states determine what the law will be in this matter. What do you think the law should be?

4. How would you define the "right to privacy"? What do you think it should protect?

5. Not everyone takes advantage of the right to vote—particularly younger voters. What could be done to encourage more people to vote?

SUMMING UP

Before you read this chapter, what did your constitutional freedoms mean to you? Had you thought about the meaning of free speech or free association? Did you realize that your right to free speech was limited in some circumstances, that your right to associate did not include criminal associations, or that your freedom to worship could be restricted?

Like all freedoms, these constitutional rights imply responsibilities. There is always a need for balance—to prevent one person's free actions from depriving another person of a basic right. In the next chapter, you will read about how the government must balance individual rights against its duty to provide order and justice.

Notes

1. *Lorillard Tobacco Co. v. Reilly*, 533 U.S. 525, 569–70, 121 S. Ct. 2404, 2429–30 (2001).
2. *Hazelwood School Dist. v. Kuhlmeier*, 108 S. Ct. 562 (1988).
3. *West Virginia v. Barnette*, 63 S. Ct. 1178 (1943).
4. *Board of Education v. Grumet*, 114 S. Ct. 2481 (1994).
5. *Bd. of Educ. of Westside Com. Sch. V. Mergens*, 110 S. Ct. 2356 (1990).
6. *Jager v. Douglas County School District*, 862 F.2d 824 (11th Cir. 1989).
7. *Santa Fe Independent School District v. Doe*, 530 U.S. 290, 309, 120 S. Ct. 2266, 2279 (2000).
8. 410 U.S. 113 (1973).
9. *Hodgson v. Minnesota*, 110 S. Ct. 2926 (1990); *Ohio v. Akron Center for Reproductive Health*, 110 S. Ct. 2972 (1990).

14 | Guaranties of Fairness

LAW TALK

arbitrary reason

due process

eminent domain

equal protection

fair manner

fundamental right

rational basis

strict scrutiny

The founders of our country had great concern for fairness in government and law. In fact, the writers of the Declaration of Independence expressed this concern explicitly when they wrote about equality:

> We hold these truths to be self-evident, that all men are created equal, that they are endowed by their Creator with certain unalienable rights, that among these are Life, Liberty and the pursuit of Happiness. . . .

Both the U.S. and Georgia constitutions put limits on government in an effort to ensure that each person is treated fairly under the laws. They provide that the government—or anyone using the powers of government—cannot take away "life, liberty, or property" without "due process of law." Moreover, everyone must be given equal protection under the law.

What these provisions mean will be explained later in this chapter. Keep in mind, however, that these provisions are like the ones described in chapter 13. They are restrictions on government action, and they apply directly only to people acting on behalf of government. These provisions can, however, be extended to private activity by the passage of other laws.

DUE PROCESS

What Is Due Process?

The due process clause (figure 14-1) requires that the government act fairly in two ways:

1. The government may not take away life, liberty, or property for reasons that are arbitrary (that is, reasons that are illogical, inconsistent, unjust, or impulsive).

2. Even if it has an appropriate reason, the government may take away these rights only in a fair manner (that is, after providing the process that is "due").

In this part of the chapter, we'll look closely at the key terms "life, liberty, or property," "arbitrary reasons," and "fair manner."

Who is protected by due process? Basically everyone subject to our laws is protected. Protection extends not only to U.S. citizens but also to

- persons from other states and foreign countries (but only under certain circumstances),
- artificial "persons," like corporations, and
- cities and counties under certain circumstances.

Protecting Life, Liberty, and Property

The government—or anyone using government powers—may not take away life, liberty, or property without due process of law. What is due process of law? It depends on what the laws and courts say it is, and that varies with the situation.

FIGURE 14-1

The Due Process Clause (Fifth Amendment)

No person shall be held to answer for a capital, or otherwise infamous crime, unless on a presentment or indictment of a Grand Jury, except in cases arising in the land or naval forces, or in the Militia, when in actual service in time of War or public danger; nor shall any person be subject for the same offence to be twice put in jeopardy of life or limb; nor shall he be compelled in any criminal case to be a witness against himself, nor be deprived of life, liberty, or property, without due process of law; nor shall private property be taken for public use, without just compensation.

Life

Depriving you of life is the most serious action that can be taken against you. Therefore the government is the most restricted in this action. It is critical that the government act for proper reasons and in a fair manner. Clearly, a person who might be sentenced to death for murder is entitled to the protection of the due process clause. What about the person in the following situation?

> **SITUATION 1** Sam was drafted into the army during the Vietnam conflict. He did not want to go. After training, he was sent into a heavy combat zone. He was killed.

Wasn't his life "taken by the government" against his will? Does the due process clause apply?

The possibility of a person in the military being killed by the enemy is outside the scope of the due process clause. It was not the government that took Sam's life. Rather, it was taken by the enemy whom he was fighting. He was fighting because he had a duty, imposed by due process of law, to defend his country.

There are, however, situations that involve the military when due process (and equal protection) would apply. The government must choose who will be drafted in a fair manner. If accused of wrongdoing while in the military, a person must be tried fairly. Because of the unique nature of military service, however, many constitutional rights enjoyed by civilians are severely curtailed. Examples are freedoms of speech and assembly.

Liberty

A government must also meet the requirements of due process when it takes away a person's freedoms.

Confinement. Physical constraint is clearly a substantial loss of liberty. For this reason, there are many restraints on the criminal justice process (discussed later). However, confinement of a person may occur outside the criminal justice system. Does due process apply in situation 2?

> **SITUATION 2** Everyone knows Herbie. When he is not doing odd jobs, he sits in the park, feeding popcorn to the birds. Everyone knows he is not very smart, but he has never harmed anyone or anything.
>
> Some people are bothered because he stares at them as they walk through the park. They want to put Herbie away. They file a petition with the court to have Herbie committed to a mental hospital.

Q Is Herbie protected by the due process clause?

Yes, he is. Being placed in an institution against one's will, whether a prison or a mental hospital, involves a loss of liberty. The government must be justified in taking away that liberty.

Individuals who are committed to a mental hospital may present a danger to themselves or to society, or they may be in need of treatment that can be provided only within the hospital. However, in all instances, an individual cannot be deprived of liberty without due process. For Herbie to be committed to a mental hospital, there must be a hearing. He must be notified of it and given an opportunity to say why he should not be confined. Then the judge will make a decision as to whether or not he should be committed.

Individual rights. Constitutional rights such as freedom of speech are also protected by the due process clause. They are considered elements of liberty, meaning that they cannot be limited for arbitrary reasons. The government can, however, regulate the "time, manner, and place" of the exercise of these rights. (The restriction must be necessary and not overly restrictive.)

The due process clause also protects individual rights not actually spelled out in the U.S. Constitution, including the right to enter into contracts, to privacy, and to travel within the United States and move about in public places (see chapter 13).

Property

The last item protected by the due process clause is property. Like the freedom to enter into contracts, the right to own property is basic to our legal system.

What constitutes property may not always be clear. Do you think the following situations show property interests that would be protected by due process?

> **SITUATION 3** Nora's welfare payments are cut off for several months. It was thought, mistakenly, that she had a new job.
>
> **SITUATION 4** Ben and Betty move into a house recently vacated by a person who has not paid his city water bill. Water service is provided to them for a few weeks. Then, late one Friday afternoon, the city cuts it off. Ben and Betty are without water for the entire weekend.
>
> **SITUATION 5** The Board of Education is advised that a school security guard had been convicted of a felony. He had not put this information on his employment application. Therefore he is fired without a chance to explain his side of the story.
>
> **SITUATION 6** Ken is not doing well at the state university medical school. His academic record is excellent, but his performance with patients is poor. In his final year, Ken appeals a decision not to let him graduate. A group of local physicians evaluate his performance. By a split decision, they recommend that he not be graduated. As a result, he is dropped from medical school.

Whether you have a right in a particular property interest is a question of law. If you feel that such a right was taken from you unfairly, you would need to know the law concerning that property interest. You would usually need to consult an attorney.

Do you have a "property interest" in your own education?

Once people receive benefits or services from the state, the law says they have a property interest in them. Drivers' licenses and welfare payments (situation 3) are such benefits. The government is not required by the constitution to provide welfare benefits. However, if it does provide them, it must do so in a fair manner.

Water (situation 4) is provided as a government service. These benefits and services cannot be taken away without due process of law. Many public employees have a property interest in their jobs (situation 5). The school security guard may be entitled to a hearing before he is fired. Ken, on the other hand (situation 6), has the legal right to attend the state university medical school if he is qualified and if space is available for admission, but there is no guarantee that mere attendance will result in graduation.

The Fifth Amendment restricts the right of governments to take property from private individuals for public uses such as for building a highway. This government right is called the power of eminent domain. However, the amendment says the government cannot take property from someone without "just compensation." It protects the individual by requiring that the government act fairly in taking property.

What if a government action reduces the value of property? For example, what if a new airport significantly inhibits a family's use of their property? The law says that this situation may be a type of "taking," and the family may be entitled to compensation from the government. In addition, the family would be entitled to notice of the taking and would have an opportunity to be heard on the issue of the value of the taking.

Only the Facts

1. What is protected by the due process clause?
2. Would any of the following be protected by the state of Georgia's due process clause? (a) a visitor to Georgia from Thailand, (b) a corporation in Savannah, (c) the city of Valdosta.
3. What aspects of liberty are protected by the due process clause?
4. Give examples of three kinds of property protected by due process.
5. How are citizens protected against the government right of eminent domain?

Think About

1. Why do you think due process is extended to noncitizens? Are all constitutional rights extended to noncitizens? Should it matter if the noncitizen is legally or illegally in the United States?

Arbitrary Decisions: What Are They?

SITUATION 7 The principal of a high school decided one morning that every student whose name begins with a vowel should walk like a duck when in the school hallways. And, at the same time, he or she must quack. Any such student who didn't do so would be "fined" $10 to be used to help fund the Botany Club.

Was this an arbitrary decision?

Of course it was—for at least three reasons. First, it was arbitrarily imposed. There was no logical or sensible reason for the principal to decide to demean any students by making them act like ducks. Second, those subject to it were arbitrarily selected. The principal had no reason to single out students whose names began with vowels. There was no indication that those students constituted a group that differed from other students. Finally, imposing a fine (that is, the "taking" of a student's property) to help fund the Botany Club was also arbitrary. It improperly put a burden on these selected students to fund an activity. Funding the Botany Club should rightly have been done either by all students or by the club members.

In contrast, the state does have a rational basis for laws requiring children to attend school. The state's interest is in seeing that its children receive an education so that they will become productive citizens. The state can require you to go to school, even though this requirement deprives you of your liberty during the school day. The requirement is logically (that is, "rationally") related to a proper interest of the government.

In effect, the due process clause says that if the government chooses to pass laws that put people into certain categories (classify them), it must have a rational basis for its actions. Its reasons cannot be arbitrary, whimsical, or irrational.

What Is a Fair Manner?

The government may act to take life, liberty, or property for an adequate reason, but it must do so in a fair—not arbitrary—manner. If the government takes a person's property for public use, it must compensate the owner for the value of what is being taken. Generally, in order to ensure fairness, the person being affected must at least be notified of the proposed action and have a hearing.

This requirement covers the manner in which trials are handled when someone is being sued or prosecuted, but should a complete trial be held every time a government acts to take away a person's liberty or property? Should a trial be required no matter how great or how little the "taking" is? Many government agencies (including schools) may act on rules that limit a person's liberty or property rights.

The courts have determined that it is not reasonable to hold court for each incident. To decide when a full trial is necessary, they have developed a series of questions. The answers to these questions serve as guidelines for making this decision.

The next two situations illustrate the use of these guidelines.

> **SITUATION 8** Wyatt is notified that he has to pay $24 to the public library in fines on eight overdue books. He says the fine should be $18. He claims he returned two of the books on time. No hearing is required by Georgia law.

> **SITUATION 9** Because of Karen's severe and continuing mental problems, her husband asks the court to commit her to an institution. Although a full-blown trial would not be required, there must be a thorough investigative hearing before action can be taken.

Due process must therefore be provided even when a trial is not held. Usually, due process means that the affected party must receive adequate notice. Some type of hearing may also be involved.

Here are the questions that the court would ask when considering whether a full-blown trial or a less formal hearing is necessary—or whether neither is required.

1. What is being lost by the individual? Is the loss irreplaceable?

   The greater the loss, the more protection the procedures should provide. Wyatt's loss (situation 8) is quite small. Further, if a mistake is made in Wyatt's fine, the library can refund his money. On the other hand, a life or period of deprived liberty can never be replaced. If Karen (situation 9) is committed to the mental institution, she can never regain that time.

2. What chance is there that the liberty or property interest will be wrongly taken away?

Karen's situation involves a difficult factual question: is Karen mentally incompetent or dangerous? The answer is not always easy to determine. There could be conflicting testimony from experts.

On the other hand, it should be easy to determine how many books Wyatt checked out and if any were returned on time.

3. Would other elements of procedure reduce the risk of error? For example, would representation by a lawyer make a difference?

It might for Karen, and she is entitled to an attorney.

4. Are there other factors that might affect the procedures?

A concern here might be cost. Would additional procedures be too costly? For example, could a library afford to have hearings regarding every fine for overdue books? Such a costly requirement might prevent the library from providing any services at all. The cost of an attorney for Wyatt would certainly be higher than his fine.

What about Karen's situation? The costs must be weighed in both time and money. How much would any added procedures cost? Would the cost be worth it, considering the possible loss of her liberty?

Notice

One basic element of due process is notice. Notice requires that a person who may be affected by a government's action be informed of it. He or she must know that the government may act (or, in some cases, may have acted) to take away life, liberty, or property.

Several factors determine whether the notice complies with the due process clause. Is it timely? Is it sufficient? Can the notice ever be given after the action has been taken?

Consider whether fair notice has been given in the fictional case that follows.

CASE OF THE STUDENT SIT-IN

Ed, Ernie, and Sharon believe it is unlawful and immoral to require registration with the selective service (for compulsory military service). They decide to protest by sitting in the school principal's office at lunchtime. On the second day of their sit-in, the assistant principal tells them to leave. They refuse. He calls the police. The police pick them up.

A crowd gathers as the police carry the protesters out. Sid, who is in the crowd, heckles the police. Sid pushes Laurie, who is standing near him. Laurie falls in front of a police officer, tripping him. Ed and Ernie then break free. It is not clear if they hit any police officers as they do so. A small riot follows.

All the students involved are sent home immediately. They are told that school officials will meet to decide their punishments. They are not told where or when. Then about 2:30 p.m., the principal calls each of them at their homes. He says, "We school officials will meet at 4:00 p.m. to decide what to do." He does not say what the charges are against the students. He does not say what action the officials might take. He says he will call later that evening to tell them what their punishments will be.

Police remove the student protesters.

Have the students—Ed, Ernie, Sharon, Sid, and Laurie—been given proper notice?

In considering whether proper notice has been given, the courts will look at what permanent effects the punishments will have. In the Case of the Student Sit-in, Ed and Ernie were expelled. Sharon and Sid were suspended for eight days. A letter of reprimand was put in Laurie's record.

Now let's look at the elements of adequate notice.

Timeliness. For Laurie, the notice could be considered timely enough. Even if it were later determined that the reprimand was improper, the letter could be removed from her file without undue harm. For the other students, however, the notice would not have been adequate. They would not have had time to prepare a defense, and they would suffer harm that could not be reversed.

Sufficiency. The laws of Georgia and the decisions of the U.S. Supreme Court provide students with certain rights.

For a short-term suspension (less than 10 days), school officials must tell students why they are being suspended. In other words, students must be told what the charges are. If the students say they are not guilty, the officials also must tell them what the evidence is against them.

For expulsion or a long-term suspension, officials must notify students and their parents of the charges and possible punishments in writing. The officials must also provide a list of the people who say the students should be suspended. Students must also be given a report, either in writing or in person, of what these witnesses say.

After the action is taken. Notice after an action is taken is adequate only if the government is able to correct any errors. In Laurie's case, the letter of reprimand could be removed. It would be too late to give notice after Ed and Ernie had lost their term of school or after Sid and Sharon's suspensions were over.

Can individuals give up their right to notice? If the students had accepted the notice they received by phone from the principal, they could have waived their right to proper notice. Would such a waiver be fair? The students may not have known their rights. It would be fair only if rules on disciplinary procedures had previously been provided to each student's family—a requirement of Georgia law.

The Hearing

The other basic element of due process is a hearing. A hearing gives an individual an opportunity to tell his or her side of the story. The courts have required that several important issues be considered. These issues concern whether a hearing is necessary and how it should be conducted.

Necessity for a hearing. There are two reasons why an individual should have a hearing. The first is to determine the facts that form the basis for the government's action. In the Case of the Student Sit-In, one question would be, What did Laurie do to cause the disturbance? A second reason is to determine the extent to which the government will act on the basis of the facts. What will be the punishments? What will be the deprivation of life, liberty, or property?

Impartiality. The question of impartiality is critical. Is there any reason why the hearing body cannot act impartially? This question is frequently asked about hearings conducted by members of a government agency. For example, can an agency that has fired someone be impartial in reviewing complaints about the firing?

Conduct of the hearing. Should those affected by the government action be able to present their side of the story? Should they be able to call witnesses or to cross-examine the government's witnesses?

Evidence. How much evidence should be necessary to prove guilt? Enough to ensure that there is no reasonable doubt? Or should a lesser standard be sufficient? In weighing these questions, a judge will keep in mind how much deprivation could be imposed. The greater the deprivation, the greater the need for tight rules of evidence.

FIGURE 14-2

Defendant Rights in School Disciplinary Actions

Possible Action	Hearing Body	Testify on Own Behalf	Call and Cross-Examine Witnesses	Represen-tation by Counsel	Record of Hearing Findings	Appeal
Letter of complaint in file	School officials	Yes	No	No	No	Yes, in all cases; through admin-istrative levels and to courts.
Short-term suspension	School officials	Yes	No	No	No	
Long-term suspension/ expulsion	School officials or school board	Yes	Yes	Yes	Yes. Local board must report to state board and to person affected.	

Note: A student can be removed from school without a hearing if school officials think he or she poses an immediate danger. In no instance is there a right to an initial hearing by a court of law. However, a hearing must be held as soon as possible.

Legal representation. Having a lawyer is a fundamental right in most criminal cases. The question here is, should the hiring of a lawyer be necessary in noncriminal cases in which substantial liberty or property interests can be taken away by the government?

Presentation of findings. Should the body that holds the hearing record the evidence presented? Should it be required to write an opinion with explanations for the action taken?

Appeal. What if the person is dissatisfied with the hearing's outcome? Should he or she have a right to appeal? If so, should the appeal go to another hearing body or to a court?

Figure 14-2 shows some of the laws applying to school expulsions and suspensions in Georgia. It is clear that the principal and assistant principal in the case of the student sit in were remarkably uninformed about the laws involved. Fortunately, that is not usually true in real-life situations. Read the chart and the discussions on the hearings. Do you think the due process rights of the students involved in the sit-in were violated?

You might consider whether you think the law ensures due process for these students. For example, should a more formal hearing be required for short-term suspensions? Should the hearing in an expulsion be before a court rather than school officials?

Some of the rules regarding short-term suspensions were established by a decision of the U.S. Supreme Court.[1] The court felt that the damage to educational opportunity and reputation justified the requirements for notice and an informal hearing. The requirement for a hearing, the court believed, would help reduce any risk of error. The court also considered the cost to schools. It felt the requirement for informal hearings would be affordable.

There is little question that due process is one of our most important protections. You will be able to look again at how it works in the discussion of the criminal justice process. In criminal proceedings, individuals risk being deprived of large amounts of liberty, property, and even life.

O n l y   t h e   F a c t s

1. Which of the following choices is wrong? A reason is arbitrary because it is (a) illogical, (b) based on untrue information, (c) unpopular, (d) not sensible.

2. What are the two basic elements of due process?

3. To determine whether a hearing meets the requirements for due process in a particular situation, what questions should be asked?

4. Which of the following are always essential to due process?
   a. timeliness of notice
   b. a 12-person jury
   c. strict rules of evidence
   d. sufficient notice
   e. an attorney for both parties
   f. a fair hearing
   g. automatic review by the U.S. Supreme Court

T h i n k   A b o u t

1. Can due process guarantee fair results? Explain your answer.

2. Why is due process one of the strongest protections against the government's power? Consider what could happen without due process protection.

3. What do you think the requirements for notice and hearing should be for a government employee likely to be suspended without pay for two weeks?

EQUAL PROTECTION

Due process concerns the basic concept of fairness. The constitutional right to due process requires that the government act fairly when it deprives a person of life, liberty, or property. The requirement of equal protection applies more generally to government actions. It is the requirement usually referred to when people talk about discrimination. It concerns another fundamental concept—equality.

You know that people are not equal in all ways. The basic intent of equal protection is to make sure that people are treated as equally as possible under our legal system. For example, it is to see that everyone who gets a speeding ticket will face the same procedures. A further intent is to ensure that all Americans are provided with equal opportunities in education, employment, and other areas.

The 1954 case *Brown v. Topeka Board of Education* (discussed in chapter 3) was a landmark step in efforts to eliminate discrimination based on race in educational opportunity. Chapter 7 discussed equal protection in the workplace. This requirement for equal protection is found in both the state and federal constitutions. The Georgia Constitution states,

> Protection to person and property is the paramount duty of government and shall be impartial and complete. No person shall be denied the equal protection of the laws. [Article 1, section 1, paragraph 2]

Laws can discriminate if there is a rational basis. Most people feel that using alcoholic beverages requires maturity, so a legal drinking age is set by law.

The U.S. Constitution makes a similar provision in the Fourteenth Amendment. It says that no state shall make or enforce any law that will "deny to any person within its jurisdiction the equal protection of the law." These provisions require the government to treat persons equally and impartially. But is it really possible to do so? Can equal protection of the law be guaranteed to everyone in all government actions? Is it possible for laws not to discriminate against some person or group? For example, a law is passed that gives some benefits to farmers. This law, therefore, classifies people as farmers and nonfarmers. Because farmers get benefits and nonfarmers don't, doesn't this law "discriminate"? Of course it does.

Actually, such classifications are used in almost all legislative acts. Many economic and social laws unavoidably affect different groups of people in different ways. It is not just any kind of discrimination that is prohibited by the constitutional guaranties of equal protection. Rather, it is classifications that

- have no rational basis,
- improperly classify people on a basis that is considered to be "suspect" by the courts (such as race), or
- deny fundamental rights without a compelling reason.

Such classifications violate the equal protection clauses of the Georgia and United States constitutions.

Rational Basis Test

Courts have generally ruled that most classifications imposed by the government do not deny persons equal protection of the laws. Generally, a legislature may make distinctions among people for any proper purpose, as long as the distinction is rational. There must be a logical relationship between the purpose of a law and any classification of people that it makes. Without this "rational basis," a law will be struck down when challenged in court.

Consider, for instance, the following law: In Georgia, children must be at least six years old on September 1 to attend first grade in public schools. It could be argued that this law discriminates unfairly against persons who are younger than six. To decide whether it violates the equal protection clause, a court would consider its purpose. Then it would decide whether there is a reasonable relationship between the purpose and the classification.

To succeed in school, children must be mature enough to stay in the classroom for an entire day. They must be ready to begin the learning process. The General Assembly determined that six years old is an age at which most children can do these things. Many other states and nations also have selected age six. This consistency suggests that the selection was sensible. Courts could be expected to find a rational basis for the classification. A similar analysis has been employed to uphold other laws treating minors (and certain types of minors) differently than other persons (for example, laws pertaining to obtaining drivers licenses, purchasing alcohol or cigarettes, and the right to be tried in juvenile court).

Strict Scrutiny Test

If a governmental action affects the "fundamental rights" of certain people or classifies them in a "suspect" way (thereby raising suspicions about why the government is taking such action), the action must pass a "strict scrutiny test." This test provides a higher standard than does the rational basis test. If the action does not pass the test, it is considered unconstitutional. To pass strict scrutiny, such an action must (a) further a "compelling" (necessary) government interest and (b) be written so that it affects the smallest group of people possible.

To survive strict scrutiny, then, a law will be questioned using both of these elements:

Compelling interest: Is the law necessary to further that governmental interest?

Narrowly tailored: Is it no broader than necessary to further that government interest?

It is very difficult to devise a law that will survive such strict scrutiny.

Fundamental Rights

Some rights are so fundamental that the government must have an extremely strong reason for limiting them. These rights are discussed in chapter 13. Courts look closely at laws that affect these rights. Are fundamental rights affected in the two situations that follow?

> **SITUATION 10** Several students at a local high school have attacked and robbed other students this year. The attackers stole the gold chains the victims were wearing. The principal has made a rule banning gold chains. Jodi, a student, feels this ban discriminates against her and others who like to wear expensive jewelry.

> **SITUATION 11** Bob moved to Savannah from New York City two weeks before the August primary election. He tries to register to vote in that election. He is told that he cannot do so. Georgia law requires that he register at least 30 days before the date of an election.

The principal has an interest in protecting students in the school (situation 10), and Jodi probably does not have a fundamental right to wear gold chains. However, in situation 11, the state law would seem to limit two of Bob's fundamental rights—the right to vote and to move between states. However, the courts have said that a state's interest in accurate voter registration is more important. As such, they have determined that this form of temporary discrimination is justifiable. In a real-life case, the U.S. Supreme Court held that a Florida Supreme Court order for a recount of votes in the 2000 presidential election was an equal protection violation that improperly treated some voters and candidates differently from county to county.

Suspect Classifications

The Supreme Court has declared certain classifications of people to be "suspect." Therefore, courts require more of a justification before such classifications will be approved as part of a government action.

Race. The clearest example of suspect classification is race. This example goes back to the Fourteenth Amendment. A major goal of that amendment was to ensure that recently freed slaves had the full benefit of their freedom.

You might think it would be easy to recognize laws that classify on the basis of race. However, consider the following situations describing actual laws and cases. Did they violate the equal protection clause by causing racial discrimination?

> **SITUATION 12** In City A, both Chinese and white persons operated laundries. The city enacted an ordinance prohibiting the construction of wooden laundries without licenses.

> **SITUATION 13** City B passed a zoning requirement limiting development throughout the city to single-family houses on lots of at least one-half acre. The effect was to prevent the building of low- and middle-income housing.

Sometimes laws may violate the equal protection clause even if their classifications appear to be neutral. This violation may result from the effect of the law, or it may result from how it is applied.

Situation 12 summarizes an early case reviewed by the U.S. Supreme Court.[2] The Court held that the ordinance caused purposeful discrimination because, as applied, 79 of 80 non-Chinese applicants had received licenses from City A. However, all 200 Chinese who applied had been denied licenses.

The effect of the zoning requirement in situation 13 also was to create racial discrimination. Fewer African Americans than white persons in City B could afford high-cost housing. However, the U.S. Court of Appeals said that the requirement did not violate the equal protection clause because there was no proof that it was intended to be discriminatory.[3]

Religion. The courts have treated with great suspicion any law that classifies people on the basis of their religion. They base this view on both the equal protection clause and the First

Amendment prohibition against the establishment of religion.

National Origin. Another suspect classification is that of national origin. Figure 14-3 describes an action against a national group.

Alienage. The courts also have treated differentiation of legal aliens as a suspect classification. An alien is a person residing in the United States who is not a citizen. Courts have struck down laws that limited the employment of legal aliens or denied them welfare benefits.

Intermediate Scrutiny Test

Because the law is constantly evolving, there are certain classifications that have not yet been declared suspect. (They are not yet subject to strict scrutiny.) These classifications have been given a "quasi-suspect" status, though, that puts the level of scrutiny somewhere between the stringent strict scrutiny and the lenient rational relationship test. To survive judicial challenges at this intermediate level of scrutiny, two factors must exist. A classification must serve an "important" governmental interest and be "substantially related" to serving that interest.

Gender. Classifications based on gender have reflected the traditional view of women in society. Recently, however, much of this gender-based legislation has been seen as inconsistent with the modern role of women. Intermediate scrutiny of gender-based classifications has become common.

Consider the following situations. Decide whether the classifications they describe violate the equal protection clause.

SITUATION 14 When a person dies without a will, the courts must appoint someone to administer the person's estate. This administrator takes care of paying for and dividing up the property. An Idaho law required that courts give preference to males over females as administrators.

SITUATION 15 Both men and women must pay an equal amount of social security tax on their wages. However, the Social Security Act at one time provided that benefits would be paid to widows, but not to widowers, responsible for children.

A Violation of Equal Protection?

During World War II, 120,000 Americans of Japanese ancestry were placed in confinement in this country. They were forced to give up property and careers. Some spent as many as three years in isolated detention camps.

The Japanese Americans were put into these camps because it was assumed that all such persons would sympathize with Japan—the enemy of the United States in that war. Officials thought that they would act as spies or try to sabotage the American war effort.

In a 1944 case, *Korematsu v. United States* (323 U.S. 214), the Supreme Court upheld the confinement. The ruling gave "great deference" to the combined war powers of the president and Congress.

Thirty years later, a congressional committee could not find a single case of subversive activity by Japanese Americans.

In passing the Civil Liberties Act of 1988, the United States government (1) acknowledged the fundamental injustice of the confinement, (2) apologized for the action, (3) established a public education fund to see that such an injustice will not happen again, and (4) paid restitution of $20,000 to each Japanese American who had been confined (or, if a person had died, to that person's spouse, children, or parents).

Both situations involve gender-based classifications that violate the equal protection clause. In situation 14, the Supreme Court held that the preference for men as administrators of estates was based on an out-of-date view of women.[4] In the case of the Social Security benefits (situation 15), the courts found that the law was not acceptable because it required persons of both genders to pay these taxes but denied benefits to one gender.[5] Why do you think the court rejected the argument that widowers are less likely to need such Social Security benefits?

Statutory Equal Protection

Congress and various state legislatures have, over the past few decades, enacted numerous laws that protect the rights of people against discrimination. These laws are based not just on suspect classifications but on other classifications that have not yet been given protection by the courts.

Age. Courts have found, under various legislative enactments, discrimination when people over the age of 40 have been denied jobs because of age. The courts have generally hesitated, though, to find that youth-based classifications violate the equal protection clause. Age limits on driving, getting married, and entering contracts have been allowed to stand. Similarly, the establishment of lower DUI standards for minors and trying minors as adults have survived equal protection challenges in Georgia.

Age, however, does give some benefit of constitutional protections. One protection includes the right to procedural due process in school disciplinary proceedings. Also, in many circumstances, freedoms and protections granted by the Bill of Rights are considered.

Poverty. Courts have never indicated that poverty, as such, is a suspect classification. They have, however, looked closely at classifications related to poor people, particularly regarding due process rights. A basic question arises: Are poor people denied equal protection because they cannot afford the costs of attorneys and courts?

All people have the right to be represented by an attorney in most criminal cases. Because the poor generally cannot afford an attorney, the Constitution requires that the government provide one without charge. The U.S. Supreme Court, however, has recently held that court-appointed attorneys—even though they are generally compelled to represent the poor, even on appeal—can withdraw if the appeal is proven frivolous. Moreover, Congress has severely curtailed funds for free legal services to the poor.

In civil cases in Georgia, as in the federal courts, poor persons can apply to proceed *in forma pauperis*, which means they do not have to pay filing fees or other court costs. Further, they may also proceed *pro se*, meaning that they may represent themselves. Poor persons are also eligible for the services of legal service organizations such as Georgia Legal Services. However,

the scope of such services is limited by the amount of government funding available, and access to such services is not constitutionally guaranteed.

The disabled. Several federal laws have extended equal protection opportunities to the disabled. The Americans with Disabilities Act of 1990 (discussed in chapter 7) protects disabled persons from discrimination in certain areas, including employment, public accommodations (restaurants, theaters, etc.), and transportation. The 1975 Education for All Handicapped Children Act requires states to provide free and appropriate education to exceptional children.

Some state constitutions prohibit discrimination on the basis of disability. Massachusetts is one such state. How far does this protection go?

SITUATION 16 Disabled inmates at a Massachusetts prison sued because they could not use the stairs to reach the library in the prison basement. They were, however, provided with alternative means of access to library materials.

Did this situation deny them equal protection?

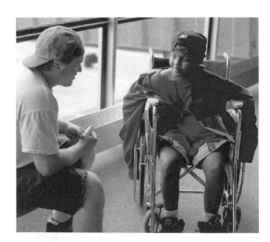

Several federal laws have extended equal protection opportunities to the disabled.

The state supreme court said no. Differing treatment alone does not violate the constitutional provision. In fact, the court said that differing treatment may be appropriate when the burden of eliminating the difference is too great or an overriding state interest justifies the discrimination.

When Equal Protection Is Denied

What happens when a government law or activity is found to violate the equal protection clause? Consider these situations:

SITUATION 17 The provision of the Social Security Act (situation 15) that denied benefits to widowers responsible for children was declared unconstitutional.

How was this violation of rights corrected?

SITUATION 18 A city school board was told by the federal court that it had to desegregate its schools. Each school was to reflect the racial makeup of the city, but the school board did not favor desegregation. It delayed making a plan for many years.

A law that violates equal protection is unconstitutional and void. Therefore it cannot be enforced. Sometimes a new law is required, as in situation 17. Congress had to amend the Social Security Act so that widowers as well as widows would receive benefits.

A more difficult problem occurs when a law is being applied in a discriminatory way. Sometimes administrators of the law have tried to get around the court's decision, as in situation 18. In such situations, the court must use its enforcement powers. In situation 18, the court might issue its own orders as to which schools the children should attend.

A final question concerns how far the courts or the government should go in terms of rectifying past discriminatory practices. Should the government merely eliminate past practices, or should it try to remedy past injustices by favoring the suspect group? Affirmative actions that try to correct past injustices against one group often, at least temporarily, discriminate against others. In other words, a preference granted to one person may mean an opportunity denied to another. The issue of rectifying past discriminatory practices is probably the most difficult one facing the courts in the area of equal protection today (for further discussion, see chapter 7).

Only the Facts

1. What kind of classifications made by laws would violate the equal protection clause?
2. Name three suspect classifications.
3. Explain the role of each branch of government in correcting violations of equal protection.
4. Do you think that the $20,000 paid to each Japanese American confined in detention camps, as described in Figure 14-3, was adequate restitution by the government? Why or why not?

Think About

1. In Georgia, a person must be at least 18 to get an unrestricted driver's license. Does this discrimination violate the equal protection clause? Explain your answer.

SUMMING UP

You now know more about due process and equal protection. Equal protection guarantees that your rights will be protected, just as it guarantees the rights of everyone else who lives in the United States. Due process helps ensure that you will be treated fairly if you ever get in trouble at school, get a traffic ticket, or have a dispute with another person or with the government. As you will see later, due process and equal protection ensure fair treatment if you are ever accused of a crime. In criminal situations, these protections are particularly important.

Notes

1. *Goss v. Lopez*, 419 U.S. 565 (1975).
2. *Yick Wo v. Hopkins*, 118 U.S. 356 (1886).
3. *Ybarra v. Town of Los Altos Hills*, 503 F.2d 250 (9th Cir., 1974).
4. *Reed v. Reed*, 404 U.S. 71 (1971).
5. *Califano v. Goldfarb*, 430 U.S. 199 (1976).

PART 4 CRIMINAL LAW

15 Crime and the System

WHAT IS A CRIME?

Every day, we read about crime in the newspaper. We watch the news and see a suspect being handcuffed. There are also law-based television programs. Some of these programs portray people committing crimes and detectives solving crimes, while others focus on the prosecution of criminals. All of the daily exposure makes us think we understand what a crime is, but do we really? What actually is a crime?

It's a Crime

Some acts definitely are crimes. For example, burglary, robbery, murder, rape, and theft by taking an automobile are all crimes. However, did you know that when a person speeds in an automobile, he or she is committing a crime—or that when someone is told never to come back to a particular store but does it anyway, he or she is committing the crime of criminal trespass? Lying to a police officer about your name or birth date is also a crime. Slapping another student in the face may be the crime of "simple battery." These are all acts that might not immediately be thought of as crimes; they are not the crimes we read about or see on television. According to the law in Georgia, however, they are crimes. People who commit these acts might be arrested and even convicted. They might be required to pay a fine, perform some community service, or serve time in jail.

Like all states, Georgia defines and describes every act that may be a crime. These definitions are contained in the Official Code of Georgia Annotated (O.C.G.A.). This Code is a series of books divided into titles according to subject. Crimes are defined in Title 16. Most acts that are crimes in Georgia are also crimes in other states (for example, murder, rape, and robbery). Some acts, however, may not be crimes in other states. Nevertheless, anyone who is in Georgia must abide by the laws in Georgia. It does no good to say, "but I didn't know this was a crime in Georgia." Anyone may familiarize him- or herself with these laws of Georgia by going to the public library or a law library and looking at Title 16 of the Georgia Code. The Georgia Code can now also be accessed on the Internet at www.ganet.org.

Legal Definition of a Crime

The Georgia legislature has defined a crime as "a violation of a statute (law) of this state in which there is a joint operation of an act or omission to act, and intention or criminal negligence." Let's take a closer look at this definition.

Let's say Jake is throwing a baseball against a neighbor's house just to see how hard he can throw the ball. Then, on the 15th throw, he breaks the neighbor's window. Has Jake committed a crime?

The act in the above example is throwing the baseball. What was Jake's intent? It was not to break the window; it was to see how hard he could throw the ball. If the law only considered actual intent, this example would not meet both elements of the definition of a crime.

However, the law also considers criminal negligence. Criminal negligence occurs when actions are taken without regard to their consequences. A judge could decide that when Jake threw the ball at his neighbor's house, he did so without considering the possibility of breaking a window when he should have known better. Therefore Jake could be guilty of a crime (criminal damage to property or criminal trespass) because of criminal negligence.

Let's take a more serious example. Henry is driving home from a party at which he drank a lot of beer. Because he is intoxicated, he veers into the wrong lane and hits an oncoming car. The other driver is killed. What was the act? Driving under the influence of alcohol. What was the intent? Surely it was not to kill the other driver. Has Henry committed a crime? Yes. Even though Henry did not intend the consequences of his act,

the law will say that he was criminally negligent when he drove while under the influence. Henry acted with complete disregard for the safety of others on the road. Therefore, he is guilty of a very serious crime (vehicular homicide).

Felonies and Misdemeanors

There are two classifications of crimes: felonies and misdemeanors. A felony is generally considered a more serious crime. Felonies include, but are not limited to, the following: possession of cocaine, heroin, LSD, and other drugs, including the possession of one or more ounces of marijuana; robbery; armed robbery; aggravated assault; burglary; theft by taking; theft by receiving stolen property; murder; rape; child molestation; and kidnapping.

Figure 15-1 lists many crimes, together with their definitions and ranges of punishment. Generally, the punishment for a felony is a prison term of a minimum of 1 year and a maximum of 20 years. The punishment time for a particular offense, however, may vary greatly. For example, possession of cocaine with the intent to distribute carries a penalty of 5 to 30 years. As figure 15-1 shows, a second conviction for that offense could carry a life sentence. Some felonies, like forgery, carry a maximum of 10 years; theft by taking property that is not an automobile carries 10 years; and entering an auto carries 5 years.

The more serious felonies—such as murder, rape, kidnapping, and armed robbery—are called capital felonies. The penalties for these crimes can be long prison terms, life imprisonment, or in the case of murder, even death. Furthermore, under recent guidelines, the minimum term for certain serious felonies, including the ones just mentioned, is 10 years without parole. (The *minimum* term for murder is a life sentence.) A person convicted of armed robbery, kidnapping, or rape will serve the full minimum term of 10 years in prison. Also, under Georgia law, if the sentence is greater than the minimum term, every day of the greater sentence will be served. This requirement means that a defendant sentenced to 20 years on one of these charges will be released only after serving the full sentence.

FIGURE 15-1

Crimes in Georgia (partial list)

CRIME	PUNISHMENT
CRIMES AGAINST THE PERSON	
Homicide	
An unlawful killing or causing the death of a human being by another human being.	
Murder	
A homicide committed with malice aforethought (that is, the murderer planned or intended to kill the victim).	Death or life imprisonment
Felony Murder	
A homicide committed while committing a felony (for example, armed robbery or rape).	Death or life imprisonment
Voluntary Manslaughter	
A homicide committed when the person acts as the result of a "sudden, violent, and irresistible passion" resulting from provocation sufficient to cause it (for example, a homicide resulting from a family quarrel).	1–20 years
Involuntary Manslaughter	
A homicide committed unintentionally while committing an unlawful act other than a felony (for example, a homicide accidentally resulting from someone firing a gun in the city limits, a misdemeanor).	1–10 years
Or a homicide committed unintentionally by committing a lawful act in an unlawful manner likely to cause death or serious bodily harm.	As misdemeanor*
Vehicular Homicide	
(See "Crimes Involving Vehicles")	
Kidnapping	
The abducting or stealing away of any person without lawful authority and the holding of that person against his or her will.	10–20 years
Kidnapping a person for ransom or injuring the person kidnapped.	Life imprisonment
Simple Assault	
An attempt to violently injure another or an act that makes another fear immediate violent injury.	As misdemeanor*
Aggravated Assault	
Assault with intent to murder, rape, or rob with a deadly weapon.	1–20 years
If victim is 65 or over.	3–20 years
If victim is a police officer.	5–20 years
Simple Battery	
Physically harming another intentionally or "making physical contact of an insulting or provoking nature with another."	As misdemeanor*
Aggravated Battery	
Maliciously harming another by depriving the person of a member of body, rendering member of body useless, or seriously disfiguring body or a member thereof.	1–20 years
If victim is 65 or older.	5–20 years
If victim is peace officer.	10–20 years
CRIMES AGAINST THE STATE	
Treason	
A breach of one's duty of allegiance to one's state or country. Levying war against the state or country or giving aid or comfort to the enemies of the state or country.	15 years–life imprisonment
CRIMES AGAINST OR IN RELATION TO PROPERTY	
Arson	
Knowingly damaging or causing another person to damage certain structures by means of fire or explosives.	
First Degree Harm to a place where people live or damage to a building that has a security interest or is insured.	1–20 years or up to $50,000 fine or both
Second Degree Harm to other types of property (that is, other buildings, vehicles, watercraft, aircraft, etc.).	1–10 years or up to $25,000 fine or both
Third Degree Damage to personal property valued at $25 or greater by fire or explosion.	1–5 years or up to $10,000 fine or both

*All misdemeanors may be punished by incarceration in a local correctional facility for up to 12 months and/or a fine of up to $1,000.

Note: This figure lists general penalties in Georgia. It does not indicate all possible fines and forfeitures.

CRIME	PUNISHMENT
Trespassing Essentially, entering upon the premises or land or vehicle (for example, auto, railroad car, aircraft, or watercraft) of another knowingly and without authority for an unlawful purpose or after being forbidden to do so. Trespass can also be not leaving when notified to leave another's property.	As misdemeanor*
Intentionally damaging the property of another (damages of $500 or less) or interfering with another's holding or use of property. In both cases, the acts would be without consent of the property holder.	As misdemeanor*
CRIMES INVOLVING SEXUAL OFFENSES **Forcible Rape** Occurs when a person has carnal knowledge (sexual intercourse) by force against the victim's will.	10–20 years or life imprisonment or life without parole or death
Statutory Rape Occurs when a person engages in sexual intercourse with another under the age of 16, not his/her spouse, even when there is consent.	1–20 years
Occurs when the victim is 14 or 15 and the offender is no more than 3 years older than the victim.	As misdemeanor*
Prostitution Offering, performing, or consenting to sexual intercourse for money.	As misdemeanor*
CRIMES INVOLVING THEFT **Armed Robbery** Taking the property of another when the offender uses a weapon.	10–20 years or life imprisonment

Burglary
Entering into the building of another without consent and with the intent to commit a felony or theft therein.
    First Offense
    Second Offense
    Third Offense
	
	1–20 years
	2–20 years
	5–20 years

Robbery Taking the property of another by force, intimidation, or sudden snatching. If victim is 65 years or older	1–20 years 5–20 years
Theft by Conversion Occurs when, having lawfully obtained money or property of another under an agreement to do something specific with it, a person knowingly converts it (takes it) for his or her own use. If amount in question is greater than $500.	As misdemeanor* 1–10 years
Theft of Lost or Mislaid Property Occurs when a person comes into control of property that he or she knows or discovers has been lost or mislaid and takes it for him- or herself and appropriates it without taking responsible measures to restore the property to its owner. If the value of the property is greater than $500.	As misdemeanor* 1–10 years
Theft by Taking Occurs when a person unlawfully takes or, after being in lawful posession of, unlawfully appropriates (takes, keeps) the property of another with the intention of depriving that person of the property. If the value of the property is greater than $500 or a firearm.	As misdemeanor* 1–10 years
Theft by Receiving Stolen Property Occurs when a person receives, disposes of, or retains stolen property that he or she knows or should know was stolen unless done with the intent to return it to its owner. If the value of the property is greater than $500.	As misdemeanor* 1–10 years

Theft by Shoplifting
Occurs when a person alone or with another intentionally takes merchandise for his or her own use without paying for it and
   — conceals or takes possession of merchandise of any store.
   — alters the price of any merchandise in any store.
   — transfers merchandise of a store from one container to another.
   — interchanges a label or price tag from one item of merchandise to another.
   — wrongfully causes amount paid for merchandise to be less than the merchant's stated price.	

*All misdemeanors may be punished by incarceration in a local correctional facility for up to 12 months and/or a fine of up to $1,000.

CRIME	PUNISHMENT
Occurs when property subject to the theft is valued at $300 or less.	As misdemeanor*
— Fourth conviction.	1–10 years
Occurs when property subject to the theft is valued at more than $300.	1-10 years
Judge may treat any theft crime as a misdemeanor.	
CRIMES INVOLVING FORGERY AND RELATED OFFENSES	
Forgery	
Occurs when a person, with intent to defraud or deceive, knowingly makes, alters, or possesses any writing using a fictitious name or so that it looks as if it was written by another. **Note:** Works of art, like paintings, can be forged as well as checks, deeds, etc.	
First Degree Delivering as well as making a forgery (for example, presenting a forged check for payment).	1–10 years
Second Degree Making or possessing a forged document but not delivering the forged document.	1–5 years
Financial Transactions (Credit Card Fraud)	
Occurs when a person, with the intent to defraud, possesses, takes, or uses unlawfully the credit card of another.	1–2 years or $1,000 fine or both
Issuing a Bad Check	
Occurs when a person writes a check knowing there are insufficient funds in the account.	
If amount is $500 or less.	As misdemeanor*
If amount is over $500.	1–3 years or fine or both
CRIMES INVOLVING VEHICLES	
Vehicular Homicide	
First Degree Occurs when a person, without malice aforethought, causes a death by committing certain traffic offenses, including hit-and-run, driving under the influence, reckless driving, or while fleeing a police officer.	3–15 years
Second Degree An unintended death resulting from traffic offense other than those described in first degree offense.	As misdemeanor*
DUI	
Driving under the influence of drugs, alcohol, certain inhalants, or any combination of two or more of these substances.	
First or Second Offense	As misdemeanor*
Third, Subsequent Offense	High and aggravated misdemeanor
Reckless Driving	
Driving in reckless disregard for the safety of persons or property.	As misdemeanor*
CRIMES AGAINST PUBLIC ADMINISTRATION	
Perjury	Not more than $1,000 and/or
Knowingly making a false statement material to the issue when under oath.	1–10 years
False Swearing	Not more than $1,000 and/or
Making a false statement on a document when under oath (for example, making a false statement after being sworn before a notary public).	1–5 years
Bribery	Not more than $5,000 and/or
Offering a public official something of value with the intent of influencing him or her, or the functions of his/her office.	1–20 years
False Alarm	
Making a false fire alarm.	As misdemeanor*
Making a false public alarm (as of a bomb).	1–5 years
CRIMES AGAINST PUBLIC ORDER AND SAFETY	
Carrying a Concealed Weapon	
Carrying a handgun in a concealed manner without a permit (except in one's home, business, or glove compartment or console of a car) or carrying a handgun with a permit in certain public places. (This law does not apply to police.) Even when there is a permit, a weapon may only be concealed in certain ways.	
First Offense	As misdemeanor*
Second Offense	2–5 years

*All misdemeanors may be punished by incarceration in a local correctional facility for up to 12 months and/or a fine of up to $1,000.

Crimes in Georgia (*continued*)

CRIME	PUNISHMENT
Rioting Two or more persons committing an unlawful act of violence.	As misdemeanor*
Affray Fighting by two or more persons in a public place, in disturbance of public tranquility.	As misdemeanor*
Terroristic Threat Threatening to commit violent crime or to burn or damage property with intent to terrorize another or to cause evacuation of a building.	Up to $1,000 and/or 1–5 years
DISCHARGING FIREARMS Discharging a firearm on or within 50 yards of a public highway or street or on someone else's property without permission or legal justification.	As misdemeanor*
DRUG OFFENSES Georgia law classifies drugs (except marijuana in its unrefined state) into five schedules.	

Schedule I and II Drugs
Considered the most dangerous. Included are methadone, LSD, opium, heroin, cocaine, amphetamines, Quaaludes, THC, and PCP ("angel dust").
Possession.
    First Offense
    Second Offense
Possession with intent to sell or selling.
    First Offense
    Second Offense
	
	2–15 years
	5–30 years
	
	5–30 years
	10–40 years or life imprisonment

Cocaine Trafficking (selling, manufacturing, delivering, or possessing 28 grams or more of cocaine with at least 10 percent purity).	Mandatory minimum: 10–30 years; and mandatory fine: $200,000–$1 million

Schedule III, IV, and V Drugs
Included are valium, uppers and downers, phenobarbital, etc.
Possession.
Possession with intent to sell or selling.
    First Offense
    Second Offense
	
	1–5 years
	
	1–5 years
	1–10 years

Marijuana Possession of 1 oz. or less. Possession of over 1 oz. but no more than 50 lbs. Possession of or selling over 50 lbs.	 Misdemeanor* 1–10 years Mandatory minimum: 5–15 years; and mandatory fine: $100,000–$1 million

*All misdemeanors may be punished by incarceration in a local correctional facility for up to 12 months and/or a fine of up to $1,000.

Misdemeanors are generally less serious crimes than felonies. Most misdemeanors are punishable by a prison term of 1 to 12 months. A misdemeanor term is always expressed in months, whereas a felony term is always expressed in years. So, if someone committed the crime of possession of marijuana and was sentenced to two years, the crime is a felony. Had the crime been a misdemeanor, the sentence would be stated in months.

Although most misdemeanors are punishable for 1 to 12 months, there are exceptions. For example, shoplifting is a misdemeanor if the value of all the items taken is less than $300. However, if someone has been convicted of shoplifting three times, the fourth charge may be considered a felony even if the value of the item taken was only $5. Therefore, the punishment may exceed 12 months. In fact, there are people facing sentences of up to 10 years for shoplifting a sandwich,

Many stores monitor customer activities to identify shoplifters.

batteries, or hair spray. These sentences represent the state's way of punishing people who commit the same crime again and again.

For some crimes, the amounts of money or drugs involved may be considered in determining whether the crime is a misdemeanor or a felony. For example, marijuana possession is a misdemeanor if less than one ounce is involved. It is a felony if more than one ounce is involved. Shoplifting also becomes a felony if more than $300 worth of goods are taken.

The punishment for intentionally damaging the property of another person without his or her consent similarly depends on the amounts of money involved. If the value of the damage is $500 or less, the crime is considered a misdemeanor offense of criminal trespass. This misdemeanor carries a sentence of 1 to 12 months. When the cost of damage is greater than $500, the accused is charged with the felony of criminal damage to property in the second degree. This felony is punishable by imprisonment for one to five years.

The sentencing ranges previously described for both felonies and misdemeanors are not mandatory jail sentences in all cases. The judge may elect to sentence the defendant to probation instead of incarceration. If the judge elects to choose probation as an alternative to incarceration, he or she usually will require certain conditions of probation, such as community service or fines. Probation programs are discussed in more depth in chapter 19.

Only the Facts

1. Distinguish a misdemeanor from a felony. What are the penalty ranges for each of these categories of crime?

Think About

1. Jules was caught shoplifting—for the fourth time. When charged with the first offense, he had stolen a carton of cigarettes; the second, a small transistor radio; the third, two CDs; and the last time, a pack of cigarettes and three candy bars. The total worth of all four thefts comes to less than $100. Yet he has been charged with a felony and will serve two years in prison. Do you think the law is being too harsh with Jules? Support your answer.

HAS A CRIME HAS BEEN COMMITTED?

You have learned about the two parts of a crime: act and criminal intent. Also, you now know the difference between a felony and a misdemeanor. Using that information and the definitions of crimes presented in figure 15-1, consider the following situations. Determine whether a crime has been committed. If so, which crime?

SITUATION 1 Mary and Barbara get into an argument. Barbara tells Mary she never wants to see her again. The next day, Mary decides to go over to Barbara's house. While she is there, Barbara says, "I told you I never wanted to see you again." However, she doesn't ask Mary to leave. Instead, Barbara calls the police. She claims that Mary is on her property without her permission.

Has Mary committed the crime of trespassing?

SITUATION 2 Bob asks his friend Mike to hold on to some marijuana for him. He'll pick it up later. Mike has never smoked marijuana before and only knows it's marijuana because Bob tells him it is. Mike stuffs the marijuana in his lunch box. Right now he's worried about a math quiz. He forgets about the marijuana. At lunch, in the cafeteria, as Mike empties his lunch box onto the table, the marijuana spills out just as the principal is walking by. He sees it and calls the police. Mike is arrested for possession of marijuana.

Has Mike committed a crime even though the marijuana was not his?

SITUATION 3 Carl offers Doug a brand new 31-inch television set for $50. Doug has been wanting a TV for a while but couldn't afford the $700 price tag that this sized set carries. Doug pays $50 and doesn't ask any questions. When Carl suggests that he be discreet and keep the deal quiet, he quickly agrees. This deal is too good to pass up. Two weeks later, a neighbor sees Doug's new TV. He immediately calls the police. The neighbor claims that the oversized set is the one that was stolen from his apartment several weeks before.

Has Doug committed a crime? After all, he paid for the television.

In situation 1, Barbara called the police because Mary came to her house after Barbara told her she never wanted to see her again. At first glance, this situation may look like a criminal trespass. However, a trespass requires notice that entry onto the property is forbidden. In this situation, Mary did not have adequate notice. Telling someone you never want to see them again is not the same as saying, "Don't ever come onto my property again." Therefore, Mary did not commit any criminal offense. What if Barbara had told Mary to leave before she called the police? In that event, Mary would be charged with the misdemeanor offense of criminal trespass. A person who is told to leave the premises and does not do so is guilty of criminal trespass.

Sometimes we do things for friends without thinking of the consequences. Mike agreed to keep Bob's marijuana for him until later (situation 2). Is he committing a crime if he keeps it? The law forbids possessing marijuana. The Code section defining this crime does not say that possessing marijuana shall be a crime unless you are holding it for someone other than yourself. Therefore Mike could be convicted of misdemeanor possession (if it was less than one ounce). Possession is possession.

In situation 3, Doug found out that the TV he had bought from Carl two weeks earlier was stolen from a neighbor, but Doug didn't steal it. He doesn't even know if in fact it was stolen. All he knows is that he paid $50. Can Doug be charged with theft by receiving stolen property?

Georgia law defines theft by receiving stolen property as follows:

A person commits the offense of theft by receiving stolen property when he receives, disposes of, or retains stolen property which he knows or should know was stolen unless the property is received, disposed of, or retained with intent to restore it to the owner.

The key in situation 3 would be whether the state is able to prove that Doug knew or should have known that the TV was stolen. What do you think? Should he have known? The fact that he paid less than 10 percent of the value of the TV would hurt his defense. It would probably be enough to show that he should have known that the TV was stolen. After all, why would someone sell a brand new TV so cheap?

Furthermore, the fact that Carl told Doug to be discreet about the deal is also very strong evidence against Doug. It shows that Doug knew or should have known that something wasn't quite right. Doug's defense attorney will have to work hard on this case. Because the actual value of the TV is more than $500, Doug is facing a felony charge.

Parties to a Crime

SITUATION 4 David is planning to rob his neighbors. He knows that they go out every Saturday night leaving their house unattended. He also knows that there is no burglar alarm. Further, a friend, Bob, has a key to the neighbors' house because he does odd jobs for them. David convinces Bob to give him the key in exchange for a share of the money he gets for the items that he steals. That Saturday night while the neighbors are out, David enters the house. He is caught just as he is carrying out the VCR.

What crime has David committed? What crime has Bob committed? After all, Bob wasn't there, and he didn't take anything. All he did was give the key to David.

Based on the law shown in figure 15-2, Bob is in trouble. He certainly aided in the commission of the crime by giving the key to David, knowing that David was going to use the key to get in and steal items from the house. It doesn't matter that David could have entered the house some other way (perhaps by breaking a window). The fact is that Bob gave David a key that he used to enter the premises and for the purpose of committing a crime.

What crime did David commit? Looking at figure 15-1, you will see a definition of the felony of burglary. People often think that a burglary requires proof that the suspect broke into the home. Actually, a person commits a burglary when he or she enters a dwelling (or building, vehicle, etc.) without authority and with the intent to commit a felony. In situation 4, David entered his neighbors' house with the intent to take their belongings. He intended to commit a felony of theft by taking. Therefore he has committed the offense of burglary.

If David had entered the house with the intent to steal and changed his mind, leaving with nothing, he would still have committed burglary. A burglary does not require that the felony act (in this case, theft) be completed. All that is necessary is that the person entered the premises without authority and intended to commit the felony. The act of burglary was complete as soon

FIGURE 15-2

O.C.G.A. §16-2-20

The Official Code of Georgia §16-2-20 defines when a person is a party to a crime.

(a) Every person concerned in the commission of a crime is a party thereto and may be charged with and convicted of commission of the crime.

(b) A person is "concerned" in the commission of a crime only if he

(1) directly commits the crime;

(2) intentionally causes some other person to commit the crime under such circumstances that the other person is not guilty of any crime either in fact or because of legal incapacity;

(3) intentionally aids or abets in the commission of the crime; or

(4) intentionally advises, encourages, hires, counsels, or procures another to commit the crime.

---

as David entered his neighbors' home with the intent to take their belongings.

David may serve time in prison. Burglary carries a penalty of 1 to 20 years; however, the sentence could be probated, meaning that David would serve his time out of jail but on probation. What about Bob? Can he receive the same term even though his role was so minor? Yes. A party to a crime is given no benefit based on the role he or she plays. A judge may take the minor role into consideration when sentencing but is not required to. Therefore Bob could be sentenced to 1 to 20 years, just like David.

The Elements of a Crime

Earlier, the two parts of a crime—an act and criminal intent—were discussed. In addition to these two necessary ingredients, each "act" has specific elements that must be proved by the state beyond a reasonable doubt. (Reasonable doubt is discussed in chapter 17.)

To understand these elements, look at the definition of kidnapping in figure 15-1. The law defines kidnapping as "the abduction or steal-ing away of any person without lawful authority and the holding of that person against his or her will." There are three elements to this crime:

1. abduction (stealing away),
2. without lawful authority, and
3. holding that person against his or her will.

Each of these elements must be proved for there to be a conviction for the crime of kidnapping. If, for example, the person being accused of the crime had lawful authority to take the victim into custody, then no kidnapping has occurred. One of the elements is missing. Two out of three is never enough. Criminal trials are often won by showing that a necessary element has not been proved.

Only the Facts

1. What does it mean to be a party to a crime?

2. Pick six crimes from figure 15-1 and list all the elements of each.

Think About

1. Consider the following scenarios. Both are slightly altered versions of situation 5:

a. What if David said to Bob, "Come with me. I need to stop over at my neighbors' house." Bob goes with David and is told to wait outside. David goes to the back of the house, breaks a window, and climbs inside. Suddenly, the neighbors come home unexpectedly, catch David inside the house, and call the police. David and Bob are both arrested. Has Bob committed a crime? Can he be charged with being party to a crime?

b. David brags to Bob about the theft he wants to commit. He even asks Bob for suggestions. Bob doesn't give him any. Bob also learns when the crime will happen but doesn't call the police to prevent it. David carries out the theft and later shows Bob what he stole. Bob still doesn't call the police. Did Bob commit a crime?

2. Should a person who plays a minor role such as driving the getaway car in a bank robbery be subject to the same sentence as the main defendant? Why or why not?

3. Do you think a person should be able to avoid conviction for a crime because one of the necessary elements could not be proved beyond a reasonable doubt? Explain.

THE CRIMINAL JUSTICE PROCESS: YOUR RIGHTS

Anyone arrested for a crime becomes subject to the criminal justice process. Generally, the criminal justice process includes all proceedings and virtually everything that happens from the time a person is suspected of committing a crime, through the prosecution, until the case is over.

This process includes formal arrest, preliminary hearings, grand jury indictments, arraignment, and trial. If the person is convicted at trial, the criminal justice process may continue through the appeals process. In subsequent chapters, the criminal justice process is examined in a case involving both adults and juveniles. In this chapter, we will look at some things that people who become a part of the process need to know about their rights.

U.S. citizens have constitutional protections that are very important to the way they live. The government cannot violate their constitutional rights. Citizens of Georgia have protections under the Georgia Constitution as well. These, too, are very important.

The first 10 amendments to the U.S. Constitution are called the Bill of Rights. They often are referred to as the fundamental freedoms. The Fourteenth Amendment to the Constitution requires the states, in prosecuting a suspected criminal, to abide by these rights in addition to any rights guaranteed by the state constitution (see figure 15-3). This amendment also guarantees all citizens equal protection of the laws.

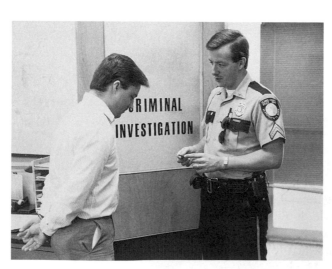

In the criminal justice process, perhaps the most important constitutional right is the right to due process.

FIGURE 15-3

Amendments to the U.S. Constitution Pertaining to the Criminal Justice Process

AMENDMENTS	EXPLANATION
Fourth Amendment (1791) The right of the people to be secure in their persons, houses, papers, and effects, against unreasonable searches and seizures, shall not be violated, and no Warrants shall issue, but upon probable cause, supported by Oath or affirmation, and particularly describing the place to be searched, and the persons or things to be seized.	**The Fourth Amendment** • protects people from unreasonable police searches and seizures. • sets requirements for search warrants.
Fifth Amendment (1791) No person shall be held to answer for a capital, or otherwise infamous crime, unless on a presentment or indictment of a Grand Jury, except in cases arising in the land or naval forces, or in the Militia, when in actual service in time of War or public danger; nor shall any person be subject for the same offence to be twice put in jeopardy of life or limb; nor shall be compelled in any criminal case to be a witness against himself, nor be deprived of life, liberty, or property, without due process of law; nor shall private property be taken for public use, without just compensation.	**The Fifth Amendment** • requires a pretrial hearing by a grand jury in felony cases. • outlaws a second trial for the same crime (double jeopardy). • protects suspects from having to answer questions that could be used against them. • guarantees fair proceedings when people are threatened by a loss of life, liberty, or property by the government. • ensures compensation for people whose property is taken by the government.
Sixth Amendment (1791) In all criminal prosecutions, the accused shall enjoy the right to a speedy and public trial, by an impartial jury of the State and district wherein the crime shall have been committed, which district shall have been previously ascertained by law, and to be informed of the nature and cause of the accusation; to be confronted with the witnesses against him; to have compulsory process for obtaining witnesses in his favor, and to have the Assistance of Counsel for his defence.	**The Sixth Amendment** guarantees an accused person the right to • a speedy and public trial by an impartial jury. • be informed of the charges and evidence. • be present when witnesses testify against him or her. • have a lawyer and to call witnesses in defense.
Eighth Amendment (1791) Excessive bail shall not be required, nor excessive fines imposed, nor cruel and unusual punishments inflicted.	**The Eighth Amendment** requires judges to • set reasonable and consistent bail. • suit the sentence to the crime.
Fourteenth Amendment (1868), excerpt . . . nor shall any State deprive any person of life, liberty, or property, without due process of law; nor deny to any person within its jurisdiction the equal protection of the laws.	**The Fourteenth Amendment** requires states to • provide due process of law in all actions, including criminal laws. • give equal protection to all citizens.

Equal protection must be given to all classes of people. For example, two people are charged with the same crime: employee #1 works for the government; employee #2 doesn't. The Fourteenth Amendment guarantees that no preferential treatment be given to employee #1 because he or she works for the government. Likewise, the treatment of people and their sentences cannot be different based strictly on their race or age.

Regarding the criminal justice process, perhaps the most important constitutional right is the right to due process, which is guaranteed by the Fifth Amendment to the U.S. Constitution as well as by article 1, section 1, paragraph 1 of the Georgia Constitution. You will often hear criminal defense lawyers protesting that the due process rights of their client are being ignored or violated. Frequently, persons accused of committing crimes are released because of violations of their constitutional rights, which in many cases is their right to due process.

Due process at its most elementary level includes the right to be heard. In other words, the accused has a right to a trial and a right to put up evidence, a right to cross-examine witnesses against him or her, a right to testify if he or she chooses, and a right to make people come to court by issuing a subpoena, among other things. These are very important rights and are generally classified as due process rights.

The Fifth Amendment is extremely important. Not only does it guarantee all persons due process of the law, it also guarantees that no one will be subject to double jeopardy: "nor shall any person be subject for the same offense to be twice put in jeopardy of life or limb." This phrase means that a person who is charged with a crime, pleads "not guilty," goes on trial, and is acquitted of the crime cannot be prosecuted a second time.

The Fifth Amendment further protects a person from being forced to give testimony against him- or herself ("nor shall [any person] be compelled in any criminal case to be a witness against himself"). This protection is what is claimed when a suspect "takes the Fifth." A suspect never has to talk about a crime if that testimony, statement, or confession will expose the suspect to criminal prosecution.

In addition to these amendments, there are others that are important, particularly in the criminal justice context. The Fourth Amendment deals with arrest and search and seizure (or the authority of the police to stop someone suspected of a crime and to search that person or his or her car). The Sixth Amendment includes the rights to a speedy and public trial, trial by jury, and the effective assistance of counsel (a lawyer).

The Eighth Amendment addresses excessive bail. What is excessive? Would $100,000 bail be excessive in a misdemeanor case of marijuana possession? Absolutely. But what about in a murder case? The Eighth Amendment also prohibits inflicting cruel and unusual punishment. As a result of these protections, a person cannot be sentenced too harshly. Once in jail, he or she cannot be beaten or deprived of medical attention.

Only the Facts

1. By what name do we commonly refer to the first 10 amendments to the U.S. Constitution?
2. Name three constitutional protections that are set forth in the Bill of Rights.
3. What does "due process" mean?

Think About

1. Do you think the protection against double jeopardy is necessary? Why or why not?
2. What do you think an appropriate bail amount would be in a misdemeanor marijuana case?

SUMMING UP

Over the years, many acts have been termed crimes by governments. Some acts—like murder—

seem very clearly to be crimes. Some, like slapping someone, may not seem like a crime but are considered to be crimes in Georgia. Some acts become crimes even though the offender didn't intend those consequences of his or her actions. Also, an act that is a crime in one state may not be a crime in a neighboring state. The state of Georgia lists and defines in the Official Code of Georgia Annotated what it considers to be crimes. Other states define crimes in their state codes.

The writers of the U.S. Constitution were very concerned about the rights of the individual. The Bill of Rights contains several amendments that deal specifically with the treatment of people accused of crimes. To understand the importance of the rights that the Constitution guarantees, imagine yourself accused of a crime that you didn't commit.

In the next chapters, we will look closely at the criminal justice process. To do so, we will follow a case involving two adults and one juvenile. You will be able to see what happens at each stage of the process. You will see how the constitutional rights previously discussed apply and how the procedures differ for adults and juveniles.

16 Arrest and Search and Seizure

You may be aware that there are many laws regulating arrest. Likewise, many laws regulate search and seizure. These laws ensure that each person is treated fairly in situations in which arrests and searches and seizures occur. In this chapter, you will discover what some of these laws are and how they protect your rights. You will also see how important it is that those making arrests or searches follow the laws. To illustrate, we will follow the Case of the Central City Drug Bust.

CASE STUDY

THE CASE OF THE CENTRAL CITY DRUG BUST

Three Central City High School sophomores went to the mall one afternoon. The three—Sandra, Alan, and Jim—were approached by a 22-year-old woman. She offered to sell them marijuana and cocaine. Jim made a purchase.

After telling his friends he'd meet them later, Jim talked with the dealer, Daisy. He asked if he could become a seller at the high school. Jim was anxious to make some money. His bike needed repairs, and he wanted to buy some stereo equipment.

Daisy suggested that they return to the "drug warehouse." There they could discuss the possibility with her supplier, Harry. They drove to an old, converted garage. They didn't know that the police had a stakeout on the garage. A raid was planned that afternoon. Jim, Daisy and Harry were arrested. (In formal terms, Jim, as a juvenile, was "taken into custody" rather than arrested.)

ARREST

Arrests are usually made by an authorized person, such as a police officer or sheriff. These officials may arrest with a warrant or, under certain circumstances, without one. A warrant is a document giving authority to do something—in this case, arrest.

With a Warrant

How do police obtain a warrant? First, a police officer or private citizen makes a sworn statement, an affidavit, before a judge (see figure 16-1). Georgia law requires that the affidavit identify

- the person to be arrested,
- the offense said to have been committed,
- the date and time it was committed,
- the person against whom the offense was committed, and
- the place of the offense.

These requirements enable the authorities to inform the accused of the specific charges against him or her. You may recall that one aspect of due process is notice. Persons likely to suffer loss of life, liberty, or property must be notified of the charges against them.

FIGURE 16-1

Affidavit for Arrest Warrant

Georgia, _____ County

Personally came _____ , who on oath says that to the best of his knowledge and belief, _____ did on the _____ day of _____ , in the year _____ , in the county aforesaid, commit the offense of _____ .

The place of occurrence of said offense being _____ and against _____ .

Said offense being described as _____
_____

and this deponent makes this affidavit that a warrant may issue for his arrest. _____
(signature)

Sworn to and subscribed before me, this the _____ day of _____ , 19 _____ .

_____ , Judge of _____ County Magistrate Court

Note that as a private citizen, you should not initiate criminal action against someone without strong reasons. If you wrongfully accuse someone of a crime, you could be sued.

The evidence presented in the affidavit must be convincing. The judge issuing the warrant must find probable cause to believe that the accused committed the offense. Probable cause means that there is more than a mere suspicion. There must be reasonable grounds to suspect that the person committed the crime. Consider situation 1:

> **SITUATION 1** It's about 10 p.m. In the apartment next to Mrs. Jones, a burglary is occurring. Mrs. Jones is looking out her window. During the next hour, in the light from the street lamp, she clearly sees the following events:
>
> a. Ms. Brown, the upstairs neighbor, puts several large boxes into her car. She seems uneasy, almost fearful. Finally, Ms. Brown jumps into her car and speeds away.
>
> b. Nick begins pacing back and forth in front of the apartment building. From time to time, he glances at his watch. Nick was arrested once before.
>
> c. The nephew of a friend of Mrs. Jones is climbing out the window of the burglarized apartment. He is carrying a small television set.

Do you think that a judge would find probable cause to issue a warrant for Ms. Brown, Nick, or the friend's nephew? Are there reasonable grounds to issue warrants?

A judge is not likely to issue an arrest warrant for burglary for Ms. Brown or Nick. The fact that Nick has been arrested before is not relevant. Ms. Brown has a legal right to put boxes in her car if they are hers. The judge has not been given enough information to indicate that the boxes belong to the neighbor being burglarized. Therefore, the judge would probably not find probable cause to issue a warrant for Ms. Brown. A judge is likely, however, to find probable cause in the case of the nephew.

Without a Warrant

Can arrests be made in Georgia without a warrant? State law allows a police officer to arrest someone without a warrant in only four situations. They are as follows:

1. when the offense is committed in the officer's presence or with his or her immediate knowledge
2. when an offender is attempting to escape
3. when there is probable cause to believe an act of family violence has occurred
4. for such other cause if there is likely to be a failure of justice because a judge is not available to issue a warrant

The reasons for exceptions one, two, and three are clear. In none of the situations would there be time to get a warrant. For example, suppose a police officer sees someone snatch a purse. In all likelihood, the person is not going to wait around while the officer goes to get a warrant to arrest him. The fourth exception gives the officers and the state (represented by the prosecutor) a general reason to argue that the arrest was valid without a warrant. Unless responding to one of these four exceptions, a police officer may arrest only with a warrant. Otherwise, the arrest is illegal.

Citizen's Arrests

As a private citizen, you have no authority to arrest anyone with a warrant. Without a warrant, you may arrest anyone who commits a misdemeanor or a felony in your presence or with your immediate knowledge. A citizen's arrest occurs when a citizen prevents a suspect from leaving a scene. Citizen's arrest most often happens in cases like shoplifting, when the store's manager detains the suspected offender. However, as the following example shows, the manager or employee cannot make such an arrest in every case.

In *Winn Dixie Stores Inc. v. Nichols*, a Winn Dixie customer complained to management that another customer stole her wallet.[1] The court held that the limited rights of merchants to detain or arrest a person reasonably believed to have committed a shoplifting offense do not authorize a merchant to detain or arrest individuals accused by store patrons of committing crimes against other patrons. To make the arrest, an employee would have had to actually see the criminal act committed. Therefore, it was ruled that management had no authority to arrest the alleged criminal. The court suggested that the only person who could have made the citizen's arrest was the robbed customer herself.

When making a citizen's arrest, a person may not use more force than is reasonable to make the arrest. Deadly force is limited to self-defense or to instances in which such force is necessary to prevent certain felonies.

It must be stressed that the right of private citizens to make a citizen's arrest is limited. They cannot arrest people for violating local ordinances or regulations because these violations are not technically crimes as defined by state law (see chapter 15). Therefore, as a private citizen, you would not have the authority to arrest a person who is creating a disturbance by making too much noise. In addition, a private person can only make a citizen's arrest for the purpose of bringing the suspect before a judicial officer.

CASE STUDY

CASE OF THE CENTRAL CITY DRUG BUST, *continued*

The police had been investigating this case for several months prior to the raid on the drug warehouse. During that time, several undercover narcotics officers (often referred to as narcs) had made "buys" from Daisy and her boss, Harry. Detective-Sergeant Penny had also witnessed two sales to other persons.

The police had presented this information to Judge Stern of Middle County Magistrate Court. The information had convinced the judge that there was probable cause to believe that Daisy and Harry had committed a crime, so he issued arrest and search warrants for Daisy, Harry, and the warehouse. The arresting officers charged Daisy and Harry with several crimes. (Not all of these crimes were identified in the warrant.) They were charged with

- possession of a Schedule II drug (cocaine), with intent to sell (possession of 28 grams or more of cocaine shows intent to sell),
- sale of a Schedule II drug,
- trafficking in marijuana (possession of more than 50 pounds), and
- contributing to the delinquency of a minor.

Harry and Daisy were, to say the least, in a great deal of trouble. (Note the stiff penalties for selling a Schedule I or II drug on page 219.)

Jim was taken into custody without a warrant. Do you know which of the four exceptions (see page 230) pertains to him? Would it help if you knew that during the raid, one officer saw him trying to get rid of bags with over 50 grams of cocaine? Harry had given them to Jim to sell at school. Also, when Jim was frisked, marijuana (less than an ounce) was found on his person.

Because Jim is under the age of 17, he was "charged" as a juvenile with the "delinquent act" of possession of less than an ounce of marijuana. This act is a misdemeanor if the accused is over the age of 17.

The police also charged Jim with possession with intent to distribute (sell) the cocaine. The charge of selling a Scheduled drug is more serious than mere possession. (A Scheduled drug is considered dangerous, and it is illegal to possess a Scheduled drug without a prescription.) How could the police charge Jim with intent to distribute the cocaine? After all, they couldn't read his mind.

The courts have held that possessing more drugs than a person can reasonably be expected to take for personal use indicates that the person intends to sell the drug. The courts also look at other factors, including whether the accused had a large sum of cash on him or her. Another factor is whether the drugs are in individual packages at the time of the arrest. For example, 10 hits of crack cocaine might be packaged in 10 vials, each containing 1 hit.

In the case of the Central City Drug Bust, Jim had bags containing over 50 grams of cocaine in all. The amount of cocaine and the manner in which it was packaged indicated he was going to sell it. Therefore, the police charged Jim with possession with intent to distribute the drug.

The police searched Harry, Daisy, and Jim. They quickly handcuffed all three. The police then "read" them their rights. What does it mean to have read them their rights?

The Miranda Warning

Due process of law requires that, before a person in custody accused of a crime can be questioned, the arresting officer must give that person the Miranda warning. The Miranda warning (figure 16-2) is made up of a number of rights derived from the Fifth, Sixth, and Fourteenth Amendments to the U.S. Constitution. In the landmark case of *Miranda v. Arizona* in 1966, the U.S. Supreme Court declared the reading of these rights to be a necessary part of due process of law.[2]

The Miranda warning is to be given once a suspect is in custody, that is, when the suspect is detained (not free to leave), even if a formal arrest has not taken place. Most important, these rights must be read and understood by the accused before he or she can be questioned.

In practice, officers do not always read these rights to every suspect. If they have failed to formally advise the suspect of his or her Miranda rights and the suspect makes a statement while in custody, the statement can be excluded from the trial of the case. The statement can also be excluded from the trial if it is shown that the suspect did not understand his or her Miranda rights or if the suspect did not make the statement voluntarily.

FIGURE 16-2

Miranda Warning

1. You have the right to remain silent.

2. Anything you say can and will be used against you in a court of law.

3. You have the right to talk to an attorney and have him present with you while you are being questioned.

4. If you cannot afford to hire an attorney, one will be appointed to represent you before any questioning if you wish.

5. You can decide at any time to exercise these rights and not answer any questions or make any statements.

Not having received a Miranda warning is not a defense for committing the crime. However, at trial the accused will certainly argue that the statements and confessions should be excluded from the evidence presented in the case. If no statement or confession is given by the defendant, then there is nothing to exclude. Therefore, no problem exists, even though Miranda rights may not have been read at the time the defendant was arrested or detained.

What happened in this famous case resulting in what everybody now knows as Miranda rights? In the *Miranda* case, a man named Ernesto Miranda was arrested and charged with kidnapping and rape. Miranda was poor, uneducated, and somewhat mentally disturbed. He was taken to the police station and identified by the victim. He was then shut in an interrogation room with several police officers. He was intensively questioned for a number of hours. Never did these police officers tell Miranda that he had the right to remain silent and not say anything that would lead toward the establishment of his guilt (in other words, that he had the right not to incriminate himself under the Fifth Amendment). Nor did they tell him he had the right to a lawyer (a right guaranteed by the Sixth Amendment). Finally, after several hours, the officers came out of the interrogation room with a written, signed confession by Miranda.

In the *Miranda* case, the U.S. Supreme Court justices made use of the exclusionary rule. The exclusionary rule says that illegally obtained evidence cannot be used to convict a person of a crime. The Supreme Court applied the rule to confessions and statements made by defendants to ensure that police officers would follow the principles laid out in their decision. Also, the court wanted to ensure that persons accused of a crime were advised of their basic rights. In the past, police officers had often questioned suspects for hours or even days until confessions were obtained (and in rare instances, even used torture).

With their ruling in the *Miranda* case, the justices wanted to prevent such behavior by the police. The court also expanded the rights of the accused to protect them from giving involuntary statements because they did not know they could remain silent. The justices did not feel that a person should be convicted of a crime on the basis of a confession illegally obtained through physical abuse or ignorance.

The courts continue to interpret the *Miranda* decision, expanding the interpretation of it in some cases and narrowing it in others. For instance, in the 1980 case of *Rhode Island v. Innis*, the Supreme Court held that the term interrogation, as used in the *Miranda* case, was not limited to express questioning by the police.[3] The court said that interrogation also included any words or actions on the part of the police (other than those that normally accompany arrest and custody) that the police should know are reasonably likely to elicit an incriminating response from the suspect.

The rights spelled out in the Miranda warning can be waived by a prisoner. However, the waiver must be given voluntarily. The prisoner must understand his or her action. There must be no trickery, promises of leniency, or threats by police officers. Figure 16-3 shows how police officers might present the waiver.

How might the Miranda ruling apply in the case of the Central City Drug Bust? What if the following events had occurred?

SITUATION 2 The police tell Jim that if he confesses to selling cocaine at the high school, they'll see that he gets off easy.

SITUATION 3 Harry has told a friend about the drug warehouse. The friend testifies to this fact in court.

SITUATION 4 A number of people are in the garage when the police arrive. As soon as the police enter, Daisy says loudly, "Well, I'm caught red-handed now."

In situation 2, the Miranda ruling would apply. Any confession obtained would not be admissible. Note that the Miranda ruling applies only to confessions made to the proper author-

ities by a person in custody who is being questioned. Harry's confession in situation 3 was not made while he was in custody. It could be used in court. Daisy's statement in situation 4 could also be admitted as evidence. She was not in custody at the time, nor was she being questioned about her involvement in the crime.

Only the Facts

1. To issue an arrest warrant, should a judge be sure there is (a) an affidavit? (b) probable cause? (c) proof that the accused committed the crime?

2. Identify at least two situations in which an arrest without a warrant would be legal.

3. Can anyone besides law enforcement officers arrest people in Georgia? Explain.

4. What does the Miranda ruling require?

Think About

1. Do you think private citizens should have the right to make arrests? Why?

2. Would you allow any more exceptions to the requirement for an arrest warrant? Explain.

3. The Miranda ruling has been controversial. Give arguments for and against it.

4. How should a person behave if arrested?

FIGURE 16-3

Miranda Warning Waiver

After the warning and in order to secure a waiver, the following questions should be asked and an affirmative reply secured to each question.

1. Do you understand each of these rights I have explained to you?

2. Having these rights in mind, do you wish to talk to us now?

SEARCH AND SEIZURE

The Fourth Amendment of the U.S. Constitution protects people from unreasonable searches and seizures (see page 225). Generally, the police must first have obtained a search warrant from a judge. Some searches are legal without a warrant, but what constitutes an illegal search can be very confusing and complicated. Only an experienced attorney can accurately explain whether a particular search is legal.

The method for obtaining a search warrant is very similar to that for obtaining an arrest warrant. To issue a search warrant, the judge must be given facts under oath. These facts must show probable cause to believe that certain illegal items will be found in the place to be searched. The items and the place that is to be searched must be specifically described. An affidavit for a search warrant is shown in figure 16-4. Figure 16-5 shows a search warrant.

In the execution of the search warrant, the officer executing it may reasonably detain and "pat-down" any person in the place at the time in order to protect him- or herself from attack or prevent the disposal or concealment of any instruments, articles, or things described in the search warrant. A pat-down involves the patting down of a person's outer clothing to discover a potential weapon or other object that could cause harm.

Exceptions to a Search Warrant

Although the Fourth Amendment declares the need for a search warrant, there are a number of general exceptions to the requirement. These exceptions relate to searches and seizures that occur

1. incident to (related to) a lawful arrest.
2. when an officer observes, in "plain view," property that has been reported stolen or is contraband or otherwise illegal. (Contraband is something a private citizen cannot legally possess.)
3. when an officer has to take immediate action (referred to as "exigent circumstances").
4. when an individual consents to the search.

Exception 1. In this exception, the search must occur in conjunction with a lawful arrest.

FIGURE 16-4

Affidavit and Complaint for Search Warrant

Georgia, _____ County   CITY OF _____ , GEORGIA

Before _____ (Name and Title of Person before whom affidavit is made)

    The undersigned being duly sworn deposes and on oath says he has reason and probable cause to believe that certain property, namely _____

_____

is now being unlawfully concealed in and upon the premises known as _____

located in the City of _____ , _____ County, Georgia, in the custody or control of

_____ and that deponent does verily believe and has probable cause to believe from facts within his knowledge as set out herein that the property heretofore described is kept and concealed in and upon said premises in violation of the laws of the State of Georgia and for the purpose of violating the same. The facts tending to establish affiant's reason for belief and probable cause for belief are as follows:

_____

_____

This affidavit and complaint is made for the purpose of authorizing the issuance of a search warrant for the person or premises described above.

Sworn to before me and subscribed in my presence this _____ day of _____ , 20 _____

_____ Signature of Affiant

Signature and Title of Officer before whom affidavit is made _____

The arresting officer can then search the person and the immediate area around him or her. The reasons for this exception are obvious. The police officer needs to know that the person is not armed. Furthermore, it is important that any evidence concealed on that person be seized to prevent it from being destroyed. However, if the arrest turns out to be unlawful, then a search under this exception will also be considered illegal.

Exception 2. This exception arises when a police officer sees an item or items that are illegal, such as stolen goods, in plain view. This exception is based on the notion that there is no intentional search if the officer has accidentally discovered the illegal item among other items visible to him or her. The officer must also have a legal right to be in the place where the search or seizure occurs. The items must be obviously illegal.

Considering these criteria, do you think the following examples would be exceptions to the requirement for a warrant?

SITUATION 5 A police officer stops a car for a traffic violation. The driver is 16. The officer sees opened beer cans on the car floor.

SITUATION 6 A person is stopped for speeding. The officer then asks the driver for a registration slip and proof of insurance. The driver opens the glove compartment to get the information. The officer sees several unusual rings and bracelets inside. She recognizes them as jewelry reported stolen by a local celebrity.

SITUATION 7 A traffic officer stops a driver for running a red light. The officer notices a strong smell of marijuana in the car. He searches the car and finds marijuana in the trunk.

If a vehicle is stopped by the police for a valid reason, then whatever the officer sees while conducting official business can be seized. This seizure is part of the plain view doctrine. In situation 5, the officer could seize the beer. He could take the underage driver into custody for possessing it.

FIGURE 16-5

Search Warrant

GEORGIA, _____ COUNTY

To _____
(name of Peace Officer making complaint)

and to all and singular the Peace Officers of the State of Georgia, "GREETINGS":

The foregoing affidavit and complaint having been duly made before me and the same, together with the facts submitted under oath contained therein having satisfied me that there is probable cause to believe that the property described therein is being unlawfully concealed in and upon the premises described therein of

_____

YOU ARE HEREBY COMMANDED to enter and search said described premises, serving this warrant, and if the property described or any portion of it be found there to seize it, leaving a copy of this warrant and a receipt for the property taken, and prepare a written inventory of the property seized and return this warrant and bring the property before me within 10 days of this date or some other judicial officer, as required by law.

Given under my hand and seal this _____ day of

_____ , 20 _____ at _____ o'clock _____ M.

_____
Signature and Title of Officer Issuing Search Warrant

In situation 6, the traffic officer had the right to stop a vehicle and ask to see proof of registration and insurance. The jewelry was not in plain view. It was only visible after the driver opened the glove compartment. However, the courts have approved this type of seizure, too, because stopping the car was lawful. Further, it was the driver who opened the glove compartment, not the officer, and he did so on his own accord, not at the request of the officer.

Situation 7 brings up the "automobile exception" to the general requirement for a warrant to search private property. This exception exists because an auto, unlike a house, can be moved out of reach of the law fairly easily. The courts have long said that when a vehicle is stopped for a legal reason, the police can search the area within arm's range of the driver without a warrant, provided there is probable cause and not just a hunch that further wrongdoing is suspected (for example, that drugs are involved) or if the driver is arrested so that the search is incident to a lawful arrest. In Situation 7, the trunk could not be searched under the circumstances unless the officers were given express permission. However, there is one caveat. If the car had to be impounded, the trunk could be searched for the purpose of conducting an inventory of the contents of the car.

Even closed containers found within a car can be searched. However, a general rule applies to all searches regardless of the circumstances. The size of the place or thing that the police search must be able to contain what they are looking for. For instance, if the police are looking in a van for illegal aliens, they cannot seize a briefcase and search it.

Exception 3. The following situation illustrates this exception:

SITUATION 8 An officer sees an armed robber holding up a drugstore, taking money and drugs. The robber leaves by foot. The officer initiates a chase. Bolting around a corner, the robber disappears into an old house.

Will the officer have to get a search warrant? If so, won't the robber have time to destroy or hide the evidence?

The third exception to the warrantless search and seizure involves "exigent circumstances" (emergency situations). Exigent circumstances occur when there is not time for the officer to obtain a warrant, as when there is a bomb threat, or as in situation 8, when police are chasing someone who has just committed a crime.

Exception 4. This exception occurs when an individual consents to a warrantless search or seizure. Consent searches are valid, but the state must prove that consent was freely and voluntarily given. To make this determination,

Is this gun in "plain view"? What if the glove compartment were closed?

the court looks at the entire circumstances surrounding the consent, including the age, education, intelligence, and length of detention of the accused; whether the accused was advised of his or her constitutional rights; the nature of questioning, especially when it is prolonged; and the use of physical punishment, if any. The psychological effect that these factors may have had are examined as well.

Let's look at some examples to understand this fourth exception. In *State v. Westmoreland,* the defendant had agreed to a search after asking if the officer had a search warrant and being told that one was not necessary.[4] The court found that this situation did not constitute voluntary consent.

In another case, *Springsteen v. State,* the court held that consent may be limited to what the consenting party wishes.[5] The search may not exceed its reasonably understood limits. Also, the consenting suspect does not need to "call a halt" when the search goes beyond the limits that were set. It is up to the state to prove that the officer did not exceed the permission that was given. However, in *McNeil v. State,* the court found that the defendant's consent for police officers to search his person for weapons and needles permitted the officers to turn his pants pockets inside out.[6] The court concluded that this search did not exceed the permission granted by the defendant.

The case of *State v. Corley* involved the search of a truck by a police officer.[7] The officer had obtained the owner's consent to search. In the course of the search, the officer opened a closed drawstring bag lying on the front seat. The court found that this action had exceeded the scope of the consent.

Consent by minors has also been an issue in some cases. The court has held that a minor's consent is not automatically invalid. A determination of validity is made by considering the circumstances under which consent is given. The court must look at whether a minor was old enough to use minimal discretion. Also, did the police act reasonably in deciding that the minor had control enough over the premises to give the consent?

In *Davis v. State*, a 10-year-old boy gave consent for police to search his parents' bedroom.[8] The youth was routinely home alone after school, with instructions not to invite friends over during those hours. The court looked at his level of maturity and understanding of consequences. It determined that his regular access to the house did not give the boy sufficient authority for the consent. The court held that young children are not able to understand and waive their own rights. How can they then understand and waive those of their parents? The boy clearly did not know the consequences of his actions in allowing the warrantless bedroom search. In *Rainwater v. State*, however, the court found that a 15-year-old could give valid consent to search.[9] In this case, the teenager called the police, saying that her brother and parents used and sold narcotics at their residence. The teen gave a police officer permission to search the yard of the family home, where a bag of marijuana was found. In upholding the search, the court found that the teen's age, almost 16, coupled with the fact that she had called the police and was a resident of

the home, permitted her to give valid consent to search the yard.

In the following situations, would you consider that valid consent has been given?

SITUATION 9 A policeman asks a suspect if he can search the trunk of the car. The suspect doesn't respond verbally, but she gives the officer the key.

SITUATION 10 A police officer arrests a suspect outside a bar. The officer asks if the police can search the suspect's apartment. The suspect, thinking he must comply, says, "Yes."

SITUATION 11 Joe, a suspect, is 16. The police ask his father if they can search his car. It is parked in the father's driveway. The father says, "Yes."

SITUATION 12 The principal has reason to suspect that a student has contraband in her locker. He searches the locker.

Regarding situation 9, Georgia courts have held that a person does not have to verbally agree to a search. Agreement can be made through actions alone.

The police do not have to inform individuals of the Fourth Amendment right to refuse a search. This determination differs from what is required under the Miranda ruling. The search in situation 10 would be valid.

Can a suspect's father (situation 11) consent to a search of the suspect's car? Yes, according to the Georgia courts. If a suspect's car is parked in his father's driveway, his father can authorize the search. What if the police thought the authorizing person was the suspect's father but he wasn't? A 1990 Supreme Court case suggests the search would still be valid. Recent court decisions have tended to give police more range in making decisions in searches.

Situation 12 poses a difficult question. A number of courts have ruled that if a school official calls in the police, then due process requirements must be met. What if school officials conduct the search? In 1985, the U.S. Supreme Court held that school officials may conduct warrantless searches, but only if they have "reasonable grounds to believe that a student possesses evidence of illegal activity or activity that would interfere with school discipline and order."[10]

Individualized Suspicion

In the previous situations, the officers have had some suspicion that a particular person (or persons) was involved in some illegal activity. But what of the situations that follow? Are these searches legal?

> **SITUATION 13** A woman is flying to California. Before reaching the airplane gate, she, her purse, and her hand luggage must be inspected by a metal detector.
>
> **SITUATION 14** A man is returning to the United States from Panama. His luggage is searched at the airport when he arrives. Unknown to him, it is also "inspected" by a drug-searching beagle.
>
> **SITUATION 15** A woman is driving to a party. On the way, she is stopped at a police roadblock set up to find DUI drivers. The woman has not taken alcohol or drugs, but on the seat beside her is a box of fireworks, which are illegal.

Protection against searches without "individualized suspicion" is seen as being at the heart of the Fourth Amendment. However, in the searches in situations 13, 14, and 15, there is no evidence of suspicion.

Situation 13 illustrates enforcement of laws permitting airport searches of persons and luggage for possible weapons. The public has generally accepted this intrusion on its right to privacy in the interest of safety. This search would be legal.

The right of customs officials to examine persons and luggage entering the country for contraband is long-standing (situation 14). Courts have also upheld the "warrantless" searches of luggage for drugs by trained dogs at airports.

The search in situation 15 would also be legal. In 1990, the U.S. Supreme Court expanded the range of "suspicionless searches" by approving the police use of "sobriety checkpoints."[11] These checkpoints are roadblocks that the police can establish to halt traffic to discover if drivers are using alcohol or drugs. In such a stop, the police can legally search the area controlled by the driver.

Many people object to suspicionless searches such as sobriety checkpoints and drug testing (chapter 7). They argue that few people are caught and that their Fourth Amendment rights

Courts have upheld the searches of luggage for drugs by trained dogs at airports.

are violated. Those in favor say tests and checkpoints deter people from abusing drugs and alcohol. What do you think?

Wiretaps (Electronic Eavesdropping)

Should a search warrant be required to overhear an oral conversation? Is a conversation the same as an illegal drug, a gun, or a document? These three items can be seized physically. That is, they are tangible objects. A conversation is only made tangible by having it recorded.

Look at the question another way. How would you feel if government officers, without your knowledge and without a search warrant, listened in on and recorded your private telephone conversation? Would this action be a physical intrusion into your home? Should the Fourth Amendment protect you from such an activity?

For many years, the U.S. Supreme Court held that there was no need for a warrant as long as there was no physical intrusion. For example, a warrant would not be needed if a public telephone booth was bugged by a device (that is, a wiretap) attached to its back wall. The warrant would be unnecessary because there would be no physical intrusion into the inside of the booth. The landmark decision of *Katz v. U.S.* readdressed this issue in 1967.[12] In it, the U.S. Supreme Court declared that the Fourth Amendment protects people (and their conversations), not just the places where they are. This interpretation means that the Fourth Amendment generally protects people from the interception and recording of any oral statements. An exception would be if one party to a conversation consented to the interception. Another would be if the conversation were held where there was no reasonable expectation of privacy.

SITUATION 16 In the case of the Central City Drug Bust, the police needed more evidence against Harry and Daisy. Without obtaining a warrant, the police put "bugging," or listening, devices on Harry's and Daisy's phones.

Would their conversations be legal evidence?

SITUATION 17 A narcotics agent overhears Harry talking to Daisy in a crowded bus. Harry said Daisy "really should work on the high school kids because sales are falling off." The agent was carrying a small recording device. She managed to tape some of their conversation. The agent, of course, had no warrant.

Could her recollection of the conversation be used as evidence in a trial? Could the tape?

SITUATION 18 Harry and Daisy were talking quietly in the office of the warehouse. They were not aware that a police sergeant was listening outside the window.

Would the overheard conversation be admissible as evidence in a trial?

Under the precedent set in the Katz decision, evidence obtained in situations 16 and 18

FIGURE 16-6

Investigative Warrants

Requirements
- Must be issued by a superior court judge.
- District attorney must apply for the warrant in writing.
- Judge must find probable cause that crime is being or has been committed.
- Judge must find that all less intrusive means have been tried.

Descriptions the warrant must include
- Place and time when eavesdropping will take place.
- Device to be used.
- Types of conversations to be recorded.
- Who is to be intercepted.

Duration of warrant (20 days)
- After information has been obtained, the police must report results of their efforts to the judge.
- The district attorney may apply for a 20-day extension if there is probable cause.

would be ruled illegal. The evidence obtained would be legal only if the police had warrants. However, in situation 17, the conversation between Daisy and Harry could probably be used in court. Daisy and Harry could not reasonably expect privacy on a crowded bus. Therefore, no search warrant would be necessary to "seize" this conversation.

Generally when the police want to use a wiretap, a warrant must be obtained. In Georgia, electronic surveillance warrants are frequently called investigative warrants. The requirements for obtaining these warrants are shown in figure 16-6.

CASE STUDY

CASE OF THE CENTRAL CITY DRUG BUST, *concluded*

The police had a search warrant that permitted them to search the warehouse and Harry's and Daisy's persons. It was based upon the sworn affidavit of Detective-Sergeant Penny, who had been posing as a drug buyer. Visits to the warehouse gave Sergeant Penny precise details about what type of drugs would be there. This information was given to Judge Stern in the affidavit.

In this case, the arresting officers had neither an arrest nor search warrant citing Jim. Did they have the legal authority to search Jim? This question is not easy to answer, and it is one that is often the subject of litigation in appellate courts. Generally, a person who is merely visiting premises that happen to be the subject of a search warrant cannot be searched unless the officer conducting the search believes he or she is armed and dangerous. In addition, the visitor's personal belongings (such as a backpack or a purse) cannot be searched if it is shown that the items belong to the visitor and the person is in fact merely a visitor as opposed to a party to the crime. However, in this case, if the drugs were in open view and in close proximity to where the visitor (Jim) was standing, the officers, upon executing the warrant, may determine that Jim is more than a visitor and is a party to the crime. If he is arrested as a party to the crime, he can certainly be searched.

In the case of the Central City Drug Bust, the police had worked very hard to break up this illegal drug-selling operation. They were especially concerned because the drugs were being "pushed" to students in the local middle and high schools. The police wanted to be sure to make their arrests and searches in a lawful manner. They did not want these offenders to get off because of a legal technicality later on at the trial. However, it is important to remember that what some people consider to be a technicality, others see as a constitutional safeguard.

Only the Facts

1. Are the following searches legal without a warrant? If they are legal, explain under what circumstances.
   a. A police officer searches someone's locked closets.
   b. A police officer searches the back seat of a stopped car.
   c. A police officer "bugs" a telephone to record conversations.

2. Define the following:
   a. probable cause
   b. exigent circumstances
   c. hot pursuit
   d. investigative warrant

Think About

1. Do you find it difficult to precisely define the following three terms from search and seizure laws? Explain your answer.
   a. immediate area
   b. plain view
   c. exigent circumstances

2. List arguments for and against general searches of school lockers by drug-sniffing dogs.

3. Why should requirements for electronic surveillance be stricter than for other searches? Do you think they are strict enough? Explain.

RESULTS OF ILLEGAL ARRESTS AND SEARCHES AND SEIZURES

The exclusionary rule was defined by the U.S. Supreme Court in the 1961 case of *Mapp v. Ohio*.[13] You have seen how the rule applies to illegally obtained confessions. It applies with equal force to illegally arrested persons and any evidence that is discovered incident to an illegal arrest. In short, it applies to any evidence seized in an illegal manner.

What can happen when the exclusionary rule is applied? A good example would be a case that the Georgia Court of Appeals decided in 1975, called here the Case of the Sleeping Drunk.[14]

CASE STUDY

CASE OF THE SLEEPING DRUNK

A man was passed out at an all-night restaurant. He was sleeping soundly on a stool. His face was buried in his folded arms on the counter. At his feet lay a half-empty bottle of rum. He smelled strongly of alcohol.

The police came into the restaurant. Seeing the man, they quickly decided he was drunk and should be arrested. They charged him with being a "public drunk," a misdemeanor in Georgia. During a brief search following the arrest, the police discovered two small plastic bags of cocaine, a Schedule II drug, in his pants pocket.

The man did not resist arrest. He was very cooperative. However, he insisted that he did not own the cocaine or know how it got in his pocket. Nonetheless, the police charged him with possession of a Schedule II drug.

In the trial, the man's attorney filed a "motion to suppress" the bags of cocaine as evidence. The attorney felt that the cocaine had been illegally obtained by the police. The attorney also sought to have the charge of public drunkenness dismissed.

The attorney argued to the court that the police had illegally arrested his client. The reason was that his client had not committed the offense of public drunkenness in their presence. Georgia law states that the person accused of the crime of public drunkenness must be loud, profane, and boisterous toward other people. The man was not showing any of these essential elements of the crime. Therefore his attorney claimed that he was illegally arrested.

Of course, if this charge were dismissed, the more serious charges of drug possession would also have to be dismissed because the drugs would then have been discovered in a search during an illegal arrest. In other words, if the arrest were declared illegal, the search would also be illegal. If the search were illegal—under the exclusionary rule—the evidence of the drugs could not be admitted. However, the trial court judge denied the motion to suppress the evidence. The man was found guilty of both charges.

On appeal, the Georgia Court of Appeals agreed with the defendant's attorney. It reversed the trial court's denial of the motion to suppress, agreeing with the defense that the arrest of a person under these circumstances was illegal. Therefore the search was also illegal. Both the public drunkenness and drug charges were dismissed. The man escaped serious felony prosecution because of the exclusionary rule.

Do you think the exclusionary rule is needed, or do you agree with those who claim that the rule makes it difficult to obtain convictions? Do you think it is too hard to follow the law as precisely as the exclusionary rule requires?

Based on what you have learned, would the following evidence be suppressed under the exclusionary rule?

SITUATION 19 A search warrant authorizes the search of a barn for a stolen auto. While looking around the barn, an officer opens a drawer in an old chest. In it, he finds plates for counterfeiting money.

SITUATION 20 The police are investigating a murder case. They interview a woman at her home. She seems uneasy, and one officer gets a hunch. Although he has neither a warrant nor consent, he pulls open a drawer in a table. He finds and seizes several vials of crack cocaine.

SITUATION 21 The same situation as 20, except the drawer is open, and the drugs are in plain view.

The evidence of counterfeiting found in situation 19 would be illegally obtained. The object of the warrant was a car, not the contents of the drawer. The officer had no right to open the drawer.

All evidence from a warrantless search that does not fit into one of the recognized exceptions would be excluded from a trial. It would be considered illegally seized. The evidence in situation 20 would have to be excluded. The officers did not have a search warrant. Situation 21 is different. The woman gave them permission to enter, and the drugs were in plain view; therefore the drugs were properly discovered and seized and would be admissible at trial. Cases in which an illegal arrest or search occurs may be dismissed. The police could then be sued by the person who has been subjected to the illegal action.

Suits of this kind can be tort actions for recovery of damages, or they may be civil rights actions. Such lawsuits would be based on a federal statute passed to protect people from unreasonable governmental actions. They are called "1983" suits because this law is found in section 1983 of title 42 of the United States Code. Police officers need to be very familiar with the law before making arrests and searches and seizures.

Only the Facts

1. What is the exclusionary rule?
2. Why is it important for police officers to be technically correct when making arrests or conducting searches?

Think About

1. How do the laws and rules regarding arrest and search and seizure protect your rights? For example, how are you protected by the requirements for different types of warrants? How are you protected by the Miranda ruling?
2. A 1984 Supreme Court ruling allowed evidence gathered as the result of an illegal search (because of a faulty warrant) to be used in court. The reasoning was that the officers had acted in "good faith." Can you think of arguments for and against the ruling?

SUMMING UP

The conflict between the need to enforce criminal laws and protect individual rights emerges clearly in the areas of arrest and search and seizure, as this chapter has shown. The U.S. Supreme Court has sometimes seemed to favor individual rights (as in decisions based on cases from the 1960s, for example). Other times, the court seems to have been more concerned about achieving greater efficiency in law enforcement, as in rulings from the 1970s and 1980s. How to balance the need to protect society and individual rights is a question that may never be entirely resolved. Perhaps maintaining a balance is itself most important. What do you think about this issue?

Notes

1. 205 Ga. App. 308, 422 S.E. 2d 209 (1992).
2. 384 U.S. 346 (1966).

3. 446 U.S. 297 (1980).

4. 204 Ga. App. 312, 418 S.E.2d 822 (1992).

5. 206 Ga. App. 150, 424 S.E.2d 832 (1992).

6. 248 Ga. App. 70 (2001).

7. 201 Ga. App. 320, 411 S.E.2d 324 (1991).

8. 262 Ga. 578, 422 S.E.2d 546 (1992).

9. 240 Ga. App. 370 (2000).

10. *New Jersey, Petitioner v. T.L.O.*, 105 S. Ct. 733 (1985).

11. *Michigan v. Rick Sitz*, 110 S. Ct. 2481 (1990).

12. 389 U.S. 347 (1967).

13. 367 U.S. 643 (1961).

14. *Peoples v. State*, 216 S.E. 2d 604 (1975).

17 The Trial

The heart of the criminal justice process is the trial. Like arrests and searches and seizures, trial procedure is regulated in part by the U.S. and state constitutions. Within the constitutional guidelines, the courts have developed a set of rules. These rules guide the participants—the judge, jury, prosecutor, and defense attorney—through the process in such a way as to guarantee that the accused is treated fairly. There are two main parts to the trial process: the preliminary proceedings and the trial itself. In effect, they form a series of steps that must be followed in each case.

PRETRIAL PROCEEDINGS

Pretrial proceedings include the following: the booking, initial appearance, preliminary hearing, indictment, and arraignment.

Booking

After a suspect is arrested, he or she is booked at the police station. Bookings are formal listings of the names of persons and the crimes of which they are accused. Usually, after booking, individuals are photographed and fingerprinted. Their personal property is taken and stored. Each person is allowed to make one phone call before being put into a jail cell.

Initial Appearance

The purpose of the initial appearance is to make sure that the person accused of a crime is aware of the charges and is given due process. The initial appearance takes place in the magistrate court. It must occur within 72 hours if there was a warrant for the arrest. Only 48 hours are permitted if an arrest was made without a warrant.

The judge will ask the accused whether he or she has an attorney. The judge will also seek to determine whether the accused is indigent (which in this situation means being unable to afford an attorney).

Until 1963, the U.S. Constitution was not interpreted as guaranteeing an indigent person the right to be represented by an attorney. This interpretation changed with the U.S. Supreme Court decision in *Gideon v. Wainwright*.[1] In this case, the court held that the state must provide an attorney to any indigent person accused of a crime that is a felony. However, the accused may waive the right to have counsel at the initial appearance.

In 1972, the U.S. Supreme Court extended the right established in *Gideon* to insist that the state provide an attorney to indigent defendants whenever imprisonment is possible, as with felonies and some misdemeanors.[2] The judge may appoint an attorney for an indigent defendant from the local members of the bar. In some jurisdictions, one or more attorneys may be appointed as public defenders. They are paid by the government to defend indigents accused of crimes in that jurisdiction.

At this initial hearing, the judge also sets bail. (For some of the more serious crimes, bail must be set by the superior court.) Bail is a certain amount of money that must be posted with the court. By posting bail, a suspect can avoid having to wait in jail until his or her trial. The money is a guarantee that the accused will appear in court for each required court appearance and for the trial.

In Georgia, a suspect is usually allowed to get out of jail by posting bail unless he or she is accused of a capital crime. (A capital crime is a crime such as murder, rape, or armed robbery that is punishable by long prison sentences, life imprisonment, or death. Bail, or surety, is generally denied by the courts for defendants accused of this type of crime.) In many cases, bail is also denied if the defendant is a repeat offender or if the crime is a violent one.

How does bail work?

SITUATION 1 Both Will and Ned have been arrested and charged with burglary. The judge sets bail for each at $5,000. Neither has that much money available.

How can they get the money so that they can be released?

By posting bail, a suspect can avoid having to wait in jail until his or her trial.

Ned is lucky. His sister agrees to pledge enough property to the court to cover the amount of the bond.

What happens if Ned does not show up for trial? His bond will be forfeited, and the property that his sister put up will be taken by the state to be sold. The money from the sale of the property will be used to cover the amount of the bond, which will then be paid to the court.

Will does what many defendants do to make bail: he contacts a bail bondsman. The bondsman stands as surety for the bail amount should the defendant fail to appear at the next appointed court date. In other words, the bondsman will have to pay the bail amount if the defendant fails to appear at the next court date. The bondsman's fee is usually 10 to 15 percent of the face value of the bail bond.

Will's bail is $5,000. He would have to pay the bondsman at least 10 percent, or $500, to be released from jail. Will doesn't have that much money, so he must remain in jail until after the trial.

There are alternatives to the bail bond system. Figure 17-1 illustrates two other approaches. The 10 percent plan is used in other states; 10 percent of the bail is paid directly to the court, thereby relieving the defendant of having to produce all the money at one time, use a bail bondsman, or rely on someone else to post bond for him or her. Release on recognizance is occasionally used in Georgia. With this approach, the defendant agrees to appear at trial, but no money is required as surety. Because the court allows the accused to be released on his or her signature, release on recognizance is often called a signature bond. Release on recognizance gives all who qualify—regardless of resources—a chance to show they are a good risk based on their word.

At the initial hearing, the judge hears arguments from the prosecutor and the defense attorney as to whether bail should be set and how much it should be. A defense attorney will attempt to get release on recognizance for the accused. Failing that, the attorney will attempt to get the judge to set the lowest possible bail.

FIGURE 17-1

How Defendants Get out of Jail before the Trial

Method	Who pays?	Cost	Requirements
Bail is set by judge unless prohibited	Defendant or	No cost if the defendant shows up for trial. Bail is then returned. All of the bail is paid if the defendant does not show up.	Sufficient cash or property to meet bail
	Bail bondsman	10 to 15 percent of amount set for bail is paid to bondsman	Sufficient funds to pay bondsman (bondsman must be willing to take risk on the defendant)
10 percent plan (10 percent of bail is paid to court)	Defendant	If the defendant shows up for trial, a small amount of that which was paid as bail is kept by the court, and the rest of the money is returned.	Sufficient funds to pay court fees (the court must be willing to take risk on the defendant)
Release on recognizance	Nobody	No charges	Defendant must qualify for enough points. Points reflect the defendant's previous record, nature of crime charged, work history, and community ties.

CASE OF THE CENTRAL CITY DRUG BUST, *continued*

Both Daisy and Harry are brought before Judge Stern. Their cases are handled separately. Judge Stern determines that Harry is able to hire his own attorney. (He hires Wanda Weill, an experienced criminal defense lawyer.) Daisy is found to be indigent, so the court appoints a public defender, Larry Block, for her.

In cases involving the sale of drugs, only a superior court judge can set bail. Harry's and Daisy's respective attorneys petition the superior court for bail for their clients. Superior Court Judge Frank sets bail at $100,000 for Harry. Harry's application for release on recognizance is denied. He has neither lived in Central City very long, nor has he held a steady job, so the court is concerned that he has no ties to the community and might leave the area to escape the trial. The judge determines that nothing other than a monetary bond will guarantee his appearance in court. Bail is set at $50,000 for Daisy. She, too, is denied release on recognizance.

Preliminary Hearing

This hearing is usually held in magistrate court. Its purpose is to determine

1. whether or not there is probable cause to believe that a crime has been committed and the defendant is the person who committed the crime.

2. whether the charges brought are appropriate to the acts committed and whether the acts constitute a felony or a misdemeanor.

In a preliminary hearing, the court is not concerned with whether or not the defendant is guilty. It simply wants to determine if there is enough evidence to indicate that the accused person should be prosecuted.

During the preliminary hearing, each side introduces evidence. The prosecution tries to show probable cause. The defense tries to show lack of it. If probable cause is established during the preliminary hearing and the case involves a misdemeanor, it is forwarded to the appropriate court, and a trial date is set. If the case concerns a felony, it is forwarded to the district attorney for presentment (presentation) to the grand jury. (Presentment may be waived by the defendant, or it may be waived by statute for less severe crimes.)

CASE OF THE CENTRAL CITY DRUG BUST, *continued*

The preliminary hearings for Harry and Daisy are held one after the other in the Middle County Magistrate Court. Acting as the prosecutor is assistant district attorney, Cindy Sharp (see figure 17-2 for the cast of characters in this case). She introduces testimonial evidence from the arresting officers. She also displays the confiscated drugs as physical evidence. She wants to show that enough probable cause exists to require the court to bind both Harry and Daisy over to the grand jury (that is, for their cases to go to a grand jury).

The defense attorneys, Ms. Weill and Mr. Block, try to discredit the witnesses. They lay the groundwork for a later motion to suppress the physical evidence, claiming that it was illegally obtained. If it were proven that the evidence was obtained illegally, the evidence could not be used at trial. However, Judge Stern decides that enough evidence has been presented by the prosecution to establish sufficient probable cause in both cases.

During a separate motion hearing, the defense attorneys ask for a reduction in the amount of bail required. A superior court judge denies their motion.

Both Harry and Daisy have convinced a bail bondsman to post their bail. They each pay the bondsman 10 percent of the original amount of bail—$10,000 for Harry and $5,000 for Daisy.

FIGURE 17-2

Cast of Characters in the Case of the Central City Drug Bust

Defendants	**Harry**. Charged with trafficking in cocaine and marijuana and contributing to delinquency of a minor. **Daisy**. Charged with trafficking in cocaine and marijuana and contributing to delinquency of a minor. **Jim**. A 16-year-old high school student. Charged with "delinquent act" of possession and intent to sell drugs. He will be tried in juvenile court (see chapter 18).
Attorneys	*Prosecutors*: **Mr. Jones**, district attorney **Ms. Sharp**, assistant district attorney *Defense Attorneys*: **Ms. Weill**, attorney for Harry **Mr. Block**, public defender, attorney for Daisy
Judges	*Preliminary hearing*: Judge Stern, Middle County Magistrate Court *Trial court*: Judge Frank, Middle County Superior Court
Witnesses for the Prosecution	***Police***: Detective-Sergeant Penny, Detective-Sergeant Brooks, and Patrolman Newmann. These officers were involved in the investigation and arrest of Harry and Daisy. ***Georgia crime lab expert***. Will testify as to authenticity and street value of drugs confiscated in the raid on the warehouse. *Other*: **Student #1**. (Sandra) Was offered marijuana and cocaine by Daisy but turned her down. **Student #2**. (Alan) Was offered marijuana and cocaine by Daisy but turned her down. **Jim**. May testify for the state against Harry and Daisy on the charges of sale of a controlled substance and contributing to the delinquency of a minor.

Because Daisy was declared indigent, a public defender was appointed to represent her in the case. You might ask, "If Daisy is indigent, how can she afford to make bail of $5,000?" The money could be borrowed from friends, relatives, or a bank. Daisy could sell an item of her property to get the money she needs. There are other ways, too, such as by posting a property bond or using a bail bondsman.

Indictment

In Georgia, all capital felonies must be presented to a grand jury. Certain cases involving other, less severe felonies like shoplifting, credit card transaction fraud, forgery, and entering an auto, are not presented to a grand jury. In these cases, the district attorney may proceed on an "accusation"

by filing a written document with the court that allows the case to go forward. This procedure helps to speed up the process. It also eliminates the need to have any witnesses present. Whether a case is presented to a grand jury or proceeds on an accusation, it will be for a grand jury to decide whether to indict persons alleged to have committed a felony. (To indict is to formally charge a suspect with a crime.)

Each county has its own grand jury made up of a group of randomly selected community citizens. In Georgia, grand juries are made up of 16 to 23 registered voters from the county in which they serve. Grand juries that serve three-month terms have varying civil powers and duties. Their chief responsibility is to determine whether to indict people who are brought before them by the district attorney.

Generally speaking, the grand jury hears only some of the evidence in a case—that is, the evidence that the district attorney chooses to present or that the grand jury requests. Defendants do not normally present evidence on their own behalf.

The grand jury decides when it has heard sufficient evidence. Then it will decide whether to accuse the defendant of the crime(s) charged. It will either issue a "true bill" of indictment or a "no bill" of indictment. If a true bill is issued, the accused is formally indicted and charged with the crime. If the grand jury feels there is not enough evidence to charge the defendant, it will issue a "no bill." The defendant will then be released and the charges dropped.

Why is a formal indictment necessary? A grand jury's review of a case is a constitutional safeguard. It ensures that there is sufficient basis for the charge that a felony has been committed and that there is evidence that the defendant may have committed it.

A grand jury decides whether to indict persons alleged to have committed a felony.

CASE STUDY

CASE OF THE CENTRAL CITY DRUG BUST, *continued*

Now that Daisy and Harry have been formally indicted at the grand jury hearing, the next step is the formal arraignment. At the arraignment, they will each have to plead guilty or not guilty after hearing the charges against them read.

Only the Facts

1. What is the first hearing after an arrest? At this hearing, what does the judge try to determine?
2. Is an attorney guaranteed to each person who is accused of a felony? of a misdemeanor?
3. What is bail? How does it differ from release on recognizance?
4. What are two purposes of a preliminary hearing?
5. Define indictment. Who determines whether persons will be indicted?

Think About

1. Do you think the bail bond system is a good one? Explain your answers.
2. The Eighth Amendment prohibits excessive bail. Are the following excessive?
   a. $50,000 for Daisy
   b. $100,000 for Harry
   c. $1 million for a wealthy person accused of trafficking in (selling) drugs to finance a business venture
   d. $250,000 for an indigent accused of robbing a convenience store at gunpoint
3. Several preliminary proceedings have so far been described. Why are all these hearings necessary to ensure due process?

Arraignment

The arraignment is held in either state or superior court. It is a formal hearing in which the judge reads the charges against the accused. Then the accused is asked for a plea—either guilty or not guilty.

Sometimes a third type of plea is accepted by the court. It is called *nolo contendere*, or a "no contest" plea. It means, "I am pleading no contest to the charges brought against me. I will not attempt to prove my innocence or disprove my possible guilt." In other words, the court is free to find defendants who plead *nolo contendere* guilty and sentence them. The persons pleading are not admitting guilt. However, for all practical purposes, their plea results in a conviction. The *nolo contendere* plea is sometimes used in traffic cases. It is also used in cases in which the person is likely to be fined but not sent to jail.

If a plea of not guilty is made, a trial date is set. The accused remains out of jail on bail or is released on recognizance or returned to jail until the trial.

A special plea of not guilty by reason of insanity may also be entered. This plea is used most often in capital crimes. If this plea is made, the court will have to hear expert testimony from psychiatrists and psychologists. Two issues must be resolved: Is the defendant now insane? Was he or she insane at the time that the alleged crime was committed?

What if a defendant is found to be insane at the time of trial or mentally incompetent to stand trial? The court can order the defendant to be confined in a state hospital until he or she is considered competent to stand trial. If the defendant becomes competent to stand trial, the trial will proceed as if the issue of mental competence had not arisen. What happens if the accused is found during the trial to have been insane at the time of the crime? The defendant will not necessarily be freed. The court may order the defendant to be committed to a state hospital or other place of confinement until he or she is considered sane. If declared sane, the accused will usually be released.

In Georgia, juries may find a person guilty but mentally ill. In these cases, the defendant serves his or her sentence in either a state hospital or a jail facility that has special treatment programs. The individual is not freed once he or she is considered well. The defendant will have to serve the length of the sentence imposed by the judge. The length of the sentence served is the same as it would be had the accused not been found to be mentally ill.

If a Person Pleads Guilty

If a person pleads guilty, the court must be satisfied that such a plea is reasonable and freely given. Furthermore, it must conclude that, in all probability, the person is guilty as charged. And the court must ensure that due process has been given to the defendant—that is, none of his or her rights can have been violated. Once the court has made these determinations, it then sets a date for sentencing. Before that date, there is usually an investigation to determine if any mitigating or aggravating circumstances exist. If so, the court will consider them in sentencing the defendant.

A judge may give a lighter sentence if there are mitigating circumstances in a case. For example, the defendant may have some problem that helps explain why the crime was committed, or the defendant may have a good record with no previous arrests. These circumstances might cause a judge to be more lenient in setting the sentence than would normally be the case.

Aggravating circumstances, on the other hand, tend to cause a judge to set a stricter sentence. Aggravating circumstances may include the fact that the defendant has a criminal history or that the crime was particularly cruel or gruesome.

Plea Bargaining

During the early stages of the trial process, the prosecutor and the defense attorney may meet to determine if the case can be settled without going to trial. These efforts are referred to as plea bargaining. Plea bargaining may begin just after the defendant obtains a lawyer.

In plea bargaining, the defense attorney sometimes suggests that the client consider pleading guilty to a less serious charge. For example, suppose the client is charged with burglary of a house, a felony punishable by a sentence of up to 20 years in prison. The defense attorney may suggest that his or her client consider pleading guilty to the less serious charge of criminal trespass. This misdemeanor is punishable by a sentence of up to 12 months in jail and/or a fine of up to $1,000.

At other times, the defense attorney may suggest that his or her client plead guilty to the charge in order to receive a recommended sentence by the prosecutor. A recommended sentence might be a sentence that is lighter or more favorable to the defendant than would usually be the case.

This plea negotiation is often carried out with the judge's knowledge and permission. Judges reserve the right, however, to make up their own minds about a sentence. A judge is not legally bound by the agreement reached by the prosecutor and the defense attorney. The judge may have reason to believe that the defendant is merely claiming guilt and is plea bargaining simply because he or she fears a trial.

The current practice is to resolve as many cases as possible through plea bargaining in order to lighten the caseload for the courts. That is not to say that a prosecutor attempts to plea bargain every single case. Each case is carefully reviewed beforehand. Factors are considered such as the amount of evidence the district attorney has against the defendant, the criminal history of the defendant, and the severity of the crime.

There has been a great deal of debate over plea bargaining. On the one hand, many people believe that our court system could not survive without plea bargaining. They argue that if it were forced to try everyone accused of a crime, the court system would collapse because of too many cases and enormous costs of so many trials. Other people oppose plea bargaining because it seems to put the responsibility of determining guilt on the prosecutor instead of on the judge and jury. They argue that plea bargaining works against a person's right to a trial by a jury of one's peers. They claim that plea bargaining enables guilty parties to get off with sentences that are too light.

CASE OF THE CENTRAL CITY DRUG BUST, *continued*

At the arraignment in the Middle County Superior Court, both Daisy and Harry plead not guilty. Daisy had been offered a plea to a charge of possession only of a Schedule II drug, a lesser charge. She declined the offer, preferring to take her chances at trial. The attorney for Harry, Ms. Weill, made a plea offer to the prosecutor. She was turned down because the district attorney's office has a policy of prosecuting all drug wholesalers.

If a Person Pleads Not Guilty: Defenses of Law

A fundamental concept in the criminal justice system of this country is that a person is presumed innocent until proven guilty beyond a reasonable doubt by the state. A defendant does not have to prove anything. He or she does not even have to take the stand in his or her own defense, and the prosecutor cannot even comment on the defendant's choice in this matter. In addition, there are certain defenses that a defendant may use at trial or even as early as during the plea bargaining stage. For each case, an attorney must decide which defenses might apply. Descriptions of the more important and commonly used defenses are shown in figure 17-3. The most common defense is to deny the charges. Witnesses and alibis are used, when possible, to support the denial. Trying to shift the blame to someone else is also an effective method of defense.

Defense attorneys may also make use of a number of pretrial motions, which can be quite important. To prevent damaging evidence being introduced at trial, the defense attorney may

FIGURE 17-3

Legal Defenses in Georgia

Alibi

Defendant must prove that he or she was someplace other than the scene of the crime when it supposedly took place.

Coercion

Defendant claims that the "crime" was committed to avoid threats of immediate death or great bodily harm. Fear must be reasonable. This defense does not apply to murder, and it applies only when the defendant is threatened, not others. Suppose a telephone caller threatened to harm you unless you stole some valuable jewelry and mailed it to him. You could not claim the defense of coercion because the threat would not be immediate. Or suppose someone threatened to harm you unless you killed another person. You could not apply this defense because it does not apply to murder.

Delusional Compulsion

The "crime" must have been committed under delusional compulsion. A delusion is a belief that is false, although the person holding it believes it is true. The compulsion must be due to mental disease, injury, or a birth defect. For example, a woman suffering from delusions may have believed that the person she killed was a large ferocious animal that was going to harm her family.

Entrapment

Defendant claims that the "crime" would not have been committed had the defendant not been tricked into it by a law enforcement officer. The officer is alleged to have participated in criminal activity to encourage the defendant to do the same. The officer must have generated the idea for the criminal activity without the help of the defendant. Often used in drug cases.

Insanity

Mental incapacitation (that is, not being capable of knowing right from wrong) at time of act must be proved.

Involuntary Intoxication

The intoxication must be involuntary. Several excuses are recognized: "excusable neglect" (example: Sandra drank punch at party without knowing it had alcohol in it); "fraud, artifice, and contrivance" (example: someone slipped LSD into Frank's punch); and "coercion" (example: Billie was physically forced to drink the punch with alcohol in it).

Mistake of Fact

Defendant claims that the "crime" was committed because of a mistaken view of the situation. For example, Jennifer shot at Herb, believing he was an "intruder." Actually, Herb is a cousin who let himself into Jennifer's house to surprise her.

Self-Defense

Can be defense of self, others, and/or home. The defendant must show justification for doing what would normally be a crime. For example, killing someone for trying to "kidnap" a pet dog would not be justifiable.

---

make a "motion to suppress evidence," claiming that the evidence was obtained illegally. Alternatively, an attorney may make a "motion for a continuance" (for the trial to be postponed) in order to have more time to prepare the case. If an attorney feels the community may be hostile to the defendant, and therefore the defendant might not receive a fair trial, he or she may make a "motion for a change of venue" (that is, a request to change the location of the trial).

CASE STUDY

CASE OF THE CENTRAL CITY DRUG BUST, *continued*

The defense lawyers get together to discuss defenses for the trial. Because this case concerns drug dealing, self-defense cannot be a defense, and neither Daisy nor Harry can claim insanity.

Harry and Daisy could not use the defense of alibi because they were caught redhanded. Entrapment is a defense that is often used in drug cases, but there is no evidence of entrapment in this case.

Daisy might consider using the defense of coercion. She could claim that Harry threatened to do her great bodily harm if she did not help him. Remember, however, that a defense must be proved in order to be successful, and no mention has been made of coercion. Consider what defenses or defense strategies Harry's and Daisy's attorneys might employ.

Only the Facts

1. What is an arraignment?
2. Match the following terms and brief definitions:
   1. aggravating circumstance
   2. plea bargain
   3. mitigating circumstance
   4. *nolo contendere*

   a. a plea of no contest to the charge
   b. an event that would cause a judge to give a lighter sentence
   c. an event that would cause a judge to give a stiffer sentence
   d. an arrangement by which a defendant pleads guilty to a lesser sentence

3. What is a (a) motion to suppress evidence? (b) motion for continuance? (c) motion for a change of venue?

Think About

1. Why would a person enter a plea of *nolo contendere* in a criminal case?
2. Do you think plea bargaining is desirable? Why or why not?
3. Do you think entrapment is a valid defense in a drug case? Why?
4. Should insanity be allowed as a defense? Why?

THE TRIAL

Criminal trials, like civil trials, can be divided into six major parts:

1. Jury selection
2. Opening statements
3. Presentation of case
4. Closing statements
5. Jury deliberation
6. Verdict

There is a major difference between a civil and a criminal trial, however. Certain constitutional guaranties apply to criminal procedures that do not apply to civil trials, including the right to have an attorney, the right of the accused to confront witnesses against him or her, and the right to a jury trial. Making sure these rights are provided is the concern of the judge in a criminal trial. In a civil trial, the judge's concern is simply to ensure that the rules of civil procedure are followed.

Why is the court more concerned about the protection of rights in a criminal trial than in a civil trial? A main reason is that the government both prosecutes and tries a criminal case. Defendants need the protection from the government that the U.S. and Georgia constitutions provide. In a civil case, both parties are considered to be on equal terms.

Another reason is the seriousness of what can happen in a criminal trial. Defendants may lose their liberty, civil rights, and even their lives (if the death penalty is imposed). In a civil trial, money, property, or a person's good name are the only things at stake.

The procedures in a criminal trial are very much like those in a civil trial (for a review, see the section "The Trial" in chapter 12). As you may recall, the two parties are called the plaintiff and the defendant in a civil case. In a criminal proceeding, they are referred to as the prosecution (or "the state)" and the defendant, respectively. In chapter 12, whenever the text refers to the plaintiff, you may assume that what is being said generally applies to the prosecution in a criminal trial.

There are many similarities between criminal and civil trials. What are some differences?

Jury Selection—*Voir Dire*

The first step, the selection of the jury, is handled as in a civil case. Each attorney asks questions aimed at determining if the jurors will be fair and impartial. Each side is permitted unlimited strikes for cause—if, for example, an attorney suspects that a potential jury member might be prejudiced or have personal knowledge of the facts.

Each attorney is also allowed a limited number of peremptory strikes. With peremptory strikes, lawyers can eliminate jurors who they feel might damage their case without having to give a reason why. However, they may never strike a juror because of race or sex. In jury selection, both the prosecution and defense try to choose jurors with whom they feel comfortable and who they think will consider the case fairly.

Opening Statements

In a criminal case, the prosecutor has the right to make the first opening statement. Opening statements are usually brief and are designed to acquaint a jury with both sides of the case. Both the prosecutor and the defense attorney say what they will try to prove during the trial.

The prosecutor outlines the formal charges made against the defendant. He or she asks the jury to consider the evidence presented in support of each charge.

In the case of the Central City Drug Bust, Harry and Daisy are being tried at the same time, but each has a separate defense lawyer. Each lawyer can make an opening statement on behalf of his or her client.

Presentation of the Case

The presentation of the case is the main part of the trial. The prosecution always has the burden of proving that the defendant is guilty beyond a reasonable doubt. The prosecution presents its evidence first, and the defense goes last. The order of presentation gives the defense the opportunity to rebut (oppose) the prosecution's evidence.

For each crime, there is a set of elements that must be proved by the prosecution. These elements are like pieces of a puzzle. Once collected and put together, they should establish a clear picture of guilt beyond a reasonable doubt.

In a crime such as in the Central City Drug Bust, the prosecutor must prove the following elements:

- that each of the defendants had in his or her possession sufficient quantities of the drugs to constitute possession for sale;
- that the drugs in question were actually drugs of the kind that the prosecutor claims them to be;
- that the defendants acted in a manner so as to be guilty of the crime of contributing to the delinquency of a minor; and
- that the defendants acted in a way that resulted in the sale of illicit drugs.

To prove its case, the prosecution presents evidence and puts witnesses on the stand to testify (see figure 17-2 for a list of witnesses who could testify for the prosecution). The police officers would testify about the arrest and the evidence seized. The prosecution also would introduce evidence such as weapons, fingerprints, drugs, and various documents.

The prosecution is permitted to introduce a defendant's previous criminal record (if any) under only two conditions:

1. the defendant introduces evidence of good moral character or
2. the previous conviction closely relates to the current crime.

The prosecution may call Jim (the student who was arrested along with Harry and Daisy) to testify. However, he would have to be provided with an attorney because his testimony might be used against him in his juvenile hearing (see chapter 18). Jim's testimony might be enlightening on two charges: contributing to the delinquency of a minor and the sale of a controlled substance. If either the prosecution or the defense calls Jim to take the stand, the judge could close the trial to the public for that portion of the case in order to protect Jim (a minor).

After each witness is presented to the jury, the defense may cross-examine him or her (see chapter 12, which discusses rules of evidence in civil cases. These rules apply in criminal cases as well).

Once the prosecution "rests its case," the defense presents its evidence. The defense's presentation is made in the same way as that of the prosecution. The prosecutor has the same opportunity to cross-examine the defense witnesses as the defense did prosecution witnesses.

Who will appear as witnesses for the defense depends on the defense strategy. For example, Daisy's attorney may decide to try to prove that Daisy was coerced into selling drugs. He would

To prove its case, the prosecution presents evidence and puts witnesses on the stand to testify.

then call witnesses and produce evidence to support that defense. If Daisy were willing, he might have her testify. (Remember that the Fifth Amendment gives individuals the right to remain silent rather than testify against themselves.)

Another strategy the defense attorney might employ would be to ask if Daisy were willing to "turn state's evidence." That is, she would testify for the prosecution against Harry. This cooperation would likely result in a lighter sentence for her.

The defense might also wish to call character witnesses for either Harry or Daisy. However, the presentation of character witnesses would permit the prosecution to introduce evidence of any previous convictions relevant to the honesty of the defendants.

In some instances, the defense may choose not to offer new evidence. Its entire case may consist of attempting to discredit the prosecution's testimony. This strategy is intended to leave the jury with a reasonable doubt concerning the defendant's guilt, in which case the jury must return a verdict of not guilty.

Closing Statements

In these statements, each attorney attempts to convince the jury that his or her case should be believed over that of the opposing side. Remember, the attorneys cannot speak about anything in their closing statements that was not presented during the trial, but either side may draw conclusions from the facts and evidence the jury has seen or heard.

Jury Deliberation and Verdict

When the presentation part of the trial is over, the judge charges the jury. That is, the judge instructs the jury about the law that must be applied to the case at hand. The judge tells the jury about the concept of burden of proof. He or she explains that the prosecution has the burden of proving beyond a reasonable doubt that the defendants are guilty of the crimes charged. The judge would say something like, "If you believe the evidence is sufficient beyond a reasonable doubt to convict the defendants of these offenses, then it is your duty to convict."

The judge reminds jurors that their duty is to reach a verdict of guilty or not guilty on each charge listed in the indictment. On each charge, if the verdict is for conviction, it must be unanimous. Finally, the judge reminds the jurors that if they do not find the evidence to be sufficient or if they have a reasonable doubt, then it would be their duty to find the defendants not guilty.

After being charged, the jurors retire to the jury room to deliberate. When they reach a verdict, the parties and jurors return to the courtroom. The judge asks the defendants to stand and face the jury. The foreman of the jury (a jury member who is selected to act as the spokesperson) then gives the verdict to the judge or court clerk to be read aloud. The judge thanks the jurors and dismisses them from further service.

If the verdict is not guilty, the defendant is freed by the court. That person cannot be tried again for that particular crime. If the verdict is guilty, the judge sentences the defendant or calls for a presentence investigation and report. When the report is ready, the judge sets a date to bring the defendant back to court for sentencing.

Only the Facts

1. What is a major difference between a civil and criminal trial?

2. What are the six major parts of the criminal trial process?

3. Opposing the defendant in a criminal trial is the _____ . In a civil trial, the defendant is opposed by the _____ .

4. Who has the burden of proof in a criminal trial?

Think About

1. Do you think the trial process is equally fair to the prosecution and the defendant? Explain your answer.

2. In a trial, what kinds of persons would the defense want to serve on the jury? Whom would the prosecution prefer?

3. Consider what might happen to the defendant in a criminal trial if the following constitutional protections were not guaranteed:
   a. the right not to testify against oneself
   b. the right to confront witnesses
   c. the right to a trial by jury
   d. the right to an attorney if the defendant is indigent and it is possible that the defendant will be imprisoned if found guilty.

SUMMING UP

This chapter has explained the trial process in a criminal case for adults. (In the next chapter, you will learn about the juvenile justice process.) You have read about the roles of defense lawyer, prosecutor, judge, and jury, as well as the differences between a criminal and civil trial. You have learned about what types of evidence may be presented and what defenses may be claimed. In the following chapter, you and your fellow students will be able to assume the roles of each of the characters in the Case of the Central City Drug Bust and act out the trial in the classroom. In this way, you will be able to gain a full appreciation for courtroom procedure and how accused persons are protected by the law.

Notes

1. 372 U.S. 335 (1963).
2. *Argersinger v. Hamlin*, 407 U.S. 25 (1972).

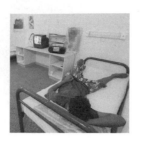

18 Juvenile Justice

LAW TALK

custody

delinquent act

formal hearing

Gault decision

informal adjustment

intake

juvenile

status offense

In the Case of the Central City Drug Bust, two of the three parties to the crime are adults (Harry and Daisy). One of them is not. The high school student, Jim, is 16 years old. Because he is under 17, his case is treated differently by the state of Georgia. It will be handled by the juvenile court in the county in which the incident occurred.

The idea of treating juveniles differently from adults in a situation in which a criminal act occurs began to take form in the early 1800s. Before then everyone—regardless of age—was treated and jailed in the same way and in the same institutions. The first juvenile court in the United States was established in Chicago in 1899. In 1906, the Georgia legislature established legal grounds for a children's court. The first juvenile court in Georgia was established in Fulton County in 1911. Today, every county in Georgia has a juvenile court.

Generally, juvenile court judges are appointed by the chief judge of the Superior Court of the circuit in which the courts are located. In small counties, a superior court judge will sometimes preside over the juvenile court. In this case, the judge functions in the dual capacity of superior court judge and juvenile court judge. In larger counties, associate judges are appointed by the chief judge of the juvenile court to assist in handling the large case loads.

Georgia juvenile courts are controlled by a 1971 law known as the juvenile code. The philosophy of the juvenile courts is to be protective of the child rather than punitive (aimed at punishment). The juvenile court is to do what is in the best interest of the child while considering the best interests of society.

Not everyone agrees with this way of treating children. Some people believe that the juvenile court is too soft on delinquents. They think more delinquents should be tried in adult courts. Others argue that children are not adults: they often go through a period of rebellion in which they do things they would not do if they were older. They say the juvenile court has worked satisfactorily. What do you think?

JUVENILE COURT

The juvenile court has jurisdiction over children under 17 years of age who are said to have committed a delinquent act or status offense. A delinquent act is one that would be a crime if it were committed by an adult. In contrast, a status offense is an act that would not be a crime if it were committed by an adult. Examples of status offenses are ungovernable behavior, being a runaway, and being truant (the behaviors listed in figure 9-2 are status offenses). The juvenile court also has jurisdiction over juveniles who commit traffic offenses. In addition, the court has jurisdiction over children aged 17 and younger who are considered to be abused, neglected, or deprived.

For youths who have been "sentenced" as juveniles, the court may retain supervision until they are 21. (Note that rather than actually being sentenced to punishment as adults are, juveniles are said to receive treatment with the goal of rehabilitation.) However, if a youth previously sentenced in juvenile court commits another offense after he or she is 17, the subsequent offense would be handled by an adult court.

The 1994 amendment to the Georgia Juvenile Court Code provides for the treatment of juvenile offenders charged with certain violent offenses as adults. It gives the superior court sole jurisdiction over any child alleged to have committed certain offenses, including murder, voluntary manslaughter, rape, aggravated sodomy, aggravated child molestation, aggravated sexual battery, and armed robbery committed with a firearm.

Before a juvenile is indicted as an adult, the district attorney may, after investigation and for "extraordinary cause," withdraw the case and submit it to the juvenile court. Also, following indictment, the superior court may, after inves-

After a youth is taken into custody, a juvenile officer explains how the juvenile justice process works.

tigation and for extraordinary case, transfer a case to the juvenile court. However, there are some capital cases that the superior court may not transfer, including cases involving murder, rape, and armed robbery committed with a firearm.

Children under 13 years of age are not believed to be capable of criminal intent. Therefore, even if they commit a capital offense, the case must be handled by the juvenile court.

TAKEN INTO CUSTODY

Consider the following scenario: Kevin, who is under the age of 17, commits a crime and is caught by the police. Because he is a juvenile, his capture is not referred to as an arrest. Instead, Kevin is said to be "taken into custody."

A youth may be taken into custody if there are reasonable grounds to believe that he or she has committed a delinquent act or a status offense. A youth may also be taken into custody if he or she has been abused and/or neglected. Neither of these events is considered an arrest, so the youth can legally claim never to have been arrested. This claim is true as long as the youth's only contact with the criminal justice system is through the juvenile court.

To understand what is likely to happen when a youth is taken into custody for committing a delinquent act, let's see what happens to Jim in the Case of the Central City Drug Bust.

CASE OF THE CENTRAL CITY DRUG BUST, *continued*

Jim was taken into custody by the police when Harry and Daisy were arrested. At the police station, Jim was taken upstairs to Detective Wade's office. Detective Wade is the juvenile officer for the Central City police department.

Officer Wade was not too surprised to see Jim. Jim had been in trouble several times during the past year. He had been stopped for racing on the highway, and his driving privileges had been taken away for six months. He had been taken into custody for shoplifting on two occasions. Each time, the store owner declined to sign a complaint against Jim. (A complaint is the document that must be filed to begin juvenile court proceedings.)

Detective Wade notified the juvenile authorities that Jim was in custody. The authorities sent someone to take Jim to the juvenile detention facility.

Detective Wade also called Jim's mother. She came to the police station as soon as she could. She was very upset. She explained that she was divorced and that she had to support herself and Jim by working long hours. It was becoming more and more difficult, she said, to get along with Jim.

Detective Wade told Jim's mother that Jim was being detained for possession of drugs, including a large amount of cocaine. If Jim were an adult, Detective Wade said, Jim would be tried for a felony. Because he was a juvenile, his case would be heard in the juvenile court, but the charges were still very serious. Detective Wade then read Jim his Miranda rights.

JUVENILE RIGHTS AND PROTECTIONS

Juveniles, like adults, have the right to remain silent when questioned about an alleged crime. They have the right to an attorney when they have been charged with a delinquent act or a status offense.

Although not required by Georgia law, it is desirable for parents, a legal guardian, or an attorney to be present when a youth is questioned by the police or anyone else. Further, the Georgia Supreme Court has indicated that parents should be present when a child waives his or her Fifth Amendment privileges.

However, the rules for determining whether a confession can be used against a defendant in court are stricter for juveniles than for adults in Georgia. A court considers whether the juvenile waived his or her rights knowingly and voluntarily. It takes into account factors such as the juvenile's age, education, and his or her understanding of the meaning of his or her rights. Interrogation methods and whether the juvenile was allowed to consult with an adult would also be considered.

The Gault Case

A minor's right to be represented by an attorney dates back only to the 1960s. Until then, juvenile courts often failed to give minors the constitutional rights guaranteed to adults. This denial resulted, ironically, from efforts to protect and aid juvenile offenders. The Gault case initiated changes in juvenile system concepts and procedures.[1]

In this case, Gerald Gault, age 15, was taken into custody for making an obscene phone call to his neighbor. His parents were not notified that he was taken into custody, nor were they told the nature of the complaint against Gerald. There were no lawyers present at the hearing. The principal witness against Gault was not the neighbor who had made the complaint but a police officer testifying as to what she had told him. The judge found Gault guilty and ordered him to attend reform school until age 21.

The Gault case was appealed, and the decision was overturned. The U.S. Supreme Court held that juveniles in danger of losing their liberty have several rights. They are entitled to be notified of the charges against them. They can confront and cross-examine witnesses. They can remain silent. They can be represented by an attorney. However, an attorney is not usually brought into a juvenile case until a formal petition is filed. Juveniles also have the right to obtain a record of their hearing and the right to an appeal.

Only the Facts

1. What is a status offense? What is a delinquent act?
2. The juvenile court in Georgia has jurisdiction over any child under the age of 17 who is alleged to have committed (a) _____, (b) _____ , or (c) _____ . It also has jurisdiction over any child aged (d) _____ or younger alleged to be deprived or abused.
3. What is the philosophy of the juvenile courts?
4. Name at least two important rights established in the Gault case.
5. Under Georgia law, what are the offenses that will result in juveniles being treated as adults?

Think About

1. Should the age of adult responsibility for crimes be 17? Give reasons to support your opinion.
2. Compare the rights of juveniles to those of adults (chapter 15). Why do you think certain adult rights are denied to juveniles?
3. How might status offenses discriminate against young people? Why are they needed?

INTAKE

The first step in the juvenile justice process is called intake. A youth taken into custody is turned over to an intake officer of the juvenile court. The intake officer immediately begins to investigate the case. Two important decisions must be made by the juvenile court within 72 hours. An intake officer must first find out whether there is enough evidence (that is, probable cause) to support the charges made against the youth. If there clearly is not, the intake officer must dismiss the case. If there is enough evidence, the intake worker must decide whether to detain the youth until a detention hearing can be held.

Detention Decisions

Juveniles may be detained for various reasons. The main ones are to prevent them from running away or hurting themselves or others. Or a youth may have nowhere else to go. Maybe his or her parents or guardians are absent or unwilling to have the child return home. Before making a decision about the detention, an intake officer must gather information by asking, What are the charges against the youth? Has he or she been in trouble with the law before? What is the situation at home and school? If detention is not considered necessary, the youth will be released to his or her parent(s) or guardian(s) until the hearing or adjustment of the case.

If the intake worker decides that the child should be detained, the parent(s) or guardian(s) must be notified. A detention hearing must be held within 72 hours of this detention decision. (For a delinquency charge, the detention hearing may be delayed if the 72-hour period ends on a weekend or holiday.) At this hearing, the judge decides two matters. First the judge considers whether it is in the best interest of the child and society for the case to proceed to a formal hearing. If so, a petition is filed. Then the judge must decide whether the child should be detained until the formal hearing. In Georgia, juveniles have the right to make bail if they are detained.

The facility in which the youth is detained depends on the offense. Those charged with delinquent acts (which are the same as adult crimes) are sent to one of the state's Regional Youth Detention Centers. Formerly, they might have been jailed in an adult facility for a delinquent offense. This form of detention was not seen as desirable and is no longer imposed except in certain situations.

As a result of the 1994 amendment to the juvenile code, certain juveniles may be placed in adult facilities. These juveniles are charged with offenses over which the superior court has sole jurisdiction. Also, public safety and protection must reasonably require their detentions in a jail. Furthermore, detention of a juvenile in an adult facility requires an order from superior court. The youths must be placed in a room separate from adults in order to prevent any physical contact between a child and an adult offender.

On the other hand, status offenders may not be kept in detention facilities for more than 72 hours (plus 48 additional hours if the juvenile court approves). Offenders must then be moved to a shelter-care facility. These facilities do not have locks on the doors. They are places for nondelinquents to stay until arrangements can be made to return them to their homes. If the natural home is not a possibility, the child may be assigned to a group or foster home.

CASE STUDY

CASE OF THE CENTRAL CITY DRUG BUST, *continued*

In Jim's case, the intake officer is Ms. Simpatica. She finds enough evidence to show that the charges against Jim should not be dismissed.

Ms. Simpatica decides to release Jim into the custody of his mother. Jim's mother promises to bring him back to the juvenile court at the proper time. She says she will try to keep him out of trouble until that time. Before they leave, the intake officer cautions Jim. "If you are picked up by the police before your next appointment," she says, "your release privilege will be taken back. I will then ask the judge to have you detained in a secure facility until your case is decided."

Youths in crisis may be assigned to shelter-care facilities. In this and all juvenile proceedings, emphasis is placed on helping—rather than punishing—the child.

Procedure Decisions

Like Jim, most children are not detained. After their release, a court worker continues the investigation. The juvenile court needs to know enough about the juvenile's background and current status (that is, whether the juvenile has a previous court record or record of being in trouble) to determine what is best for the child and society as a whole. There are several possible courses of action.

Release. If the intake officer finds that the evidence against the youth is not sufficient, the youth will be released from the court's jurisdiction.

Informal adjustment. The intake officer may decide to proceed with an informal adjustment. Informal adjustment is unique to the juvenile justice system. When the court proceeds with an informal adjustment, it does not hold a formal hearing but retains jurisdiction over the youth for three months. (The judge can extend this period for another three months.)

For there to be an informal adjustment, the youth must have admitted wrongdoing. Also, the youth and his parents must agree to the process. Generally, informal adjustments are used with first offenders of minor delinquent acts.

The purpose of informal adjustment is to improve the youth's behavior. To help ensure improved behavior, delinquent or unruly youths may be required to attend school on a regular basis. Counseling or special programs may be required. Furthermore, a juvenile may have to make restitution (that is, pay for any damages caused by their behavior), or he or she may be expected to do community service.

Formal hearing. Before a petition for a formal hearing can be filed, the court must find that it is in the best interest of the child and society. If the decision is made to proceed with a formal hearing, a petition charging delinquency (or unruliness or deprivation, as appropriate) must be signed by the complaining witness. The witness could be a police officer, a school official, or an injured citizen.

Once the judge signs the petition, a date is set for the formal hearing. The parents and child are notified by a summons. The summons requires those named in it to appear in juvenile court at a certain time and date. A copy of the petition, detailing the charges against the child, accompanies the summons to the parents.

CASE STUDY

CASE OF THE CENTRAL CITY DRUG BUST, *continued*

Ms. Simpatica has reviewed the entire record and the investigation report. She has decided that there is enough evidence to proceed with a formal petition of delinquency. This document will be signed by the police officer who took Jim into custody at the warehouse. Jim and his mother will be notified of further proceedings.

Only the Facts

1. What is the role of an intake officer?

2. For what reasons might a youth be detained before a formal hearing?

3. Under what conditions can a juvenile be detained in an adult facility? What kind of housing arrangement must the jail provide?

4. What is an informal adjustment? What is required for there to be an informal adjustment?

5. What is necessary before a formal hearing may be held?

Think About

1. Why is there no procedure like informal adjustment in the adult criminal justice process?

FORMAL HEARING

The primary goal in the formal hearing for juveniles is to do whatever is in the best interest of the child, whereas in a trial, it is to determine whether the defendant (an adult or juvenile who is being treated as an adult) is guilty or not guilty. (See figure 18-1 to compare the differences between formal hearings for juveniles and trials for adults.)

In some juvenile courts, the arraignment is held at the same time as the detention hearing (previously discussed). This procedure is similar to that for adults but is less structured. At the arraignment, youths hear the charges against them and admit or deny them. If the arraignment is not held, youths are informed of the charges and plead guilty or not guilty at the formal hearing.

A formal hearing has two parts. The first part is the adjudicatory hearing, which is basically the same as an adult trial. Its purpose is to determine whether the child committed a delinquent or unruly act. The adjudicatory hearing must be held within 10 days of the detention hearing if the juvenile remains in custody. It must take place within 60 days of arraignment if the youth is not held in detention. After listening to all of the evidence, the judge decides whether the child committed the offense charged. If the judge finds the youth did not commit the offense charged, the youth will be released. If the judge finds that the juvenile did commit the offense charged, then a dispositional hearing will be held.

The second part of the formal hearing is the dispositional hearing. It may immediately follow the adjudicatory hearing, but it often takes place at a later date. If the disposition is to take place later, the judge may order a predisposition investigation if a party requests one. In the dispositional hearing, the judge decides what the treatment is to be. It is similar to a sentencing hearing after an adult trial.

At the dispositional hearing, the prosecution and the defense can call witnesses and present evidence in an effort to influence the judge regarding the type of treatment he or she orders. Remember, the goal of the judge is to order whatever he or she thinks is in the best interests of the juvenile.

FIGURE 18-1

How a Formal Hearing for a Juvenile Differs from an Adult Trial

	Formal Hearing	Adult Trial
Purpose	To do what is best for the child and to decide if the child is guilty of committing a delinquent act.	To determine whether the defendant is innocent or guilty of charges.
Prosecutor	Presents case, determines facts, and considers best interest of the child.	Presents evidence to prove the state's charges against the defendant.
Defense	Defends the child against charges and sees that the child gets a fair hearing and that best interest of the child is served.	Defends the accused against charges; ensures that the accused gets a fair trial.
Evidence	The rules of evidence are set by the judge in each individual case.	There are strict rules of evidence (see chapters 12 and 17).
Jury	Defendant has no right to a jury. (See discussion in "Formal Hearing.")	The defendant has a right to trial by jury.
Press and public	Spectators or press are allowed only with permission of judge. Restrictions are to protect the child.	Generally, the press (written media) and spectators are allowed.

Juveniles do not have the right to a trial by jury. In the early 1970s, the Supreme Court determined that using a jury in juvenile cases would bring the delay, formality, adversarial nature, and "clamor" of adult jury trials—factors that would not necessarily be in the best interest of the child.[2] Some Supreme Court justices disagreed with this opinion. They argued that the consequences of juvenile hearings are the same as adult trials and there should be similar procedures. What do you think?

Disposition of the Case

After hearing the evidence, the judge has several treatment choices:

1. Release the child to the custody of the parent or legal guardian with no court supervision.
2. Place the child on probation with certain conditions.
3. Commit the child to the Department of Juvenile Justice.
4. Detain the juvenile at a youth detention center for up to 90 days.
5. Send the juvenile to an outdoor program or boot camp.

Usually, a commitment to the Department of Juvenile Justice is for two years. However, if the offense the child committed comes under the Designated Felony Act (outlined in figure 18-2), there will be a special hearing to decide whether restrictive custody is needed. If the judge finds that restrictive custody is necessary, the child will be committed to the Department of Juvenile Justice for five years.

A juvenile 13 years of age or older who is convicted of an offense over which the superior court has exclusive jurisdiction is committed to the Department of Corrections. Until the juvenile reaches the age of 17, he or she is housed separately from adults in a youth confinement unit designed to provide rehabilitation. (In some cases, however, the superior court can transfer the case to juvenile court. Figure 18-2 illustrates alternative penalties for certain felony offenses.)

COMMITMENT TO THE DEPARTMENT OF JUVENILE JUSTICE

If a juvenile is committed to the Department of Juvenile Justice, the department will determine where he or she will be placed and for how long. Initially, a screening committee of the department—including a representative of the juvenile court and parent(s)—makes these decisions. (Some placement options are listed in figure 18-3.)

Before the early 1800s, there were no separate facilities for youth offenders; adults and children were imprisoned in the same institutions. In

FIGURE 18-3

What Can Happen to Juveniles Who Have Committed a Delinquent Act

Probation or Court Supervision	Committed to Department of Juvenile Justice
General conditions	**Options**
Not to break any laws	Conditional release to parents
To attend school regularly	Intensive supervision
To report to probation officer	Nonresidential community treatment or day center
To obey parent(s) or guardian(s)	Special residential treatment center or program (for job training, drug and alcohol abuse, wilderness program, etc.)
Not to use drugs or alcohol	Youth development campus (assignment based on sex, public risk, and treatment needs)
Other possible conditions	Out-of-home placement in a group home or shelter
A curfew	Boot camp (military style)
Limits on places or associations	Detention at a youth detention center
Community service	
Intensive probation	
Restitution	
Special educational programs	
Counseling	
Suspension of driver's license	
Essays or reports	
Testing	
Supervision fee	
Special residential treatment program	

1825, the House of Refuge was opened in New York City as a place to house offenders who were minors. Since that time, many similar facilities have been opened in the United States. They have often been called reform schools.

Georgia did not make a legal distinction between adults and children in the criminal justice system until 1905. In that year, the General Assembly established the Georgia State Reformatory for persons 16 years old and younger. Today, Georgia has a network of juvenile detention facilities. Regional youth detention centers house youths who are detained for short periods of time and provide short-term programs. There are also youth development campuses and a youth development facility for youths serving longer terms. These facilities have schools and rehabilitation programs. The state also has day program centers and some special residential treatment centers for those who abuse drugs and alcohol. Following release, the juvenile receives aftercare, a program that helps with readjustment to home and community life.

CASE STUDY

CASE OF THE CENTRAL CITY DRUG BUST, *continued*

In the Middle County Juvenile Court, Jim's case is called *In re Jim*, which is how juvenile cases are usually titled. The title means "about Jim" or "the matter of Jim." The juvenile court judge, Judge Brown, presides.

Jim, his mother, and his attorney are in the courtroom. All of the witnesses for both sides are sequestered during the trial. That is, they are kept away from the proceedings until it is their turn to testify so that one does not hear the testimony of another. As such, Ms. Simpatica, and Detective Penny are present but are not inside the courtroom.

An adjudicatory hearing is less structured than an adult trial. When it begins, Judge Brown asks the prosecutor to present the petition against Jim. The charges are read as follows:

— possession of less than one ounce of marijuana; and

— possession with intent to sell Schedule II drugs (cocaine).

Judge Brown asks if Jim knows his rights in this hearing. There has not been an arraignment, so she asks if he admits or denies the charges. Jim denies the charges.

As in an adult trial, both the prosecution and the defense present witnesses. The attorneys cross-examine the witnesses. Judge Brown asks several questions. When both sides have given testimony, she calls for closing statements, during which the lawyers summarize their cases.

If Jim is found to have committed the acts charged, the dispositional hearing will follow. It is also less formal than an adult procedure. One of the witnesses in the dispositional hearing may be a court service worker who can provide a social history of the child (similar to the information provided in figure 18-4, "Life Histories of Jim").

After hearing both sides, the judge will decide the appropriate treatment for Jim. Do you think she will choose probation or commitment to the Department of Juvenile Justice? Note that Jim could face many other penalties for a conviction for selling or using drugs. If put on probation, he would lose his driver's license.

If Jim were an adult, the penalties for his offense would be more severe. State laws passed in 1990 to curb drug abuse restrict the ability of any adult with a drug-use conviction to be licensed as a professional by the state, to obtain a student loan for college, to collect a state pension, or to receive a state contract.

Regional youth detention centers like this one in Rome, Georgia, house youths who are detained for short periods of time and provide short-term programs.

FIGURE 18-4

Life Histories of Jim

1. "It's a Hard Knock Life"

Life has not been kind to Jim. His father abandoned him and his mom when Jim was only six. They have heard nothing from his father since.

When her husband deserted her, Jim's mother had no job skills. She took an evening job as a waitress while she trained to be a hairdresser. Now she works in a beauty shop.

Jim is not close to his mother. Secretly, he blames her for his father's desertion. He blames her for the fact that they are poor. She's a nervous person, always pestering Jim about picking up his things. She gets angry if Jim is late coming home. She complains if he doesn't tell her everything he does.

Jim likes school. He's not a great student—except in math, where he shines. He'd like to go to college, but he'd have to get a scholarship or a loan. Most of his grades aren't that good.

He likes school, too, because that's where he sees his friends. He doesn't bring them home much. His mother says they're a wild bunch. She's right. Jim does a lot of things he otherwise might not do to impress his friends. For example, when he got that speeding ticket, it was his friend Bob's dare that started the whole thing. And the second time he got caught shoplifting, he lifted some hairspray for Bob's girlfriend.

2. "Life in the Fast Lane"

Jim grew up in a hurry. As a baby, he was quick to walk and talk. As a teenager, he was quick to date, to drink, and to experiment with drugs.

Jim's parents have been divorced since he was six. A restless man, his dad picked up new money-making schemes as quickly as he dropped old ones, but none really panned out.

Jim's mother is entirely different. She's always worrying, particularly about what others might "say." She worries about having enough money to pay bills. In Jim's eyes, she is always working—at her job, around the house. She never seems to have any fun.

Jim's dad comes to town occasionally. He sometimes brings lavish—if impractical—gifts. (He's not consistent about sending child-support checks, however.) Jim adores his father. Acquaintances say Jim is just like his dad. They mean this as a warning. Jim takes it as a compliment.

In school, Jim is well known. He sometimes excels in creative work, but his grades are low, and he never studies. His friends are impressed by Jim's special skills. He knows how to use a fake credit card for charging long-distance calls. He knows how to get booze without an ID. And, Jim's good at getting out of trouble. He's only been caught for shoplifting twice, and only once has he failed to talk his way out of a speeding ticket.

Only the Facts

1. Explain how a formal hearing for juveniles differs from an adult trial.

2. Explain the three basic treatment options that can be ordered by a juvenile judge for a youth who is found to be delinquent.

3. How were youthful offenders treated in the early 1800s in Georgia?

4. Name at least three possible conditions of probation.

5. Name at least two treatment options of the Department of Juvenile Justice.

Think About

1. Should juveniles be entitled to trial by jury for acts that might keep them incarcerated for over a year? Should the jury consist of juveniles or adults? Explain your answer.

2. Juvenile court proceedings are generally private. Explain why you agree or disagree with this practice.

3. The goal of treatment for youths is to change behavior so that they won't get into trouble again. Which of the options discussed do you think will work? What other methods might be effective?

4. Think back to what you have learned about adults in the criminal justice system. Do you think youthful offenders are handled as fairly or as carefully as adults?

SUMMING UP

Youths are treated differently in the juvenile justice system than are adults in the criminal justice system. This different treatment is a relatively modern idea; the juvenile justice system evolved in Georgia during the past century. In this chapter, you have learned about the types of offenses committed by juveniles. Some offenses may result in juveniles being tried as adults in superior court; for other offenses, they may be treated as juveniles, and their cases may be handled in juvenile court. You have learned about the procedures of juvenile court and how they differ from procedures in superior court, the rights and protections of juveniles, and the treatment options available to youthful offenders. In the next chapter, you will learn about the final stage in the criminal justice process: sentencing. (Recall that juveniles are said to receive "treatment" rather than "sentencing.") As you continue to read, think about the goal of the adult criminal justice system, which is primarily to punish rather than rehabilitate. If you had to reshape this system, would you borrow any ideas from the juvenile justice process?

Notes

1. *In re Gault*, 387 U.S. 1 (1967).
2. *In re Burrus and McKeiver v. Pennsylvania*, 403 U.S. 528 (1971).

19 Consequences

I n the Case of the Central City Drug Bust, suppose Harry and Daisy are found guilty. What would happen? Would they immediately be whisked off to prison?

In Georgia, the judge sentences the defendant in non-death penalty cases. Sentencing occurs after the defendant is found guilty or pleads guilty. A plea of guilty is often the result of a plea bargain. Before giving a sentence, the judge will order a presentence hearing and may order a presentence investigation to obtain as much information about the defendant as is possible.

PRESENTENCE INVESTIGATION AND HEARING

In Georgia, presentence investigations are conducted by the probation officers of the Georgia Department of Corrections. Each superior court has probation officers. Besides conducting presentence investigations, these officers supervise all persons who are put on probation by the court.

In the presentence investigation, a probation officer compiles data on the defendant's background. This information includes any previous criminal record, plus facts about employment, education, social contacts, and community ties. The judge uses this information in deciding the sentence. In cases involving physical, psychological, or economic injury to the victim, the probation officer may tell the court what impact the crime had on the victim. During the hearing, the judge also listens to both the defense and prosecution presentations concerning the defendant's good and bad qualities.

The defense attorney seeks to minimize the defendant's sentence. He or she will try to downplay the role of the defendant in the crime or

LAW TALK

death penalty

fine

incarceration

parole

probation

restitution

sentence

highlight the weaknesses in the evidence at trial. The defense attorney may also explain how the defendant's problems in life contributed to the defendant's state of mind, which caused him or her to commit the crime. The defense attorney will also point out the lack of a criminal record on the part of the defendant (assuming that is the case) and perhaps discuss the defendant's level of cooperation in the case. The defense lawyer points out any factors that would tend to mitigate the sentence (that is, make the sentence lighter than usual). On the other hand, the prosecutor stresses the impact of the crime. He or she will call the judge's attention to any "aggravating circumstances," which could make the sentence more severe.

To see how this process works, look at the facts from the presentence investigation reports on Daisy and Harry in figure 19-1. What facts might the prosecutor stress? What facts might each defense attorney stress?

When this hearing is over, the judge may immediately issue a sentence, or he or she may postpone sentencing in order to consider the information that has been gathered.

SENTENCING

Options

In deciding a sentence, a judge has various options, depending on the defendant's crime and its circumstances. The judge may also be influenced by the defendant's age and criminal history. A judge's options are as follows:

Incarceration. To be incarcerated means to be put into jail or prison. A judge may order a jail or prison term within the limits fixed by law for the particular crime.

If a person is convicted of a misdemeanor, his or her time may be spent in a county (or city) jail or a county prison camp. Jails are designed to hold people who are either awaiting trial or who have been sentenced for 12 months or less. Most people who are convicted of less serious offenses spend time in jail.

Generally, people who are incarcerated for felony crimes and receive sentences of one year or more are sent to state prison rather than jail. Prisons are designed for long-term incarceration. However, sometimes felons spend time in jail while waiting to be transferred to prison.

FIGURE 19-1

Presentence Investigation Reports

Harry

27 years old.

Convicted six years ago for selling a Schedule II drug.

College degree in business.

Single.

Currently employed as salesman for an insurance firm. Has been employed there for two years and is a valued employee.

Biological father left home when Harry was two.

Has two older brothers, both of whom have criminal records.

Daisy

22 years old.

First offense.

Dropped out of high school after three years.

Divorced, supports a three-year-old son. Receives no child-support payments from child's father.

Had a steady job for two years at a processing plant, laid off, no steady work for past three years.

Occasional churchgoer.

Parents still married and help support Daisy.

For most felony crimes, the penalties will be a range of years in prison (see figure 15-1 in chapter 15). The specific term is decided upon by the judge, who considers the circumstances surrounding the crime and the background of the defendant. For instance, if the sentence for burglary in Georgia is anywhere from 1 to 20 years, a person convicted for the second time on burglary charges could receive a minimum two-year sentence rather than a minimum one-year sentence. For a third burglary conviction, a person may face a minimum five-year sentence. The maximum sentence for all burglaries is 20 years. The judge decides an appropriate sentence within the ranges provided by the statute for each crime committed.

Probation. The judge may put defendants on probation instead of sending them to prison. Probation can be defined as a treatment program. Defendants do remain free from incarceration, but they must follow the conditions imposed on their freedom by the court. These conditions are either "general" or "special."

General conditions of probation are those that are required in every case. They include the following:

- not violating any law;
- avoiding injurious and vicious habits;
- avoiding persons and places of disreputable or harmful character;
- reporting to the probation officer as directed;
- working faithfully at suitable employment; and
- not changing one's present place of abode, not moving outside the jurisdiction of the court, or leaving the state for any period without prior permission of the probation officer.

On the other hand, special conditions relate to the case itself. For example, in a simple battery or stalking case, a special condition might be no contact with the victim. Performing community service would be a special condition. In a drug case, the court might order drug treatment as a special condition. If the victim suffered damages (for example, a broken window), restitution might be ordered. A special condition is any condition that is not required in every case. Imposing a special condition allows a judge to impose conditions that more closely pertain to the specific charge.

People on probation are supervised by and must meet regularly with probation officers, usually once a month. Probation officers are responsible for making sure that defendants comply with the conditions of their probation. In addition, they try to help the defendants they supervise. The probation officer may involve the defendant in group therapy sessions, or the officer may help the defendant get a job. Persons on probation are expected to be employed and to pay a monthly fee to the probation officer when circumstances allow. The probation officer may also counsel the defendant about how to avoid further run-ins with the criminal justice system.

Georgia has several special probation programs. One is "intensive probation," in which probationers are closely monitored. Intensive probation usually requires an evening curfew and frequent visits to the probation officer. Other special probation programs include house arrest, electronic surveillance, or day work programs. The term of probation is established by the court in accordance with the law.

If the conditions of probation are violated, the court may revoke (or take back) the probation. The court will hold a hearing to determine if the person did in fact violate the probation. If the judge finds a violation of probation, he or she may revoke some or all of the probationary period. The judge can then send the person to jail or prison or impose alternative punishment. Other possible sentences include enrollment in a residential drug rehabilitation program or attendance at a probation detention center or diversion center where the person will work to pay off fines and restitution. There are two ways to violate probation:

- technical violation—occurs when a defendant has either failed to pay the monthly fee or to perform the assigned community service or has violated a special or general condition of probation. Commonly, a technical violation results when a defendant has not reported to the probation officer as required.

- substantive violation—occurs when the defendant commits another criminal offense.

Community service. This option is becoming increasingly popular with the courts. Rather than incarcerating offenders, the judge can require them to provide some form of community service in the city or county in which they live or were convicted. The service is usually arranged through the probation department, and it can be any service the judge orders. Community service might be typing at a publicly funded work center or clean-up work around the jail or courthouse. The laws pertaining to driving under the influence of intoxicants (DUI) specifically require performance of community service upon conviction.

Fines. A fine is a cash payment to the court. The use of fines as a penalty for committing an offense has been commonplace for centuries. Fines are charged for many offenses, particularly traffic violations, misdemeanors, and drug-related crimes. For misdemeanors, the person usually pays a fine instead of serving a jail or prison sentence. For felonies, such as drug cases, the offender is often heavily fined in addition to serving a prison term or being subject to other conditions of probation if the defendant is sentenced to probation instead of to a prison term.

Restitution. Restitution means paying the victim for damages. Restitution may be made by returning the amount of money or property stolen. In the case of injury, restitution is made by paying the victim for the cost of medical treatment. In the case of damage to property, restitution is made by paying for necessary repairs or replacement of the property.

Special probation programs include house arrest, electronic surveillance, or day work programs.

Imprisonment and probation. The judge may sentence the defendant to serve part of the sentence in jail or prison and the remainder on probation. This type of sentence is called a split sentence.

Special programs. The problem of overcrowded prisons has prompted courts to consider alternatives to incarceration. Georgia is recognized as a leader in this area. It has a program called special alternative incarceration, a 60- to 120-day program of strict discipline and regimen often imposed on first offenders or those who have light criminal records. It is intended to discourage those sentenced to the program to become repeat offenders. Informally, it is referred to as a prison "boot camp."

Definite versus Indefinite Sentencing

Except for death penalty cases tried by a jury, the judge decides the nature and length of sentence within the ranges set by law, referred to as indefinite sentencing. Some people feel that such flexibility leads to unfair sentencing practices. Sometimes—for almost identical crimes and circumstances—one judge will give a minimum sentence. Another will give a maximum sentence. To illustrate, consider situations 1 and 2:

> **SITUATION 1** Andrew is convicted of robbery by sudden snatching when he steals a purse containing items worth over $500. It is his first offense. He has been laid off his job for five months. He commits the crime impulsively because he is desperate.
>
> **SITUATION 2** Carl is convicted of snatching a purse containing items worth over $500. It is his first conviction, but he has been arrested several times before for similar crimes. He has never been convicted because no one could ever identify him positively. As a juvenile, he had a history of truancy and unruly behavior.

The law allows a sentence of 1 to 20 years for the crime of robbery. What if Andrew were sentenced to five years (situation 1), but Carl was sentenced to one year (situation 2)? This type of unfairness can result when the statute providing the penalty for the crime establishes a range of punishment, resulting in indefinite sentencing. To avoid unfairness in sentencing, some state legislatures favor a system of definite, predetermined sentences for every crime. The circumstances of the crime would not matter. Everyone would receive the same sentence for committing the same type of crime.

Judges argue that a definite sentence system is too inflexible. For many crimes, the only reasonable alternative to prison that judges can impose is probation. Judges contend that definite (prison) sentences would force them to award probation in cases in which they felt the definite sentence was too harsh. Probation, however, might be too lenient for the crime and circumstances.

Look again at situations 1 and 2. Under a definite sentence system, the law might impose a sentence of two years in prison for a first offense of robbery by snatching. That would mean Carl and Andrew would get equal sentences. Would that be fair? Would it be fairer if Andrew was given probation? Is a system of definite sentences fairer than one in which a judge determines the sentence? However important, achieving fairness in sentencing is not easy.

Purposes of Sentencing

Before sentencing, the judge must know the background of the convicted defendant and the range of punishment the law allows for the crime. If the defendant is convicted of more than one crime, then the judge must also decide whether the sentences should run concurrently (at the same time) or consecutively (one after the other).

Underlying these laws and decisions is a philosophical question: Why do we punish people for their crimes? There are four basic purposes of punishment:

1. Retribution—Essentially, to seek revenge. It is best expressed by the biblical Old Testament concept of "an eye for an eye and a tooth for a tooth."

2. Deterrence—To discourage persons from committing crimes.

3. Rehabilitation—To help criminals change their behavior; to help them become responsible citizens.

4. Incapacitation—To protect society from dangerous, lawbreaking persons.

All criminal sentences are based on one or more of these purposes.

CASE STUDY

CASE OF THE CENTRAL CITY DRUG BUST, *concluded*

If Harry and Daisy are found not guilty, they would be released. If they are found guilty, they would be sentenced. In determining the sentence, a judge considers

—each defendant's past, as revealed in the presentence reports,

—the possible punishments for the crimes,

—whether the sentences should run concurrently or consecutively, and

—the purposes of punishment.

Often, the task of sentencing someone is very difficult.

Only the Facts

1. What is the purpose of a presentence investigation and hearing?
2. Name and define the sentencing options of a judge in Georgia.
3. What are four purposes of punishment?

Think About

1. Consider some of the penalties confronting defendants in the Case of the Central City Drug Bust. Some people feel that the penalties for being found guilty of contributing to the delinquency of a minor are light. Do you agree? If so, explain why. Why are people fined as well as imprisoned for selling drugs?
2. What is your opinion of a system of definite sentences? Would it result in fairer sentencing? Explain.
3. In your opinion, what is the most important of the four purposes of punishment? Rate the four in terms of their importance, and defend your rating.

Persons sentenced to prison in Georgia are placed in the custody of the Georgia Department of Corrections.

IF SENTENCED TO PRISON

What happens to people when they are sentenced to prison? Where will they be sent? For how long?

Prison—The Place

Persons sentenced to prison in Georgia are placed in the custody of the Georgia Department of Corrections. They may be freed on bail if there is an appeal and the crime committed was not too serious. Offenders convicted of committing a misdemeanor have an absolute right to an appeal bond except in cases involving domestic violence or DUI.

Prior to being permanently assigned to a facility, offenders are taken to a holding facility.

A holding facility is a place where prisoners are evaluated before being transferred to a prison. The evaluation determines the special needs of each prisoner. These needs involve security, physical and mental health, and job skills. Following this evaluation, the department assigns the prisoner to one of the state's numerous institutions. Assignment depends on the prisoner's previous record, current conviction, and needs.

Compared with other states and Western countries, Georgia has a high rate of incarceration, and its prisons are overcrowded. Older facilities create inhumane conditions. To maintain an acceptable environment in prisons and avoid costly lawsuits by inmates and human rights groups, the state continues to provide money for new prisons. An important question is whether building new prisons is a good use of tax dollars. Time in prison doesn't necessarily deter crime, and peoples' opinions differ as to whether prison is more effective than other options, at least in some cases. Moreover, maintaining the prison system is expensive. It generally costs many times more to keep a person in prison than to put someone on probation.

What do you think Georgia should do to solve its problems with overcrowded prisons? Consider the following viewpoints:

Viewpoint A: The state should not put any more money into building prisons. Incarceration does little or nothing to change the behavior of inmates. There are many recidivists (persons who commit additional crimes after having served a sentence for been punished for their first crime). Instead of putting so many offenders in prison, the state should put as many as possible in community-based programs. These programs can help offenders stop their criminal behaviors and lead productive lives.

Viewpoint B: Sentencing practices should be tougher. Recidivism occurs because punishments are too light. Not enough criminals go to prison, nor are criminals kept in prison long enough. The state should build more prisons. If necessary, taxes should be raised to meet the costs. Public safety is worth it.

Which viewpoint would you favor? Why?

Prison—The Time Served

A person's philosophy about punishment for criminal acts will affect how he or she feels about current practices that shorten the sentences of prisoners. Prisoners do not always serve the full sentence given by the judge. They may be released early to relieve prison overcrowding. Their sentence may be reduced as a reward for good behavior in prison, or they may be paroled (unless their sentence prohibits parole).

An offender who is put on parole is released from prison and allowed to serve the rest of his or her sentence in the community under the supervision of a parole officer. Prisoners look forward to reaching their parole date. This date marks the minimum time a person must serve before being considered for parole.

Usually, the state Board of Pardons and Paroles decides whether a prisoner will receive parole. In some cases, the board's decision is restricted by statutes enacted by the state legislature. These laws are aimed at reducing recidivism as well as sending a message to potential criminal offenders. For example, in 1995, the Georgia legislature enacted a statute requiring that a person convicted of certain serious and violent crimes (such as armed robbery, murder, rape, kidnapping, aggravated sexual battery, aggravated child molestation, and aggravated sodomy) would serve at least 10 years before being granted parole.

The board consists of citizens appointed by the governor. When an eligible prisoner requests parole, the board reviews the prisoner's stay in prison. It considers the nature of the crime for which he or she was imprisoned and other factors. Then the board determines whether the person is ready for parole.

If parole is granted, the paroled offender must obey the conditions set by the parole board. Paroled offenders must not associate with known criminals or get into trouble with the law. They must see a parole officer on a regular basis. They are expected to get and keep jobs. The paroled offender is under the parole officer's supervision until the jail sentence is complete.

To better understand how a sentence and parole works, let's look back at the Case of the Central City Drug Bust. Assume that the judge sentences Harry to serve five years in prison followed by three years of probation (see figure 19-2). If Harry is paroled after serving two years, he will be supervised on parole for the remaining three years of his prison term. After he has completed those three years successfully, he will be on supervised probation for another three years to complete the sentence ordered by the judge.

Like many other aspects of the criminal justice system, parole is controversial. Arguments for and against it are in figure 19-3.

The Board of Pardons and Paroles has other powers. Governors in other states may grant a pardon or reprieve to a person who has been condemned to death. (A reprieve is the temporary suspension of a sentence.) In Georgia, however, the governor has no power to give pardons or reprieves; they are granted only by a majority vote of the Pardons and Paroles Board.

FIGURE 19-2

What Penalties Do Harry and Daisy Face?

If Convicted of—	Prison/Fine
Possession of a Schedule II drug with intent to sell	
1st conviction	2–15 years
2nd conviction	5–30 years or life imprisonment
Sale of a Schedule II drug	
1st conviction	5–30 years
2nd conviction	10–40 years or life imprisonment
Trafficking in marijuana	
(more than 50 lbs.; greater penalties if more than 2,000 lbs.)	5–15 year mandatory minimum plus $100,000–$1 million mandatory fine
Contributing to the delinquency of a minor	
1st conviction	1–5 months and/or $200–$500 fine
2nd conviction	3–12 months and/or $400–$1,000 fine
3rd conviction	1–3 years and/or $1,000–$5,000 fine

FIGURE 19-3

Parole—Pros and Cons

Pro

By allowing early release, parole helps control prison overcrowding.

Prisoners behave better when they are working toward parole.

Parole costs taxpayers less than prison.

Parolees have incentives for good behavior. They know they may be sent back to prison if they aren't acting like law-abiding citizens.

A parolee can get a job, support family, pay taxes, and contribute to the economy.

Con

Caseloads for parole officers are large, and they can't provide the supervision their parolees need.

The best parole supervision can't keep a parolee from committing another crime.

Parolees often have trouble getting jobs.

Decision to parole is inexact. The more deserving may be denied parole and the less deserving given it.

THE DEATH PENALTY

Pro and Con

People have been arguing about the use of the death penalty for centuries. The debate involves some basic questions:

1. Does the state have the moral right to take a person's life? Those in favor of the death penalty say yes. If a person kills another, it is right for the state to take the killer's life. Those opposed to the death penalty say that two wrongful acts (the act of the killer and the state's act of taking the killer's life) do not make one right act.

2. Does imposing the death penalty reduce the number of serious crimes committed? Those favoring the death penalty say yes. They reason that the threat of death makes many potential killers consider their actions. Those opposing it point to studies that seem to indicate that the death penalty has not been shown to prevent people from committing such crimes.

3. Does the death penalty violate the rights of due process and equal protection contained in the Fifth and Fourteenth Amendments to the Constitution? Those favoring it argue that it does not. In 1976, the U.S. Supreme Court ruled that the death penalty was not a cruel and unusual punishment in violation of the Eighth Amendment.[1] Furthermore, the court allows many appeals. It has required that methods for deciding when to impose capital punishment should be fair. Those who oppose the death penalty say that it does violate constitutional rights. In practice,

poor people who cannot afford the best lawyers are often those who are executed.

In addition to these arguments against the death penalty, some people claim that death penalty sentences are racially biased. This argument was made in the Georgia case of *Mc-Clesky v. Kemp*.[2] The defendant based his claim that death penalty sentences are racially biased on a university study that showed that defendants were four times more likely to receive a death sentence for killing a white person than for killing an African American. The U.S. Supreme Court disagreed. The court acknowledged that the criminal justice system is not entirely free of racial bias. However, it said that the presence of some bias was not enough to invalidate Georgia's death penalty statute.

There are other arguments. Those in favor of the death penalty argue that most Americans support it. They say that putting someone to death is less costly than a long prison term. Those opposing the death penalty say that because of the costly appeals process (discussed in the next section), it can actually cost as much or more to execute someone than to keep that person in prison for life. Also, death penalty opponents point out the fact that the death penalty is irreversible. Every year people are released from prisons upon discovery of new evidence that may have changed the verdict of their trials from guilty to not guilty.

The Capital Case Process

Because of the finality of the sentence, cases involving capital offenses are handled somewhat differently than other felony cases. Although certain crimes like armed robbery and rape are still called capital crimes, they are no longer truly capital crimes because the death penalty cannot be imposed. A death sentence may be imposed only for murder, which makes it the only type of capital case. In Georgia, the jury usually decides whether the defendant is guilty, and the judge determines what the sentence will be. However, a jury that reaches a verdict of guilty

in a murder case must also decide whether the defendant should be sentenced to death, to life imprisonment, or to life without parole.

Before imposing the death penalty, the jury must determine if there are aggravating circumstances. These circumstances must be supported by evidence heard in the trial or during the presentence hearing. Georgia law lists 10 major aggravating circumstances, including whether the defendant has been previously convicted of a capital felony or whether he or she committed the murder for hire).

The jury also hears evidence of mitigating circumstances, such as a person's age. For example, although the U.S. Supreme Court has said that states may execute minors, Georgia law prohibits the state from seeking the death penalty for anyone under 17.

The jury must reach a unanimous decision on the death penalty. If all jury members do not agree, the judge must make the sentence life imprisonment.

Because execution is final, the death row inmate is provided with many opportunities to appeal the decision (that is, to try to get the sentence changed). This appeals process has become long and complex. To simplify it somewhat, some states (including Georgia) have adopted a unified appeal system. In this system, all of the issues on which a defendant can appeal must be incorporated into one document. This document can be submitted to the state and federal appellate courts only once.

In addition to appeals, death row inmates can file up to three *habeas corpus* petitions in both state and federal courts. These petitions must be based on constitutional issues. Usually, they allege that there has been a denial of fundamental rights during the trial or sentencing phases of the criminal justice process. Typically it may take 9 to 10 years for these appeals and petitions to go through the courts.

Some people think the number of *habeas corpus* petitions should be limited. Others believe these protections are important to avoid taking a life unjustifiably. What do you think?

Only the Facts

1. Define parole. How does parole differ from probation?
2. What is a recidivist?
3. Give two arguments for and two against the death penalty.
4. Explain the responsibility of a jury in a case in which the death penalty is possible.

Think About

1. In one kind of community-based program, offenders live in prison at night and work in the community during the day. Defend or argue against such a program. What attitude toward punishment would such a program reflect?
2. Suppose you had to release some prisoners to relieve prison overcrowding. You must choose whether to release persons convicted of (a) forgery, (b) child abuse, (c) involuntary manslaughter, (d) burglary, or (e) arson. In what order would you allow release of these prisoners? Explain your reasons for deciding which prisoners to release first.
3. Would the fact that polls show most Americans favor the death penalty be a good argument for imposing it? What about the fact that many death row inmates have had their convictions overturned after DNA evidence has been discovered and/or analyzed years after their trials but before they were executed? Explain your answer for each question.

SUMMING UP

Sentencing and punishment are areas of controversy as well as areas of change. Centuries ago in England, people were hanged for offenses for which they might receive only probation today. Nowadays, types of punishment in other countries vary considerably compared with Georgia. Some countries impose more lenient punishments; others impose harsher punishments. Much of the variation can be traced to the question, why do we punish criminals?

Many people in the United States favor harsher punishments than are currently imposed and are willing to pay (through taxes) to keep more criminals in prison for longer periods. Other people are willing to risk safety in favor of better rehabilitation programs outside prison.

Notes

1. *Gregg v. Georgia*, 428 U.S. 153 (1976).
2. 481 U.S. 279 (1987).

20. Immigration and Citizenship

20 Immigration and Citizenship

Immigration has affected every aspect of life in America. Look around at your classmates, neighbors, and friends. Look at the foods you eat and the music you hear. With the exception of Native Americans, we are all products of immigration. The United States is often described as a "melting pot" because of the many different cultures, races, and religions that make our nation unique. For more than 300 years, various ethnic, cultural, and social groups have come to this country to reunite with loved ones, seek jobs, and find a haven from religious and political persecution. Because America was built on immigration, it is important to study immigration law.

SOURCE OF IMMIGRATION LAW

As with every aspect of the law, the U.S. Constitution is the starting point for laws governing immigration. Article I, Section 8.4 of the Constitution gives Congress the power over immigration and naturalization. This power is justified by the duty Congress has to keep the United States safe and secure. After all, our country's relationship with other nations and their citizens can affect national safety and security.

Congress's power over immigration is broad and largely unchallenged. Overseeing the process of people from other countries entering the United States is part of this duty. General authority to administer immigration laws has been delegated by Congress to the Department of Homeland Security. Immigration-related matters are handled on a day-to-day basis by three of the department's bureaus: the Bureau of Citizenship and Immigration Services, the Bureau of Immigration and Customs Enforcement, and the Bureau of Customs and Border Patrol. In addition, there is the Executive Office of Immigration Review, which includes the immigration courts and an appellate court. The Executive

Office of Immigration Review is also called the Board of Immigration Appeals. These courts make final determinations regarding immigration matters. Most of these agencies are better known by their previous name, the Immigration and Naturalization Service (INS). This name was changed in 2003 with the creation of the Department of Homeland Security. The authority of the department and its bureaus is defined by law. The primary law is called the Immigration and Nationality Act. The laws governing the implementation of this act are found in the Code of Federal Regulations.

The ways in which immigration laws are applied to particular cases are determined by courts and administrative bodies (for example, agencies such as the Bureau of Citizenship and Immigration Services and its review board, the Board of Immigration Appeals). A case may begin by someone filing an application for an immigration benefit such as protection under asylum laws (discussed later in this chapter). The application is submitted to the bureau, which then makes a decision. If the bureau decides to deny the benefit sought, that denial is reviewed by an immigration judge. The immigration judge's decision is then reviewed by the Board of Immigration Appeals. In some cases, the board's decisions are reviewed by the federal courts.

Other governmental bodies assist in executing immigration laws. For example, in certain employment-related cases, the Department of Labor must consider how immigration will affect the labor market. Such a decision can be very important in determining whether a work visa will be granted or denied.

Only the Facts

1. List three reasons why people immigrate to the United States.
2. Name the federal agency that oversees immigration law on a day-to-day basis.
3. What is the name of the primary immigration law?

Think About

1. Can you think of ways in which immigration affects your life?
2. Why does the Constitution give power to Congress to oversee immigration and naturalization?
3. Whom do immigration laws regulate? What activity do these laws regulate?

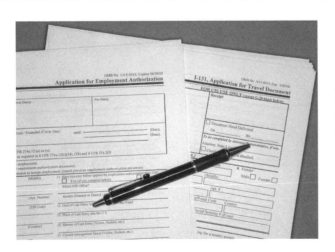

An application for an immigration benefit is first submitted to the Bureau of Citizenship and Immigration Services.

CITIZENS

Most people are familiar with the concept of citizenship. To help you understand more precisely who is a citizen, remember two words: soil and blood.

SITUATION 1 Juan is born in the United States to parents who are citizens of Spain but are vacationing in Florida.

Can he claim U.S. citizenship?

SITUATION 2 Maria is born in Brazil to parents who are U.S. citizens.

Can Maria claim U.S. citizenship?

Soil

According to the Fourteenth Amendment to the U.S. Constitution, persons born in this country are citizens of the United States. This constitutional provision comes from a historical principle that says that a person's nationality is determined by his or her place of birth. This concept has a legal name: the doctrine of *jus soli*. *Jus* is the Latin word for "law," and *soli* means "soil." Anyone born in the United States is therefore a citizen. The United States includes any of the 50 states, Puerto Rico, the Virgin Islands, American Samoa, Guam, or any other island or territory that is considered to be part of the United States. Additionally, certain persons born in the Canal Zone (Panama) while it was under U.S. control may also be considered citizens. Under current laws, there is only one exception to the doctrine of *jus soli*: a child born in the United States to parents who are in the diplomatic service of another country does not acquire U.S. citizenship at birth.

Blood

Some people become citizens through derivative citizenship. That is, they become citizens of the United States because even though they are born outside the country, they are born to at least one parent who is a U.S. citizen. The concept of derivative citizenship also has a legal name: the doctrine of *jus sanguinis*. *Sanguinis* is a Latin word that means "blood." Thus, under this doctrine, a child's nationality depends on the nationality of his or her parents.

Citizens born in the United States can prove their citizenship with their birth certificates. Derivative citizens can apply for a certificate of citizenship for the purpose of proving that they also are citizens. The Bureau of Citizenship and Immigration Services is in charge of considering the evidence in support of claims of derivative citizenship and determining whether or not a person is a citizen. If citizenship is determined, the bureau will issue the certificate. The U.S. Passport Agency can also make this determination, but it must defer to the bureau in cases in which the evidence presented to support the claim of derivative citizenship is not clear.

A person who is not born in the United States and who is not a citizen because one or both parents were citizens at their birth can nevertheless apply to become a U.S. citizen under certain conditions. The process for applying for citizenship is called naturalization. (Naturalization will be discussed in greater detail later in this chapter.)

Only the Facts

1. What is the doctrine of *jus soli*?
2. What is the one exception to the doctrine of *jus soli*?
3. What is a certificate of citizenship?

Think About

1. Explain the concept of derivative citizenship.
2. Would a child born in a U.S. military hospital outside the United States be considered a citizen?

ALIENS

According to immigration laws, people are either citizens or noncitizens (aliens). Immigration laws do not affect U.S. citizens. Rather, they apply to aliens who are in the United States temporarily or permanently. Immigration laws determine how aliens can visit, live, work, and study in the United States. They also determine if, how, and when aliens can become citizens. Immigration laws cease to affect an alien once he or she becomes a citizen of the United States.

There are basically two types of aliens: those who come to the United States for a temporary stay and those who come with the intention of staying permanently.

Nonimmigrants

Nonimmigrants are aliens who come to the United States temporarily. Their stay here is usually authorized by one of the nonimmigrant visa categories created in the Immigration and Nationality Act. There are numerous nonimmigrant visas available for various purposes (see figure 20-1). Each visa provides for a certain period during which the nonimmigrant can stay in the United States. In addition to nonimmigrant visas, immigration laws provide other ways for aliens to enter or remain in the United States for temporary periods of time. Temporary protective status gives temporary legal status and work authorization to aliens from specific countries that the U.S. government has determined are not safe to return to because of significant natural disasters or war. For example, a few years ago a volcano destroyed a substantial part of the island of Monserrat. Following that natural disaster, the U.S. government issued temporary protective status for aliens present in the United States who were citizens of or last resided in Monserrat. The authorization to live and work in the United States is in effect for those aliens until the U.S. government decides that the situation in Monserrat has improved enough for its citizens to return safely.

FIGURE 20-1

Immigration Visas

Visa Type	Granted to
A	ambassadors, diplomats, and others working in the diplomatic service
B	those who are pursuing business or pleasure (tourists)
C	people catching connecting flights destined for other countries
D	crew members (those working on ships or planes that are docked temporarily in the United States)
E	investors and traders (those making substantial investments in imports or exports)
F	students (aliens studying in an accredited school or university)
G	representatives of international organizations
H	professionals, nurses, and seasonal laborers
I	foreign media personnel
J	exchange students
K	husbands, wives, children, fiancés/fiancées, or children of fiancés/fiancées of U.S. citizens
L	intracompany transferees (as with international countries)
M	vocational students
N	those who are in the United States for some purpose related to the North Atlantic Treaty Organization (NATO)
O	scientists, artists, educators, and athletes
P	internationally recognized athletes or entertainers
Q	Irish Peace Process Program workers (who come to learn about conflict resolution techniques)
R	religious workers
S	informants (that is, persons who are brought into the country to provide information in criminal investigations)
T	victims of trafficking (such as forced prostitution)
TN	those who are involved in the North American Free Trade Agreement (that is, truck drivers, salespeople, or distributors temporarily conducting business in the United States as a result of NAFTA)
U	victims of criminal activity
V	spouses and children of permanent residents

Another type of temporary status is called parole. Parole allows the Bureau of Citizenship and Immigration Services to bring an alien applying for admission to the United States into the country on a temporary basis prior to the formal admission being granted. Paroles are granted on a case-by-case basis when there is urgent humanitarian need or a significant public benefit to be gained. Examples of persons who have been or can be paroled include

- refugees from Cuba,
- those who are applying to become permanent residents of the United States but who need to travel abroad temporarily and then return to continue with their pending applications, and
- those who need to travel to the United States temporarily for humanitarian purposes (such as an operation) but who do not qualify for any of the other nonimmigrant visas.

Parole is generally approved for a specific period of time, and the alien must use the parole document prior to its expiration.

O n l y t h e F a c t s

1. What is a nonimmigrant?
2. List three visas currently provided by the Immigration and Naturalization Act.
3. Immigration laws affect aliens even after they become citizens. True or False?

T h i n k A b o u t

1. Give an example of a situation in which temporary protective status might be granted. Give an example of a situation in which parole might be granted.
2. Look at the list of visas in figure 20-1. For which nonimmigrant visas would an Olympic ice skater or a French news reporter qualify?

Immigrants

Unlike nonimmigrants, who come to the United States for a temporary period of time, immigrants come to the United States to work and live permanently. The goal of an alien who wants to be an immigrant is to become a lawful permanent resident. To do so, the alien must obtain a permanent resident alien card (a "green card"). Once the green card is granted and the alien becomes a permanent resident, he or she is allowed to live, work, and travel in the United States on a permanent basis. Furthermore, permanent residents have the right to become naturalized citizens if they meet all of the requirements.

Aliens generally want to immigrate to the United States for one or more of four reasons: to be united with family, to work or make professional advancements, to flee persecution in their home countries, or to make a better life for themselves and their families. For example, the Hispanic population in Georgia has grown rapidly because immigrants are seeking jobs and to be with family members who are already in the state (see figure 20-2).

Family-Based Immigration

SITUATION 3 Ly Tien immigrates to the United States and becomes a naturalized citizen. As soon as he becomes a citizen, he applies for immigration visas for his wife, three unmarried children, and his brother. He believes that as a citizen he can bring all family members to the United States.

Is he correct?

Most legal immigrants, nearly three-fourths, come to the United States to be close to family members who are already here. U.S. citizens may apply for an immigrant visa on behalf of the following family members: spouses, children (including minor, adult, unmarried, or married children; stepchildren, in certain cases; and adopted

FIGURE 20-2

Georgia Tops Nation in Hispanic Growth

The Hispanic population grew faster in Georgia than in any state in the nation from 2000 to 2002, according to an analysis of U.S. Census Bureau figures.

Lured by jobs and relatives, a net gain of about 102 Hispanics a day came to Georgia in the two-year period from Latin America, mainly Mexico, and from states with much larger Hispanic populations, such as California, Texas, and Illinois.

Georgia's Hispanic community grew 17 percent, to about 516,500, the latest evidence of profound transformation of a state long cast in black and white.

The pattern repeated itself around the Southeast, in places with little sustained history of Hispanic settlement. The eight states with the fastest growing Hispanic populations included North Carolina, Kentucky, South Carolina, Virginia, and Alabama.

The analysis also shows that metro Atlanta experienced the most rapid Hispanic growth rate among the nation's 20 most populous metro areas. The census says rural Dawson County, about 60 miles north of downtown Atlanta, had the most dramatic increase in Hispanic population—59 percent growth—though only 2 percent of people in Dawson County are Hispanic.

Gwinnett County has the highest concentration of Hispanics—13 percent—of the 29 counties that meet the federal definition of metro Atlanta.

About 6 percent of Georgians and 7.5 percent of metro Atlantans are Hispanic.

Source: Mark Bixler, "Georgia tops nation in Hispanic growth," *Atlanta Journal-Constitution*. ajc.com/Metro. Accessed September 18, 2003.

Employment-based immigration allows employers to bring skilled workers into the United States.

children), parents, and siblings. Lawful permanent residents are allowed to apply on behalf of only spouses and unmarried children. Approval of an application for a family immigrant visa can take several years. Once the visa is approved, the alien relative may immigrate to the United States, or if the relative is in the United States on a nonimmigrant visa, the alien may obtain permanent resident status.

The relationship of the applicant to the alien who wants to become an immigrant affects the length of the process. For instance, the spouse of a U.S. citizen can qualify for permanent resident status immediately once the husband-wife relationship is formed, but the spouse of a lawful permanent resident must wait 4 to 8 years. The brother or sister of a U.S. citizen can wait 20 years or more to acquire permanent resident status.

Employment- or Talent-Based Immigration

The second type of immigration, employment-based immigration, allows employers to bring skilled workers into the United States. This complex process is coordinated between the Bureau of Citizenship and Immigration Services and the U.S. Department of Labor to ensure that foreign workers are not hired for jobs that U.S. citizens could do. Only a few workers per employer are allowed. Before bringing immigrant workers to the United States through an employment-based immigrant petition, employers must show that there are no qualified Americans available to fill the job. However, once the immigrant workers are in the United States, they can petition to become lawful permanent residents and, eventually, U.S. citizens. They can also bring with them to the United States a spouse and children who are unmarried minors.

For example, Mrs. Pascal is an engineer with specialized skills who lives in France. A U.S. company wants to hire her. The company believes that she can do the job that needs to be performed better than anyone else. The first thing the company must do is show the U.S. Department of Labor that there is no one currently in the U.S. labor market who could do the work. The company must then file for an immigrant worker visa for Mrs. Pascal. If approved, it will enable her, her husband, and their children to come to the United States, acquire permanent resident status, and eventually acquire U.S. citizenship (if desired). Aliens who are considered to have unique skills or who have won prestigious awards (such as the Nobel Prize) can apply for an immigrant work visa without the support of an employer or a decision from the Department of Labor.

Refugees and Asylees

Most people are familiar with the saying on the Statute of Liberty that reads, "Give me your tired, your poor, your huddled masses yearning to breathe free." The saying is fitting because the United States was founded in part by those who fled countries in which they were being persecuted for political or religious reasons. U.S. immigration laws reflect the ongoing responsibility that the nation has assumed to offer protection to individuals who are at risk of persecution because of their race, nationality, religion, ethnicity, or political or social activities. This protection is offered to people who are referred to as refugees or asylees. A refugee is an alien wanting protection who has obtained formal permission to enter the United States while he or she was outside the country. An asylee is an alien who is already in the United States and then applies for and is granted asylum (or protection).

Regardless of how an alien enters the United States, whether legally or not, he or she can apply for asylum once in the United States. Aliens become asylees only after their applications for asylum have been granted. Both asylees and refugees are eligible to apply for lawful permanent

The Statute of Liberty is a powerful symbol of welcome for immigrants to the United States.

resident status after they have held their asylee or refugee status for at least one year. The spouses and children of asylees and refugees can also be considered asylees and refugees.

Certain immigrants are ineligible for asylee or refugee status, including terrorists, drug traffickers, those who have serious criminal convictions, those who have persecuted others, and those who pose a serious threat to national security. There are more limited forms of protection in some cases for individuals in these categories.

SITUATION 4 Gerry McGuyver and Martin Flanagan are citizens of Ireland experiencing religious persecution in the Catholic and Protestant struggle in that country. They want to come to the United States.

Would they come as asylees or refugees?

Special Immigrants

There is a catchall provision in the Immigration and Nationalization Act for aliens such as widows and orphans of citizens, certain juveniles, Amerasians (that is, children of U.S. and Asian citizens), victims of domestic violence, and religious workers. These aliens may apply for a special immigrant petition. If approved, this petition can lead to an adjustment in status so that the person can become a lawful permanent resident.

Persons Who Are in the United States Illegally

Aliens who are in the United States without formal permission are in the country illegally. Some illegal aliens intend to stay temporarily, whereas others intend to stay permanently. Illegal aliens come to the United States in one of two ways: they overstay or violate their visa or they cross the border illegally.

Visa overstays/violators. Any alien who enters the United States legally with a nonimmigrant visa but who either overstays the period of time allowed under the terms of the visa or performs an activity not allowed under the terms of the visa is considered to be in the country illegally. For example, Marco, a tourist, enters with a "B" visa (see figure 20-1) and, upon entry, is granted 30 days of stay. If he stays beyond the 30 days or engages in work during the 30 days (tourists are not authorized to work), he becomes an illegal alien. While here, he is offered a job and takes it. Because tourists are not authorized to work, accepting a job has made Marco an illegal alien.

Aliens who cross the border illegally. Aliens who cross the border into the United States without presenting themselves to an immigration checkpoint for inspection are also illegal aliens. For example, a person who enters the United States through the Mexican or Canadian border hidden in the trunk of a car is an illegal alien.

Illegal aliens in these categories face obstacles to obtaining legal status. Most illegal aliens apply for asylum or temporary protective status or acquire lawful permanent resident status through a family member or employer. Under a limited provision in the law, qualified illegal aliens may obtain a family-based or employment-based visa by paying a financial penalty and by meeting a variety of other qualifications and time limitations. Visa overstays or violators may obtain permanent resident status without paying such a penalty only when they are applying as the spouse or minor child of a U.S. citizen. Persons who cross the border without passing through inspection may not petition for permanent resident status without paying the penalty.

Only the Facts

1. What is a green card?
2. What is the reason why most people immigrate to the United States?
3. What is the difference between a refugee and an asylee?
4. Name the two types of illegal aliens.

Think About

1. Why do you think an employer can bring only a few workers into the United States under employment-based immigration? Must the workers be skilled? Explain your answer.

Immigrants who cross the border into the United States are required to present themselves to an immigration checkpoint.

2. U.S. immigration laws reflect the responsibility that our nation assumed historically to support human rights. Explain how immigration laws accomplish this purpose.

ACQUIRING AND LOSING LEGAL STATUS

Engaging in any criminal act that violates the immigration law definition of good moral character can prevent an alien from gaining legal (that is, permanent resident) status. It can also mean losing legal status already obtained. Convictions for not only murder, rape, drug trafficking, child molestation, and fraud but also lesser charges such as theft or assault and battery may be obstacles to obtaining or retaining legal immigration status. Further, lying to the U.S. government to obtain an immigration benefit constitutes fraud and misrepresentation and can jeopardize an alien's status now and in the future. For example, if a married alien tells the Bureau of Citizenship and Immigration Services that he or she is not married and the bureau grants permanent resident status based on this assertion but later learns of the lie, the bureau can take away the alien's lawful permanent resident status.

In some cases, an alien who has a criminal conviction or who has committed fraud and misrepresentation may submit a waiver (that is, a kind of apology) to the Bureau of Citizenship and Immigration Services in order to achieve or retain permanent resident status. Waivers are usually allowed when an extreme hardship would be inflicted on a citizen or resident spouse or child if the alien's status were to be denied or taken away. Nevertheless, aliens who engage in criminal activity or fraud and misrepresentation (two of the most common acts) may face deportation. Other reasons for being deported include overstaying a visa and entering the country illegally.

Moreover, if the Bureau of Citizenship and Immigration Services believes that an alien is likely to be a burden on the welfare system, it may deny that alien's application for permanent resident status. The U.S. citizen or permanent resident who files the petition on behalf of the alien must therefore show that he or she makes enough money to support the alien or that there is another citizen or resident who is willing and able to support the alien. This person is called a sponsor. Alternatively, the alien seeking to become a resident can show that he or she is employable and is unlikely to become a burden on the welfare system.

Aliens may lose their eligibility to become residents if they lose their sponsor. For example, if the company that wants to hire Mrs. Pascal, the engineer from France, changes its mind and withdraws the offer of employment, Mrs. Pascal will not be able to seek permanent resident status. Likewise, if a permanent resident has a daughter and the permanent resident dies before the daughter can acquire her own permanent resident status, her application will be denied. There are several humanitarian exceptions to the loss of a sponsor.

Other ways in which a permanent resident may lose his or her status once it is granted include the following:

- The permanent resident abandons his or her status. A permanent resident may lose his or her status if there is a lengthy absence from the United States. The outcome depends on the circumstances surrounding the absence and whether or not the resident intended to abandon his or her status.

- The permanent resident renounces his or her status. A resident may renounce (that is, deliberately give up) resident status at any time by submitting the appropriate form to a Bureau of Citizenship and Immigration Services officer (or a U.S. consulate or embassy in another country).

- The Bureau of Citizenship and Immigration Services rescinds (or repeals) the permanent resident's status. The bureau can rescind the permanent resident status of an alien within five years of granting it if the bureau discovers that the alien was not eligible for the status when it was initially granted (for example, if it is discovered that an alien lied about his or her qualifications when applying for permanent resident status).

- The permanent resident is deported. Permanent resident status will be revoked if the resident commits an offense that results in deportation.

O n l y   t h e   F a c t s

1. Which activities can result in an alien not being able to obtain legal status or will cause him or her to lose it?
2. What is a sponsor?

T h i n k   A b o u t

1. Explain the concept of a waiver.
2. A permanent resident goes on a two-week trip to Mexico. While there, he has a car accident and is in a coma for two years. Three years after his departure, he attempts to reenter the United States. He is stopped by immigration officers, who must determine whether he abandoned his status by being outside the United States for three years. Given what you know, how would you decide the case?

ACQUIRING CITIZENSHIP

Recall that persons who are not born in the United States and who do not derive citizenship through their parents can apply to become U.S. citizens under certain conditions through a process called naturalization. Naturalization applications are filed with the Bureau of Citizenship and Immigration Services, which has sole power to determine whether an alien can become a naturalized citizen. Citizenship obtained through naturalization carries with it the privilege of full participation in government, including the right to speak freely, to criticize the government, to work for the government, and to promote changes in the law. Naturalized citizens are not second-class citizens. In fact, there are very few differences between citizenship by birth and naturalization, except in two important respects: naturalized citizens cannot run for the office of President of the United States and, in extreme cases, naturalized citizens can be denaturalized (a process that is explained later in this chapter).

Naturalization Requirements

Physical and Legal Presence Requirements

To be eligible for naturalization, an alien must meet the requirements for residency and physical presence established by the Immigration and Nationality Act:

- The alien must have been a lawful permanent resident of the United States for a minimum of five years (or three years, if he or she is married to a U.S. citizen) before applying for naturalization.
- The alien must show that he or she has been physically present in the United States for at least half of the time during the past five years.
- The alien must show that he or she has lived in the city in which he or she is applying for naturalization for at least three months.

There are less stringent requirements for those who reside outside the United States but who work for the United States (such as the military). Furthermore, aliens who serve in the U.S. military during a time of war do not have to show that they had lawful permanent resident status prior to applying for naturalization.

Oath of Allegiance

To gain citizenship through naturalization, an alien must understand the oath of allegiance and

be able and willing to take it. Under the oath, the alien promises

- to support the Constitution of the United States;

- to "renounce and abjure absolutely and entirely all allegiance and fidelity to any foreign prince, potentate, state, or sovereignty of whom or which the applicant was before a subject or citizen";

- to support and defend the Constitution and laws of the United States against all enemies, foreign and domestic;

- to bear true faith and allegiance to the United States; and

- to bear arms on behalf of the United States, perform noncombatant service in the Armed Forces of the United States, or perform work of national importance under civilian direction when required by law.

Age Requirement

With the exception of adoption and those individuals who have honorably served in an active duty status in the Armed Forces during a time of war, aliens must be at least 18 years old to qualify for naturalization.

Mental Competency Requirement

An alien must be legally competent at the time he or she takes the examination for naturalization, which is part of the naturalization application, and at the time the oath of allegiance is administered. That is, the alien must understand the purpose of naturalization and the responsibilities that come with citizenship. Past history of mental incompetence, such as having been confined to a mental institution, is not an impediment, provided that during the time of the application and when the oath is administered the alien has overcome the problem sufficiently to understand the concept of U.S. citizenship and to desire to be a U.S. citizen.

English Language Requirement

Aliens who apply for naturalization must be able to speak, read, write, and understand English. An interview is conducted in English, giving aliens an opportunity to hear and answer questions and demonstrate their ability to speak and understand the language. The Bureau of Citizenship and Immigration Services officer will also ask the alien to read a randomly selected sentence and to write down a simple phrase (such as "I want to become a citizen") dictated by the bureau officer. Aliens must be able to read and write the sentences clearly and accurately.

Good Moral Character Requirement

A person must be considered to have "good moral character" in order to be approved for naturalization. Good moral character is defined by the Immigration and Nationality Act by reference to a list of specific, prohibited activities. However, there is also a discretionary aspect to good moral character; that is, the Bureau of Citizenship and Immigration Services may consider other activities not necessarily listed in the act. Generally, an alien is not considered to be of good moral character if he or she

- is habitually drunk,

- has been convicted of certain crimes such as theft or violence,
- is a practicing prostitute or is one who procures prostitution,
- engages in commercial vice,
- smuggles other aliens,
- is a practicing polygamist,
- has been convicted of a controlled substance violation,
- has an income derived principally from illegal gambling activities,
- has given false testimony or perjury to obtain an immigration benefit,
- has made false claims in order to obtain U.S. citizenship or to vote in elections,
- has failed to pay a child support obligation,
- has failed to file taxes, or
- is a man who is eligible for but fails to register with the Selective Service.

All naturalization applicants are required to be fingerprinted so that a Bureau of Citizenship and Immigration Services officer may request a copy of the applicant's record from the Federal Bureau of Investigation. The bureau officer has the right to review the alien's complete immigration file and history. Lying on an application for naturalization is unwise. For example, if the record shows that a small crime was committed but the applicant has lied about the incident, even though the crime may not block the way for naturalization, the applicant will not be considered to have good moral character because he or she lied. That is, the lie is more harmful than the incident that the alien tried to conceal. Moreover, if the applicant has lied under oath, he or she has committed perjury, and that offense is considered to be even more serious.

Knowledge of U.S. History and Government Requirement

In addition to demonstrating an understanding of the English language, naturalization applicants must pass an examination to show a knowledge and understanding of the fundamentals of U.S. history and the principles and form of U.S. government. Applicants may obtain a list of the government and history questions from the Bureau of Citizenship and Immigration Services prior to taking the exam. A bureau officer generally asks 10 questions that are chosen randomly from 100 possible questions. The questions, which are answered orally, are designed to assess basic knowledge ("What are the branches of government?"), locally specific knowledge ("Who is the mayor of your city?"), and lesser-known facts ("Who wrote the *Star Spangled Banner*?"). The applicant must be able to answer at least 60 percent of the questions correctly.

Exceptions

SITUATION 5 Cheluchi Ukwu is a sick, elderly Nigerian woman. One of her greatest wishes is to become a U.S. citizen before she dies, but she does not know the English language and is blind.

Can she become a citizen through the naturalization process?

Because of a medical handicap, advanced age, or religious beliefs, some people may be unable to complete all of the prerequisites for naturalization but nevertheless may be eligible for citizenship. An applicant who has a physical disability that renders him or her incapable of learning to speak the English language (for example, a person who is deaf or mute) may be exempt from the English language requirement. Persons who are blind have also been exempted from the requirement, even though blindness itself is not an impediment to learning language. For other physical conditions, a medical doctor must show that the disability is such that the applicant is unable to acquire the language skills (that is, the ability to speak, write, read, and understand English). Likewise, because of this inability to learn, the requirement of knowledge of U.S. history and government may be waived. However, aliens who lose their cognitive abilities as a direct result of illegal drug use do not qualify for this exemption.

In addition to the disability exception, aliens who have been long-time lawful permanent residents of the United States and are of an advanced age may qualify to have their naturalization interview and government and history test conducted in their native language. Aliens who are over 50 years of age and have been living in the United States as permanent residents for at least 20 years or who are over 55 years of age and have been living in the United States as permanent residents for at least 15 years are covered by this exemption.

> **SITUATION 6** Padmaj Srinivason, who is from India, wants to become a U.S. citizen. However, because of his religious beliefs, he cannot take the full oath of allegiance.
>
> **Q** Will he be denied citizenship because he does not take the oath?

Some persons may be exempted from taking the full oath of allegiance because their religious convictions prevent them from voting, serving on juries, pledging allegiance to the flag, bearing arms, engaging in politics, or otherwise participating in government. The U.S. Constitution protects freedom of religion just as it creates the right to become a naturalized citizen. Because these constitutional provisions may conflict, immigration laws provide that eligible applicants may become naturalized without having to violate basic tenets of their religious beliefs.

Denaturalization

Naturalization may be revoked if a person who is seeking citizenship by naturalization conceals a material fact or intentionally misrepresents him- or herself (that is, lies) during the application process. The process of revoking a person's citizenship is known as denaturalization. In a denaturalization proceeding, the government must prove that

1. the naturalized citizen misrepresented or concealed some fact,
2. the misrepresentation or concealment was willful (or deliberate),
3. the fact was material (that is, important to the decision of granting citizenship), and
4. the naturalized citizen obtained citizenship as a result of the misrepresentation or concealment.

When the government seeks to revoke naturalization because of either concealment or misrepresentation, it must show that the naturalized citizen actually intended to deceive the government. That is, the government must show that the naturalized citizen knew that his or her statements were lies. Denaturalization is considered the most serious of all immigration law proceedings, and any decision made by the Bureau of Citizenship and Immigration Services against a naturalized citizen is reviewed carefully by the U.S. courts.

Only the Facts

1. What is naturalization?
2. Name two ways in which this form of citizenship differs from citizenship by birth.
3. List three requirements that must be completed before a person can become naturalized.
4. List the four things that must be shown for a citizen to become denaturalized.

Think About

1. Should a naturalized citizen be allowed to run for President? Can you think of other important American government leaders who were

naturalized citizens? Hint: Think back to the Founding Fathers as well as recent political figures.

2. Is the English language requirement part of the naturalization process fair? Why or why not?

3. Would a person who lost his or her ability to learn because of taking prescription drugs be exempt from the English language and knowledge of U.S. history and government requirements of the naturalization process? What if the drugs had been prescribed to another family member? Do you think a person who has "kicked" a drug habit but remains learning-disabled should be exempt from the English language and knowledge of U.S. history and government requirements? Why or why not?

Suppose a woman lied about her age when she was naturalized because she suffered from dementia and mental delusions. Should this woman be denaturalized? Explain your answer. Would she be eligible for naturalization in the first place?

SUMMING UP

In this chapter, you have learned about the fundamental principles of immigration law. Obtaining citizenship can be as simple as being born to a parent who is a U.S. citizen or as complicated as seeking protection under asylum laws, receiving lawful permanent resident status, and ultimately applying for citizenship through the naturalization process. Immigration laws affect the future of individual lives and our nation. We become better-informed citizens by understanding immigration law and the immigration process.

Glossary

These terms are defined as they are used in this book and according to Georgia law. The definitions are not formal legal definitions.

abandonment—leaving children without intending to return; forsaking parental responsibilities.

actuarial table—a set of figures used to predict how long a person is likely to live. It is based on the average life expectancies of a large number of people.

adjudicatory hearing—the first part of a formal hearing for a juvenile. Its purpose is to determine the facts in the case. Did the youth commit a delinquent or unruly act? Is the youth deprived? See *dispositional hearing, formal hearing*.

administrative law—rules and regulations created by government agencies enabling them to carry out the duties assigned to them by Congress, a state legislature, or a local government.

adoption—the legal process of substituting adoptive parents for a child's biological parents.

affidavit—a written statement that is sworn to be true before an authorized official such as a judge.

affirmative action—steps taken by an organization to remedy past discrimination in hiring, promotion, and recruitment. Such steps may be required by the government. Typically, affirmative action involves the selective hiring of persons in a status category (such as race) to balance worker populations.

age of majority—the age when a person is considered an adult, as defined by state law. In Georgia, this age is 18 years old.

aggravating circumstances—facts about a crime or criminal that might influence a judge to be tougher in sentencing.

alibi—the defense that claims that a person was somewhere else at the time a crime was committed.

alien—a noncitizen. Regardless of how an alien enters the United States, whether legally or not, he or she can apply for asylum once in the United States.

alimony—support payments that a person is ordered by a court to make to a divorced spouse.

alternative dispute resolution (ADR)—alternative methods to going to court when attempting to solve disputes between parties.

ADR is often much less formal and complex than a court proceeding. Most often, it is also less costly. See *arbitration, mediation, negotiation.*

analogy—a type of logical thinking basic to legal reasoning. It is based on the idea that if two things agree in some ways, they will agree in other ways. When used in law, it means looking at cases with similar situations and applying their resolutions to another similar case at hand.

annulment—a court declaration that a marriage never existed because it was not valid from the start.

answer—a legal document filed with the clerk of court in which the defendant admits or denies the claims made in the complaint.

appeal—a request that a higher court review the decision of a lower court. The higher court may uphold, reverse, or modify the decision.

appellate court—a court that reviews the decisions of trial courts to determine whether the law was properly applied in the cases reflected in those decisions.

arbitrary reason—a reason that is not sensible or logical; it has no rational basis. One requirement of the due process clause is that life, liberty, and property not be taken away for arbitrary reasons.

arbitration—a method of settling disputes in which a third party hears the arguments and facts from both sides and decides how to resolve the dispute.

arraignment—a court hearing in the criminal justice process during which the judge reads the charges against the defendant and the defendant enters a plea of guilty, not guilty, or *nolo contendere.*

arrest—to take a person into physical custody and charge him or her with committing a crime.

arrest warrant—a document that gives an authorized person, such as a police officer, permission to arrest someone.

assault—an intentional tort or crime in which there is an attempt to inflict bodily injury or a threat of attack by someone capable of carrying out that threat.

assumption of the risk—one of two main defenses against a charge of negligence when it is alleged that the risk or injury was foreseeable and that the plaintiff proceeded to act despite the possibility of harm.

asylee—an alien who is already in the United States and then applies for and is granted asylum (or protection).

attachment—a court-authorized method of collecting a debt. The county sheriff takes possession of a debtor's property and sells it to repay the creditor.

automobile exception—the case law exempting certain automobile searches from the general requirement for a search warrant.

bail—a sum of money or property pledged to the court to assure that an accused person will appear to stand trial. Once bail is posted, the accused is released from police custody until the trial.

bait and switch—a deceptive sales technique. It consists of luring customers into a store by advertising goods or services at low prices with the intent of suggesting a substitute of a more expensive item.

balloon payment—the last payment of a loan that is much larger than the other payments.

bankruptcy—a proceeding in court that takes place because a person is not able to pay his or her debts. The person's property may be used to pay some of the debts. The remaining debts are cancelled.

battery—an intentional tort or crime in which one person intentionally touches another without consent.

benefit—a privilege given to an employee by the employer, such as paid vacation, paid sick days, insurance coverage, or a Christmas bonus.

bigamy—the crime of being married to more than one person at a time.

biological parent—the natural parent of a child.

bondsman—a person whose business consists of loaning money for bail. The bondsman posts bail, taking the risk that the accused will not show up for trial—which would result in the bondsman losing the bail money. For taking this risk, the bondsman charges the accused a percentage of the bail, usually 10 to 15 percent.

booking—the procedure of officially recording an arrest by a law enforcement agency such as the police department in a certain city or county.

breach—failure to meet a legal responsibility.

building code—a collection of laws that sets standards for constructing, altering, and repairing buildings.

Bureau of Citizenship and Immigration Services—agency in charge of considering the evidence in support of claims of derivative citizenship and determining whether or not a person is a citizen. If citizenship is determined, the bureau will issue the certificate.

capital felony—the most serious type of crime, the penalty for which may be life imprisonment or death.

case law—court interpretations of statutory, constitutional, or common law.

caveat emptor—a Latin phrase meaning "let the buyer beware." Called the first law of consumer protection, it indicates that the buyer should be careful about the quality of products and services purchased.

ceremonial marriage—a marriage created by formal ceremony, blood test, and marriage license.

character witness—one who testifies about the lifestyle, background, and personality of a defendant, rather than the facts of a case.

charge—(1) a judge's instructions to a jury; (2) the formal accusation of a crime.

charter—a state law that creates a city and acts as its constitution.

child labor laws—laws that create special restrictions on the use of children in the marketplace. These laws usually limit the type of work, hours, and ages of working children.

child support—payments from a parent to a person with legal custody of the child (guardian or other parent) to be used in caring for the child.

citizen—a constitutional provision that comes from a historical principle that a person's nationality is determined by his or her place of birth. Some people are citizens because they are born to a parent who is a citizen, even if they are born outside the United States.

civil disobedience—the act of breaking civil laws that one considers unjust in order ultimately to have them changed.

civil judgment—a court decision in a civil suit that requires one party either to pay a sum of money or to take certain actions as a result of the breach of some legal duty.

civil law—all areas of law except those involving crime.

clear and present danger—a possible effect of speech that makes such speech exempt from First Amendment protection. For instance, if a court determines that a person's speech could incite people to unlawful action, that speech would not be protected and could be declared illegal.

closing—the final meeting in the sale of real property in which the property is formally transferred from seller to buyer.

closing argument—summary remarks made to the jury by attorneys for both sides after all evidence is presented in a trial.

code—a collection of laws, such as the laws of the State of Georgia. See *Official Code of Georgia Annotated*.

codify—to organize laws by subject matter.

coercion—a defense that claims that the defendant was forced to commit the crime against his or her will.

collateral—property that can be sold or retained by a creditor if the debtor fails to pay the debt.

collective bargaining agreement—a contract between the employer and the employees' union setting wage scales, hours, and working conditions.

collision insurance—the coverage for damage to one's motor vehicle caused by impact with another motor vehicle.

commercial speech—speech or written material intended solely to make money, such as advertising. It receives less constitutional protection than other forms of speech.

common law—the legal rights and duties that courts declare to exist in the absence of statutes; generally based on the English system of law at the time the United States was founded.

common law marriage—a marriage created without a legal ceremony by a couple living together and publicly presenting themselves as married.

community service—a sentencing option in which the defendant is assigned to work for a certain length of time at a public service job, such as providing janitorial services at a government building (such as a courthouse).

comparative negligence—one of two main defenses against a charge of negligence. In this defense, both parties share responsibility for negligence, but the plaintiff can recover damages if his or her negligence was less than that of the defendant. See *contributory negligence*.

complaint—(1) the first legal document filed in a civil lawsuit, detailing the claim, court of jurisdiction, and remedies requested; (2) in a criminal case, a formal document, submitted to the prosecution by the victim or a witness, that accuses a person of committing an offense.

comprehensive insurance—the coverage for damage to a motor vehicle other than by collision.

condominium—an individually owned dwelling unit in a complex of such units. Each unit owner also owns a share of the common property, such as halls or yards.

consideration—something of value offered by each party in making a contract.

constitutional law—the legal basis or framework of law in American society as found in the U.S. Constitution and the individual state constitutions. Although written and intended to have a permanence in structure, constitutional laws can be changed. Making such a change is called amending a constitution.

constitutional right—a basic right or protection provided by a constitution or its amendments that cannot be denied by the government. Also called *fundamental right*. See also *First Amendment rights*.

consumer—a buyer of goods and services.

consumer credit—loans for family, personal, or household purposes, as opposed to business loans.

consumer law—the body of laws that govern personal, family, and household purchases.

consummation—a requirement for a valid marriage. In a ceremonial marriage, consummation is accomplished by obtaining a license and having a ceremony.

contempt of court—a ruling by a judge that a person is intentionally obstructing order in a court or failing to obey a judge's order. It is punishable by a fine or a jail sentence.

contract—a legally enforceable agreement by two or more parties in which each has an obligation to the other(s).

contractual warranty—a type of warranty that is agreed to by the parties, such as a bill of sale limiting the seller's responsibility for defects in a product.

contributory negligence—a rule of law governing a situation in which the plaintiff and defendant share responsibility for negligence. Under this rule, the plaintiff may not recover any damages. This rule has been replaced in Georgia by the rule of *comparative negligence*.

conversion—an intentional tort whereby a property owner is deprived of the property either permanently or for an indefinite period of time.

court—see *appellate court, juvenile court, magistrate court, probate court, state court, superior court, trial court.*

credit—(1) the purchase of goods or services with a delayed payment schedule; (2) money that is loaned. See *consumer credit, open-end credit, secured credit, unsecured credit.*

credit bureau—a business that collects information on individuals and issues credit reports used to determine whether a consumer is a good credit risk.

credit sale—the purchase of goods "on time" (in installments).

creditor—a person who provides credit, loans money, or delivers goods or services before full payment is made.

crime—an act that harms others physically, financially, or psychologically and that is declared a crime by a statute.

criminal justice process—all proceedings between the time a person is suspected of a crime until that person is unconditionally freed by the government.

criminal law—the body of law that deals with acts that are declared crimes by the government.

cross-examination—the questioning of witnesses for the opposing side during a trial or hearing.

custody—the care and keeping—legal or physical—of something or someone, such as a child or a prisoner. See *joint custody.*

damages—money that would compensate a plaintiff for some injury, loss, or inconvenience caused by another and that is asked for in a civil lawsuit.

death penalty—the ultimate penalty given to someone found guilty of committing certain capital crimes. Not all states use the death penalty.

debtor—a person who owes money or buys on credit.

deed—a document that represents the passing of property from the seller to the purchaser.

deed to secure debt—a document that establishes the buyer's real property as collateral for a loan.

defamation—an intentional tort in which a written or spoken expression about someone is false and damaging to that person's reputation.

default—failure to fulfill a legal obligation, such as not repaying a loan or not filing an answer to a plaintiff's claim.

defendant—the party accused of wrongdoing in a civil or criminal case.

definite sentencing—a system of assigning penalties in which the judge has no choice about the type or duration of the penalty.

degrees of consanguinity or **affinity**—a measure of blood or marriage relationships, as set forth in the Official Code of Georgia Annotated. Marriage is prohibited between people who have these specific relationships.

delay—a pretrial tactic popular with defense attorneys that consists of putting off the trial by using various legal maneuvers.

delinquent act—an act by a juvenile that if committed by an adult would be criminal.

delusional compulsion—a defense to a criminal accusation in which the defendant claims that he or she acted because of a compelling belief in the truth of something that is, in fact, false.

denaturalization—the process of revoking a person's citizenship acquired by naturalization. Naturalization may be revoked if a person who is seeking citizenship by naturalization conceals a material fact or intentionally misrepresents him- or herself (that is, lies) during the application process. When the government seeks to revoke naturalization because of either concealment or misrepresentation, it must show that the naturalized citizen actually intended to deceive the government.

deportation—the removal from a country of an alien whose presence is unlawful. Aliens who engage in criminal activity or fraud and misrepresentation may face deportation. Other reasons for being deported include overstaying a visa and entering the country illegally.

deprived child—a child who has been abused or neglected.

derivative citizenship—citizenship determined by the nationality of a person's parents. Derivative citizens can apply for a certificate of citizenship for the purpose of proving that they are citizens.

desertion—leaving one's spouse with no intention of returning. Usually, one year's absence is required, by law, to prove desertion.

deterrence—one of four philosophic viewpoints about the purpose of sentencing. This one maintains that the purpose of punishing an offender is to discourage people from committing crimes.

direct examination—the questioning of a witness during a trial by the attorney who called the witness.

directed verdict—(1) in criminal law, a verdict of not guilty entered by the judge when the prosecution has not shown enough evidence to prove the accusation; (2) in civil law, a verdict entered by the judge agreeing with one party's claim that the other party cannot possibly prove its case.

discovery—the pretrial exchange of information between opposing sides.

dispositional hearing—a juvenile court hearing to determine the most appropriate form of treatment for a delinquent, status offender, or dependent. This is the second part of a formal hearing for a juvenile. See *adjudicatory hearing*, *formal hearing*.

dispossess—to evict a tenant or reclaim property if payment owed is not made.

distress warrant—a court-authorized document that enables a landlord to recover overdue rent by having a tenant's possessions sold at auction.

divorce—the ending of a marriage by court order.

doctrine of *jus sanguinis*—citizenship determined by the nationality of a person's parents. *Jus* is the Latin word for "law," and *sanguinis* is Latin for "blood." Also known as *derivative citizenship*.

doctrine of *jus soli*—citizenship determined by a person's place of birth. *Jus* is the Latin word for "law," and *soli* means "soil."

due process—the principle that the government must act in a fair and reasonable manner when it threatens to deprive individuals of life, liberty, or property. It is embodied in the Fifth,

Sixth, and Fourteenth Amendments to the U.S. Constitution.

DUI (driving under the influence)—the unlawful operation of a motor vehicle while under the influence of alcohol or drugs.

earnest money—a deposit paid to the seller of real property by the potential buyer upon the signing of the purchase contract.

easement—a document that grants certain uses of property to persons other than the owner of the property. It can also limit the owner's use of the property.

elastic clause—a passage in the U.S. Constitution (art. 1, sec. 8) that gives Congress the right to pass all laws necessary for carrying out the tasks delegated to it.

emancipated minor—a person under the age of 18 who is declared by a court to be capable of surviving independently of parents. Such a minor can enter into contracts for necessities.

eminent domain—the power of a government to take property for public purposes, such as building a highway, from private individuals (for just compensation).

entrapment—a defense to a criminal charge. It consists of proving that the defendant was induced by law enforcement officials to commit a crime that he or she would otherwise not have committed.

environmental regulations—laws that affect land use and property ownership in order to keep the environment clean and healthy for all of its inhabitants.

equal employment opportunity (EEO)—a federal mandate that prohibits certain employers from discriminating against individuals on the basis of status categories, such as age, gender, race, or handicap.

equal protection—a principle guaranteed by the U.S. and Georgia constitutions that requires the government to treat all persons equally and impartially.

equity—the power of a court *not* to apply an established rule of law to a particular situation in order to avoid an unjust result.

eviction—a procedure by which a landlord forces a tenant who has defaulted on paying the rent to move out. See *dispossess*.

evidence—matters of fact that tend to prove or disprove other matters of fact. See *hearsay evidence, real evidence, testimonial evidence*.

exclusionary rule—a rule that prohibits the use of illegally obtained evidence in a criminal trial.

exigent circumstances—a rule allowing warrantless searches and seizures in emergency situations. These circumstances usually occur when the police are in hot pursuit of someone who has just committed a crime.

expert witness—a person who, because of training, work, or experience, is qualified to testify on the technical or special facts of a case.

express warranty—a warranty created by certain actions of the seller, such as a written or spoken promise, description, or display of a sample or model.

fair manner—the requirement necessary to due process that there can be no government action against someone unless done in a fair manner. Generally, fair manner requires that the person affected be given notice of the proposed action and a hearing in order to oppose the action if desired.

false imprisonment—an intentional tort in which one person is unlawfully detained against his or her will by another.

Federal Trade Commission (FTC)—a federal agency with the authority to issue regulations concerning certain business transactions and to sue companies for violations.

felony—a serious crime punishable by a prison sentence of a year or more. Examples are murder, kidnapping, armed robbery, arson, rape, and forgery.

fighting words—expressions likely to cause a breach of the peace. Such expressions are not protected by the First Amendment right to free speech.

finance charges—the cost of credit, including interest, late charges, service charges, and insurance on the loan.

fine—a penalty imposed upon a convicted person by a court, requiring that he or she pay a specified sum of money to the court.

First Amendment rights—freedom of assembly, association, religion, speech, and of the press as guaranteed in the Bill of Rights of the U.S. Constitution. See *constitutional right, fundamental right.*

fixture—an item of personal property so attached to real property that it is considered part of the real property.

Food and Drug Administration (FDA)—a federal agency that sets standards for and regulates the safety of foods, drugs, cosmetics, and other household products.

foreclosure—the process of satisfying an unpaid debt by obtaining the collateral and selling it.

foreman—a juror elected by the jury to act as its spokesperson and leader.

formal hearing—a court hearing to determine if a juvenile is in need of state protection or treatment. It has two parts: the adjudicatory and the dispositional.

formal petition of delinquency—a document that must be filed by the complaining witness before a formal hearing of a juvenile case can be held.

foster parent—a temporary guardian licensed by the state or designated by a court to care for a child.

fraud—a deception, lie, or dishonest statement made to cheat someone. Fraud can prevent a meeting of the minds in making a contract.

freedom of assembly, association, religion, speech, and **of the press**—rights guaranteed by the First Amendment of the U.S. Constitution. These are explained in chapter 13 of the text.

full warranty—a type of warranty that assures a buyer that goods are totally free of defects when sold. Full warranty includes an obligation that the seller will repair or replace the goods within a specified time period after purchase if they are not of the assured quality.

fundamental right—a protection guaranteed by the U.S. Constitution or its amendments. See *constitutional right.*

gag order—a court order prohibiting publicity before and during a trial.

garnishment—a court-authorized method of collecting debts from a third party holding assets of the debtor. Collection may be done through payroll deductions, from a checking account, or by other methods.

Gault decision—a U.S. Supreme Court decision establishing several rights for juveniles in danger of losing their liberty. These include the juvenile's right to be notified of charges, to remain silent, to have an attorney, to cross-examine witnesses, and to obtain a record of the hearings. The decision also establishes the rights of parents to be informed when children are taken into custody.

grace period—a short period (several days) after a rent payment is due, during which a tenant may not be evicted for late payment.

grand jury—a group of 16 to 23 registered voters selected to serve for three-month periods. Their main responsibility is to decide whether there is enough evidence to indict people accused of felonies. They may also investigate the conduct of government agencies or affairs, inspect government buildings, etc.

green card—a permanent resident alien card. Once the green card is granted and the alien becomes a lawful permanent resident, he or she may live, work, and travel in the United States.

grounds—legal reasons for a lawsuit (for example, reasons that a court will accept as valid for divorce) or for an appeal.

guarantor—a person who promises to pay a debt if the debtor does not.

guardian—an adult who has the legal responsibility for a child and/or the child's property.

***habeas corpus* petition**—an appeal by a prisoner to be brought before a judge to evaluate the lawfulness of the detention. Usually at issue is whether the prisoner's fundamental rights were denied him or her during the trial or sentencing phase of the criminal justice process. *Habeas corpus* is a part of due process and is guaranteed by the U.S. Constitution.

habitual violator—a driver who has committed certain serious traffic offenses multiple times (individually or in combination with others). Once declared a habitual violator by the Department of Public Safety, a driver will be treated much more severely than would normally be the case for any further traffic offense.

hearing—a proceeding in which arguments, witnesses, or evidence are heard by a judge in order for the judge to make some decision relative to the case. See *adjudicatory hearing, dispositional hearing, formal hearing, preliminary hearing, presentence hearing.*

hearsay evidence—testimony that usually is not admissible in an adult trial because it is not based on the personal knowledge of a witness. It is a repetition of another's statement and considered unreliable.

holding facility—a place in which prisoners are evaluated before being transferred to a jail or prison.

homicide—the killing of a person.

illegitimate child—a child whose parents are not married to each other when the child is conceived and do not marry later. Under Georgia law, such a child is referred to as one "born out of wedlock."

immigration—to enter a country for permanent residence.

immunity—exemption from penalties or duties. For example, government officials may have immunity for liabilities from losses or harm caused by official actions.

implied warranty—see *statutory warranty.*

incapacitation—one of four philosophic viewpoints about the purpose of sentencing. This viewpoint maintains that the purpose of punishing an offender is to protect society from dangerous people who would break the law.

incarceration—the jailing or imprisoning of an offender.

incest—sexual relations between members of a family or persons who are too closely related to each other to be legally married. These relationships are defined by the laws of consanguinity and affinity.

indefinite sentencing—a system in which judges determine the appropriate sentences for defendants found guilty in their courts. The sentences must be within the range set for the crime(s) by the legislature. In this system, the parole authority actually controls the amount of time served.

indictment—a formal accusation, usually of a felony, by a grand jury.

indigent—a defendant too poor to afford an attorney.

informal adjustment—a treatment option for a juvenile delinquent or status offender that is like an informal short-term probation. However, it is determined before a formal petition or hearing occurs and is offered only to first or minor offenders who admit their wrongdoing and have a good record.

injunction—a court order to guard against future harms. It may stop or require an action.

insanity—a defense to a criminal charge that declares, in effect, that the defendant may have committed the act but was not responsible for his or her behavior due to mental problems.

insurance—see *collision insurance, comprehensive insurance, liability insurance, uninsured motorist insurance.*

intake—the first steps in the juvenile justice process.

intentional tort—a deliberate act that damages a person or his/her property. Many, but not all, intentional torts are also crimes.

interest—one of the costs of credit; a percentage of the amount loaned that is added to each payment to be made over a certain period of time.

interrogatory—a discovery technique. Written questions are sent by one party's attorney to the attorney for the other party. They must be answered in writing and under oath.

intestate—having no will.

investigative warrant—an electronic surveillance warrant. A document that allows the police to gain evidence in a criminal case using a wiretap or other eavesdropping methods.

jail—a local government facility used for incarcerating persons generally for no more than a year.

joint custody—an arrangement in which parents share custody of a child after a divorce. See *custody.*

judge—the person who presides over a court and controls the conduct of a trial.

jurisdiction—(1) the authority of a court to resolve a particular controversy. Jurisdiction may be determined by geographic location, subject matter, or persons involved in the case; (2) the area of authority of a government. See *personal jurisdiction, subject matter jurisdiction,* also chapter 3.

jury—see *grand jury, trial jury.*

jury deliberation—the consideration that a jury gives when deciding a case. Deliberation begins after the presentation part of the trial ends. See *verdict.*

jury panel—a group of local citizens chosen at random. Trial juries are selected from this panel.

justification—one of three general types of defenses against an intentional tort. The defendant admits doing the acts complained of by the plaintiff but denies that the acts were wrong, claiming instead that they were justified.

juvenile—a person under the age of 18. Age determination is used to decide juvenile court authority in delinquency and unruliness cases as well as in cases involving abuse and neglect.

juvenile court—a court that hears cases involving juveniles. Every Georgia county has a juvenile court with jurisdiction over children who are delinquent, unruly, deprived, abused, or in need of treatment or who have committed a traffic offense.

labor union—an organization which workers agree to allow to represent them when dealing with the owners (management) of the company for which they work. The two main types are craft unions for workers in the same profession and industrial unions for workers in the same industry.

landlady, landlord—the owner of leased or rented property.

law—all rights and duties that can be enforced by the government (or one of its parts) as well as the means and procedures for enforcing them. See *administrative law, child labor laws, civil law, common law, consumer law, criminal law, right-to-work laws, statutory law, sunshine law, usury laws.*

layoff—when a worker is not given work or wages, usually temporarily, because of a shortage of demand for the product. A laid-off worker may sometimes collect unemployment compensation.

leading question—a question that is phrased so as to suggest the desired answer. It is not allowed on direct examination in court.

lease—a contract to rent property.

legal duty—an obligation that can be enforced by the government.

legal right—a privilege that is guaranteed by the government.

legal separation—an arrangement in which a married couple lives apart, with terms set by court order. This separation is not a divorce and does not end a marriage.

liability insurance—a type of automobile coverage required by Georgia law. When the insured person is at fault, this insurance provides payment of damages to other parties who suffered injuries or property loss in the accident.

liable—responsible for committing the tort and, therefore, for paying damages.

libel—the intentional tort of writing, printing, or broadcasting false information damaging to someone.

licensing and examining boards—commissions created by state governments that set standards and qualifications for performing certain services and certifying practitioners in certain professions (such as accounting, psychology, nursing).

lien—a legal hold on property until some legal obligation is fulfilled.

limited warranty—an incomplete warranty; one that offers less than a full warranty.

litigation—using the judicial process (from filing a lawsuit through appeal) to solve a dispute.

loan—the money borrowed from a bank, finance company, other lending institution, or person under an agreement that it will be paid back over a specific period of time.

local government—the government of a city or county.

lockout—a tactic used by an employer to force an agreement with a union. The employer closes the workplace, suspending all wages.

long-arm statute—a state law that allows a court to have jurisdiction over cases involving, for example, products manufactured in another state but used by a consumer in the court's jurisdiction. See *jurisdiction*.

magistrate court—a Georgia trial court that hears relatively minor civil claims and criminal pretrial proceedings.

malicious prosecution—an intentional tort in which one person, with intent to harm, causes another person to be arrested and prosecuted without just cause.

marriage—a legally enforceable agreement between two people promising to be husband and wife. See *ceremonial marriage*, *common law marriage*.

marriage license—a document issued by the judge of the probate court that must be obtained before a formal marriage ceremony can be performed.

mediation—the process of solving a dispute through an impartial third party who guides disputing parties in working out a solution.

meeting of the minds—a requirement for a legal contract in which the parties must know and understand what is expected of each.

minimum wage—the least hourly amount that can be paid to employees whose employers are subject to federal wage and hour laws.

Miranda warning—a statement of the rights of a person in police custody that are taken from the Fifth, Sixth, and Fourteenth Amendments to the U.S. Constitution. The reading of these rights to a suspect in custody before interrogation is a necessary part of due process. See chapter 16.

misdemeanor—a crime less serious than a felony. A misdemeanor carries a maximum penalty of one year or less in jail and/or a fine of $1,000 or less. Examples are speeding and theft of less than $500.

mitigating circumstances—circumstances surrounding the commission of a crime that may reduce the blameworthiness of the defendant and influence a judge to give a lenient sentence.

mitigation—one of three general types of defenses against an intentional tort. The defendant admits doing the act and that it was wrong, but he or she attempts to reduce the amount of damages by showing good faith, a lack of malice, or lack of intent to cause harm.

mortgage—a type of loan in which a house or real property is given as collateral.

motion, pretrial—see *pretrial motion*.

motion for a change of venue—a request from an attorney to a trial judge to change the location of a trial from one jurisdiction to another.

motion for continuance—a request from an attorney to a trial judge to postpone a trial to allow for more time to prepare the case.

motion to suppress evidence—a request from an attorney to a trial judge to prevent the introduction of evidence that would damage that attorney's side of the case.

natural parent—see *biological parent*.

naturalization—the process by which persons born in other countries apply for U.S. citizenship. Although naturalized citizens have the right to speak freely, to criticize the government, to work for the government, and to promote changes in the law, they cannot run for the office of President of the United States.

negligence—an unintentional tort that occurs when loss or damage results from a person failing to perform a legal duty or to exercise a reasonable standard of care for others. See *comparative negligence, contributory negligence*.

negotiation—a method of resolving disputes in which the parties (or their representatives) talk with each other to attempt to reach a compromise (and thus a settlement) on the issues in dispute.

1983 suit—a civil rights lawsuit against a public official claiming that the plaintiff's civil rights were violated as a result of some government action (so called because of the federal statute in section 1983 of the Federal Code upon which such a suit would be based).

no bill—the refusal of a grand jury to return an indictment against a person accused of a crime.

no-fault divorce—divorce in which neither party is held to be responsible for the breakup of the marriage.

nolo contendere—a Latin phrase meaning, "I will not contest it." This statement can be a defendant's formal answer in court to criminal charge(s). In this answer, the defendant is not contesting the charge(s) but is not admitting guilt. Often used in cases in which a fine but not jail is likely.

notice—a basic element of due process that involves informing a person that the government may act to take away his or her life, liberty, or property. Also, a requirement in civil law that each party keep the other informed of any actions taken.

nuisance—an intentional tort involving continued inconvenience to persons, which usually affects the use or enjoyment of their property.

obscene material—material not protected by the First Amendment because it appeals to the prurient interest, depicts sexual conduct in an offensive way, and lacks serious literary, artistic, political, or scientific value.

Official Code of Georgia Annotated (O.C.G.A.)—compilation of all of Georgia's statutory law. The code is divided into titles according to subject.

open-end credit—credit in which the borrowed amount is not fixed, such as in credit card purchases. Sometimes called revolving credit.

opening statement—a brief introduction to the case given by the attorneys for each side at the start of a trial.

ordinance—a law created by a local (city or county) government.

overtime—work hours in excess of 40 per week. Workers are often paid a higher hourly wage for this extra work.

parole—(1) supervised release from prison before a sentence has been completed; (2) the temporary status granted to an alien who is waiting for his or her application to formally enter the country to be processed. Such a parole is granted for a specific period of time on a case-by-case basis when there is urgent humanitarian need or a significant public benefit to be gained.

parties—(1) persons involved in committing a crime; (2) opponents in a lawsuit; (3) persons having obligations in a contract.

part-time work—working less than 40 hours per week.

pension—an arrangement for paying a worker after retirement, generally based on the worker's income and length of service with the employer.

peremptory strike—in the pretrial jury selection, an attorney's dismissal of a potential juror without stating a reason.

periodic tenancy—a lease for a definite length of time. As opposed to a *tenancy-at-will*.

personal jurisdiction—a court's authority to act with respect to the parties before it.

personal property—all types of property, tangible or intangible, except real property.

petit jury—see *trial jury*.

plain view doctrine—a rule that the police, when acting without a search warrant, can seize only those items in sight of the officer(s).

plaintiff—the party initiating a civil lawsuit.

plea bargaining—negotiations between a defense attorney and prosecutor in which a defendant pleads guilty in exchange for a lesser charge or sentence.

pleadings—the documents that form the factual and legal issues to be determined in a civil trial (for example, the plaintiff's complaint and the defendant's answer).

police powers—the authority behind many state and local government laws to ensure public health, safety, and well-being.

power of the state—a court's authority to require one party to perform a legal duty.

precedent—a rule of law established by a court decision and applied in deciding similar cases.

preliminary hearing—a pretrial proceeding held to determine whether there is probable cause in a criminal case.

preliminary proceedings—the first part of the criminal trial process. It consists of booking, initial appearance, preliminary hearing, indictment, and arraignment.

prenuptial agreement—rights and duties regarding marriage and possible divorce or property settlements that a couple agrees to before marriage.

presentence hearing—A hearing that may be scheduled after a jury has found a defendant guilty and before sentencing. This hearing allows time for a presentence investigation.

presentence investigation—research about a defendant who is found guilty. Compiled by a probation officer, this research might include aggravating or mitigating circumstances, criminal record, background, and community status of the defendant.

pretrial motion—a request from an attorney to a trial judge to suppress evidence, postpone the case, change the location of the trial, etc.

principal—the original sum of money borrowed in a loan.

prison—a state-operated facility designed to confine adult offenders sentenced to a year or more.

probable cause—reasonable grounds (sufficient evidence) to make an accusation.

probate court—a Georgia trial court of limited jurisdiction. It has authority to probate wills, handle the estates of those who die without wills, appoint guardians, issue marriage licenses, etc.

probation—a sentence releasing an offender into the community under the supervision of a probation officer.

property—see *personal property, real property*.

property ownership—having rights in property that are superior to anybody else's.

prosecution—the party bringing a criminal case against a defendant; the government.

prosecutor—the government's attorney in a criminal case. In superior courts, the district attorney, or DA.

proximate cause—an act that caused or led to an injury and without which the injury would not have happened.

public housing—government-owned and -operated housing for low-income persons. All or part of the rent for this housing is paid by the government.

Public Service Commission (PSC)—a state government board that regulates privately owned companies supplying energy, communications, and transportation to the public.

puffery—advertising claims that exaggerate the good points of a product. These claims are legal because they concern matters of opinion, not fact.

pure democracy—a type of government in which all of the citizens, rather than their elected representatives, decide upon the laws. See *representative democracy*.

Pure Food and Drug Act—the first major bill (1906) to protect consumers in the United States. It established standards for labeling food, liquor, and medicine.

question of fact—an issue concerning the facts of a case, such as whether the defendant did actually commit the act charged.

question of law—an issue concerning the legal procedures or principles that apply to a case.

rational basis—a reasonable relationship between the purpose of a law and any classification of people that the law establishes or applies to.

real estate broker—also called real estate agent; the person who brings the buyer and seller of real property together to negotiate the sale.

real evidence—tangible items used to prove or disprove a point in a trial; one of two principal types of evidence in a trial.

real property—land and whatever is attached to or growing on it, such as houses or crops.

recidivism—the repetition of criminal behavior by a person previously convicted of a crime.

redirect—additional questioning of a witness by the attorney who called the witness. It follows cross-examination of the witness by the other attorney or comes at the close of one side of the case.

reform school—a prison for juveniles. In Georgia, this term is no longer officially used. See *regional youth detention center, youth development campus*.

refugee—an alien desiring protection who has obtained formal permission to enter the United States while he or she was outside the country.

regional youth detention center (RYDC)—a short-term facility for incarcerating juveniles convicted of committing delinquent acts. These facilities may also be used to detain juveniles charged with delinquency until a hearing.

rehabilitation—one of four philosophic viewpoints about the purpose of sentencing. This viewpoint maintains that the purpose is to change a person's criminal behavior to socially desirable conduct.

reject for cause—in the pretrial jury selection, to dismiss a potential juror for some reason, such as a relationship with a party in the case.

release on recognizance (ROR)—a pretrial release in which the defendant signs a promise to appear for trial but does not have to post bail.

repossession—a legal method for the creditor to reclaim an item used as collateral if the debtor fails to repay the debt.

representative democracy—the type of government existing in the United States, in which representatives are elected by the people to make laws.

request for production—a pretrial discovery technique in which one attorney asks the opposing attorney to make certain documents available for inspection.

restitution—a court requirement that an offender pay money or provide services to the victim of the crime or provide services to the community.

retribution—one of four philosophic viewpoints about the purpose of sentencing. This viewpoint maintains that the purpose is to gain revenge for the harm for which the criminal is responsible. The biblical concept of "an eye for an eye and a tooth for a tooth" illustrates this viewpoint.

right—see *constitutional right, fundamental right, legal right, right of petition, visitation rights.*

right of petition—the right of individuals to seek access to all government officials and agencies, as specified in the First Amendment to the U.S. Constitution.

right-to-work laws—state laws that prohibit collective bargaining agreements that require all workers to join a union. A minority of states, including Georgia, have such laws.

ROR—see *release on recognizance.*

RYDC—see *regional youth detention center.*

search warrant—a document issued by a judge that authorizes a police search at a specified location for a certain item and the seizure of that item.

secured credit—a debt that has been guaranteed by a third party or secured with collateral.

security deposit—a sum paid to the owner of rental property by the tenant before moving in. It is to be returned when the tenant moves out unless it is needed to pay for any damages beyond normal wear and tear caused by the tenant.

security interest—a creditor's right to reclaim collateral to pay a debt should the debtor default.

self-defense—a justification for an act that would otherwise be a crime. The person committing this act reasonably believed that it was necessary to protect self or property from immediate danger.

sentence—the penalty imposed by a court upon a person convicted of a crime.

separation—see *legal separation.*

separation of church and state—the constitutional principle prohibiting the government from promoting or discriminating against any religion.

settlement—a mutual agreement between two sides in a lawsuit that ends the dispute before the case is decided in court; an agreement settling financial and other matters in a divorce.

shelter-care facility—a short-term facility that provides temporary care for juveniles in a physically unrestricted environment.

slander—a spoken expression about a person that is false and damages that person's reputation.

Social Security—a U.S. government insurance plan. Every person who contributes to this plan during working years collects payments after retirement or becoming disabled. Benefits are paid to dependents if the contributor dies.

standard of care—a measurement used by a court in a negligence case to determine a person's responsibility with regard to keeping others from harm. It is determined by comparing an act with the imaginary conduct of a reasonable and prudent person.

stare decisis—the principle whereby a previous court decision must be applied to another case when the facts are similar.

state court—a Georgia trial court created to lessen the load of superior courts. It has jurisdiction over misdemeanors and many civil disputes.

status category—a group of people who have historically experienced discrimination because of characteristics beyond their control, such as race, old age, or gender. See *suspect classification.*

status offense—an act such as truancy, disobedience, or running away that is only an offense when committed by a juvenile.

statutory law—laws made by representatives elected to the legislative branch of government.

statutory warranty—a warranty imposed on a transaction by law. Statutory warranties include the warranties of title, merchantability, and fitness. Also called *implied warranty.* See *warranty.*

strict liability—a legal responsibility for injuries or damages even if the fault was not through negligence or intentional conduct.

strict scrutiny—a test to determine whether a governmental action affecting the fundamental rights of certain people or classifying them in a "suspect" way is constitutional.

strike—a tactic used by employees to force an agreement between union and employer. The workers refuse to work, often forming a picket line in front of the workplace to discourage anyone from entering.

subject matter jurisdiction—a court's power to act with respect to the kinds of issues involved in the dispute.

summons—a written order issued by a judge requiring a person to appear in court.

sunshine law—a law that requires governments to hold open meetings when official actions (other than those involving personnel matters) are to be taken.

superior court—a Georgia trial court with general jurisdiction. It has exclusive jurisdiction over certain cases including felony and divorce cases and can hear appeals from lower courts.

suspect classification—a group of people that is identifiable, shares an unchangeable characteristic, and has a history of prejudice against it. Under the Fourteenth Amendment's equal protection clause, laws that discriminate purely on the basis of these classifications are unconstitutional.

symbolic speech—an act that is protected by the First Amendment to the U.S. Constitution because it has the same intent as speech, such as protesting by flying the flag upside down or wearing an armband.

temporary protective status—gives temporary legal status and work authorization to aliens from specific countries that the U.S. government has determined are not safe because of significant natural disasters or war.

tenancy-at-sufferance—the situation when a tenant remains in possession of the premises after the term of the lease runs out. The tenant may stay only as long as the landlord allows.

tenancy-at-will—a lease for an indefinite period of time.

tenant—a person renting real property.

testimonial evidence—statements or depositions by witnesses in a trial. One of two principal types of evidence.

title—a document that proves ownership of property.

tort—a wrongful act or failure to act that harms or interferes with a person or property. Torts can be unintentional (negligence) or intentional. Some intentional torts are also crimes. A tort is always tried in a civil lawsuit. See *intentional tort, negligence.*

tortfeasor—the defendant or accused wrongdoer in a civil lawsuit involving a tort.

transaction—a business activity (buying, selling, leasing, etc.).

traverse jury—see *trial jury.*

trespass—an intentional tort or crime involving unauthorized entry onto the real property of another or damage to or temporary interference with the property of another.

trial—the examination in a court of the issues of fact and law in a case for the purpose of reaching a judgment.

trial court—courts in which cases are originally heard and decided. Cases decided here may be appealed later.

trial jury—a group of local citizens (usually 12) chosen to hear a trial and render a verdict. Also called *petit* or *traverse jury.*

true bill—a document formally submitted to the court by a grand jury accusing a suspect of a felony. See *indictment.*

unemployment compensation—a government-run program that provides temporary payments for a certain period of time to employees who have lost their jobs.

unified appeal system—a process of combining into one document the appeals for a defendant sentenced to death.

Uniform Commercial Code (UCC)—a body of law adopted in most states that governs commercial transactions. It establishes certain implied warranties.

uninsured motorist insurance—a type of coverage that protects the insured driver from financial loss in accidents involving uninsured drivers who are determined to be at fault.

unsecured credit—a loan without a guarantor or collateral; the creditor relies on the debtor's good financial record and promise to repay.

usury laws—state laws limiting the maximum amount that can be charged for interest on a loan.

variance—an exception to the zoning regulations granted to the owner of a piece of property by the local zoning board.

vehicular homicide—a felony traffic violation in which a person is killed by an automobile driven by a driver who was operating the vehicle illegally (for example, was DUI, driving recklessly, fleeing from police).

venue—the geographical location in which a court with jurisdiction may hear and determine a case.

verdict—the decision of a jury or judge about whether a defendant is guilty as charged. See *directed verdict.*

visitation rights—a parent's or relative's right to be with a child. These rights apply generally after a divorce or legal separation.

void—not legally binding; able to be cancelled.

voir dire—the pretrial process in which opposing lawyers question potential jurors to select an impartial jury.

waive—to voluntarily give up some right, privilege, or benefit.

warrant—a document issued by a judge authorizing some action, such as an arrest or a search. See *arrest warrant, distress warrant, investigative warrant, search warrant.*

warranty—a guarantee made by a seller or manufacturer concerning the quality or performance of goods. See *contractual warranty, express warranty, full warranty, limited warranty, statutory warranty*.

warranty of fitness, of merchantability, and **of title**—the three types of statutory or implied warranties, defined in chapter 4. See *statutory warranty*.

will—a document that states how an individual wants his or her property to be distributed after death.

wiretap—electronic eavesdropping.

witness—(1) a person who testifies in a trial or hearing; (2) a person who watches the signing of a document, such as a will. See *character witness, expert witness*.

workers' compensation—a program run by state governments to pay employees who have been injured on the job.

youth development campus (YDC)—a long-term facility for juveniles convicted of committing delinquent acts.

zoning regulations—local government laws that limit the purposes for which owners can use real property.

Index

Note: Glossary entries are indicated in **bold type**; figures appear on pages followed by f.

Consumer Product Safety
Commission, 47

Consumers, **299**

Consummation, 104, **299**

Contempt of court, 175, **300**

Contract cohabitation, 106

Contracts, 6, **300**
  employment, 86–93
    hours, 94
      minimum wage, 93
    unwritten, 92*f*
  enforcing, 41–42
  home purchase, 79
  language used, 41*f*, 41
  marriage contract, 103–104
  requirements, 38–41
  spoken and written, 41
  summing up, 43
  unconscionable, 40
  voiding, 42–43

Contractual warranty, 46, **300**

Contributory negligence, 144, **300**

Conversion, **300**
  of real property, 137

Corporations, liability, 142

Counterclaims, 164

Counties, 14

County ordinances, 14–15

Court reporters, 164*f*

Courts
  basic function, 20–21
  changing court-made law, 33
  how they make laws, 29–32

Courts of concurrent jurisdiction, 23

Courts of general jurisdiction, 23

Courts of limited jurisdiction, 23

Covenants (subdivision), 84

Credit, **300**
  collecting debts, 64–67
  cost of, 62–64
    examples, 57*f*, 62*f*
  credit basics, 57–60
  economic role, 56
  how to become a good
    credit risk, 61*f*
  investigating applicants, 51
  mortgage loans, 79–80
  obtaining, 60–64
  protection for consumers, 66
  protection from
    discrimination, 61–62

sources (listed), 60*f*

Credit bureaus, 61, **300**

Credit Card and Credit Card Bank
Act, 59

Credit cards, 59
  what your application must
    say, 63*f*

Creditor, 56, **300**

Credit sales, 57, **300**

Credit transactions, 56

Crime(s), 5, **300**
  defined, 130
  elements of, 223
  examples, 214
  legal definition, 215
  torts compared, 6, 131*f*

Criminal justice process,
224–226, **300**
  amendments to Georgia
    Constitution and, 225*f*
  defenses, 251–253, 252*f*

Criminal law, **300**
  disagreements, 21–22
  purpose, 131
  titles of cases, 22
  when you need a lawyer, 162*f*

Criminal negligence, 215

Cross-examination, **300**
  civil cases, 172, 173–174
  criminal cases, 255

Cruel and unusual punishment, 226

Custody, 259–260, **300**

D

Damages, 6, **300**
  amounts, 143
  types of, 142–143
  verdict for, 175

Davis v. State (1992), 237

Death penalty, **300**
  capital case process, 278
  due process, 199
  pro and con, 277–278
  reprieve (pardon), 276
  serious felonies, 215

Debt collection practices, 65

Debtors, 56, **300**

Deceptive sales practices, 49

Decisions by judges, 29*f*, 29

Deeds, 81, **300**

Deeds to secure debt, 81, **300**

Defamation, 134–135, **300**

Default, 64, 65, **300**
  court proceedings, 66

Defective products, 46–47

Defendants, 22, 131, **300**

Defense, 173–174
  types of, 251–253, 252*f*

Definite sentencing, 273–274, **300**

Degrees of consanguinity (or affinity),
103, **300–301**

Delays, 252, **301**

Delinquent acts, 259, **301**
  detention facilities, 262
  what can happen to juveniles, 266*f*

Delinquent taxpayers, 81

Delusional compulsion, 252*f*, **301**

Denaturalization, 294, **301**

Department of Corrections, 275

Department of Family and Children
Services (DFCS), 118*f*, 118

Department of Homeland
Security, 282–283

Department of Juvenile Justice, 265

Deportation, 291, **301**

Depositions, 166–167

Deprived child, 123, **301**

Derivative citizenship, 284, **301**

Desertion, 109, **301**

Designated Felony Act, 265

Detention hearings, 261

Deterrence, 274, **301**

DFCS. *See* Department of Family
and Children Services

Directed verdict, 173, **301**

Direct examination, 171–172, **301**

Disability exceptions, 293–294

Discipline, parental, 119

Discovery, 165–166, **301**

Discrimination
  credit, 61–62
  housing, 85
  jobs, 87–90
  jury selection, 170
  married men, 107
  statutory equal protection,
    209–211

Dispositional hearing, 264, **301**

Dispossess, 71, **301**

Acknowledgments

Design: Dianne Johnson; **Layout and Production**: Lisa Carson; **Production**: Reid McCallister; **Editing**: Jayne Plymale; **Proofreading**: Allison Adams; **Indexing**: Francine Cronshaw

Photos: Picture sources are listed in the order that the images appear on the page from left to right, top to bottom.

The following abbreviations are used in this list:

CA = ClipArt.com
CD = ArtExplosion
EJ = Ed Jackson
PSD = Adobe Photoshop stock art
PTG = Photos to Go
RM = Reid McCallister
spice = Webspice.com
xChg = stock.xchng

Cover: Piedmont College; xChg; Steve/Mary Skjold/Index Stock. **Chapter 1**: 2:CD; CD; CD. 4:CA. 7:CA. **Chapter 2**: 12:CA; CD; CA; EJ. 10:CA; CD; CD. **Chapter 3**: 20:CA; CA; CA. 21:RM. 25:EJ. 32:RM. **Chapter 4**: 38:CA; CA; CA. 45:RM. 52:CA. 55:CA. **Chapter 5**: 56:CA; PSD; CA. 58:RM. 59:xChg. **Chapter 6**: 68:CA; CD; CD. 71:xChg. 79:PSD. 80:CA. **Chapter 7**: 86:CA; CA; CA. 89:PTG. 91:CA. 96:CA. 99:CA. **Chapter 8**: 102:CD; CA; CA. 103:RM. 108:CA. **Chapter 9**: 116:CD; CA; CA. 120:CA. 122:CA. 125:CA. **Chapter 10**: 130:CA; spice; CA. 132:CA. 137:CA, CA, CA, CA. 139:CA. **Chapter 11**: 146:CA; CA; CD. 148:RM. 155:CD. 159:CA. **Chapter 12**: 160:spice; EJ; CA. 161:CA. 162:CD. 167:EJ. 169:RM. **Chapter 13**: 180:spice; Paul Efland; EJ. 184:CA. 187:CA. 189:CA. 190:EJ. 192:Bill Winburn. 196:EJ. **Chapter 14**: 198:CA; CA; CA. 201:Walker Montgomery. 203:CA. 206:EJ. 210:CA. **Chapter 15**: 214:CA; xChg; spice. 220:Shmuel Thaler/Index Stock. 222:spice; xChg; RM; Walker Montgomery. 224:EJ. **Chapter 16**: 228:spice; spice; CA. 232:Julian Treadwell; 236:RM. 238:xChg. **Chapter 17**: 244:CA; RM; EJ. 245:RM. 249:RM. 254:EJ. 255:EJ. **Chapter 18**: 258:CA; CA; CA. 259:Julian Treadwell. 262:CA. 267:Georgia Department of Juvenile Justice. **Chapter 19**: 270:CA; Walker Montgomery; Walker Montgomery. 273:CA; 275:CA. **Chapter 20**: 282:CA; CA; CA. 283:RM; 287:CA. 288:CA. 289:CA. 292:CA; CA; CA; CA.

Contributors: Lee Creasman Jr., **Chapter 1**; Patrick Lee Lail, **Chapter 2**; Marla S. Moore, **Chapter 3**; April R. Roberts, Emily J. Culpepper, **Chapter 4**; Laura Bedingfield Herakovich, Brian C. Harms, **Chapter 5**; Randy H. Luffman, Jaimie N. Johnson, **Chapter 6**; Alisa L. Pittman, **Chapter 7**; Laura W. Hyman, **Chapter 8**; John P. Brumbaugh, **Chapter 9**; Kenneth N. Winkler, **Chapter 10**; Gary Blaylock Andrews Jr., **Chapter 11**; Kelly Michael Hundley, **Chapter 12**; Trishanda Hinton, **Chapter 13**; Alexandra O. Liner, **Chapter 14**; Julianne H. Lynn, **Chapter 15**; Jonathon W. Hickman, **Chapter 16**; Cheri Alison Grosvenor, **Chapter 17**; Civia L. Gerber, **Chapter 18**; David A. Stevens, **Chapter 19**; Carolina Colin-Antonini, **Chapter 20**.